Lecture Notes in Computer S

Edited by G. Goos, J. Hartmanis, and J.

Springer
Berlin
Heidelberg
New York
Barcelona
Hong Kong
London
Milan
Paris
Tokyo

Siegfried Reich   Manolis M. Tzagarakis
Paul M.E. De Bra (Eds.)

Hypermedia:
Openness, Structural
Awareness, and Adaptivity

International Workshops OHS-7, SC-3, and AH-3
Aarhus, Denmark, August 14-18, 2001
Revised Papers

 Springer

Series Editors

Gerhard Goos, Karlsruhe University, Germany
Juris Hartmanis, Cornell University, NY, USA
Jan van Leeuwen, Utrecht University, The Netherlands

Volume Editors

Siegfried Reich
Salzburg Research
Jakob-Haringer-Str. 5, 5020 Salzburg, Austria
E-mail: sreich@salzburgresearch.at

Manolis M. Tzagarakis
Computer Technology Institute, Research Unit II
61 Riga Ferraiou str., 26221 Patras, Greece
E-mail: tzagara@cti.gr

Paul M.E. De Bra
Eindhoven University of Technology, Dept. of Computer Science
PO Box 513, 5600 MB Eindhoven, The Netherlands
E-mail: debra@win.tue.nl

Cataloging-in-Publication Data applied for

Die Deutsche Bibliothek - CIP-Einheitsaufnahme

Hypermedia: openness, structural awareness, and adaptivity : international
workshops ; revised papers / OHS-7 ... Aarhus, Denmark, August 14 - 18,
2001. Siegfried Reich ... (ed.). - Berlin ; Heidelberg ; New York ;
Barcelona ; Hong Kong ; London ; Milan ; Paris ; Tokyo : Springer, 2002
  (Lecture notes in computer science ; Vol. 2266)
  ISBN 3-540-43293-0

CR Subject Classification (1998):H.5.4, H.5.1, H.4, H.3, C.2, D.4

ISSN 0302-9743
ISBN 3-540-43293-0 Springer-Verlag Berlin Heidelberg New York

Springer-Verlag Berlin Heidelberg New York
a member of BertelsmannSpringer Science+Business Media GmbH

http://www.springer.de

© Springer-Verlag Berlin Heidelberg 2002
Printed in Germany

Typesetting: Camera-ready by author, data conversion by PTP-Berlin, Stefan Sossna
Printed on acid-free paper   SPIN 10846220   06/3142   5 4 3 2 1 0

Preface

This volume contains the final proceedings of the Seventh Workshop on Open Hypermedia Systems (OHS7), the Third Workshop on Structural Computing (SC3), and the Third Workshop on Adaptive Hypermedia (AH3). All workshops were held at the 12th ACM Conference on Hypertext and Hypermedia in Aarhus, Denmark, August 14–18, 2001.

Introductions, agendas, lists of program committee members and participants, and, of course, the papers can be found in the individual sections of the workshops.

This volume would not have been possible without the support of Springer-Verlag, Heidelberg. In particular, we would like to thank the executive editor of the LNCS series, Mr. Alfred Hofmann.

November 2001

Sigi Reich
Manolis Tzagarakis
Paul De Bra

Table of Contents

The Seventh Workshop on Open Hypermedia Systems (OHS7)

The Third Workshop on Structural Computing (SC3)

The Third Workshop on Adaptive Hypermedia (AH3)

The Seventh Workshop on Open Hypermedia Systems (OHS7)

Program Committee Members of OHS7

The following people have served on the Program Committee of the Seventh Workshop on Open Hypermedia Systems. Their support is gratefully acknowledged.

Kenneth M. Anderson, University of Colorado, Boulder, US
Wernher Behrendt, Salzburg Research, AT
Leslie Carr, University of Southampton, UK
David DeRoure, University of Southampton, UK
Stuart Goose, Siemens Corporate Research, US
Dave L. Hicks, Aalborg University Esbjerg, DK
Dan Joyce, University of Plymouth, UK
David E. Millard, University of Southampton, UK
Luc Moreau, University of Southampton, UK
Monica M.C. Schraefel, University of Toronto, CA
Jim Whitehead, University of California, Santa Cruz, US
Uffe K. Wiil, Aalborg University Esbjerg, DK

List of Presentations at OHS7

Sigi Reich, *Introduction to Workshop and Wrap Up*
Kenneth M. Anderson, *Using Open Hypermedia to Support Information Integration*
Jörg M. Haake, *Applying Collaborative Open Hypermedia Concepts to Extended Enterprise Engineering and Operation*
Yuzuru Tanaka, *Meme Media and Meme Pools for Re-editing and Redistributing Intellectual Assets*
David DeRoure, *Introduction to Sotonoid Papers*
Don Cruickshank, *The Pipeline of Enrichment: Supporting Link Creation for Continuous Media*
David E. Millard, *Auld Leaky: A Contextual Open Hypermedia Link Server*
Neil Ridgway, *FOHM+RTSP: Applying Open Hypermedia and Temporal Linking to Audio Streams*
Uffe K. Wiil, *Development Tools in Component-Based Structural Computing Environments*
Peter J. Nürnberg, *Peer-Reviewed, Publishable Hypertexts*

List of Participants at OHS7

Kenneth M. Anderson, University of Colorado, Boulder, US
Dimitris Avramidis, Computer Technology Institute, Patras, GR
Leslie Carr, University of Southampton, UK
Don Cruickshank, University of Southampton, UK
David DeRoure, University of Southampton, UK
Luke Emmet, Adelard, UK
Erich Gams, Salzburg Research, AT
Jörg M. Haake, FhG-IPSI, Darmstadt, DE
David L. Hicks, Aalborg University Esbjerg, DK
Duncan Martin, University of Nottingham, UK
David E. Millard, University of Southampton, UK
Kenji Naemura, Keio University, JP
Ted Nelson, Keio University, JP
Peter J. Nürnberg, Aalborg University Esbjerg, DK
Digly Ofer, BrowseUp, IL
Kevin Page, University of Southampton, UK
Andrew Pam, Glass Wings, AU
Sigi Reich, Salzburg Research, AT
Neil Ridgway, University of Southampton, UK
Alon Schwartz, BrowseUp, IL
Susanne Sherba, University of Colorado, Boulder, US
Yee-Wai Sim, University of Southampton, UK
Yuzuru Tanaka, Hokkaido University, Sapporo, JP
Mark Thompson, University of Southampton, UK
Mark Truran, University of Nottingham, UK
Manolis Tzagarakis, Computer Technology Institute, Patras, GR
Frank Wagner, Roskilde University, DK
Jim Whitehead, University of California at Santa Cruz, US
Uffe K. Wiil, Aalborg University Esbjerg, DK

Introduction to OHS7

Sigi Reich

Salzburg Research
Jakob Haringer Straße 5
5020 Salzburg, Austria
sreich@salzburgresearch.at

An Open Hypermedia System (OHS) is typically a middleware systen which
provides hypermedia functionality to front-end applications on the users' desk-
tops. Hence, existing tools and applications can be hypermedia-enabled using
the functionality provided by the OHS. Additionally, OHSs integrate with the
backend layer, i.e., file systems, databases, and the Internet.

Starting with OHS1 (held at ECHT '94 Edinburgh, Scotland [24]), a series of
workshops on the overall theme of open hypermedia has been organized: OHS2
(held at Hypertext '96 Washington, D.C. [23]), OHS3 (held at Hypertext '97
in sunny Southampton, UK [20]), OHS4 (held at Hypertext '98 in Pittsburgh,
PA [21]), OHS5 (held at Hypertext '99 in Darmstadt, Germany [22]), and finally,
OHS6 (held at Hypertext '00 in San Antonio, TX [14]).

This year's workshop followed on from that tradition. 9 of 13 papers were
selected by the workshop programme committee for presentation and publication
as post-workshop proceedings. 30 people participated at the workshop.

1 Overview of Papers Presented

The list of papers and presentations given at the workshop covers a broad range
of topics. The papers started with Ken Anderson's and Susanne Sherba's InfiniTe, a framework whose design is heavily influenced by open hypermedia concepts. Jörg Haake then demonstrated how concepts of Collaborative Open Hypermedia Systems (COHS) can be applied in order to support engineering and
operation of extended enterprises (EE).

Yuzuru Tanaka and his colleagues, introduced "meme media", in particular
the distribution of media assets. Then, Richard Beales et al. presented "The
Pipeline of Enrichment", a paper on the application of open hypermedia concepts to continuous media. Danius Michaelides et al. described a contextual
open hypermedia server that extends the existing FOHM (Fundamental Open
Hypermedia Model) with context. Following on to that, Neil Ridgway and Dave
DeRoure discussed issues in extending FOHM towards streaming of link data.

Uffe Wiil demonstrated that development tools can lower the entry barrier for
developers considerably, in particular, their tools are based on standard UML as
a notation for specifying hypermedia services. Finally, Pete Nürnberg and Dave
Hicks discussed issues for publishing hypertexts, in particular, they focused on
publishing the structures (only) rather than the contents enriched with some
links to references or related work.

S. Reich, M.M. Tzagarakis, P.M.E. De Bra (Eds.): OHS/SC/AH 2001, LNCS 2266, pp. 4–7, 2002.
© Springer-Verlag Berlin Heidelberg 2002

2   Discussion of New Research Directions

While the research this year concentrated on the issues outlined above, the discussion went further on to general research issues for middleware systems (see also for example [5, 6, 11, 12]). In the following we will briefly describe these and derive specific issues for open hypermedia systems.

Looking at a closely related community — the multimedia middleware community — which has organised a workshop at the ACM Multimedia 2001 Conference [12], we see that these researchers put emphasise on streaming services, quality of service (QoS) aspects, and issues of configuration and flexibility.

At the OHS workshop, a list of research issues based on an investigation by *Geihs* [5] has been discussed. Based on participants' feedback we can outline the research issues for hypermedia middleware systems as follows:

- Enterprise application integration (EAI): participants felt that this was an important topic of research and that the open hypermedia community could contribute well to that research area. Integration of different data sources as well as dealing with legacy applications have long been issues of the OHS community (see e.g. [1, 3, 19]).
- Quality of service (QoS) for links and/or meta data in general. This issue is already been addressed by several papers of this workshop, in particular [2, 16].
- Nomadic mobility and mobile link servers: this aspect has been raised at last year's workshop [18]. Issues include the evolution of hypermedia link services to support the structuring of ad hoc information spaces. Part of this issue are features for dynamic configuration of middleware services.
- Programming models: this issue has been discussed with some depth at the workshop. People felt very strongly about design patterns — this may be due to the fact that the OHS community has developed a lot of design experiences over the past years by working on interoperability standards [13].
- Architectural issues, which by the very nature of OHSs as an integrating concept, are very important. For instance, the issue of a reference architecture for CB-OHS has been discussed at several previous workshops (see e.g., [8]). In particular with respect to systems supporting mobile users architectural issues will become more important (such as how to access mobile link servers, etc. — see also "nomadic mobility" above).
- Collaboration, as an aspect with a long tradition in OHS, see e.g. [7, 9, 15, 17].
- Media aspects, in particular content based retrieval and navigation (in non-textual media). This is an established — albeit unsolved — research issue, see [10] in these proceedings.

Summary

The large number of participants at OHS7 shows that there is a continuing interest in systems issues in the hypertext community. Furthermore, The above list of research issues bears witness to an active research community.

References

1. Kenneth M. Anderson. Integrating open hypermedia systems with the world wide web. In *Proceedings of the '97 ACM Conference on Hypertext, April 6-11, 1997, Southampton, UK*, pages 157–166, April 1997.

2. Richard Beales, Don Cruickshank, David DeRoure, Nick Gibbins, Ben Juby, Danius Michaelides, and Kevin R. Page. The pipeline of enrichment: Supporting link creation for continuous media. In Siegfried Reich, Manolis Tzagarakis, and Paul DeBra, editors, *Proceedings of the 7th Workshop on Open Hypermedia Systems, ACM Hypertext '01 Conference, Aarhus, Denmark, August 14-18*, 2001.

3. Hugh C. Davis, Simon Knight, and Wendy Hall. Light hypermedia link services: A study of third party application integration. In *ECHT '94. Proceedings of the ACM European conference on Hypermedia technology, Sept. 18-23, 1994, Edinburgh, Scotland, UK*, pages 41–50, 1994.

4. Hugh C. Davis, Antoine Rizk, and Andy J. Lewis. OHP: A draft proposal for a standard open hypermedia protocol. In Wiil and Demeyer [23], pages 27–53. UCI-ICS Technical Report 96-10, Department of Information and Computer Science, University of California, Irvine.

5. Kurt Geihs. Middleware challenges. *IEEE Computer*, pages 24–31, June 2001.

6. Rachid Guerraoui. *Middleware 2001. IFIP/ACM International COnference on Distributed Systems Platforms. Heidelberg, Germany, November 2001.* Springer Verlag, LNCS 2218, 2001.

7. Kaj Grønbæk, Jens A. Hem, Ole L. Madsen, and Lennerth Sloth. Cooperative hypermedia systems: a Dexter-based approach. *Communications of the ACM*, 37:64–74, February 1994.

8. Kaj Grønbæk and Uffe K. Wiil. Towards a reference architecture for open hypermedia. *Journal of Digital Information (JoDI). Special Issue on Open Hypermedia Systems*, 1(2), 1997.

9. Jörg M. Haake. Structural computing in the collaborative work domain? In Reich and Anderson [13], pp. 108–119.

10. Moritz Neumüller. Because i seek an image, not a book. In Siegfried Reich, Manolis Tzagarakis, and Paul DeBra, editors, *Proceedings of the 7th Workshop on Open Hypermedia Systems, ACM Hypertext '01 Conference, Aarhus, Denmark, August 14-18*, 2001.

11. Peter J. Nürnberg, John J. Leggett, and Uffe K. Wiil. An agenda for open hypermedia research. In *Proceedings of the '98 ACM Conference on Hypertext, June 20-24, 1998, Pittsburgh, PA*, pages 198–206, 1998.

12. Thomas Plagemann and F. Eliassen. M3W 2001 technical program. October 5th, 2001 Ottawa, Canada. The Workshop was held in conjunction with ACM MM 2001, 2001.

13. Siegfried Reich, Uffe K. Wiil, Peter J. Nürnberg, Hugh C. Davis, Kaj Grønbæk, Kenneth M. Anderson, David E. Millard, and Jörg M. Haake. Addressing interoperability in open hypermedia: The design of the open hypermedia protocol. *New Review of Hypermedia and Multimedia*, 5:207–248, 1999.

14. Siegfried Reich and Kenneth M. Anderson, editors. *Open Hypermedia Systems and Structural Computing. Proceedings of the 6th Workshop on Open Hypermedia Systems (OHS-6) and the 2nd Workshop on Structural Computing (SC-2). San Antonio, TX, USA.* Springer Verlag, September 2000. Lecture Notes in Computer Science (LNCS) No. 1903.

15. Olav Reinert, Dirk Bucka-Lassen, Claus A. Pedersen, and Peter J. Nürnberg. CAOS: A collaborative and open spatial structure service component with incremental spatial parsing. In *Proceedings of the '99 ACM Conference on Hypertext, February 21-25, 1999, Darmstadt, Germany*, pages 49–50, February 1999.
16. Neil Ridgway, David De Roure. Fohm+rtsp: Applying open hypermedia and temporal linking to audio streams. In Siegfried Reich, Manolis Tzagarakis, and Paul DeBra, editors, *Proceedings of the 7th Workshop on Open Hypermedia Systems, ACM Hypertext '01 Conference, Aarhus, Denmark, August 14-18*, 2001.
17. John L. Schnase, Edward L. Cunnius, and Bruce S. Dowton. The StudySpace project: Collaborative hypermedia in nomadic computing environments. *Communications of the ACM*, 38(8):72–73, August 1995.
18. Mark Thompson, Roure David De and Danius Michaelides. Weaving the pervasive information fabric. In Reich and Anderson [14], pages 87–95.
19. James E. Whitehead. An architectural model for application integration in open hypermedia environments. In *Proceedings of the '97 ACM Conference on Hypertext, April 6-11, 1997, Southampton, UK*, pages 1–12, 1997.
20. Uffe Kock Wiil, editor. *Proceedings of the 3rd Workshop on Open Hypermedia Systems, Hypertext '97, Southampton, England, April 6-11*, 1997. Scientific Report 97-01, The Danish Centre for IT Research.
21. Uffe Kock Wiil, editor. *Proceedings of the 4th Workshop on Open Hypermedia Systems, Hypertext '98, Pittsburgh, PA, June 20-24*, June 1998. Technical Report CS-98-01, Aalborg University Esbjerg.
22. Uffe Kock Wiil, editor. *Proceedings of the 5th Workshop on Open Hypermedia Systems, Hypertext '99, Darmstadt, Germany, February 21-25*, February 1999. Technical Report CS-99-01, Aalborg University Esbjerg.
23. Uffe Kock Wiil and Serge Demeyer, editors. *Proceedings of the 2nd Workshop on Open Hypermedia Systems, ACM Hypertext '96, Washington, D.C., March 16-20. Available as Report No. ICS-TR-96-10 from the Dept. of Information and Computer Science, University of California, Irvine*, March 1996. UCI-ICS Technical Report 96-10, Department of Information and Computer Science, University of California, Irvine.
24. Uffe Kock Wiil and Kaspar Østerbye, editors. *Proceedings of the ECHT '94 Workshop on Open Hypermedia Systems*, September 1994. Tech. Report R-94-2038, Dept. of Computer Science, Aalborg Univ.

Using Open Hypermedia to Support Information Integration

Kenneth M. Anderson and Susanne A. Sherba

Department of Computer Science
University of Colorado, Boulder
430 UCB
Boulder CO 80309-0430
{kena, sherba}@cs.colorado.edu,
http://www.cs.colorado.edu/users/{kena, sherba}

Abstract. The task of information integration challenges software engineers on a daily basis. Software artifacts, produced during software development, contain many implicit and explicit relationships whose sheer numbers quickly overwhelm a software team's ability to understand, manipulate, and evolve them. We are developing an information integration environment to aid software engineers in tackling this difficult task and are making use of open hypermedia techniques to enable critical characteristics of the environment, such as third-party tool integration, typed links, and a partitioned information space through the use of contexts, traditionally referred to as composites. We describe our prototype implementation of the information integration environment, focusing on how open hypermedia has either influenced the design of the environment, or contributed directly to its functional capabilities.

1 Introduction

Software engineers create software artifacts, such as source code, requirements documents, test cases, etc., during the course of a software development project. These artifacts often have numerous relationships, both implicit (such as a requirements traceability link between a source file and a design document) and explicit (such as "See also Document A, Section 3...", between them [2]. A key challenge in software engineering is managing these relationships: How does a software team create, track, and evolve the hundreds of thousands of relationships that can exist in large-scale software development projects? We refer to this task as *information integration,* since establishing a link between two documents typically signifies that information in one document is semantically-related to information in the other document. Open hypermedia [14] is well suited to supporting information integration [4]. In particular, it provides:

- **Advanced Hypermedia Data Models**: Open hypermedia provides data models that can support the complex nature of relationships between software artifacts, including support for n-ary relationships and "links between links."

S. Reich, M.M. Tzagarakis, P.M.E. De Bra (Eds.): OHS/SC/AH 2001, LNCS 2266, pp. 8–16, 2002.

- **External Links**: Open hypermedia provides links that are stored separate from the information they relate. This feature enables, for instance, the ability to have different sets of relationships over the same set of software artifacts to support different tasks such as change impact analysis or requirements traceability.
- **Third-Party Application Integration**: Software engineers make heavy use of tools, and they are unwilling to adopt a new technology if it requires them to abandon their favorite tools. Open hypermedia integrates hypermedia services directly into third-party tools [8,16,17], allowing software engineers to retain their current tools while gaining the information integration benefits of open hypermedia.

However, while open hypermedia enables these critical characteristics, open hypermedia systems often lack the tools that can help to automate the process of information integration. Automating information integration in a large-scale software development project requires the ability to understand the content of the documents and employs techniques not typically provided by open hypermedia systems, such as automatic link generation facilities, keyword extraction and document clustering tools, image analysis, etc. As such, we are building on our past experience in open hypermedia [1,2,3,4] to develop an information integration environment that provides tools to help automate the information integration process and whose design is influenced by the results of the open hypermedia research community. Our environment is called InfiniTe (pronounced like "Infinity"), and we have implemented a proof-of-concept prototype to help us explore various research issues such as the use of XML (eXtensible Markup Language [6]) to support information integration [5] as well as the issues encountered in integrating open hypermedia into such an environment, which is the focus of this paper.

The rest of this paper is organized as follows. We briefly present the InfiniTe architecture and describe our prototype implementation. Then, we discuss the open hypermedia issues surrounding InfiniTe. Next, we briefly discuss related work, and then offer a few conclusions.

2   InfiniTe Information Integration Environment

A model of the information integration environment appears in Figure 1. The model consists of users, data sources, integrators, translators, contexts, a repository, and an open hypermedia layer. The basic idea is that information is brought into the information integration environment by invoking a *translator*. The translator retrieves information from a *data source* and stores it in a *repository*. (The previous sentence may imply that translators are "batch processors," however this is not the case. InfiniTe places no restrictions on the implementation architecture of its translators.) The repository consists of multiple *contexts*; contexts store information (using XML) along with attributes, which serve to provide meta-data on the information. Contexts can contain sub-contexts. In addition, the documents of a context can be linked together in arbitrary relationships; relationships can span multiple contexts and can have type information associated with them (e.g. a requirements traceability link, a consistency relationship, etc.). Relationships can be stored as XLinks [9] or within the open hypermedia layer.

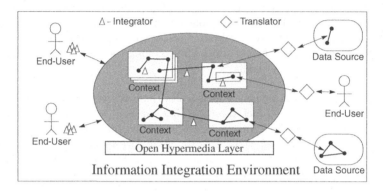

Fig. 1. InfiniTe's Conceptual Architecture

Integrators aid users in finding, creating, maintaining, and evolving *relationships* within the repository. While our main focus is on relationship management, integrators are free to create new contexts and to store information within them while performing their tasks. For instance, an integrator that searches documents for particular keywords, may store the location of discovered keywords in a document separate from the documents being searched. It may then create a new context and include pointers to the searched documents plus the document that it created.

Since InfiniTe is intended to support software development, the issue of versioning must be addressed. We initially intend to support versioning using contexts and relationships. That is, a translator will be able to query the repository to see if it has translated a particular document before (assuming that the document's name and location hasn't been changed in the meantime). If so, the translator can create a new context and translate the document into the new context. It can then compare the newly translated document with the previous instance to see if anything has changed. If so, the translator can create a version relationship between the two translated documents. Note, in this discussion we have been careful to use the word "can" rather than "will," since whether or not a particular translator supports versioning will be up to the translator's developer. However, the operations needed to support this type of versioning will be available from the application program interface of the repository.

Finally, the relationships that are generated by integrators can be imported into the open hypermedia layer and then made available to the original data source using its native editing tools. This feature allows software engineers to submit a set of artifacts to the repository, make use of integrators to discover relationships contained in those artifacts, and then view the generated relationships within the native editing environment of the original artifacts. This capability is critical to enabling the adoption of the information integration environment, and is discussed in more detail below; while it is true that our approach requires the use of a new environment to perform information integration tasks, the results of those operations can be made available to the software engineers within their own tools. Software engineers, thus, gain access to tools and techniques to perform information integration tasks, but they are not required to give up the tools they already use to gain these capabilities.

3   Open Hypermedia Issues

We have implemented a proof-of-concept prototype of InfiniTe to explore a variety of research issues (See Figure 2). The implementation makes use of a set of Java Servlets that can invoke integrators and translators on XML documents stored in the repository. XSLT [7] is used to translate repository information from XML into HTML for presentation in a Web browser. In addition, repository relationships can be extracted from the environment as a set of XLinks that can then be imported into an open hypermedia system for display in the documents of integrated third-party applications. This aspect of the InfiniTe project complements our past work in the area of XLinks and open hypermedia [13], in which we evaluated the utility of open hypermedia systems to serve as authoring environments for XLinks.

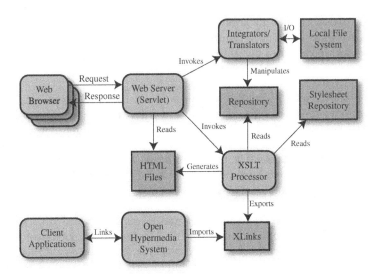

Fig. 2. InfiniTe's Prototype Architecture

In particular, the information integration environment raises some interesting issues with respect to open hypermedia. The first issue concerns open hypermedia's ability to influence the design of other systems. First, InfiniTe is designed to support heterogeneity: As long as a translator can be constructed for a particular application's data types, its documents can be included in the repository and its information can contribute to the relationships being discovered and managed by InfiniTe's integrators. (Thus, both textual and binary source files can be translated into InfiniTe.) Second, InfiniTe makes use of advanced hypermedia concepts. In particular, an InfiniTe context is very similar to an open hypermedia composite [11] and provides similar information organization properties. Additionally, InfiniTe supports the creation of n-ary relationships between imported documents and within and between contexts. This raises our second issue which concerns realizing support for these open hypermedia concepts outside of an open hypermedia system.

Both contexts and InfiniTe's support for relationships are realized in the current prototype using XML and XLink. Each file translated into the repository, is assigned an id. A file can be included in a context by storing its id in the context's associated XML file. Files can thus participate in multiple contexts. Additionally, contexts can contain other contexts allowing for fine grain partitioning of the information space. Furthermore, each context is assigned an id that can be included in a relationship. Thus, even though the context containment hierarchy is implemented as a tree structure, it is possible to have relationships span between arbitrary members of that tree structure. Relationships are currently realized using XLinks. These XLinks are stored in separate files and make use of XPointers [10] to refer to information contained in other repository files and contexts. The XLinks and XPointers store enough information to enable the construction of open hypermedia LocSpecs [12] upon import into an open hypermedia system. We have implemented a proof-of-concept prototype of this feature, which constitutes our third open hypermedia issue within the InfiniTe environment.

Our proof-of-concept prototype involves the translation of text (e.g. ASCII) documents into the repository, running a keyword extractor to discover keywords in these documents, and then exporting the keyword information as a set of anchors and links into an open hypermedia system (Chimera [4]) for display on the original text documents. The first requirement in achieving this functionality is that each translator must record the location of the original file that gave rise to the translated file in the repository. Currently, we store this information as an absolute file path, although in the future this information can be stored more abstractly as a URI or as an identifier from a naming service [15]. Second, a mapping between the location of a word in the translated document and the location of the same word in the original document must be established. In our example, text documents were stored in simple XML documents that had a root tag of <text> and where each line of the text file was contained by a <line> tag. In addition, if a keyword is discovered in a document, it is placed in a

<keyword> tag. As such, the mapping of the location for a particular word in a translated document to its location in the original document is:

1. If x equals the line number of the word in the translated document, x-2 equals the line number of the word in the original document. This accounts for the two lines at the start of a translated file that consists of the standard XML declaration and the <text> tag. In general, the line number of the word in the original file is x-y where y equals the number of header lines in the XML file before the first line of the document is reached.

2. If x equals the character position of the first character of the word in the translated document for its particular line, then x - (19 * y) - 6 equals the character position of the first character of the word in the original file for its particular line. y is the number of keywords that appear before the word in question. This formula is derived by considering the following factors: Each line begins with a <line> tag, which consumes 6 characters. And, each time a keyword appears in a line, 19 characters are consumed by the <keyword> and </keyword> tags. If a word appears before any keywords in a line, then y equals 0 and the character mapping reduces to x-6.

This map must be codified within a translator of the InfiniTe environment. It can then be applied to any number of keyword-processed documents to produce a set of XLinks that describe relationships between a keyword index and the instances of a particular keyword in the set of documents. These XLinks are then imported into Chimera using the following process:

1. A *hyperweb* is created with the same name as the name of the context which includes the translated files and the generated keyword index. If these files span multiple contexts, our current implementation simply picks the name of the context containing the first keyword document that it processes.
2. The absolute file path to the original file is turned into a Chimera *object* [4].
3. This object is combined with a Chimera text *viewer* (e.g. Emacs) to create a *view*.
4. LocSpecs are created to represent each found keyword.
5. The attributes of the LocSpec are calculated using the mapping process described above.
6. Each LocSpec is then converted into a Chimera *anchor*.
7. Finally, Chimera *links* are established between the anchors in the keyword index and the anchors in the keyword documents themselves. These links are created by the Chimera XLink importer which makes direct use of Chimera's API.

The result of this process allows a user of an integrated text editor to open one of the original text documents and have all keywords appear as selectable anchors, which lead to a new keyword index document when clicked. (The new index document is exported directly to the local file system using an additional InfiniTe translator.)

In this fashion, InfiniTe is able to make its relationships viewable to software engineers within their favorite tools. While we have focused on text-only documents, we believe this process is generalizable to other document types.

4   Related Work

We now briefly review two related systems. The GeoWorlds environment [18] is an information analysis environment that allows users to retrieve documents off the Web, organize them into collections, and apply a variety of analyses upon them. GeoWorlds is strictly focused on the World Wide Web and can only import information from Web-based data sources. We intend to support both remote and local information sources, with particular attention to supporting legacy, third-party, data formats. This will allow our environment to be applied to both existing and new software development projects. In addition, GeoWorlds services are focused more on information analysis while our focus will be on relationship management. Our environment will thus have greater capabilities for discovering, viewing, and manipulating relationships than what is found in the GeoWorlds environment.

The second related system is located at `http://www.xlinkit.com/`. It is a link generation engine that allows consistency relationships to be specified over software artifacts. The basic idea is that a software engineer writes consistency rules for a set of documents and then submits those rules along with a set of documents. (Documents must be converted to XML before the link generation engine can process them.) The link generation engine then checks the documents to see if they follow the submitted consistency rules. As output, the engine generates a report that displays the results of the analysis: instances of the rules are highlighted and information is provided to show, for each instance, if the rule was followed or violated. Our environment can be used to check consistency relationships over software artifacts, but it is also intended to support a broader spectrum of relationship types. For instance, we intend to build integrators that can aid the process of generating requirements traceability links, similar to the results we achieved with Northrop Grumman using only the Chimera open hypermedia system [2]. Rather than providing a rule-based language for a single relationship type, our environment will provide APIs to software engineers that will allow them to construct their own translators and integrators to manage the relationships relevant to their software development projects. This does not mean that rule-based languages are not helpful in automatic link generation; indeed the experience with xlinkit demonstrates the benefits of this technique. In fact, we plan to leverage the results of the xlinkit experience, along with other work in hypermedia link generation, to create a generic rule-based integrator that can support various rule sets via a plug-in mechanism. In addition, our use of open hypermedia will allow the relationships discovered in the environment to be viewable within the native editing context of the original software artifacts. Thus, while both of these systems require a translation step into XML, our approach will allow information to flow back to the original artifacts.

5   Conclusions

Open hypermedia plays an important role in providing realistic support for information integration tasks. Its characteristics (outlined in the Introduction) are necessary to eliminate adoption barriers by software engineers, since the use of InfiniTe does not prevent engineers from using their favorite tools to develop software. Having constructed an initial implementation of the InfiniTe architecture, our future plans will focus on validation. In particular, we plan to apply InfiniTe to the software artifacts of open-source software development projects. This experiment has two goals: One, to see if InfiniTe has the capacity to handle the artifacts of medium- and large-scale projects and, two, to evaluate whether InfiniTe has the ability to generate integrated (e.g. linked) information that is useful to the developers of these projects.

References

1. Anderson, K. M. (1997). Integrating Open Hypermedia Systems with the World Wide Web. In *Proceedings of the Eighth ACM Conference on Hypertext*, pp. 157-166. Southampton, UK. April 6-11, 1997.
2. Anderson, K. M. (1999). Issues of Data Scalability in Open Hypermedia Systems. *The New Review of Hypermedia and Multimedia*, 5: 151-178.
3. Anderson, K. M., Och, C., King, R., and Osborne, R. M. (2000). Integrating Infrastructure: Enabling Large-Scale Client Integration. In *Proceedings of the Eleventh ACM Conference on Hypertext*, pp. 57-66. San Antonio, TX, USA. May 30 - June 4, 2000.
4. Anderson, K. M., Taylor, R. N., and Whitehead, E. J., Jr. (2000). Chimera: Hypermedia for Heterogeneous Software Development Environments. *ACM Transactions on Information Systems*, 18(3): 211-245.
5. Anderson, K. M., and Sherba, S. A. (2001). Using XML to support Information Integration. In *Proceedings of the 2001 International Workshop on XML Technologies and Software Engineering (XSE 2001)*. Co-located with the 2001 International Conference on Software Engineering. Toronto, Ontario, Canada. May 15, 2001.
6. Bray, T., Paoli, J., and Sperberg-McQueen, C. M. (1998). Extensible Markup Language (XML) 1.0, W3C Recommendation, 10-February-1998. http://www.w3.org/TR/REC-xml.
7. Clark, J. (1999). XSL Transformations (XSLT) Version 1.0 W3C Recommendation, 16 November 1999. http://www.w3.org/TR/xslt.html.
8. Davis, H. C., Knight, S., and Hall, W. (1994). Light Hypermedia Link Services: A Study of Third Party Application Integration. In *Proceedings of the Sixth ACM Conference on Hypertext*, pp. 41-50. Edinburgh, Scotland. September 18-23, 1994.
9. DeRose, S., Orchard, D., and Trafford, B. (1999). XML Linking Language (XLINK). http://www.w3.org/TR/xlink/.
10. DeRose, S., and Daniel, R. (1999). XML Pointer Language (XPointer). http://www.w3.org/TR/WD-xptr/.
11. Grønbæk, K. (1994). Composites in a Dexter-Based Hypermedia Framework. In *Proceedings of the Sixth ACM Conference on Hypertext*, pp. 59-69. Edinburgh, Scotland. September 18-23, 1994.
12. Grønbæk, K., and Trigg, R. H. (1996). Toward a Dexter-Based Model for Open Hypermedia: Unifying Embedded References and Link Objects. In Proceedings of the Seventh ACM Conference on Hypertext, pp. 149-160. Washington DC, USA. March 16-20 1996.

13. Halsey, B., and Anderson, K. M. (2000). XLink and Open Hypermedia Systems: A Preliminary Investigation. In *Proceedings of the Eleventh ACM Conference on Hypertext*, pp. 212-213. San Antonio, TX, USA. May 30 - June 4, 2000.

14. Østerbye, K., and Wiil, U. K. (1996). The Flag Taxonomy of Open Hypermedia Systems. In *Proceedings of the Seventh ACM Conference on Hypertext*, pp. 129-139. Washington DC, USA. March 16-20, 1996.

15. Tzagarakis, M., Karousos, N., Christodoulakis, D., and Reich, S. (2000). Naming as a Fundamental Concept of Open Hypermedia Systems. In *Proceedings of the 2000 ACM Conference on Hypertext*, pp. 103-112. San Antonio, TX, USA. May 30 - June 3, 2000.

16. Whitehead, E. J., Jr. (1997). An Architectural Model for Application Integration in Open Hypermedia Environments. In *Proceedings of the Eighth ACM Conference on Hypertext*, pp. 1-12. Southampton, UK. April 6-11, 1997.

17. Wiil, U. K., and Leggett, J. J. (1997). HyperDisco: Collaborative Authoring and Internet Distribution. In *Proceedings of the Eighth ACM Conference on Hypertext*, pp. 13-23. Southampton, UK. April 6-11, 1997.

18. Yao, K., Ko, I., Eleish, R., and Neches, R. (2000). Asynchronous Information Space Analysis Architecture Using Content and Structure-Based Service Brokering. In *Proceedings of the 2000 ACM Conference on Digital Libraries*. San Antonio, TX, USA.

Applying Collaborative Open Hypermedia Concepts to Extended Enterprise Engineering and Operation

Jörg M. Haake

GMD - German National Research Center for Information Technology
IPSI - Publication and Information Systems Institute
Dolivostr. 15, D-64293 Darmstadt, Germany
haake@darmstadt.gmd.de

1   Introduction

An Extended Enterprise (EE) is a new form of organizing Business-to-Business (B2B) cooperation among business partners. Here, independent companies form a network to develop and deliver a product to a customer. An EE extends the concept of a virtual enterprise because it persists even after the product is delivered. Thus, the EE serves as a container for knowledge captured during product development and delivery, which can be used to aid partner acquisition and project organization for future projects. In an EE, cooperation occurs across organizational boundaries. Distributed teams must be formed and supported when defining and executing a joint business process. Hence, different computing infrastructures used by the different partners within an EE must be integrated. Likewise, access to the joint business process and sharing of information resources among partners must be facilitated. We believe that concepts from collaborative open hypermedia systems [10] can help to solve these problems. In this paper, first the problem of supporting engineering and operating an EE is analyzed. Then, previous approaches to supporting an EE are summarized. Next, our approach of supporting an EE using collaborative open hypermedia concepts is presented. This approach has been developed and is currently applied in the IST-1999-10091 project EXTERNAL funded by the CEC. Finally, some conclusions are presented.

2   Problem Analysis

An extended enterprise is defined as a number of partner organizations, which combine their individual capabilities and business processes, in order to perform a joint business process. As a result, a product is delivered to a customer, and it is believed that such an organization is able to deliver a product faster and cheaper compared to traditional companies. It is argued that the benefits of an EE stem from combining complementary capabilities, which would otherwise need to be acquired by a single company (which would need time and money).

S. Reich, M.M. Tzagarakis, P.M.E. De Bra (Eds.): OHS/SC/AH 2001, LNCS 2266, pp. 17–27, 2002.

However, in order to realize such a benefit, good partners need to be found, and cooperation between the partners needs to be defined, coordinated, and efficiently executed. The main idea here is to collaboratively define and execute a joint business process, which reflects the needs of the product to be delivered and the capabilities of the partners. The joint business process combines the individual work processes already present within each partner company. It serves as a kind of meta work process layer, which combines and extends the individual work processes of each partner into a joint work plan for the whole EE. This work plan needs to be defined and executed. Whenever the need arises, the joint work plan needs to be changed. In order to support continuous improvement, the work process execution should be captured and made available for later analysis and sharing as best practice, if necessary. Finally, the definition and execution of such a shared work plan requires support, which operates across organizational boundaries. Specifically, the different computing infrastructures in use by the different partners need to be integrated into an Extended Enterprise Network (EEN), which comprises all tools and repositories needed to share the joint work plan.

We believe that such a heterogeneous environment, which requires collaborative work on heterogeneous information items (such as work process descriptions, and documents), is an ideal application area for collaborative open hypermedia systems concepts. Some requirements of such an EEN are listed below:

- Shared representation of joint work plan/work process (including links into individual partners' work processes), partners' skills and capabilities, and overall organization (e.g. actors and roles);
- Collaborative access to and manipulation of the shared representation by all partners;
- Coordination support for executing the joint work process (including enactment of work processes, and adaptation to emergent needs);
- Communication support facilitating cooperation among members of distributed teams;
- Learning support, which facilitates learning of the work process as well as capturing of best practice examples and debriefing of work process execution.

Collaborative open hypermedia systems concepts can help to

- integrate the individual partner's work processes into a coherent whole (i.e. help maintain relationships between work processes, capabilities, and organizations),
- facilitate cooperative browsing and editing of such information structures,
- aid coordination by providing enactment support for work process structures, and
- provide multiple presentations of the hyperstructures (e.g. for definition, enactment, and learning purposes).

3   Related Work

Traditionally, work execution support in enterprises has been the goal of research in workflow management systems (WFMS). Here, a few workflow designers define standard processes (so called schemas), which are then instantiated and executed by a workflow engine. At execution time, the workflow system offers tasks to be executed to employees, which are upon acceptance presented with the necessary documents and tools for carrying out the task. After task completion, results are forwarded to the next task in the work process. Ad-hoc workflow systems support the ad-hoc definition of work processes by defining next tasks on the fly. However, WFMS support only individuals in defining a work process (mostly workflow designers) instead of supporting teams in negotiating a joint work process. Furthermore, WFMS only reference work objects (such as documents) instead of maintaining integrity and facilitating cooperative access to shared information resources. Thus, a WFMS solution does not address the cooperative and emergent nature of an EE.

Shared workspace systems support asynchronous and synchronous access to shared objects by distributed team members [7]. In addition, they provide awareness services [5], which help team members to perceive presence and activities of team members. Thus, coordination is facilitated. An example for a purely Web-based system using Web browsers as clients and Web servers with extensions is BSCW [2]. To support structuring of the information space BSCW only provides document lists in folders, but no task-related structure. Additionally, BSCW focuses on asynchronous work. Therefore, awareness mainly concentrates on document related events. Since version 3.2 of BSCW, synchronous awareness is provided through a user presence and activity monitor via additional Java applets. Communication is supported by a "talk" facility implemented using a Java applet. Since BSCW is Web-based, every kind of document can be up- and downloaded and opened with an installed application using the helper applications specification of Web-browsers. However, these applications usually are single user applications so that synchronous work is not possible. Additionally, on some machines corresponding applications might be missing and then users might not be able to access the documents. In general, shared workspace systems such as BSCW do not provide support for work process description, and enactment. Instead, work planning and execution remains under the responsibility of the users. Thus, the work orientation and coordination requirements of an EE remain to be addressed.

HyperDisco [17] supports shared workspaces containing hypermedia objects and external application files that can be accessed and manipulated by heterogeneous tools. It also provides an open protocol to integrate new tools into its infrastructure. It supports asynchronous cooperative authoring with heterogeneous tools. CAOS [11] is a component-based open hypermedia system, which focuses on spatial parsing and collaboration support. Posties is a WebDAV application for collaborative work [5]. It supports asynchronous cooperative authoring over the Web. Open hypermedia systems, e.g., HyperDisco, focus on linking and integrating heterogeneous tools (and the information objects the tools work on) into an open hypermedia. They also adopt a component-based approach for developing open hypermedia services (e.g., navigational hypertext service and spatial hypertext service), but this architecture focuses on interfaces and not on run-time extensibility.

Some cooperative hypermedia systems were developed to support cooperative work process definition and execution. For example, Kacmar et al. [8] demonstrated the ability to integrate workflow management in a collaborative hypermedia environment through computability and a process-based model. This approach provided task and document management, while also providing cross-system capabilities in either real-time or batch-oriented services by monitoring the states of multiple hypertexts. Further, the workflow model was created in the same environment as document authoring thus providing a homogeneous work setting for all user activity. CHIPS [14] provided a shared hypermedia workspace where authors could define and execute work processes synchronously and asynchronously, and where work processes and work objects were represented in the same shared hypermedia workspace.

Other open hypermedia systems include the one developed in the EuroCODE project [6], which aims at a Dexter-compliant architecture for supporting sharing of hypertexts. The hypertext model provides many structuring possibilities, but processes are not explicitly modeled in the described system. It provides a variety of cooperation modes on shared documents, but focuses on asynchronous cooperation. It uses an event notification and locking mechanism based on an object-oriented database system. Integrating the hypermedia architecture with an application sharing tool providing non-cooperation aware clients supports synchronous work. For explicit communication a conferencing system is used. A few cooperative open hypermedia systems based upon the open hypermedia model exist, such as Manufaktur [9]. In Manufaktur, spatial workspaces can be cooperatively created and populated with linked objects. However, Manufaktur does not support process modelling and enactment.

As a result of this analysis we can state that previous approaches do not address all requirements of EE engineering and operation, as stated in section 2. In the next section, our approach is presented.

4   Supporting Extended Enterprise Engineering

In the IST-1999-10091 project EXTERNAL we develop infrastructure, tools and a methodology for supporting the engineering and operation of Extended Enterprises. In this paper, we focus on infrastructure and tools.

4.1   Approach

Our approach can be summarized as providing a cooperative open hypermedia system, which:

- uses open hypermedia to represent descriptions of work processes, organizational descriptions (e.g. actors, roles, capabilities) and work objects (e.g. documents) as a nested hypermedia graph (called an EE model);

- provides a shared repository for the EE model and use collaborative open hypermedia concepts to enables cooperative access to the shared EE model by all participants;
- provides open hypermedia clients as cooperative tools for browsing and manipulating the EE model stored in the repository;
- supports enactment of work processes by providing a workflow structure service in the cooperative open hypermedia system (COHS).

In the following sub sections we discuss each issue in more detail.

4.2   Representing the EE Model

In order to support definition and coordination of the joint business process of the EE, descriptions of work processes, organizational descriptions (e.g. actors, roles, and capabilities) and work objects (e.g. documents) are represented as a nested hypermedia graph (called an EE model). Since many components of this EE model stem from the EE partners, this EE model hyperstructure serves as a meta information structure, which binds the partners' components together. Thus, heterogeneous information resources must be linked into a common structure. In addition, the types of objects to be linked will change over time (e.g. induced by changes of the environment). Thus, extensibility and tailorability need to be supported.

In EXTERNAL, we use open hypermedia concepts to support the integration of arbitrary information resources. The key concept is a wrapper node type [12]. Here, a wrapper implements a shared object reference. Basically, the wrapper represents an external information resource as a node. The content attribute of this node type contains an URL pointing to the information resource. In addition, attributes are used to define which tools can be used to manipulate the content object. This way, any information item can be linked into the EE model structure, and the cooperative tools provided by the COHS can be used to display and manipulate its content (see below). By employing sub typing, new types of information objects can be added at run-time (thus, supporting extensibility).

4.3   Shared Repository

In order to make the shared EE model available to all partners, a shared repository containing the EE model is provided. Sharing the EE model requires two prerequisites: Firstly, a common interchange format or data model needs to be defined. In EXTERNAL we use a common XML DTD to represent the EE model in XML. Secondly, a standardized interface to the repository is needed, so that clients can access and share data via the repository. The COHS provides a repository server, which enables asynchronous and synchronous access to its content.

4.4   Cooperative Tools

Cooperative tools for browsing and manipulating the EE model, which is stored in the repository, serve as clients of the cooperative open hypermedia system. A number of such clients are provided. Native clients (i.e. clients which have been written in the COHS implementation environment as described in the next section) include [12]:

- Cooperative content editors (e.g. for text, graphics, images),
- Cooperative search tool for executing queries on the shared EE model,
- Orientation tool for displaying hierarchical overviews on the nested EE model (including group awareness),
- Process definition and enactment worktop, which provides an EE portal to the users (offering links to the shared EE model and to tools working on it, including tailoring support).

In addition, tools and work environments already present at the EE partner infrastructure needs to be integrated as well. Two approaches are used:

- Document centric integration: Tools are associated with the documents/ resources they operate on (like MIME types). Thus, wrapper types can be used to encapsulate such documents/resources and to define which tool should be opened in which way on that content object. Users or COHS clients can trigger execution of the tools when traversing the structure.
- Process centric integration: explicit calls to the tools are stored as macro commands (e.g. persistent queries or persistent commands) on the worktop. Here, the API provided by the tools, which are to be called, is used to configure proper execution of the tool.

Using both approaches, a variety of external tools have been integrated in the EXTERNAL EE engineering and operation environment [16]:

- The SimVision simulation tool for probabilistic simulation of work processes,
- The METIS visual process modelling tool,
- The Workware work enactment environment.

In the above cases, the necessary data provided by the shared repository is specified and the target application is called. Data is either translated from the repository into the target data format (in the case of the SimVision tool) from the COHS or extracted by the called tool (in case of METIS and Workware, which can deal with the native XML format).

To support cooperative work using external (non-cooperative) tools, the COHS was integrated with the NetMeeting environment [12]. Thus, any non-cooperative tools can be shared in an application sharing session. For this purpose, the COHS uses its knowledge about the members and contact details of the current session, and creates a new NetMeeting session with the same members. In this session, the specified tool will be started on the respective document, and shared.

4.5   Support for Process Execution

To support definition and execution of the joint business process, hypermedia types for representing work processes and a process execution engine, which enacts work process descriptions, are provided [12]. Here, the workflow engine is provided as a structure service in the cooperative open hypermedia system (COHS). This service interprets the shared EE model as a workflow structure. Corresponding to the server functionality in the COHS a process browser is provided as a COHS client. In this browser users can get an overview about the structure and current status (e.g. status of tasks, presence of co-workers, results of previous tasks) of the work process (see Figure 1). In addition, they can trigger execution of tasks, which are ready for execution. The browser then displays the documents needed for finishing the task, and also provides access to the tools needed for the job (using the above mentioned tools, tool integration methods).

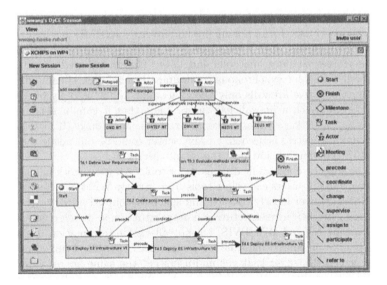

Fig. 1. XCHIPS Browser

In addition to process enactment, users can at any time use the browser to modify the (so far not enacted) work process description. The changes immediately take effect for continued enactment. Using the cooperative tools provided, users can execute the tasks together (e.g. instead of working on a task alone).

5 Implementation

The infrastructure provides access to and manipulation of shared hypermedia-based EE models. It serves as a basis for integrating tools and for supporting cooperative engineering and operation of extended and virtual enterprises. For wider accessibility and interoperability internet standards are used preferably. The system architecture of our approach can be characterized as client-server-based (see Figure 2). The EE models are stored in the COHS server using XML according to a hypermedia-based XML Document Type Definition (DTD). XML extends HTML because you can define your own set of tags by means of a DTD. The EE models can reference any other web resources. The server provides access to the enterprise models on the object level. Using its services, enterprise models can be created, manipulated, versioned, locked, merged, cloned and executed consistently.

The server supports the HyperText Transfer Protocol (HTTP) for asynchronous access to the EE models. Asynchronous access means that usually the server sends no notifications of other user's interactions to the clients whereas synchronous access is characterized by typically fine-grained notifications of the activities of other users [3]. In order to provide synchronous access to the EE models the server uses Java's remote method invocation (RMI) in a bi-directional way for special clients. Java RMI allows Java programs running in two different virtual machines to share methods and data. This distributed object mechanism is well suited for synchronous communication between clients and server. Some very restrictive firewalls only allow incoming traffic as reply to a request. A client behind such a firewall has the problem that it cannot get notified at any time by the server so that it has to work asynchronously. If in such a case also synchronous access is needed, a proxy server could be put inside the firewall handling the communication with the remote server.

This architecture allows flexible usage of tools. All tools work on the shared EE models and end-users can select tools from strictly What You See Is What I see (WYSIWIS) over loosely coupled and specially coupled until not coupled at all depending on their infrastructure and usage situation and preferences. Loosely coupled means relaxed WYSIWIS, i.e. not all-visible information is shared or not all changes on shared information are notified. Specially coupled means individual screen design so that the end-users get the same shared information presented differently. For WYSIWIS, loosely coupled or specially coupled tools synchronous Groupware clients are needed because of the notifications from the server to the clients.

Our current prototype implementation is called XCHIPS ("eXtensible Co-operative Hypermedia Integrated with Process Support"). It is implemented in pure Java using DyCE ("Dynamic Collaboration Environment"), a Client/Server-based Java framework for the development of Groupware components [13]. Figure 3 shows the system architecture of XCHIPS. The DyCE server provides persistence for shared objects, shared object types and mobile Groupware components as well as management services, e.g. uploading and downloading of components, shared data types and shared data, transactional support for accessing

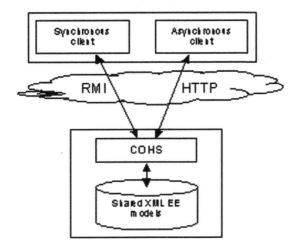

Fig. 2. System Architecture

and modifying shared data. The client provides a desktop for accessing components, registered to the server, and shared data, components work on. For XCHIPS, we have modeled shared hypermedia with process support on top of DyCE's shared object model and we have created several components.

Our prototype system includes the cooperative hypermedia editor, the cooperative navigation tool, the cooperative search tool, a chat tool and an audio conferencing tool based on the Java Media Framework, a shared whiteboard, a shared Web browser, a shared text editor and a shared brainstorming tool.

6 Conclusions

In this paper, a COHS-based solution for supporting engineering and operation of an EE was presented. XCHIPS, a prototypical implementation of the approach, uses an OHS-based approach to represent and manipulate shared EE models. COHS-features such as a collaboration structure service supporting for synchronous and asynchronous manipulation of EE models are used to facilitate cooperative work in the EE. A workflow structure service is provided, which coordinates work in the EE by enacting the EE model.

This work goes beyond existing approaches for EE support. Compared to WFMS, the COHS approach presented maintains both WF structure and work objects in a unified open hypermedia workspace. Using wrappers and tool integration methods new tools and information resources can be supported by the COHS. The COHS approach goes beyond shared workspace systems due to its process support and hypertext functionality (thus, leading to an open and tailorable solution [15]). Compared to other OHS and COHS systems this work

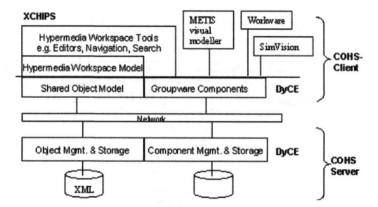

Fig. 3. XCHIPS Architecture

supports truly open collaboration via its support for native as well as legacy applications and through its run-time extensibility.

First usage experiences with the prototype in the EXTERNAL project indicates that the approach works well for providing a unified portal to all documents and tools relevant for work coordination and execution. However, difficulties experienced include the configuration of the firewalls and the coordination of concurrent access to shared repository data from non-native tools. Here, currently a locking approach is used, which seriously limits concurrent work (this does not apply to native tools, since they underlie the more fine-grained concurrency control of the COHS server).

In the future, we will address above issues. In addition, the system will be evaluated in three real-world user communities in the EXTERNAL project.

References

1. Anderson, K. M. (1999). Issues of Data Scalability in Open Hypermedia Systems. *The New Review of Hypermedia and Multimedia*, 5: 151-178.
2. Bentley, R., Horstmann, T., Trevor, J., The World Wide Web as enabling technology for CSCW: The case of BSCW, Computer-Supported Cooperative Work: Special issue on CSCW and the Web, Vol. 6 (1997), Kluwer Academic Press.
3. Delen, D., Benjamin, P. C., Erraguntla, M. An Integrated Toolkit For Enterprise Modeling And Analysis, Proceedings of the 1999 Winter Simulation Conference, IEEE Press, Dec. pp. 289-297.
4. Dourish, P. and Bellotti, V. Awareness and Coordination in Shared Workspaces. In Proc. of the ACM 1992 Conference on Computer Supported Cooperative Work, Toronto, Nov. 1-4, pp. 107-114.
5. Feise, J. Posties: A WebDAV Application for Collaborative Work. In Proceedings of Hypertext'00, ACM Press, San Antonio, Texas, U.S.A, pp. 228-229
6. Grønbæk, K., Hem, J.A., Madsen, O.L., Sloth, L. Systems: A Dexter-based Architecture. In Communications of the ACM 37, 2, 1994, pp. 65-74

7. Haake, J. M. Facilitating Orientation in Shared Hypermedia Workspaces. In: Stephen C. Hayne (Ed.): Group'99. Proceedings of the International ACM SIG-GROUP Conference on Supporting Group Work (November 14-17, 1999, Embassy Suites Hotel, Phoenix, Arizona, USA), pp. 365-374, New York, ACM Press, 1999.

8. Kacmar, C., Carey, J., and Alexander, M. 1998. Link processes: Supporting work-flow management using a hypermedia scripting language. Information & Software Technology. 40, 381-396.

9. Mogensen, P. and Grønbæk, K. Hypermedia in the virtual project room - toward open 3D spatial hypermedia. Proceedings of the eleventh ACM on Hypertext and hypermedia, 2000, 113-122. ACM Press: New York.

10. Reich, S., Wiil, U. K., Nürnberg, P. J., Davis, H. C., Grønbæk, K., Anderson, K. M., Millard, D. E., Haake, J. M. Addressing Interoperability in Open Hypermedia: The Design of the Open Hypermedia Protocol. The New Review of Hypermedia and Multimedia, Taylor Graham Publishing: London. January 2000.

11. Reinert, O., Bucka-Lassen, D., Pederson, C.A., Nürnberg, P.J. CAOS: A Collaborative and Open Spatial Structure Service Component with Incremental Spatial Parsing. In Proceedings of Hypertext'97, ACM Press, Southampton, U.K., pp. 49-50

12. Rubart, J., Haake, J. M., Tietze, D. A., Wang, W. Organizing shared enterprise workspaces using component-based cooperative hypermedia. Proceedings of the 12th ACM Conference on Hypertext and Hypermedia (Aarhus, Denmark, August 14-18, 2001). ACM Press: New York. In print.

13. Tietze, D. A., Steinmetz, R. Ein Framework zur Entwicklung komponenten-basierter Groupware. Proceedings der Fachtagung D-CSCW 2000, München, September, 2000.

14. Wang, W., and Haake, J.M. Flexible Coordination with Cooperative Hypermedia. In: Proceedings of ACM Hypertext'98 (HT98), pp. 245-255, June, 1998.

15. Wang, W., and Haake, J.M. Tailoring Groupware: The Cooperative Hypermedia Approach. In Computer Supported Cooperative Work: The Journal of Collaborative Computing, Vol. 9, No. 1, 2000, Kluwer.

16. Wang, W., Haake, J. M., Rubart, J., Tietze, D. A. Hypermedia-based Support for Cooperative Learning of Process Knowledge. Journal of Network and Computer Applications, Vol. 23, pp. 357-379, Academic Press, 2001.

17. Wiil, U.K. and Leggett, J.J. Workspaces: The HyperDisco Approach to Internet Distribution. In Proceedings of Hypertext'97, ACM Press, Southampton, U.K., pp. 13-23.

Meme Media and Meme Pools for Re-editing and Redistributing Intellectual Assets

Yuzuru Tanaka, Jun Fujima, and Tsuyoshi Sugibuchi

Meme Media Laboratory
Hokkaido University
Sapporo, 060-8628 Japan
{tanaka, fujima, buchi}@meme.hokudai.ac.jp

Abstract. While the current Web technologies have allowed us to publish intellectual assets in world-wide repositories, to browse their huge accumulation, and to download some assets, we have no good tools yet to flexibly re-edit and redistribute such intellectual assets for their reuse in different contexts. This paper reviews the IntelligentPad and IntelligentBox meme media architectures together with their potential applications, proposes both the use of XML/XSL or XHTML to define pads, and a world-wide web of meme pools. When applied to Web documents and services, meme media and meme pool technologies allow us to annotate Web pages with any types of meme media objects, and to extract and make any portions of them work as meme media objects. We can functionally combine such extracted meme media objects with each other or with other application meme media objects, and redistribute composite meme media objects for their further reuses by other people.

1 Meme Media for Re-editing and Redistributing Knowledge

Nowadays the research topics of science and technology are diversified and segmented into more and more categories. The number of interdisciplinary research topics has also increased. With increasingly sophisticated research on science and technology, there is a growing need for interdisciplinary and international availability, distribution and exchange of the latest research results, in re-editable and redistributable organic forms, including not only research papers and multimedia documents, but also various tools developed for measurement, analysis, inference, design, planning, simulation, and production. Similar needs are also growing for the interdisciplinary and international availability, distribution and exchange of ideas and works among artists, musicians, designers, architects, directors, and producers. We need new media technologies that externalize scientific, technological, and/or cultural knowledge fragments in an organic way, and promote their advanced use, international distribution, reuse, and re-editing.

These media should be able to carry a variety of intellectual assets. A media object denotes such a medium with a content intellectual asset. Such media objects can replicate themselves, recombine themselves, and be naturally selected

S. Reich, M.M. Tzagarakis, P.M.E. De Bra (Eds.): OHS/SC/AH 2001, LNCS 2266, pp. 28–46, 2002.

by people reusing them. We call them "meme media" since they carry what Richard Dawkins called "memes". In his book, "The Selfish Gene" [1] published in 1976, Dawkins suggested provocatively that ideas (he called them memes) are like genes and that societies have meme pools in just the same way as they have gene pools. Whereas genes exist in a physical environment, "memes" exist within a society. M. J. Stefik at Xerox PARC also pointed out, in 1986, the importance of developing new knowledge media that work as memes [2]. A fundamental and necessary framework for the growth and distribution of "memes" is a "meme pool". A "meme pool" is an accumulation of "memes" in a society and functions like a gene pool. "Meme media", together with a "meme pool" provide a framework for the farming of knowledge. When economic activities are introduced, a "meme pool" becomes a "meme market" where providers and distributors of "memes" should be able to carry out their business without prohibiting the replication, re-editing and redistribution of "memes" by users.

Hypermedia research groups have mainly focused their efforts on the linking services among intellectual assets for the navigation and the interoperability among them. They basically assumed that hypermedia contents were just viewed without making their copies, re-editing, nor redistributing them among people. Over the last seven years, the Open Hypermedia Working Group (OHSWG) has been working on a standard protocol to allow interoperability across a range of application software components. The group first focused on the separation of link services from document structures, which enables different hypermedia systems to interoperate with each other, and client applications to create, edit, and activate links which are managed in separate link databases [3]. Microcosm [4] and Multicard [5] are examples that worked as reference systems of link servers. The hypertext community also focused on the interoperability with database systems, which introduced higher level functionality: for example HyperBase [6] on a relational foundation, and HBI [7] on a semantic platform. The interoperability with databases also leads to the idea of separating component storage, run time and document content issues. The Dexter Hypertext Reference Model [8] proposed a layered architecture to separate them. As an alternative to such a layered architecture, the open hypertext community collaboratively developed a standard protocol OHP [9] for interdependent different services to interoperate with each other. These architectures worked as a basis to apply link services to the Web [10,11]. HyperDisco [12] and Chimera [13] proposed such interoperable service models, which were later applied to the Web [14,15].

The OHSWG approach was basically based on the following principles: the separation of link services, and the standardization of a navigational and/or functional linking protocol among different applications and services. The standard protocol may rely on either API libraries or an on-the-wire communication model using such a standard transport medium as socket. The group is further expanding the linking service functionality by introducing collaborative spatial structures [16], computational aspects, or dynamically defined abstract communication channels [17].

Meme media research that has been conducted independently from the open hypertext community has been focused on the replication, re-editing, and redistribution of intellectual assets. To achieve this goal, our group adopted a visual-wrapper architecture. Any component, whether it is an application or a service, small or large, is wrapped by a visual wrapper with direct manipulability and standard interface mechanism. These wrappers work as media to carry different types of intellectual assets. A media object denotes an intellectual asset wrapped by such a standard wrapper. Our wrapper architecture allows users to define a composite media object by combining primitive media objects. Composite media objects allow further recombination. Users can exchange those composite media objects through the Internet.

Application of meme media technologies to OHS technologies simply means that objects in the latter framework are wrapped by meme media wrappers, which will introduce meme media features to those objects without loosing any of their OHS features. The purpose of this paper is to propose such possibilities.

We have been conducting the research and development of "meme media" and "meme market" architectures since 1987. We developed 2D and 3D meme media architectures IntelligentPad and IntelligentBox respectively in 1989 and in 1995 [18,24], and have been working on their meme-pool and meme-market architectures, as well as on their applications and revisions.

Meme media and meme pool architectures will play important roles when they are applied to a reasonably large accumulation of intellectual assets. The current situation of the WWW, for example, satisfies this condition. While the current Web technologies have allowed us to browse such a huge accumulation of intellectual assets published on the Web, we have no good tools yet to flexibly re-edit and redistribute these intellectual assets for their reuse in different contexts. We need OHS technologies for the advanced reuse of Web-published intellectual assets. Meme media and meme pool technologies, when applied to the Web, will play similar roles as such OHS technologies for users to annotate Web- published assets; they further allow people to re-edit and redistribute some portions of their copies, without changing their originals, for their reuse in different contexts together with different applications.

In this paper, we review the IntelligentPad and IntelligentBox architectures together with their various applications we have developed up to now, proposes both the use of XML/XSL or XHTML to define pads, and to embed another pad, and a world-wide web of meme pools. We also propose new application frameworks of meme media for DB visualization/materialization and virtual laboratories for interactive scientific simulations. All these applications are decomposable, and re-editable. Their components can be reused in different contexts. Our world-wide web of meme pools will allow us to redistribute and re-edit all these applications. When applied to Web documents and Web services, meme media and meme pool technologies allow us to annotate Web pages with any types of meme media objects, and to extract and make any portions of them work as meme media objects. We can functionally combine such extracted meme media objects with each other or with other application meme media objects, and redistribute composite meme media objects for their further reuses by other people.

2   IntelligentPad and IntelligentBox

IntelligentPad represents each component as a pad, a sheet of paper on the screen. A pad can be pasted on another pad to define both a physical containment relationship and a functional linkage between them (Figure 1). When a pad P_2 is pasted on another pad P_1, the pad P_2 becomes a child of P_1, and P_1 becomes the parent of P_2. No pad may have more than one parent pad. Pads can be pasted together to define various multimedia documents and application tools. Unless otherwise specified, composite pads are always decomposable and re-editable.

In object-oriented component architectures, all types of knowledge fragments are defined as objects. IntelligentPad exploits both an object-oriented component architecture and a wrapper architecture. Instead of directly dealing with component objects, IntelligentPad wraps each object with a standard pad wrapper and treats it as a pad (Figure 1). Each pad has both a standard user interface and a standard connection interface. The user interface of a pad has a card like view on the screen and a standard set of operations like "move", "resize", "copy", "paste", and "peel". Users can easily replicate any pad, paste a pad onto another, and peel a pad off a composite pad. Pads are decomposable persistent objects. You can easily decompose any composite pad by simply peeling off the primitive or composite pad from its parent pad. As its connection interface, each pad provides a list of slots that work as connection jacks of an AV-system component, and a single connection to a slot of its parent pad (Figure 1). Each pad uses a standard set of messages–'set' and "gimme"–to access a single slot of its parent pad, and another standard message "update" to propagate its state change to its child pads. In their default definitions, a "set" message sends its parameter value to its recipient slot, while a "gimme" message requests a value from its recipient slot. Figure 2 shows a set of pulleys and springs that are all represented as pads, and a composition with them. Each of these pulleys and springs is animated by a transparent pad.

IntelligentBox is the 3D extension of IntelligentPad. Users can define a parent-child relationship between two boxes by embedding one of them into the local coordinate system defined by the other. A box may have any kind of 3D representations. Figure 3 shows a car composed with primitive boxes. When a user rotates its steering wheel, the steering shaft also rotates, and the rack-and-pinion converts the rotation to a linear motion. The cranks convert this linear motion to the steering of the front wheels. This composition requires no additional programming to define all these mechanisms. Suppose for example that someone published an animation of a flying eagle that is composed of a wire-frame model of an eagle that was covered by special boxes that apply deformation to a wire-frame model (Figure 4). One could easily replace this eagle with a wire-frame model of a 3D letter "A" to obtain a flying letter "A".

A pad as well as a box consists of a display object and a model object (Figure 5). Its display object defines its GUI, while its model object defines its internal state and behavior. Each display object further consists of a controller object and a view object. Its view object defines its view on the display screen, while its controller object defines its reaction to user events.

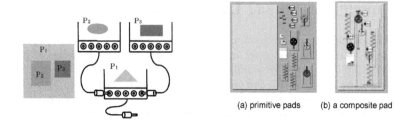

(a) primitive pads   (b) a composite pad

Fig. 1. A composite pad and slot connections. **Fig. 2.** An example pad composition.

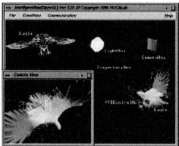

(a)   primitive boxes. (b) a composite box.

Fig. 3. An example box composition.   **Fig. 4.** Flying eagle animation.

When a pad (a box) P_2 is pasted on (connected to) another pad (box) P_1, the IntelligentPad (IntelligentBox) constructs a linkage between their view parts (Figure 6). This defines a dependency from P_1 to P_2. If P_1 has more than one slot, we have to select one of them to associate it with P_2. The selected slot name is stored in a register of the child pad (child box) P_2 named connectslot. A child pad (box) can send either "set ↑ connectslot ⟨value⟩" message or "gimme ↑ connectslot" message to its master, while the parent pad (box) can send all of its child pads (boxes) an "update" message without any parameter. The up arrow before connectslot means that the slot name stored in connectslot becomes the real parameter. The interpretation of the update message again depends on the implementation of the sender and the receiver pads (boxes). It usually informs the child pads (boxes) of a parent's state change. IntelligentPad (IntelligentBox) allows us to enable/disable each of these three standard messages. The two messages "set s v" and "gimme s" sent to a pad (box) P are forwarded to its parent pad (box) if P does not have the slot s.

The display object and the model object of a primitive pad are usually defined as C++ code, which makes it difficult for non-programmers to develop a new pad. Some pads have very simple internal mechanism that requires no coding. They include multimedia documents with some parameters exported through

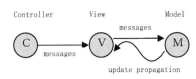

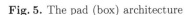

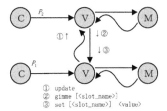

Fig. 5. The pad (box) architecture   **Fig. 6.** The interface between pads

their pad slots. For the definition of such a document, we may use XHTML, or a pair of XML and XSL to define its content and style, which requires no programming expertise. You may specify any of its phrases enclosed by a begin-tag and an end-tag to work as a slot value. An IEPad, when provided with a document content in XML and a style in XSL, generates the corresponding XHTML text to view on itself. It also generates a slot for each specified phrase in the original XML or XSL texts. For the development of an IEPad, we wrapped Microsoft InternetExplorer with a pad wrapper, and provided it with the slot-definition capability.

Figure 7 shows a parameterized XHTML that displays any text string in the specified orientation. Two parameters are parenthesized with tags to specify that they work as slots. Figure 8 shows its viewing by an IEPad, which has two child pads; one is used to input a string, while the other is to specify the angle. In addition to these functions, an IEPad allows us to embed any composite pad in an XHTML text using a special tag, and generates this pad on itself when viewing this XHTML text. The XHTML text in Figure 7 embeds a composite pad working as an analog clock, while Figure 8 shows the composite analog clock pad embedded in the document viewed by an IEPad.

3   Intellectual Assets on Meme Media

IntelligentPad and IntelligentBox have versatile application fields. They have a capability of covering all kinds of client application systems that use 2D and 3D graphical representations. Each application may require the development of new primitive pads or boxes. Some primitive pads or boxes may be too complicated to call them primitive pads or boxes, and require professional programmers to develop them.

Figure 9 shows PIM (Personal Information Management) tools developed as composite pads, while Figure 10 shows a GIS (Geographical Information System) using IntelligentPad and a legacy GIS database engine. Sapporo Electronic Center has developed an experimental GIS system for the urban design and administration of Sapporo City using IntelligentPad in cooperation with Fuji Xerox, Hitachi Software Engineering, and Fujitsu. As Nigel Waters, a professor in the Department of Geography, University of Calgary, pointed out the poten-

```
<?xml version="1.0" ?>
<html xmlns=http://www.w3.org/1999/xhtml xmlns:ip="http://ca.meme.hokudai.ac.jp/IntelligentPad">
  <head>
    <title>IEPad example</title>
    <script language="VBScript">
      <![CDATA[
      Sub func_caption(caption)
                lblActiveLbl.Caption = caption
      End Sub

      Sub func_angle(angle)
                lblActiveLbl.Angle = angle
      End Sub
      ]]>
    </script>
    <ip:slotlist>
      <ip:slot name="caption" func="func_caption">Meme Media Lab.</ip:slot>
      <ip:slot name="angle" func="func_angle">90</ip:slot>
    </ip:slotlist>
  </head>
  <body>
    <h2>This is an IEPad viewing a XHTML text that defines two slots and embeds one composite pad.</h2>
    <object classid="clsid:99B42120-6EC7-11CF-A6C7-00AA00A47DD2" id="lblActiveLbl" width="250" height="250">
      <param name="FontSize" value="20" />
      <param name="angle" value="90" />
      <param name="caption" value="Meme Media Lab." />
    </object>
    <object id="ipclock" classid="clsid:7D4FE1B3-05AC-463C-A30D-930194AA4D58" />
  </body>
</html>
```

Fig. 7. An XHTML text defining two slots and one embedded pad

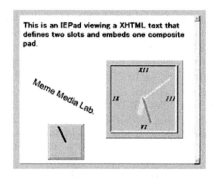

Fig. 8. The viewing of the parameterized XHTML text in Figure 7

tial application of IntelligentPad to GIS [25], a map display, a traffic simulation model, a video image of an intersection, and a display in graph form are all represented as mutually interacting pads. Such a GIS is not only a great pedagogical device, but is also invaluable for planning.

Seigo Matsuoka of Editorial Engineering Laboratory Inc. applied Intelligent-Pad to the production of a digital archive system "The Miyako" of Kyoto cultural heritage. It stores all the multimedia contents in a relational database management system, and uses IntelligentPad for its front-end interface to provide full

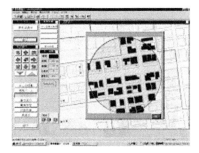

Fig. 9. PIM tools as composite pads   **Fig. 10.** GIS using legacy GIS engine

interactivity so that users can navigate through the huge contents library using various types of association search based on Japanese culture.

As to IntelligentBox, we have already developed two important generic application frameworks; one for interactive database visualization and the other for interactive scientific visualization. Our DB visualization framework provides visual interactive components for (1) accessing databases, (2) specifying and modifying database queries, (3) defining an interactive 3D object as a template to materialize each record in a virtual pace, and (4) defining a virtual space and its coordinate system for the information materialization. These components are represented as boxes, i.e., components in the IntelligentBox architecture. Figure 11 shows an example composition for information materialization. It specifies the above mentioned four functions as a flow diagram from left to right. The leftmost box is a TableBox, which allows us to specify a database relation to access; it outputs an SQL query with the specified relation in its "from" clause, leaving its "select" and "where" clauses unspecified. The database is stored in a local or remote database server running an Oracle DBMS. When clicked, a TableBox pops up the list of all the relations stored in the database, and allows us to select one of them.

The second box is a TemlateManagerBox, which allows us to specify a composite box used as a template to materialize each record. It allows us to register more than one template, and to select one from those registered for record materialization. When we select a template named t, the TemplateManagerBox adds a virtual attribute, "t" as TEMLATENAME, in the "select" clause of the input query, and outputs the modified SQL query. The database has an additional relation to store the registered templates. This relation TEMPLATEREL has two attributes; TEMPLATENAME and TEMPLATEBOX. The second attribute stores the template composite box specified by the first attribute. In the later process, the specified SQL query is joined with the relation TEMPLATEREL to obtain the template composite box from its name. When we register a new template composite box, the TemplatManagerBox accesses the database DDD (Data Dictionary and Directory) to obtain all the attributes of the relation specified by the input SQL query. It adds slots with these attributes

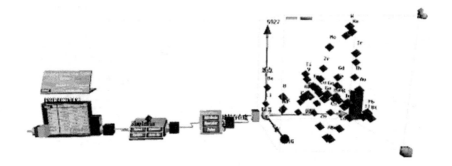

Fig. 11. An example composition for information materialization

to the base box of the template composite box. In the later process, the record materialization assigns each record value to a copy of this template box, which decomposes this record value to its attribute values and store them in the corresponding attribute slots of the base box.

The third component in the example is a RecordFilterBox, which allows us to specify attribute attr, a comparison operator θ, and a value v. This specification modifies the input query by adding a new condition attr θ v in its "where" clause. The RecordFilterBox accesses the database DDD to know all the accessible attributes.

The last component in this example is a ContainerBox with four more components, an OriginBox, and three AxisBoxes. A ContainerBox accesses the database with its input query, and materializes each record with the template composite box. While an OriginBox specifies the origin of the coordinate system of the materialization space, each AxisBox specifies one of the three coordinate axes, and allows us to associate this with one of the accessible attributes. It also normalizes the values of the selected attribute. These two components also use query modification methods to perform their functions.

In addition to the components used in the above example, the framework provides two more components, a JoinBox and an OverlayBox. A JoinBox accepts two input SQL queries, and defines their relational join as its output query. It allows us to specify the join condition. An OverlayBox accepts more than one query, and enables a ContainerBox to overlay the materialization of these input queries. From the query modification point of view, it outputs the union of input queries with template specifications.

By using a ContainerBox together with an OriginBox and AxisBoxes as a template composite box, we can define a nested structure of information materialization as shown in Figure 12. Thei displacement of the origin of each record materializing ContainerBox from the map plane indicates the annual production quantity of cabbage in the specified year at the corresponding prefecture, while each record materializing ContainerBox shows the cabbage production changes during the last 20 years.

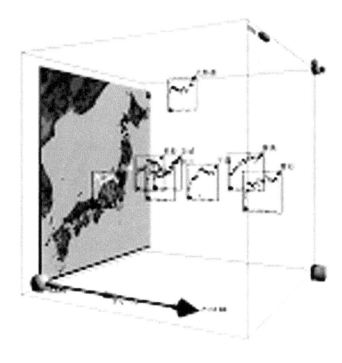

Fig. 12. A nested structure of information materialization

As an application of our information materialization framework, we have been collaborating with Gene Science Institute of Japan to develop an interactive animation interface to access cDNA database for the cleavage of a sea squirt egg from a single cell to 64 cells. The cDNA database stores, for each cell and for each gene, the expression intensity of this gene in this cell. Our system that was first developed using our old information materialization framework without query modification components animates the cell division process from a single cell to 64 cells. It has two buttons to forward or to backward the division process. When you click an arbitrary cell, the system graphically shows the expression intensity of each of a priori specified set of genes. You may also arbitrarily pick up three different genes to observe their expression intensities in each cell. The expression intensities of these three genes are associated with the intensities of three colors RGB to highlight each cell of the cleavage animation. Keeping this highlighting function active, you can forward or backward the cell-division animation. The development of this system took only several hours using the geometrical models of cells that are designed by other people. The cDNA database is stored in an Oracle DBMS, which IntelligentBox accesses using Java JDBC. We have applied our new information materialization framework to the same application. This

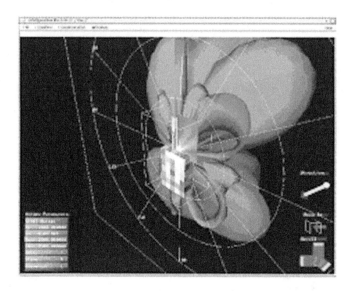

Fig. 13. Virtual Lab System using IntelligentBox technologies.

extension enabled us to dynamically construct the same functionality within 15 minutes without writing any program codes or any SQL queries.

For interactive scientific visualization, IntelligentBox provides a generic linkage mechanism with AVS system. This allows us to define a box as a program module of AVS so that combination of such boxes defines a composition of an AVS program, and that the manipulation of such a box changes parameter values of its corresponding AVS program module. These allow us to define a virtual laboratory in which we can construct a scientific simulation world through direct manipulation of an a priori given components, directly manipulate objects in this world to change situations, and interactively observe the simulation result in this world. Figure 13 shows a virtual laboratory for experimenting on the antenna of a cellular phone. Users can directly change the location and the length of the antenna to observe the changes of the radiation pattern, the electric field, and the surface current on the phone body. The system uses NEC2 as a numerical computation solver, which is invoked through AVS.

All these application pads and boxes are decomposable. User can reuse some of their components for different applications, or customize them by replacing some of their components with others and/or by adding new components to them.

4   Meme Pool Architectures

In order to make pads and boxes work as memes in a society, we need their worldwide publication repository that works as a meme pool. As described in Section 2, an IEPad allows us to embed any composite pad in an HTML text using a special tag, and generates this pad on itself when viewing this text. This enables us to publish any composite pads by embedding them in arbitrary Web pages. Users can drag these embedded pads out of Web pages into local environments. Since we have already developed the IntelligentBox runtime environment as an ActiveX control, and also as a pad called an IBPad, we can play with a IntelligentBox system on a Web page that is viewed by an IEPad, and apply a clip-and-paste operation to any box components in the system to import them into our own local envirionment. An IEPad, however, requires the writing of an HTML definition to publish a pad. Users like to use drag-and-drop operations not only to retrieve pads from WWW but also to publish pads to WWW. Furthermore, users of Web browsers have to ask Web page owners by sending, say, an e-mail to include his or her information in other's Web pages, or to span links from other's Web page to his or her page. This is similar to the situation between tenants and owners. While the owner-tenant system works well to emergently form the clustering of similar information contents, we also like to provide a large public marketplace for people to freely open their stores or galleries of pads.

"Piazza Web" is a world-wide web of piazzas, each of which works as such a marketplace. We can browse through Piazza Web, using a PiazzaBrowserPad. Each piazza has a corresponding file that stores a set of pads together with their geometrical arrangement. Such a file may be stored locally, or in a special remote server called a piazza server. Each piazza is also represented as a pad called a PiazzaPad. Pads can be drag-and-dropped to and from a PiazzaPad to upload and download pads to and from the associated remote server file. When a PiazzaPad is opened, all the pads registered to the associated server file are immediately downloaded onto this pad, arranged in their registered locations, and become available. A PiazzaPad has a slot to specify a piazza server with its URL address. When given an update message, a PiazzaPad saves all the pads on itself with their current states and current locations into the corresponding server. When given a new URL address, a PiazzaBrowserPad either generates a new PiazzaPad on itself or uses the old PiazzaPad, depending on its specified mode, and sets this URL address to the file address slot of the PiazzaPad to download the registered pads. An entrance link to a piazza is also represented as a pad, and can be put on another piazza to define a link. When clicked, the entrance link pad sends its stored URL address to the underlying PiazzaBrowserPad, which then opens this piazza. A PiazzaBrowserPad has a save slot, which, when accessed by a set message from, say, a buttonPad connected to this slot, sends an update message to its child PiazzaPad to make it save its child pads to the server. Users are welcome to install their Piazza servers anywhere, anytime, and to publish their client pads. Piazza enables end users to open their own gallery of pads on the Internet, or to exhibit their pads in some other private or public space. Such pad galleries work as flea markets, shops, shopping centers, community message boards, community halls, or plazas. We have also extended an IBPad so that its IntelligentBox environment may import boxes that are temporarily held by the clip-board. Using such an IBPad on a piazza, we can clip-and-paste boxes between any piazza and our local environment. The upload of boxes requires the pushing of the save button on the PiazzaBrowserPad.

Transportation of pads and boxes undefined at their destination requires their cross-platform migration; their execution on the destination platform requires that all the libraries necessary for their execution should be available there in advance. These libraries include pad definition libraries, API libraries, and class libraries. These are defined as DLLs (Dynamic Link Libraries), and dynamically called when required. Migration of a new pad to a different platform requires migration of all the required DLLs that the destination lacks. Pads that someone has uploaded to a PiazzaPad can be downloaded from the same PiazzaPad and executed if and only if the destination platform has all the required DLLs. Each PiazzaPad allows privileged users to upload a new pad together with its required DLLs. When another user opens this PiazzaPad, it checks if the destination platform has all the required DLLs. If yes, this user can drag this pad out of the PiazzaPad. If not, the PiazzaPad asks the user if he or she wants to download the missing DLLs. Only after the required downloading, he or she can drag this pad out of this PiazzaPad. The automatic DLL migration by Piazza systems simplifies the distribution of pads among users.

Ikuyoshi Kato's group at Graduate School of Physics, Hokkaido University, applied IntelligentPad and Piazza to the international availability, distribution and exchange of nuclear reaction experimental data and their analysis tools (Figure 14). For example, a user A may open a piazza and drag-and-drops a chart showing his experimental result. Another user B later accesses the same piazza to see what user A has published. He drags this pad out into his own environment, and overlays his own experimental result on this chart by drag-and-dropping his data pad onto this chart pad. Then he may drag this updated pad into the same piazza together with the data pad showing also the bibliographic information. He may also drop a massage pad into this piazza to inform user A of this update.

5   Meme Media Technologies and the Web

While the current Web technologies have allowed us to browse such a huge accumulation of intellectual assets published on the Web, we have no good tools yet to flexibly re-edit and redistribute these intellectual assets for their reuse in different contexts. We need OHS technologies for the advanced reuse of Web-published intellectual assets. Meme media and meme pool technologies will play similar roles as such OHS technologies for people to annotate Web pages with any types of meme media objects. they further allow people to extract and make any portions of Web pages work as meme media objects. We can functionally combine such extracted meme media objects with each other or with other application meme media objects, and redistribute composite meme media objects for their further reuses by other people.

Figure 15 shows a Web-annotator composed with an IEPad and a WebAnnotationPad. A WebAnnotationPad has a double layered structure with its base

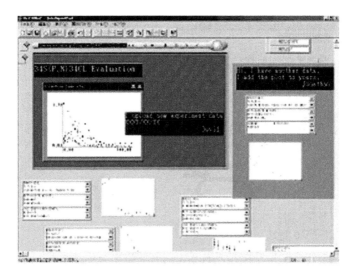

Fig. 14. International distribution and reuse of nuclear reaction data and analysis tools.

layer and its surface layer, and three different operation modes; the transparent mode, the translucent mode, and the hiding mode. The surface layer works as a transparent or translucent film covering the base layer and its child pads if any. In its transparent mode, a WebAnnotationPad makes its surface layer inactive, and the background of this layer transparent, only showing what are drawn or pasted on this layer; every user event, including pad pasting events, passes through the surface layer. You may use this mode to paste an IEPad directly on the base layer of a WebAnnotationPad; this IEPad is inserted between the base layer and the surface layer. In its translucent mode, a WebAnnotationPad makes its surface layer active, and the background of this layer translucent; only those user events that are not processed by this layer passes through the surface layer. In its hiding mode, a WebAnnotationPad makes its surface layer and all the child pads of this layer in inactive and invisible; every user event passes through the surface layer.

In its translucent mode, a WebAnnotaionPad allows you to paste any pad on its surface layer. The pasted pad works as a child pad of the surface layer. Any pad pasted on a WebAnnotationPad in its transparent or hiding mode becomes a child of the topmost pad at this location under the surface layer. The surface layer also works as a drawing tool. This function allows you to draw any figures as annotations to the Web page shown by the inserted IEPad. When an inserted IEPad scrolls its page, the WebAnnotationPad also scrolls its surface layer for the same distance so that every child pad and every figure on the surface layer keep their original relative locations on the Web page shown by the inserted IEPad.

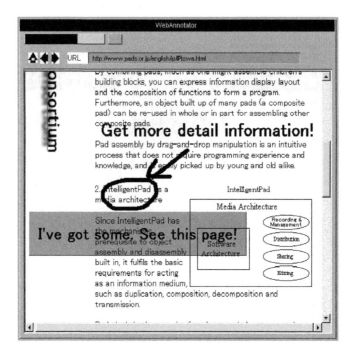

Fig. 15. WebAnnotatorPad with an inserted IEPad, an annotative anchor pad, and an annotative drawing.

Each WebAnnotationPad has its associated local or remote file, and allows you to save its annotation information there, including its child pads and annotation figures, together with the URI of the Web page shown by the inserted IEPad. When we change the URI of the inserted IEPad, this new URI is informed by this IEPad to the base layer of the WebAnnotaionPad through a slot connection, which accesses its associated local or remote file to load the previously saved corresponding annotation information if any. A reference to any object as an annotation may use an annotative anchor pad with the URI of this object. You may paste such an annotative anchor pad at any location on a WebAnnotationPad in its translucent mode. A click of such an annotative anchor pad sets its content URI to the URI slot of the WebAnnotationPad, which tells the inserted IEPad to read the new URI; both the inserted IEPad and the WebAnnotationPad will respectively load the corresponding Web page and annotation information. Figure 15 shows an annotative comment "Get more detail information!" with an arrow pointing to a system name in the Web page. It also has an annotative anchor pad with a caption "I've got some. See this page", which points to another Web page. When clicked, this anchor pad sets a new URI to the WebAnnotationPad and its inserted IEPad.

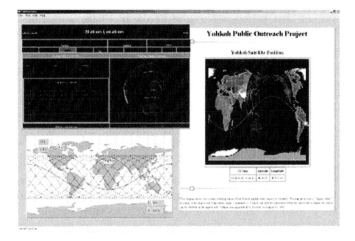

Fig. 16. Live copies of the two satellites' location information, and their reuse in a different context to visually compare their orbits.

The Web annotator in Figure 15 is also a pad, and hence allows you to transport this composite pad together with its contents to other users through the Internet. The transportation of contents actually sends only the two URIs.

Figure 16 shows our recent research achievement called LiveDocument, which allows us to cut out any portion of an arbitrary Web page through mouse operations, and to make its live copy as a pad. Such a copy is alive in the sense that it periodically polls the source server to update its state. You may paste such a pad on another pad to define a slot connection, and periodically sends its recent value to its parent pad. Figure 16 shows two Web browsers, left top one and the right one, showing the current locations of a space station and a satellite Yohkoh. Their longitudes and latitudes are extracted as 4 live pads. They are pasted on a world map in the left bottom quadrant with appropriate slot connections to plot these satellite locations. The map shows the orbits of these satellites with two different colors, blue and red. You may use the Piazza system to redistribute this composite map with 4 live pads. This composite pad is kept alive at any destination.

6 Concluding Remarks

If we retrospect the last three decades of computer systems, we can summarize them as follows. In 1970s, we focused on the integrated management of enterprise or organization information, and developed database technologies. In 1980s, we focused on integrated environment of personal information processing and office information processing, based on the rapid development of personal computers and workstations that began in the late 1970s. In 1990s, we focused on publication and browsing of intellectual assets, based on the rapid development of WWW and browser technologies.

One of the possible scenarios for the coming decade may be the further growing need for interdisciplinary and international availability, distribution and exchange of intellectual assets including information, knowledge, ideas, works, and tools in re-editable and redistributable organic forms. Meme media and meme pool system architectures work as the enabling technologies for this need. They will significantly accelerate the evolution of memes in our society.

We have been applying meme media technologies for a variety of information systems, including PIM systems, GISs, over-the-counter financial consultation systems, multimedia presentations, education tools, database visualization and materialization systems, and virtual laboratory systems, to prove the generic potentialities of meme media architectures. First of all, we have observed significant reduction of man-month in developing these applications. Second, we have experienced significant reuse of components and frameworks of one application in other applications. Third, we have learned much from using IntelligentPad and IntelligentBox systems how to decompose application system for better reuses of components. Finally, we have also experienced the difficulties in understanding the functions of unfamiliar components. These difficulties are similar to those we experience when we first encounter a new product unfamiliar to us. Before a new product becomes a commodity, it needs to be accompanied by a set of manuals. It is useful for a new product to follow some convention in naming its connectors in such a way as video, L, R for AV cable signals. However, we still need to solve this problem for those meme media objects with immature usage conventions.

While current Web technologies have already allowed us to access a huge accumulation of intellectual assets, we have no good tools yet to flexibly re-edit and redistribute these intellectual assets for their reuse in different contexts. We need OHS technologies for the advanced reuse of Web-published intellectual assets. We have shown in this paper that meme media and meme pool technologies play similar roles as such OHS technologies to annotate Web pages with any types of meme media objects. They futhrer allow us to extract and make any portions of Web pages work as meme media objects. We can functionally combine such extracted meme media objects with each other or with other application meme media objects, and redistribute composite meme media objects for their further reuses by other people.

Application of meme media technologies to OHS technologies may introduce memetic features to open hyper media systems; it will allow people to re -edit and redistribute intellectual assets published in open hypermedia systems. This application simply means that objects in the latter framework are wrapped by meme media wrappers, which will introduce meme media features to those objects without loosing any of their OHS features.

References

1. R. Dawkins. *The Selfish Gene*. Oxford Univ. Press, Oxford, 1976
2. M. Stefik. The next knowledge medium. *The AI Magazine*, 7(1):34-46, January 1986.
3. L. Carr, W. Hall, D. De Roure. The Evolution of Hypertext Link Services, ACM Comput. Surv. 31, 4es, Dec, 1999.
4. A. M. Fountain, W. Hall, I. Heath, H. C. Davis. Microcosm: An Open Model With Dynamic Linking. Proc. ACM European Conference on Hypertext '90 (ECHT '90), Versailles, France, 298-311, Nov. 1990.
5. A. Rizk, L. Sauter. Multicard: An Open Hypermedia System, Proc. ACM European Conf. on Hypertext '92 (ECHT '92), Milano, 4-10, Dec. 1992.
6. H. Schütt, N.A. Streitz. Hyperbase: A Hypermedia Engine Based on a relational Database Management System, Proc. ACM European Conf. on Hypertext '90 (ECHT '90), Versailles, 95-108, Nov. 1990.
7. J.L. Schase, J.J. Legget, et.al.. Design and Implementation of the HBI Hyperbase Management System. Electronic Publishing: Origination, Dissemination and Design, 6(2), 35-63, 1993.
8. F.G. Halasz, M.D. Schwartz. The Dexter Hypertext Reference Model. Communications of ACM, 37(2), 30-39, Feb. 1994.
9. H.C. Davis, A. Lewis, A. Rizk. OHP: A Draft Proposal for an Open Hypermedia Protocol. ACM Hypertext '96, Open Hypermedia Systems Workshop, Washington DC, March 1996.
10. K. Grønbæk, N.O. Bouvin, L. Sloth. Designing Dexter-Based Hypermedia Services for the World Wide Web, Proc. ACM Hypertext '97, Southampton, UK, 146-156, 1997.
11. K. Grønbæk, L. Sloth, P. OrbÊk. Webvise: Browser and Proxy Support for Open Hypermedia Structuring Mechanisms on the WWW. Proc. the Eighth International World Wide Web Conference, 253-268, 1999.
12. U.K. Will, J.J. Leggett. The HyperDisco Approach to Open Hypermedia Systems, Proc. ACM Hypertext '96, Washington DC, 140-148, March 1996.
13. K.M. Anderson, R.N. Taylor, E.J. Whitehead. Chimera: Hypertext for Heterogeneous Software Environments, Proc. ACM European Conference on Hypermedia Technology (ECHT '94), Edinburgh, Scotland, 94-106, Sept. 1994.
14. U.K. Will, J.J. Leggett. Workspaces: The HyperDisco Approach to Internet Distribution, Proc. ACM Hypertext 97, Southampton, UK, 13-23, April 1997.
15. K.M. Anderson. Integrating Open Hypermedia Systems with the World Wide Web, Proc. ACM Hypertext '97, Southampton UK, 157-167, April 1997.
16. O. Reinert, D. Bucka-Lassen, C.A. Pedersen, P.J. Nürnberg. CAOS: A Collaborative and Open Spatial Structure Service Component with Incremental Spatial Parsing, Proc. ACM Hypertext '99, 49-50, Darmstadt, Germany, 1999.
17. L. Moreau, N. Gibbins, et. al.. SoFAR with DIM Agents, An Agent Framework for Distributed Information Management, Proc. Fifth Int'l Conf. and Exhibition on the Practical Application of Intelligent Agents and Multi-Agents, Manchester UK, Apr. 2000.
18. Y. Tanaka, and T. Imataki. IntelligentPad: A Hypermedia System allowing Functional Composition of Active Media Objects through Direct Manipulations. In *Proc. of IFIP'89*, pp.541-546, 1989.
19. Y. Tanaka, A. Nagasaki, M. Akaishi, and T. Noguchi. Synthetic media architecture for an object-oriented open platform. In *Personal Computers and Intelligent Systems, Information Processing 92, Vol III*, North Holland, pp.104-110, 1992.

20. Y. Tanaka. From augmentation media to meme media: IntelligentPad and the world-wide repository of pads. In *Information Modelling and Knowledge Bases, VI* (ed. H. Kangassalo et al.), IOS Press, pp.91-107, 1995.
21. Y. Tanaka. A meme media architecture for fine-grain component software. In *Object Technologies for Advanced Software*, (ed. K. Futatsugi, S. Matsuoka), Springer, pp.190-214, 1996.
22. Y. Tanaka. Meme media and a world-wide meme pool. In *Proc. ACM Multimedia 96*, pp.175-186, 1996.
23. B. Johstone. DIY Software. *New Scientist*. Vol.147, No.1991:26-31, 1995.
24. Y. Okada and Y. Tanaka,. IntelligentBox: a constructive visual software development system for interactive 3D graphic applications. *Proc. of the Computer Animation 1995 Conference*, pp.114-125, 1995.
25. N. Waters. POGS: Pads of Geographic Software. *GIS World*, 8(11): 82, 1995.

The Pipeline of Enrichment: Supporting Link Creation for Continuous Media

Richard Beales, Don Cruickshank, David DeRoure, Nick Gibbins, Ben Juby, Danius T. Michaelides, and Kevin R. Page

Intelligence, Agents, Multimedia,
Department of Electronics & Computer Science
University of Southampton, SO17 1BJ, UK
rmb00r@ecs.soton.ac.uk

Abstract. The application of open hypermedia to temporal media has previously been explored with respect to the link service, in particular link delivery and generic linking. This paper is based on the notion of *continuous metadata*, in which we use metadata in a temporally significant manner to capture and convey the information required to support linking. With a focus on link creation and *live* processing, our approach enriches hypermedia content with additional metadata at a number of points between capture and delivery. We illustrate this approach with a tool which assists metadata capture by annotation of continuous media according to a simple ontology.

1 Introduction

Previously we have investigated the application of open hypermedia to temporal media [7]. This paper extends this work in three ways: we address link creation rather than link resolution and delivery; we generalise link or anchor/endpoint streams to be instances of *continuous metadata* and we consider this metadata throughout the system; we support live processing rather than assuming we are working with stored media.

The scenario which motivates this work involves capturing an event, such as a seminar or meeting, and making this available retrospectively as a hypermedia resource. We will focus on video recordings and associated presentational material as this is the resource we have available for study, but we are looking towards the richer set of information that might be obtained from "smart" environments where the event is supported by augmented (and possibly virtual) reality. In this respect, our work is informed by the meeting room scenario discussed in [21].

Our goal here is to provide a user with a means to annotate (enrich) the original material with metadata which will support linking. We see this as an example of processing that may occur several times during the capture, production and use of the material: the pipeline of enrichment. The annotation is related to an agreed vocabulary (a simple ontology) for describing the event, and different events will have different ontologies. We are interested in generating the annotation interface automatically from the ontology. In the smart

S. Reich, M.M. Tzagarakis, P.M.E. De Bra (Eds.): OHS/SC/AH 2001, LNCS 2266, pp. 47–58, 2002.
© Springer-Verlag Berlin Heidelberg 2002

workshop scenario, we envisage a variety of personalised interfaces which enable live annotation by those involved in the event.

In the next section we introduce our notion of continuous metadata that underlies this work, enabling us to generalise link streams and address live processing throughout. This is followed in section 3 by a description of our tool which supports continuous metadata. In section 4 we consider the simple ontology, based on RDF. Section 5 combines the tool and the ontology, and there is a discussion in section 6.

2 Introduction to Continuous Metadata

In previous papers we have introduced the notion of *continuous metadata* [18, 5], built upon earlier work linking temporal media in the audio domain [10,6]. We view metadata simply as data about data, which can be encapsulated in a number of formats. In this situation it is not the type nor content of the metadata that is of premier importance; we are more concerned with its temporal relevance and continuous nature.

We define a *mediadata* flow to be the streamed content from and against which continuous metadata flows are derived and synchronised. The mediadata flow would normally be a multimedia stream, such as audio and/or video, transported using a real-time network protocol. The metadata, distributed as a separate flow (possibly through a number of intermediate filter nodes) might be generated on a "just-in-time" or live basis, but cannot be downloaded in its entirety before presentation begins. Although it might be the case that it is the volume of metadata that warrants streaming, we do not presume that the continuous metadata flow will be saturated with a non-stop transfer of information.

3 The HyStream System

3.1 The Temporal Linking Service

The Temporal Linking Service (TLS) was built to demonstrate the concepts of mediadata flows and metadata flows. The TLS comprises of a streaming media server, a continuous metadata server and a client that can receive and synchronise the resultant streams from both servers.

The prototype media server uses the Java Media Framework (JMF) to stream media to the client using the Real-time Transport Protocol (RTP) [19]. The client application also uses JMF to view the incoming media flow. The JMF component of the client maintains a media clock, which JMF uses internally to maintain a steady video image. The client application also uses this media clock to synchronise the incoming metadata with the media.

The persistence of metadata within the server is performed by an XML backend. The stored form of the metadata consists of:

1. A start point for the link (a URI [2] which points to the media for which the link is relevant).

2. An endpoint (a URI to the destination of the link).
3. A human readable label for the link.
4. The time period for which the link is relevant in the respective media flow.

3.2   The Temporal Linking Transfer Protocol

The Temporal Linking Transfer Protocol (TLTP) is used between components of the TLS, and is described in more detail in [5]. In this protocol, on-time delivery of metadata is preferred over guaranteed delivery. To support small devices and features of the network layer with small buffering capability, we opt to transmit metadata "just-in-time". Since we cannot usefully incorporate late metadata into a continuous media flow the desired behaviour is to simply drop late metadata. Due to the timeliness of metadata, we dispense with the requirement for the client to acknowledge the arrival of particular fragments of data, as the server cannot usefully retransmit the data into the metadata stream.

As part of the setup process between a TLS server and client, the client determines the effective latency of payloads from the server to the client. To achieve this, the client requests the server to return the time value of the server's local clock. The client records the value of its local clock when the response is received. This action allows the client to determine the effective time difference of server to client messages. This method does not assume that the local clock on either the client or the server has been set correctly.

After calculating the effective time difference between the client and the server, the client then informs the server of this difference. Thus the server is capable of determining at any time whether a metadata payload is too late for delivery, allowing it to drop such metadata.

3.3   The Seminar Application

Our first application of the HyStream system was to deliver seminar activities held at the IAM group with metadata on slide changes. Generally, this involves a speaker, a set of presentation slides and a video camera at the event. This metadata takes the form of links into a publicly available set of slides that correspond to the ones given in the video. Figure 1 shows a clip of a seminar presentation at the IAM group. The top left of the figure shows the video of the seminar, and the temporal metadata is shown below the video, in the form of hypertext links. The section to the right of the window shows the resultant slide of the visible link.

The target of a link is determined by the mime type of the endpoint. If the mime type of the endpoint is a media type supported by the Java Media Framework, the video window is redirected to that endpoint. If the Mime-Type is not supported by JMF, the endpoint is invoked on the right hand side of the window. This allows the metadata producer to augment the continuous metadata stream with links that refer to other video resources, either live or stored.

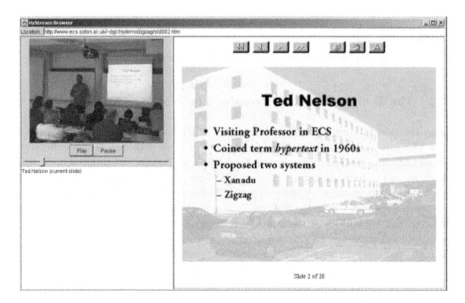

Fig. 1. The HyStream seminar application

The buttons above the presentation slide contain links that refer to other slides within the same presentation, allowing the viewer to navigate the presentation slides independently of the video window. During the seminar, the current slide is always available as a link under the video window, allowing the user to "synchronise" back with the presenter.

4   Authoring Continuous Metadata

Earlier research, including the HyStream system, has focused on the mechanisms to distribute and deliver continuous metadata. This work complements technologies such as RTP [19], RTSP [20], and Quality of Service provision [3,4] for network transportation of continuous mediadata. Synchronised presentation of such material within an Open Hypermedia System is usually based on concepts introduced in the Amsterdam Hypermedia Model [11] and latterly included in SMIL [1].

In this paper we will focus on the creation of continuous metadata to accompany streamed multimedia, the beginning of a branching and repetitive process of authoring and annotation; a pipeline of data enrichment.

Several standards are already defined within the broadcast entertainment industry which utilise metadata:

– TV Anytime [8] annotates media to allow navigation and integration between and within temporal content (stored on a user's device from broadcast) and external Web based data.

- MHEG marks up multimedia as collections of related objects for interchange and synchronised presentation, with a procedural language to describe interaction and presentational semantics [9].
- The Multimedia Content Description Interface, MPEG-7, defines a core set of quantitative measures of audio-visual features and structured relationships between them, associated with the original media as metadata [15].

These standards focus on augmenting content with metadata about the media itself, normally within a combined media and metadata stream. For our workshop scenario we will record continuous metadata not directly represented within or by the streamed content (video); we will represent people, objects, and events as abstract data entities. More specifically, we will record information about the workshop attendees, the video recording of the proceedings, presentation slides, and any annotations a participant might add (perhaps from a personal linkbase). However, before any such metadata can be authored, we must specify a structure to define any relationships between the entities, as well as the entities themselves - an ontology.

The Resource Description Framework (RDF) [12] is an infrastructure that enables the encoding, exchange, and reuse of structured metadata. RDF does not prescribe semantics for each particular resource description community, instead it provides the ability to define new metadata elements as needed using an XML syntax. Its data model defines a *resource* as any object uniquely identified by a URI (Uniform Resource Identifier) [2], and resources have *properties* which express the relationships of *values* associated with that resource. The values can be either atomic (strings, numbers etc.) or other resources (which may have their own properties) [14].

Collections of properties about a particular resource form a *description*; collections of properties used to describe resources within a particular resource description community form a *vocabulary*. RDF includes a mechanism for declaring and publishing vocabularies as XML Schemas, so that RDF can support any number of descriptive requirements without needing to define them. For example, the Dublin Core Metadata [22] is a simple vocabulary designed for resource discovery on the WWW which is defined within RDF. Vocabulary semantics can therefore be understood, reused and extended, in a modular manner using the XML namespace mechanism by any system supporting RDF.

Once an RDF vocabulary has been defined, gathering the metadata itself can be a manual or automated process; for a simple scenario such as ours it is trivial to collate the information by hand, however technology is already available to aid generation and, at least in part, do so transparently:

- On registering at a conference, it is usual for a delegate to be given a bar coded name badge; whenever the delegate enters a workshop or seminar room the bar code is manually scanned, compiling an attendance list typically used for marketing purposes, but also ideal for creating metadata.
- Presentation resources (such as Power Point, AppleWorks, and so on) can be parsed to build self-describing RDF sequences. Meaningfully cataloguing

resources not contained within a standard presentation format (for example demonstrated software applications) would be more involved, requiring a background application to monitors file activity for the duration of the presentation.

Nonetheless, the laborious operation of temporal annotation - identifying and recording when a person is speaking, or a resource is displayed - still remains. *Smart spaces* leverage pervasive technology, combining computing embedded within the existing infrastructure with mobile devices such as PDAs [13]. Use of smart spaces, combined with more recent audio and video analysis could be applied to automate this process of temporal annotation:

− Proximity identification systems such as RFID, coupled in the longer term with speaker recognition and video analysis may be employed to reliably identify the current speaker.
− The Palette project [17], developed at Xerox FX Palo Alto Laboratory, offers a more novel approach to identifying the current slide than video analysis. Paper printouts of the slides to be shown are produced, each carrying a barcode that uniquely identifies that slide. To display their chosen slide, the speaker places the paper representation under a barcode reader, which is linked to the presentation PC. By distributing pen-style barcode readers and printed booklets of slides amongst the audience, during a question and answer session, an audience member may quickly select for display the slide which they wish to query. Thus this technology offers instant tangible benefits during the presentation, in addition to expediting the production of metadata for future use.
− Video and audio analysis techniques such as gesture recognition may allow the mood of the workshop to be captured, allowing someone to, for example, search for instances in the presentation when the speaker looked uncomfortable.

Within the IAM Group at Southampton we are investigating how pervasive computing devices can exploit RDF to communicate wirelessly within a smart environment. Other work in the group involves the exchange of relevant links between participants in a H.323 video-conference, by piping metadata over a T120 data channel. Combining these ideas in the scenario of a workshop or conference, members of the audience could exchange links amongst themselves that they find relevant as the presentation proceeds. Such ambient metadata may also be captured, potentially offering a fascinating insight into the audiences first impressions; the extent to which this information can be usefully exploited will of course depend on the richness of the ontological structure in which it is defined.

   The scope for automatic metadata capture in the future is so vast that ultimately rather than simply adding new metadata, the authoring process may be as much concerned with filtering that metadata which has already been electronically harvested, to produce a personalised view or window onto the event.

5   Extending HyStream with RDF Metadata

In the context of the workshop scenario, we have extended the HyStream seminar application to interact with an RDF knowledge base when creating the link data. By describing the smart space with a set of RDF entities, we can produce an interface within the HyStream application which contains all the possible links that can occur during the meeting. In our mock-up smart space, we have produced a set of RDF descriptions that would have been created by our smart room (figure 2).

The RDF vocabulary, shown as a simplified overview in figure 3, contains:

1. Video / Media - defined by the URI of the media on the server
2. Person - expressed in the VCard schema. A number of Person entities would attend the workshop
3. Presentation - given by a particular Person(s), which will contain
4. Slide - the separate slides within a Presentation, which the HyStream viewer can display along with the workshop video
5. Relevant Link - an annotation offered by a Person (not necessarily the Person giving the Presentation) linking to some relevant information. This might be generated at the workshop, or at a later point when the Person is viewing the recorded Presentation

To deliver this content when displaying the workshop video the HyStream application queries the Temporal Linking Server as before. To generate the continuous metadata stream using TLTP, the server now locates valid entities for

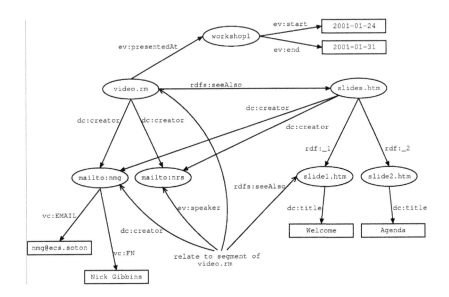

Fig. 2. RDF Entity Diagram

each particular time point within the RDF description of the workshop, and then sends the data to the client.

The HyStream client can also be used to author the original metadata or annotations, as shown in figure 4. A customised HTTP server generates a dynamic user interface derived from the RDF description, delivering the resources as click-able hypertext links. Each dynamically generated link is accompanied by two extra links, labelled "appear" and "disappear", which can be used to inform the HTTP server of events that happen in the media. The authoring links invoke JavaScript to encode the current time from the media window (which can be paused to allow more accurately timed annotations) into the HTTP request. Upon receiving the HTTP requests, the server adds the new events into the RDF knowledge base.

Events that are captured by the HTTP server relate to a precise time during the video. This must be the case during a live recording, because the period of time that the event remains is unknown when the event is recorded. When the metadata is played back to the user through the continuous metadata stream, the links have time ranges. This does not pose a problem when we author and view the metadata stream sequentially. If we try to perform these in parallel, we find that we cannot deliver metadata with a known end-time. This area requires further research. Our current solution is to deliver the link with a preset duration when the duration is not known.

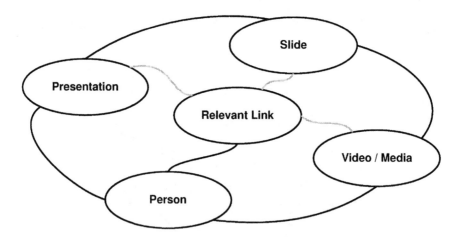

Fig. 3. Simple RDF relationships

6   Discussion

6.1   Further Enhancements to the HyStream Client Using RDF

The current mechanism for creating metadata through the HyStream viewer is limited. Although the authoring interface is generated dynamically, the HTTP server expects an RDF vocabulary that conforms to the Person, Video / Media, Presentation, Slide and Relevant Link entities we have used. This should be extended so than a similar authoring interface can be generated from an arbitrary RDF knowledge base using a vocabulary previously unknown to the server.

The ontology we have used includes some basic relationships between entities. For example, a name and email together define a "person"; that person can then be labelled as a "creator of" a resource, and that resource in turn can have other creators attached. While it is currently assumed that any resource which is part of an RDF sequence represents a slide, a sequence might also be used to refer to a number of audio clips, or even odours released during the presentation. If the application is to sensibly handle types of resources previously unknown to it, then a hierarchy of relationships is required. The odours released might form part of a workshop on perfumery. It cannot be reasonably expected that a generic application such as ours will have in-built knowledge of this area. However a series of relationships can be defined, to explain that any particular fragrance is a member of a super class "fragrances", and that objects of super-class "fragrance" have odour and visual image, but do not emit sound. The application can then follow this hierarchy of relationships until it reaches a concept that it can handle - i.e. visual image, and place the resource accordingly within its user interface.

Rich ontological relationships will provide a further benefit. Each workshop is currently viewed as an isolated event, and it is not possible within the current ontological structure to reliably express the far-reaching professional networks that invariably connect such events in the real world. If rich relationships are employed, then, provided that they derive from a common set of base classes, a network of relationships between workshops can be established, allowing these lines of professional network to be traversed electronically through our application.

6.2   Representing Time in Hypermedia

Although the HyStream/RDF system has an awareness of time - it must do to serve continuous metadata - it does not store this as an intrinsic part of the RDF entities, nor as a direct relationship between them. Instead, when querying the server we specify a time parameter which returns all the objects valid at that moment - it is these objects which have relationships between themselves, not with time - the server *superimposes* a temporal perspective.

Thus, a slide is related to a video and is valid for a set time, rather than both the slide and video being related to a "first class" time entity.

Does this matter? As far as the user is concerned the result is the same. Could the way we discern time impact upon our ability to exchange metadata

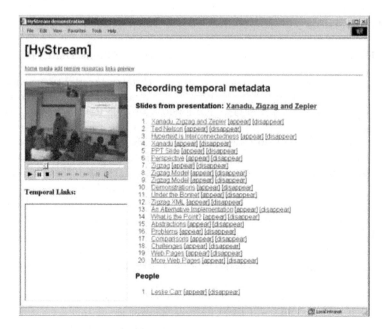

Fig. 4. The HyStream authoring window

between hypermedia systems? Certainly the MPEG-7 group are not using RDF for storing metadata because of the lack of linking to spatio-temporal sections of data [16].

The predominant view of temporal media is of a discrete "block" within a hypermedia system - it is the synchronised presentation of the media with other hypermedia elements that has received the most attention. As such we tend to use mechanisms to jump to or from particular time indexes within the media - again, the timeline is superimposed so that we can synchronise hypermedia elements. For instance, within the HyStream/RDF application a point in the video is accessed as a link to the video itself appended with a time index.

The situation is further complicated when the temporal media becomes unbounded, such as in a live scenario. Here it becomes more difficult to deal with the media as a block within a carefully scripted hypermedia presentation, because the block has an infinite length.

So how could we represent time? One way might be to introduce time as a separate entity to which other entities are related. Although this sounds simple it changes the manner in which we create presentations - we would have to maintain a constant temporal perspective - and this would significantly complicate the system. Another alternative might be to use time as a context - viewing an entity from a particular time context could resolve that entity to the correct data for that moment.

Acknowledgements. This research was partially funded by EPSRC projects HyStream (GR/M84077), AKT (GR/N15764/01) and EQUATOR (GR/N15986). We are grateful to our colleagues in these projects for their support of this work, especially Luc Moreau, Nigel Shadbolt, Wendy Hall, Dave Millard and Paul Lewis. We also wish to thank Hugh Glaser and Jian Meng for the Sheffield AKT workshop case study.

References

1. Jeff Ayars, Dick Bulterman, Aaron Cohen, Erik Hodge, Philipp Hoschka, Eric Hyche, Ken Day, Kenichi Kubota, Rob Lanphier, Nabil Layaïda, Philippe Le Hégaret, Thierry Michel, Muriel Jourdan, Jacco van Ossenbruggen, Lloyd Rutledge, Bridie Saccocio, Patrick Schmitz, Warner ten Kate, and Ted Wugofski. Synchronized multimedia integration language (SMIL 2.0) specification, September 2000.
2. T. Berners-Lee, R. Fielding, and L. Masinter. Uniform resource identifiers (URI): Generic syntax, August 1998.
3. S. Blake, D. Black, M. Carlson, E. Davies, Z. Wang, and W. Weiss. An architecture for differentiated services, December 1998.
4. R. Braden, D. Clark, and S. Shenker. Integrated services in the internet architecture: an overview, June 1994.
5. Don Cruickshank, Luc Moreau, and David De Roure. Architectural design of a multi-agent system for handling metadata streams. In *The Fifth International Conference on Autonomous Agents*, pages 505–512, May 2001.
6. David De Roure, Steven Blackburn, Lee Oades, Jonathan Read, and Neil Ridgeway. Applying open hypermedia to audio. In Kaj Grønbæk, Elli Mylonas, and Frank M. Shipman, editors, *Hypertext '98*, pages 285–286. ACM SIGLINK, 1998.
7. David C. DeRoure and Steven G. Blackburn. Amphion: Open hypermedia applied to temporal media. In Uffe K. Wiil, editor, *Proceedings of the 4th Open Hypermedia Workshop*, pages 27–32, June 1998. Technical Report CS-98-1, Department of Computer Science, Aalborg University Esbjerg, Denmark.
8. S. Draper, H. Earnshaw, E. Montie, S. Parnall, R. Toll, D. Wilson, and G. Winter. TV Anytime. In *Proceedings International Broadcasting Convention (IBC 99)*, pages 103–108. IBC, 1999.
9. Wolfgang Effelsberg and Thomas Meyer-Boudnik. MHEG explained. *IEEE Multimedia*, 2(1):26–38, 1995.
10. S. Goose and W. Hall. The development of a sound viewer for an open hypermedia system. *The New Review of Hypermedia and Multimedia*, 1:213–231, 1995.
11. Lynda Hardman, Dick C. A. Bulterman, and Guido van Rossum. The amsterdam hypermedia model: Adding time and context to the dexter model. *Communications of the ACM*, 37(2):50–62, February 1994.
12. Ora Lassila and Ralph R. Swick. Resource description framework (RDF) model and syntax specification, February 1999.
13. W. Mark. Turning pervasive computing into mediated spaces. *IBM Systems Journal*, 38(4):677–692, 1999.
14. Eric Miller. An introduction to the Resource Description Framework. *D-Lib Magazine*, May 1998.
15. Frank Nack and Adam T. Lindsay. Everything you wanted to know about MPEG-7: Part 1. *IEEE Multimedia*, 6(3):65–77, September 1999.

16. Frank Nack and Adam T. Lindsay. Everything you wanted to know about MPEG-7: Part 2. *IEEE Multimedia*, 6(4):64–73, October 1999.
17. Les Nelson, Satoshi Ichimura, and Elin Ronby Pedersen. Palette: A paper interface for giving presentations. In *CHI*, pages 354–361, 1999.
18. Kevin R. Page, Don Cruickshank, and Dave De Roure. Its about time: Link streams as continuous metadata. In *Hypertext '01*, pages 93–102. ACM, August 2001.
19. H. Schulzrinne, S. Casner, R. Frederick, and V. Jacobson. RTP: A transport protocol for real-time applications, January 1996.
20. H. Schulzrinne, A. Rao, and R. Lanphier. Real time streaming protocol (RTSP), April 1998.
21. Mark Thompson, David De Roure, and Danius Michaelides. Weaving the pervasive information fabric. In S. Reich and K.M. Anderson, editors, *Open Hypermedia Systems and Structural Computing, 6th International Workshop, OHS-6, 2nd International Workshop, SC-2, San Antonio, Texas, USA, May 30-June 3, 2000 Proceedings*, volume 1903 of *Lecture Notes in Computer Science*, pages 87–95. Springer-Verlag, September 2000.
22. S. Weibel, J. Kunze, C. Lagoze, and M. Wolf. Dublin core metadata for resource discovery, September 1998.

Auld Leaky: A Contextual Open Hypermedia Link Server

Danius T. Michaelides, David E. Millard, Mark J. Weal, and David DeRoure

Intelligence, Agents, Multimedia,
Dept. of Electronics and Computer Science, University of Southampton, UK
{dtm, dem, mjw, dder}@ecs.soton.ac.uk

Abstract. The work of the Open Hypermedia Systems Working Group (OHSWG) has lead to the creation of several hypermedia models and a common protocol for Navigational Hypertext. However none of these include a working model of context. In this paper we present how we have extended the Fundamental Open Hypermedia Model (FOHM) to include context and behaviour. We then present Auld Leaky, a lightweight contextual link server that stores and serves structures represented in FOHM, using Context to filter query results.

1 Introduction

The Open Hypermedia Systems Working Group (OHSWG) has spent several years developing and defining the Open Hypermedia Protocol (OHP) [3] in an attempt to achieve interoperability between Open Hypermedia Systems. This development effort relied on both the definition of a suitable Hypermedia model and also a protocol (either text or API-based) to manipulate it. As Hypermedia is a wide field, the protocol was split into several different domains (Navigational, Spacial and Taxonomic) and OHP-Nav was developed as a text-based protocol that addressed only the Navigational domain. However, it has been argued that the community should have concentrated on the model rather than the protocol [11], particularly as several areas of the model, including Context, Behaviour and Computation, were never formally agreed.

Individual research groups within the OHSWG have taken the OHP-Nav model and extended it. Within the IAM group at Southampton we have developed the Fundamental Open Hypermedia Model (FOHM) [12] based on the OHP model, but capable of representing structures from all the discussed domains.

FOHM was always intended to include Context and Behaviour [10]. Recently we have turned our attention to producing a firm definition of context in FOHM and producing a contextual link server that would be flexible and general enough to use within several projects within our lab.

Version one of this link server will be known as Auld Linky, however the beta-version we are currently using is affectionately known as Auld Leaky.

S. Reich, M.M. Tzagarakis, P.M.E. De Bra (Eds.): OHS/SC/AH 2001, LNCS 2266, pp. 59–70, 2002.
© Springer-Verlag Berlin Heidelberg 2002

1.1 Requirements

Before construction of Auld Leaky began we set down several simple requirements. These were based around our main goal of creating a simple link server that could be easily installed. This meant that we would be aiming at a single executable with a simple API. We wanted the link server to be as lightweight as possible and not require large infrastructures such as databases or middleware systems. The link server should just serve links with no need to access external services. Finally, and most importantly, the link server needed to act contextually. To this end we envisaged extending FOHM to allow context and behaviour objects to be attached to each of the hypermedia objects.

2 FOHM

In its work on interoperability, the OHSWG considered the requirements of several domains of hypertext. The three most frequently mentioned were Navigational [6,1,7,15,2], Spatial [9,8,14] and Taxonomic [13,4,5]. The OHP protocol was always more concerned with Navigational Hypertext, however FOHM, which is based on the OHP-Nav data model, is capable of expressing all three domains.

2.1 The Model

In FOHM we describe four first-class objects that are analogous to the objects in the OHP data model. *Associations* are structures that represent relationships between *Data* objects. These Data objects are wrappers for any piece of data that lies outside of the scope of the model. They normally represent a document although one could represent any file, stream or other item.

Data objects are not directly placed in the Associations. Instead *Reference* objects are used, these either point at Data objects in their entirety or at parts of those Data objects, for example the second paragraph of a text document, or the second scene of a film. They are attached to the Association object via *Bindings*. Each Association also has a structure type and a feature space; each Binding must state its position in that feature space, effectively stating how it is bound to the Association's structure. A FOHM Navigational structure is illustrated in Figure 1.

Essentially, an Association relates different objects. The Bindings attach References to the Association. The References point to objects in the system. In the illustration the objects are items of Data, but References can also point to other Associations.

2.2 Navigational Hypertext in FOHM

Navigational Hypertext is the most common of the domains that can be represented in FOHM. Its notion of directed links can be modelled easily by a single Association feature "direction" to which Data objects are bound with either a "source", "destination" or "bi-directional" value.

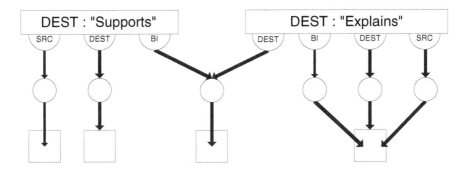

Fig. 1. Link Structures in FOHM

Figure 1. shows a Navigational structure described within the FOHM model, in this case two links. The first is a link across three different data objects (one of which is referenced in its entirety), the second is a link across one area of one document and three different areas within a second document. Notice that Associations can share References and that References can share Data objects.

3   Auld Leaky

The Auld Leaky implementation is written in Perl, it consists of a number of components that can be compiled into a single executable. The core is built around a FOHM implementation which provides basic container objects and APIs for matching structures together. FOHM objects are grouped into linkbases, which are managed by the link server. The link server provides APIs for storing, looking up and querying stored linkbases. The final component consists of a module to expose the link server as a web-server-like process, using HTTP and XML.

3.1   Communication

Auld Leaky communicates using FOHM structures that have been serialised into XML. These are then sent over HTTP connections. Similar to a web server, Leaky responds to the standard HTTP request types:

GET   requests are sent with an ID (a simple string), the relevant
            object is located in the linkbase and returned in the form
            of XML.
POST   requests are sent with a FOHM object in the content of the
            message. This is then pattern-matched against the objects
            in the linkbase (this is explained further in Section 3.2).
PUT   requests are sent with a FOHM object in the content of
            the message. Leaky then adds this object to the linkbase.
DELETE   requests are sent with an ID, the relevant object is located
            in the linkbase and removed.

3.2   Pattern Matching

The basic mechanism for querying in Auld Leaky is pattern matching. To perform a query, a FOHM structure is constructed and then matched against each structure stored in the link server. The matching of two structures proceeds in a tree-like prefix depth first search, meaning that when matching two FOHM objects, first each of their attributes are matched, followed by the matching of any sub-objects. Matching immediately fails when any attribute or object matching fails.

In order to facilitate powerful queries, we add extra attributes to the FOHM objects. Firstly, an attribute called **state** indicates the nature of the structure with respect to matching. The attribute has four values; *undefined* and *defined* indicate whether the particular object is in a defined state or not (where being undefined means being set to nothing, or null). A third state, *variable*, marks an object as being a variable. Variables are objects that match any other object of the same type, they are currently anonymous, and can contain some form of constraint to allow for complex matching. Our current implementation allows for constraints expressed as perl expressions (utilising perl's **eval** in a sandbox), but other constraint languages and suitable evaluators could be used. The fourth value of state, *lookup*, is used for linkbase loading, and not for matching purposes. Linkbase loading is discussed in section 3.5.

Whilst the use of the state attribute is sufficient for constructing queries, it can often lead to quite verbose structures. Specifically, queries often contain just a few concrete values and the remaining values are variable or just not set to anything (for example an author might want to create an Association without a description attribute). To avoid this, we introduce an extra attribute, called **missing** which has two values: *variable* and *undefined*. This attribute indicates what state a field in an object should assume if the field is unspecified.

Note that our query objects are FOHM structures which means that we can store them in linkbases.

3.3   Matching Bindings

The Bindings contained within an Association are a special case for matching purposes. The Bindings in an Association are a bag of Binding objects. This presents a problem to our matching algorithm, since there is a choice. For all other FOHM structures there is a strict correspondence between objects in each structure to be matched. To match Binding objects, we have to employ an exhaustive search algorithm to try and find a solution such that all Bindings have been matched with a Binding in the other Association. The algorithm uses a recursive method of attempting to match a Binding to each available Binding in the other Association. For each successful match, the Bindings are marked as unavailable and a recursive call is made. If the recursive call returns unsuccessfully, then matching continues with the next available Binding; if there are none, then the routine fails. If the recursive call returns successfully then a configuration of Binding matches has been found where all the Bindings have been matched.

Binding objects also have extra attributes to control how they are matched. The `optional` attribute indicates that a Binding does not have to be matched against another Binding. For the matching algorithm, this attribute simply means that it can ignore optional bindings and return successfully if only optional Bindings remain unmatched.

The `repeatable` attribute allows for a Binding to be matched against more than once. This is typically used to match against Associations where the number of Bindings in unknown. For example, the right hand Association in Figure 1. has a `src`, two `dest` and a `bi` (directional) Binding. A query to find all the links from the source document would include the `src` Binding but it would also include a variable Binding for the `dest` Bindings to match against. In this case the variable Binding is marked as repeatable, so that it can match any number of `dest` Bindings.

3.4   Querying

The process of performing a query entails constructing a FOHM structure to be used in the pattern matching and making a `POST` HTTP call to the link server. The link server receives the XML data and converts it into an internal FOHM structure. This is then matched against each object in the linkbase; any matches are accumulated. It is possible for the query to specify the linkbase or scope the search by specifying a more restrictive path in the HTTP request. The matching results are converted to XML and returned to the client. The client will then typically reconstruct the results back into FOHM objects.

3.5   Linkbases, Naming, and Loading

Associations, References and Data objects are first class in FOHM; they have an `id` value. Linkbases are collections of FOHM structures. We try and preserve URL semantics so that an object can be referenced by:

```
http://servername:port/<linkbase name>/<object id>
```

The naming scheme used within the linkbases is up to the author, but using a hierarchy, if appropriate, is consistent with the URL scheme. Structures can also have local identifiers denoted by `#value`. Local identifiers are given to structures which do not have their own identity, but need to be referenced, e.g. for cyclic structures. The identifier is only valid within the scope of the communication.

Links are typically loaded into Auld Leaky when the service is started, but can also be stored using the `PUT` method. Note that since link servers load up their structures from URLs, its possible that a URL can be supplied that points to another link server, possibly even a query.

Structures stored can be references to other objects, using the `lookup` value of the state attribute. The `id` attribute on such structures, indicates the destination of the reference. Primarily, lookup structures are used for shared objects or for separating out the FOHM structures for easier authoring of linkbases. An open issue is the action of the linkbase when faced with a unknown identifier. The id could be a URL; this leads to a number of distributed link service possibilities.

The simplest case is that the link server would just store that it is a reference to an unknown object (although the type is known). The reference would have to be resolved by the client. During the matching process its not clear how the link server should treat the reference. The link server is faced with the problem of matching a (known) FOHM object against just a reference.

It could just assume that the structure matches and let the client decide for itself. An alternative would be for the link server to make a query to the remote link server passing on the structure to be matched; a kind of distributed search/query. This sounds quite attractive, but it does required that the reference points to a link server capable of performing the query. This approach is the subject of future work.

An alternative solution to the problem of a reference is to lookup the object from the specified location and store that structure locally. Hence when a structure is loaded into the link server, the server will also load remote structures referenced, so it has all the data it requires. This process could possibly be recursive. The link server effectively has a copy of the actual remote structures, and this raises a number of caching and consistency issues. This solution does mean that the link server is able to perform its matching unhindered.

3.6   Context and Behaviour

Context and Behaviour objects can be attached to all parts of the FOHM structure as is shown in Figure 2. These objects are opaque to the FOHM description and are defined separately. Any link server that deals in FOHM structures is required to understand the Context definitions, however the Behaviour objects are used only by clients and need not be understood (although they still have to be served).

Auld Leaky implements the context object of the FOHM structures as a set of key value pairs called contextvalues. Although a relatively simple mechanism for representing context it is deceptively powerful. Figure 3. shows an example context object.

From this Context object the following information can be identified:

1. The value of context item location is given as "office".
2. The context item time has a constraint attached to it that defines time as being later than 19:05.

This last time-based context is an interesting example. Notice that the type of the object is not specified, i.e. the time is represented as a string 19:05. The contextvalue also has a constraint attached to it. Constraints can be used on any element where the default matching (a string comparison) is not sufficient, in this case by invoking a greater than comparison.

The Context object itself also has a Perl constraint that indicates that a successful match requires that the contextvalue with the key "passed_deadline" should not exist.

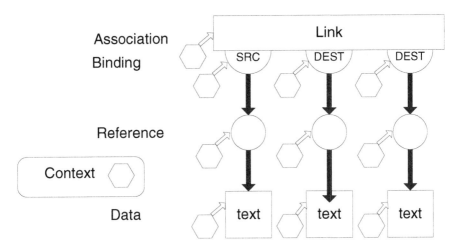

Fig. 2. Context Placement on FOHM Data Structures

```
<context>
  <contextvalue key="location">office</contextvalue>
  <contextvalue key="time" state="variable">
    <constraint> ( $_[0] gt "19:05"); </constraint>
  </contextvalue>
  <constraint>(!$_[0]->contextvalue("passed_deadline"));</constraint>
</context>
```

Fig. 3. XML Representation of Context Object

```
<behaviour event="display">
  <behaviourvalue key="passed_deadline">true</behaviourvalue>
</behaviour>

<behaviour event="traversal">
  <behaviourvalue key="location">home</behaviourvalue>
  <behaviourvalue key="time">+00:05</behaviourvalue>
</behaviour>
```

Fig. 4. XML Representation of Behaviour Object

Behaviour objects are implemented in Auld Leaky in much the same way as Context objects.

For example, Figure 4. shows two Behaviour objects. The first could be attached to a Data object. Each Behaviour object has an event type associated with it. In this case, the event "display" is used to indicate that the Behaviour should be carried out when the object is displayed. This is client dependant and in no way enforced by Auld Leaky. In this case the client interprets the Behaviour in such a way that upon display of this Data item it sets the "passed_deadline" flag in the clients context to be true.

The second Behaviour object could be attached to an Association object. The event here is traversal rather than display. When the client follows the Association above the value of time in the client's context will be increased by five minutes and the location is changed to home.

These two Behaviour objects are fairly simple and both result in modifications to the client's user context which are then used to carry out further matching in the application in which they are used. The Behaviour object need not be used in this way and could just as easily be constructed to trigger additional events in the system or to allow objects to express the specifics of how they are displayed.

3.7   Querying in Context

There are two important ways that Context can be used in Auld Leaky. Firstly, since Context objects can be attached to FOHM structures it becomes possible to attach them to the structures sent in queries, these structures then only match if their contexts match as well. Secondly, Context objects can be attached to the queries themselves. This Context object acts like a filter on query results. Objects that are returned from the query matching are matched against the supplied query Context. Objects whose Context does not match the query Context are removed from the result set. The Context matching filters down the FOHM structures so that sub-objects can be removed.

For example, this means that if a Binding matches the Context but that the Data object it binds does not, then the Binding, the Data object and the Reference that joins them are all removed from the results set.

An issue raised with this context filtering is that a structure could be filtered such that it would no longer match the original query. For example, a query that required a source binding to a particular URL could find that, due to filtering, all the source bindings had been removed.

The solution we have implemented to this problem is to re-match any structures that get filtered against the original query.

4   Applications

As well as allowing contextual filtering of Navigational links it is possible to use Auld Leaky as a contextual structural engine to drive novel applications. In this section we shall briefly explain some of things we have been exploring.

4.1 Hypertext Short Stories

One of the applications constructed using Auld Leaky is the cgi based Hypertext Story Engine. This constructs short stories for the reader on the fly from data and links stored within the linkbase. The client maintains a user profile, in the form of a context, that it uses to find the next appropriate story fragment.

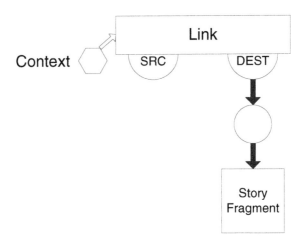

Fig. 5. The Short Story Link

A story is constructed from fragments of text. These are stored as data objects in the linkbase. To link all of these story fragments together, Associations exist within the linkbase. These Associations contain one source Binding that is totally generic (will match any Data item). However, the Association has a Context attached to it. The client constructing the story queries the linkbase with the user context and is returned all of the Associations that match that Context. Figure 5. shows the association structure used in the application.

The story fragments are not directly linked to each other. Instead, the client uses the current readers context to offer the reader a selection of story fragments to view. Viewing the story fragment will modify the readers context , based on Behaviour objects attached to the Association and Data objects, resulting in a different set of fragments being offered next time.

We are currently using Context and Behaviour as a way of keeping track of time, characters and also plot progression (for example to restrict basic exposition and background information to the beginning of the story when the scene is being set).

4.2 Contextual Information Systems

Auld Leaky can also be used as a way of accessing factual information. We designed an applet that dynamically builds a document about the history of the City of Glasgow. It does this based on the interest preferences that the user has selected (choosing from areas such as Culture, Industry and Government). Alongside the web server that serves the applet we run a copy of Auld Leaky which is responsible for providing the necessary FOHM structures to the applet.

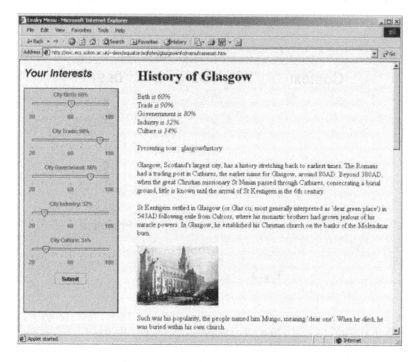

Fig. 6. The Level of Detail Applet

The dynamic document is represented in FOHM as a transclusive tour (this means that the tour is compiled into a single document). Each item in the tour is a secondary Association which we call 'level of detail' (LoD). Each LoD is a list which contained Data items ordered by their length. Context objects attached to each Data item described how relevant that item is to each interest.

The applet uses the interests selected by the user to construct a user context and then queries the whole tour. The link server returns the tour with each LoD included but with Data items that do not match the context removed. The applet then uses the first positioned Data item in each LoD to build the dynamic document.

Figure 6. shows a screen shot of the applet. The user has set the sliders on the left to represent their interests and the applet has dynamically built a document describing the History of Glasgow on the right, using the tour and LoD structures served up by Leaky.

5   Conclusion

In this paper we have presented Auld Leaky, a contextual Link Server that is architecturally light and yet has the ability to manipulate structures from multiple hypertext domains in a consistent way.

Although Leaky's use of context and behaviour is quite sophisticated the actual model of context used (a vector of key value pairs) is simple. We are currently working to produce a more complex ontology of context that would make some of the semantics and relationships within Context objects explicit.

The Architectural simplicity of Leaky also makes it an ideal component in a peer to peer distributed system. There are a number of opportunities for incorporating distributed aspects into the link service. In particular further work is needed to provide a strong naming strategy and investigate issues of caching structures. In addition we have identified a number of interesting distributed query issues which need to be explored.

We are also interested in developing the use of context. In particular in regard to narrative structures, where we are looking at using context to produce dynamically generated 'tours' of material where the tour contains a narrative structure with a recognisable 'beginning', 'middle' and 'end'. Such dynamic guides can also be tailored towards users' interests and may vary according to a required length (e.g. a user might request a five minute description). The Glasgow applet and Hypertext Story Engine represent our initial work in this area.

References

1. Kenneth M. Anderson, Richard N. Taylor, and E. James Whitehead. Chimera: Hypertext for Heterogeneous Software Environments. In *ECHT '94. Proceedings of the ACM European conference on Hypermedia technology, Sept. 18-23, 1994, Edinburgh, Scotland, UK*, pages 94–197, 1994.
2. Tim Berners-Lee, Robert Cailliau, A. Luotonen, Henrik Frystyk Nielsen, and A. Secret. The World Wide Web. *Communications of the ACM*, 37(8):76–82, 1994.
3. Hugh Davis, Siegfried Reich, and David Millard. A proposal for a common navigational hypertext protocol. Technical report, Dept. of Electronics and Computer Science, 1997. Presented at 3.5 Open Hypermedia System Working Group Meeting. Aarhus University, Denmark. September 8-11.
4. Parunak H. Van Dyke. Don't Link Me In: Set-Based Hypermedia for Taxonomic Reasoning. In *Proceedings of the '91 ACM Conference on Hypertext, Dec. 15-18, 1991, San Antonio, TX*, pages 233–242, 1991.
5. Parunak H. Van Dyke. Hypercubes Grow on Trees (and Other Observations from the Land of Hypersets). In *Proceedings of the '93 ACM Conference on Hypertext, Nov. 14-18, 1993, Seattle, WA*, pages 73–81, 1993.
6. Andrew M. Fountain, Wendy Hall, Ian Heath, and Hugh C. Davis. MICROCOSM: An Open Model for Hypermedia With Dynamic Linking. In A. Rizk, N. Streitz, and J. André, editors, *Hypertext: Concepts, Systems and Applications (Proceedings of ECHT'90)*, pages 298–311. Cambridge University Press, 1990.
7. Kaj Grønbæk and Randall H. Trigg. Design issues for a Dexter-based hypermedia system. *Communications of the ACM*, 37(3):40–49, February 1994.

8. Catherine C. Marshall and Frank M. Shipman. Spatial Hypertext: Designing for Change. *Communications of the ACM*, 38:88–97, 1995.
9. Catherine C. Marshall and Frank M. Shipman. Spatial Hypertext and the Practice of Information Triage. In *Proceedings of the '97 ACM Conference on Hypertext, April 6-11, 1997, Southampton, UK*, pages 124–133, 1997.
10. David Millard and Hugh Davis. Navigating Spaces: The Semantics of Cross Domain Interoperability. In Siegfried Reich and Kenneth M. Anderson, editors, *Open Hypermedia Systems and Structural Computing. Proceedings of the 6th Workshop on Open Hypermedia Systems (OHS-6) and the 2nd Workshop on Structural Computing (SC-2). San Antonio, TX, USA* (Sept. 2000), Springer Verlag. Lecture Notes in Computer Science (LNCS) No. 1903. (ISSN 0302-9743), pages 129–139, 2000.
11. David Millard, Hugh Davis, and Luc Moreau. Standardizing Hypertext: Where Next for OHP? In Siegfried Reich and Kenneth M. Anderson, editors, *Open Hypermedia Systems and Structural Computing. Proceedings of the 6th Workshop on Open Hypermedia Systems (OHS-6) and the 2nd Workshop on Structural Computing (SC-2). San Antonio, TX, USA.* Springer Verlag, September 2000. Lecture Notes in Computer Science (LNCS) No. 1903, pages 3–12, 2000.
12. David E. Millard, Luc Moreau, Hugh C. Davis, and Siegfried Reich. FOHM: A Fundamental Open Hypertext Model for Investigating Interoperability Between Hypertext Domains. In *Proceedings of the '00 ACM Conference on Hypertext, May 30 - June 3, San Antonio, TX*, pages 93–102, 2000.
13. Peter J. Nürnberg, Erich R. Schneider, and John J. Leggett. Designing digital libraries for the hyper-literate age. *Journal of Universal Computer Science*, 2(9), 1996.
14. Olav Reinert, Dirk Bucka-Lassen, Claus A. Pedersen, and Peter J. Nürnberg. CAOS: A Collaborative and Open Spatial Structure Service Component with Incremental Spatial Parsing. In *Proceedings of the '99 ACM Conference on Hypertext, February 21-25, 1999, Darmstadt, Germany*, pages 49–50, February 1999.
15. John L. Schnase, John L. Leggett, David L. Hicks, Peter J. Nürnberg, and J. Alfredo Sánchez. Design and implementation of the HB1 hyperbase management system. *Electronic Publishing—Origination Dissemination and Design*, 6(1):35–63, June 1993.

FOHM+RTSP: Applying Open Hypermedia and Temporal Linking to Audio Streams

Neil Ridgway and David DeRoure

Intelligence, Agents, Multimedia,
University of Southampton, Dept. of Electronics and Computer Science,
Southampton, UK
{cnhr, dder}@ecs.soton.ac.uk

Abstract. The World Wide Web (WWW) was originally designed to handle relatively simple files, containing just text and graphics. With the development of more advanced Web browsers and streaming media protocols, it can now be used for the real-time delivery, display and playback of different types of media, including audio and video. The *Synchronized Multimedia Integration Language* (SMIL) has also been developed, to create and stream multimedia presentations over the Web. Both the WWW and SMIL however embed the hypertext link information, to the different types of media, within their documents. This makes the link information easier to transport but considerably harder to maintain. As a result of this problem, the WWW is sometimes referred to as a "closed" hypermedia system. This paper describes how *Open Hypermedia Systems* (OHSs) can be used to solve this problem of embedded links. It also describes how a streaming media protocol, the *Real Time Streaming Protocol* (RTSP), can be extended to support Open Hypermedia and temporal linking, specifically in the audio domain.

1 Introduction

The *World Wide Web* (WWW) and *Open Hypermedia Systems* (OHSs) have both been used to create links to and from text and images. Temporal media such as audio and video however has always been regarded, by the WWW and the majority of OHSs, as "something" to be linked to. On the WWW for instance, activating links to this type of media would traditionally make the Web browser download the entire media file to the user's machine. The browser would then execute an external application to playback the media.

Handling temporal media in this way is fine for small low-quality files. However as the quality of the media increases, so does its file size. The process of downloading a larger, higher-quality file can take a substantial amount of time, especially if the network connection was poor. To overcome this problem, and also to deal with live media, *streaming media* protocols were developed. When a client requests a streaming media file, for example an audio sample or a video clip, the server splits the file into more manageable packets and then transmits them to the client. On receiving the packets the client will buffer enough of them to ensure the quality of the playback is reasonable.

S. Reich, M.M. Tzagarakis, P.M.E. De Bra (Eds.): OHS/SC/AH 2001, LNCS 2266, pp. 71–81, 2002.
© Springer-Verlag Berlin Heidelberg 2002

The development of streaming media protocols have resolved the problems of delivering the media. However the WWW can only create links *to* audio and video. The *Synchronized Multimedia Integration Language* (SMIL) can be used to create links to and from audio and video streams. However the WWW and SMIL both embed the link information within their respective documents. This makes the link information easier to transport but considerably harder to maintain.

The Open Hypermedia approach involves managing the hypermedia link information separately from the documents (or media). Making links into 'first class citizens' in this way has a number of advantages in terms of the functionality of hypermedia systems, especially for adaptive information systems whereby the presentation is personalised to the reader. However, the approach also requires systems to be engineered differently.

Open Hypermedia Systems have not used streaming media protocols. While OHSs such as Microcosm and HyperWave have provided tools to create links to and from the audio domain, these tools use audio files that are stored on the same machine as the OHS. Also, a limited amount of research has been carried out into video, but there has been very little research into the audio domain.

This paper discusses how two Open Hypermedia Systems have attempted to handle the audio domain. A brief description of SMIL, streaming media protocols and IPv6 is then given. Finally this paper describes how an existing streaming media protocol can be extended to support Open Hypermedia and temporal linking, specifically in the audio domain, using finite stored media.

2   Open Hypermedia Systems and Audio

Traditionally, the audio domain has been neglected in the development of hypermedia systems. There are several reasons for this:

- The lack of technology. The first generation of hypermedia systems did not have the computer technology to manipulate audio data. Over time this technology has improved.
- The HCI challenges, such as browsing audio information. For example, audio does not have a unique visual representation and therefore developing intuitive graphical interfaces, to manipulate audio, is quite difficult.
- The problems of the audio file formats. Currently there are several file formats which can be used to store audio data. However with each format the file size increases as the quality of the audio recording increases. As a result, high quality recordings can rapidly consume large amounts of disk space. Working in the compressed domain raises some new challenges.

These problems have caused the majority of hypermedia systems to concentrate mainly on the authoring of links between text, images and video; the *visual* domain. With the development of more powerful computers, sound cards and "open" hypermedia however, it has become possible to develop applications that can be used in conjunction with these systems, to manipulate the audio domain. Two of these are described in more detail below.

2.1   The SoundViewer Tool for Microcosm

The SoundViewer Tool [19] was developed for Microcosm [1,12,24,25] to provide a meaningful visual representation of audio within a hypermedia context. It can be used as a standalone application but when it used with Microcosm, links can be visually authored to and from the audio domain. The tool consists of two windows; the first is a scrollbar representing the length of the entire audio file and the second is a zoomed in view of an area within the scrollbar. This second window displays the link information for a particular section of the audio file. The SoundViewer tool can only create links to and from audio files, stored on the same machine as the Microcosm system.

2.2   The Harmony Audio Player for HyperWave

The Harmony Audio Player [9] supports digital audio and it can be used as a standalone application or with the HyperWave [7,8] system. When used with HyperWave, the tool will be executed when a user selects an audio document from the session manager. This will create a connection to the server and download the audio file. The audio sample is then displayed in the viewer as a waveform, with a scrollbar representing the current position in the audio file. The player contains the normal controls to playback, stop and pause the audio sample. Users can author links to other documents by selecting the sample or a portion of the sample. These areas will then be marked as links, which users can then follow by simply clicking on these areas.

2.3   SMIL for the WWW

The Synchronized Multimedia Integration Language (SMIL) [22] is a declarative language designed to combine, both spatially and temporally, independent media objects into a synchronised multimedia presentation. These presentations can then be streamed over the WWW.

The language provides a common timeline in which media objects can become active at specific times. It is possible, using SMIL, to give the impression that a particular presentation activates links to images and text, when a specific time range is reached within an audio or video file. However this link was not activated by the media, it is activated when the time range is reached on the time-line. Links can be created from audio and video, however the browser has to support this functionality and at the moment most browsers only support a limited subset of the SMIL language. These links would also be embedded within the SMIL document.

3   The Fundamental Open Hypermedia Model

In recent years the open hypermedia research community has turned its attention to the problem of interoperability and the creation of standards. They realised that OHSs could not interoperate because each system used its own proprietary protocols for communication between the clients and the server. As a result of this the Open Hypermedia Systems Working Group (OHSWG) started the development of the *Open Hypermedia Protocol* (OHP) [10,21], which focused primarily on a protocol for interoperability.

As work continued, the protocol steadily grew in size until the group realised that a single protocol could not be used, to handle all of the aspects of open hypermedia. The functionality of OHP was reduced so that it handled the traditional form of navigational hypertext and it was renamed to *OHP Navigational* (OHP-Nav) [6,11]. OHP-Nav defines a protocol for communication and the data structures required to handle navigational hypertext. It was successfully demonstrated at Hypertext 98 held in Pittsburgh USA and at Hypertext 99 in Darmstadt Germany.

After these conferences the Southampton members of the group focused on the development of a higher-level structure, that could work across the three main hypertext domains; navigational, spatial and taxonomic hypertext. This structure is called the *Fundamental Open Hypermedia Model* (FOHM) [3,4,5] and it is defined using an *eXtensible Markup Language* (XML) [26] DTD. This model however, does not describe an interoperable communication protocol; it just describes an associational structure for interoperability. Therefore to use this model, over heterogeneous networks and distributed systems, an underlying transport protocol has to be used. The work presented here is one of two such 'bindings' of FOHM to a communications model; the other uses a software agent communication language in a multi-agent framework.

4   Streaming Media Protocols

The *Internet Engineering Task Force* (IETF) have developed two protocols, that can be used for the real-time delivery of audio and video streams over the Internet. Implementations of these streaming media protocols use IPv4 [14], the current Internet Protocol, for the control and delivery of the media data and they are described in more detail in the following sections.

4.1   The Real-Time Transport Protocol

The Real-time Transport Protocol (RTP) [2] has recently become an Internet Standard and it provides end-to-end delivery services, such as payload type identification, timestamping and sequence numbering, for data with real-time characteristics e.g. audio streams. RTP itself does not provide all of the functionality required for the transport of data and therefore applications usually run it "on-top-of" a transport protocol such as UDP [14]. UDP however is a connectionless protocol and therefore is not reliable. To ensure that the real-time data will be delivered on-time, if at all, RTP must be used in conjunction with other mechanisms or protocols that will provide a reliable service.

4.2   The Real Time Streaming Protocol

The Real Time Streaming Protocol (RTSP) [13] is a proposed Internet standard and it is described as being an *application-level* protocol, which controls the delivery of streaming media with real-time properties. RTSP itself does not actually deliver the media data; this is handled by a separate protocol such as RTP. Therefore RTSP can be described as a "network remote control", to the server that is streaming the media.

The underlying protocol, that is used to control the delivery of the media, is determined by the scheme used in the RTSP URL [13]. For example the "rtsp" scheme identifies a reliable protocol, such as TCP, for the delivery of the commands; whilst the "rtspu" scheme denotes an unreliable protocol such as UDP.

RTSP is intentionally similar, in syntax and operation, to the *HyperText Transfer Protocol* (HTTP/1.1) [17], which is an Internet draft standard. There are several reasons for this:

− Any future extensions to HTTP/1.1 can also be added to RTSP, with little or no modification.
− RTSP can be easily parsed by standard HTTP or MIME parsers.
− It can adopt HTTP's work on web security mechanisms, caches and proxies.

However, one of the fundamental reasons why RTSP is based on HTTP/1.1 is because the current version of HTTP (HTTP/1.0) was not designed to cope with the transmission of real-time data over the Internet [20]. What limited capabilities HTTP/1.0 has in this area have already been exhausted. By making RTSP similar in operation and syntax to HTTP/1.1, the designers have essentially provided HTTP-level services to the real-time delivery of streaming data.

4.3   The Future − IPv6

The current Internet Protocol, IPv4 [14], became an Internet standard in 1981 and at that time, the Internet was a community of approximately one thousand systems. In 1999 this number had grown to approximately 100 million and it has been estimated that an increasing number of devices will become "Internet-aware". As the number of these devices has grown, so has the demand for more addresses.

IPv4 has an address length of 32 bits and this provides about four billion possible addresses. However this is a theoretical limit and the actual number is constrained, by several factors, to a few hundred million. With the current rate of growth it has been estimated that these addresses will run out between 2002 and 2012.

Temporary solutions to this problem have already been developed and they include the *Network Address Translator* (NAT) [16]. The IETF decided however, that a more permanent solution would be required, to overcome this problem and several other limitations of IPv4. As a result they have developed the next generation of Internet Protocol called *IPng* or *IPv6* [18].

IPv6 became a standard in 1998 and it consists of five main changes to IPv4. These include expanded addressing capabilities (128 bits), header format simplification and flow label capability, which will possibly provide real-time services for streaming media. There is no doubt within many organisations and research communities that IPv6 will eventually replace IPv4.

5   Extending RTSP to Support FOHM

To extend RTSP to support Open Hypermedia a new implementation of the protocol had to be developed. The IETF require at least two reference implementations of a protocol, before it can even be considered to be an Internet standard. These implementations could of been used, however they had very limited functionality and they were based on draft proposals. Therefore it was decided that a new implementation, of the current proposed standard, would be developed.

RTSP runs "on-top-of" the current Internet Protocol, IPv4. During the design of the new framework however, the IETF were developing the next generation of Internet Protocol, IPv6. This new protocol is backwards compatible with IPv4 and therefore it was decided that the new RTSP implementation would support IPv6. This ensures that the RTSP client and server would be able to communicate using either protocol.

By extending RTSP to support FOHM, users would be able to create, display and follow links using an open interoperable linkbase format. This combination is mutually beneficial because the protocol provides a communication mechanism for FOHM and the model provides the open hypermedia functionality for RTSP.

5.1   The New Methods for RTSP

To extend the new RTSP implementation, to support the creation, display and traversal of links, several new methods were developed and they are described below.

The AVAILABLE_LINKS Method. Linkbases contain a considerable amount of information to ensure that the associations they contain can be used across hypermedia domains. Therefore they are too large to stream down at the same time as the audio. The AVAILABLE_LINKS method is used to download the linkbase(s) before the actual audio stream. It is possible to stream down multiple linkbases.

When a client calls this method, each linkbase is streamed down to the client and stored in a temporary file. This file is then validated using the FOHM linkbase DTD and a XML parser. Once validated the linkbase(s) are then parsed, so that all of the required information can be retrieved and stored in a temporary cache. This cache contains:

- A link identifier, which is used for searching and retrieving the link.
- A source and a destination URI [23], which are the begin and end points of the association respectively. The source URI references the audio stream in the RTSP presentation.

- The source URI begin and end times, which are used to determine when the source URI is active and for how long.
- The destination URI begin and end times, which are used to determine when the destination URI is active and for how long.
- A found flag, which is used to determine if this link had already been displayed.

The begin and end times for each URI are optional and when there are no time values, the link is active for the entire duration of the presentation.

After the cache has been created and initialised, with the values from the linkbase, the links are then displayed. During playback of the presentation the links will also be displayed, at the relevant times. The linkbase(s) are only downloaded once. Any subsequent requests, by the user, to display the links or playback the presentation, will use the values stored in the cache.

The FOLLOW_LINK Method. This method can only be used after all of the link information, from the linkbase(s), have been streamed down to the client and the cache has been initialised. After the cache has been initialised, users can then follow these links by using their link identifiers. The **AVAILABLE_LINKS** request will have automatically displayed these identifiers upon completion.

When users issue a command to follow a link, using its identifier, the client searches for this link within the cache. Once found all of the relevant information for this link is then used by the client to decide how to handle the link. The client can handle three different types of link:

1. A link to non-continuous media such as text, images and graphics. In this situation the destination URI uses the HTTP protocol for the delivery of the media. Since the RTSP server only handles streaming media, the client handles this type of URI by activating an external Web browser. There is no communication between the client and server, when this type of link is followed. FOHM can be used to create links to non-continuous media, such as a link to an anchor in the middle of a document. However this functionality is not required in this situation and therefore the begin and end times, for this URI, are not relevant.

2. A link to a different part of the current presentation. This is analogous to the forward and rewind buttons of a CD player. When a user issues a command to resolve this type of link, a **FOLLOW_LINK** request is sent to the server. This request contains the destination URI and if relevant a destination range, which represents both the begin and end time for this URI. On receiving the message the server pauses the presentation and changes the current position of the audio stream, within the presentation, to the new range. The server then re-starts the playback from the new position. If no range value is given, then the presentation will be played back from the beginning.

3. A link to a new presentation or stream. With this scenario the existing presentation is closed down because a new presentation can not be created within an existing presentation. When a user issues a command to follow this type of link, the client sends a request to the server to close the current presentation. When this has happened the client uses the destination URI,

from the link, to start a new RTSP session with the server. Several messages will be passed between the client and server, to ensure that the session is initialised properly and all of the required resources are created and setup. When this is complete the client will send a message, to the server, to playback the new presentation.

The CREATE_LINK Method. This method can be used to create links from an audio stream within a presentation. It cannot be used to create links when a presentation is being played back.

When a user wants to create a link, the client checks to see if the current session contains either a single stream or a presentation. If the session contains a single stream, then the client returns an error because temporal linking in RTSP requires more than one stream; to handle the audio and the FOHM linkbases. Only a presentation can handle multiple streams and therefore, a single stream cannot be used to create, display and follow links.

If a presentation already contains a linkbase and this method is called, then the client checks to see if a link, with the user's new link identifier, already exists in the cache. If it does, the client informs the user that this link already exists and no further action will be taken. Otherwise a CREATE_LINK request, containing the source and destination URIs and any range values, is sent to the server.

Once received, the server finds the first linkbase within the presentation and seeks to the end of this file. The server then creates a new FOHM association, with the URIs and the values from the request, and append it to the end of this linkbase. When this is complete, a reply is sent to the client.

On receiving the reply the client adds the URIs and the values, from the original request, to the cache. This ensures that the user can see and use the link immediately, without having to call the AVAILABLE_LINKS method first. However if this command is used then the current cache is removed, a new cache is created and then all of the links, including the new ones, are streamed down to the client. The cache is created in the normal way and it will now contain all of the new links.

The display of the link information during the playback of the presentation, is unaffected by the CREATE_LINK method because it relies on the cache. As described in the previous paragraph, any new links are immediately inserted into the cache, when the client receives CREATE_LINK reply.

If the presentation does not contain a linkbase then a CREATE_LINK request, with the source and destination URIs and their range values, is sent to the server. The server, when it has received this request, creates a new linkbase file. The URI to this linkbase is appended to the presentation's container file, which consists of all of the URIs to the files and hence the streams, used within this presentation. After this the new linkbase is opened and a new FOHM association, containing the source and destination URIs and their ranges, is inserted. The server then sends a reply to the client.

At this stage however, the server will have only modified the container file, created the linkbase and inserted the new link information. A stream for downloading this information, to the client, will not have been created. In fact the server will still be dealing with the original presentation, which does not contain a linkbase. Therefore this presentation will have to be closed down and re-opened, so that a new stream for the linkbase will be created and initialised.

On receiving the reply, the client sends a message to the server to close down the current presentation. After the server has notified the client that this request has succeeded, the client then sends several other requests to re-open the presentation. These requests will return information, to the client, about all of the streams in the presentation, including the new linkbase stream. The client uses this information to create and initialise all of the required resources. When this is complete, the client then sends an **AVAILABLE_LINKS** request to download all of the link information. The cache is then initialised in the normal way.

If the user decides to create more links, then the link information will be inserted into the new linkbase, which has just been created.

6   Conclusion and Future Work

The research, outlined in this paper, has shown that it is possible to extend the Real Time Streaming Protocol (RTSP) to support an open interoperable linkbase format, i.e. the Fundamental Open Hypermedia Model (FOHM), using the next generation Internet Protocol (IPv6). This combination is mutually beneficial because the protocol provides a communication mechanism for FOHM and the model provides the Open Hypermedia functionality, so that links can be created to and from the audio domain.

In this study, streaming is used for delivery of stored media. With live one-way or two-way streams, hypermedia linkbases cannot always be preloaded. Support for hypermedia link streams as 'live metadata' is the subject of current research [15].

Acknowledgements. This research was partially funded by the EPSRC HyS-tream project (GR/ M84077). We are grateful to our colleagues in this project and the IAM Research Group for their support, especially Don Cruickshank, Kevin Page and David Millard.

References

1. A. M. Fountain, W. Hall, I. Heath and H. C. Davis. MICROCOSM: An Open Model for Hypermedia with Dynamic Linking. In *Hypertext: Concepts, Systems and Applications*. INRIA, Cambridge University Press, November 1990.
2. Audio-Video Transport Working Group. *RFC 1889, RTP: A Transport Protocol for Real-Time Applications*. IETF,
   http://www.ietf.org/rfc/rfc1889.txt?number=1889, January 1996.
3. D. E. Millard and H. C. Davis. Navigating Space: The Semantics of Cross Domain Interoperability. In *Proc. of the 2nd International Workshop on Structural Computing, Hypertext 2000*, pages 129–139, San Antonio, Texas, USA, May-June 2000. ACM.

4. D. E. Millard, H. C. Davis and L. Moreau. Standardizing Hypertext: Where next for OHP? In *Proc. of the 6ᵗʰ International Workshop on Open Hypermedia Systems, Hypertext 2000*, pages 3–12, San Antonio, Texas, USA, May-June 2000. ACM.

5. D. E. Millard, L. Moreau, H. C. Davis and S. Reich. FOHM: A Fundamental Open Hypertext Model for Investigating Interoperability between Hypertext Domains. In *Proc. of the 6ᵗʰ Workshop on Open Hypermedia Systems, Hypertext 2000*, pages 93–102, San Antonio, Texas, USA, May-June 2000. ACM.

6. D. E. Millard, S. Reich and H. C. Davis. Reworking OHP: the Road to OHP-Nav. In *Proc. of the 4ᵗʰ Workshop on Open Hypermedia Systems*, pages 48–53, Pittsburgh, Pennsylvania, USA, June 1998. ACM.

7. F. Kappe. Hyper-G: A Distributed Hypermedia System. In Barry Leiner, editor, *Proc. of INET*, San Francisco, California, August 1993. Internet Society.

8. F. Kappe and H. Maurer. Hyper-G: A large Universal Hypermedia System and some spin-offs. In *Computer Graphics - online*, May 1993.

9. G. Geiger. A Digital Audio Player for the HyperWave Internet Server. Master's thesis, Graz University of Technology, January 1997.

10. H. C. Davis, A. Rizk and A. Lewis. OHP: A draft proposal for a standard open hypermedia protocol. In *Proc. on the 2ⁿᵈ Workshop on Open Hypermedia Systems*, pages 27–53, Washington, D.C., March 1996. ACM, Technical Report No. ICS-TR-96-10, University of California. Eds, U. K. Will and S. Demeyer.

11. H. C. Davis, S. Reich and D. E. Millard. A proposal for a common Navigational Hypertext Protocol. Technical report, Presented at 3.5 Open Hypermedia System Working Group Meeting, Aarhus University, Århus, Denmark, September 1997.

12. H. C. Davis, W. Hall, I. Heath, G. J. Hill and R. J. Wilkins. Towards an Integrated Environment with Open Hypermedia Systems. In *Proc. of the ACM Conference on Hypertext*, pages 181–190, Milan, Italy, December 1992. ACM.

13. H. Schulzrinne, A. Rao and R. Lanphier. *RFC 2326, Real Time Streaming Protocol (RTSP)*. IETF, http://www.ietf.org/rfc/rfc2326.txt?number=2326, April 1998.

14. J. Postel. *RFC 791, Internet Protocol: DARPA Internet Program Protocol Specification*. Information Sciences Institute, http://www.ietf.org/rfc/rfc0791.txt?number=0791, September 1981.

15. K. R. Page, D. Cruickshank and D. DeRoure. Its About Time: Link Streams as Continuous Metadata. In *Proc. of the 12ᵗʰ ACM Conference on Hypertext and Hypermedia*, pages 93–102, Aarhus University, Århus, Denmark, August 2001. ACM.

16. P. Srisuresh and M. Holdrege. *RFC 2663, IP Network Address Translator (NAT): Terminology and Considerations*. IETF, http://www.ietf.org/rfc/rfc2663.txt?number=2663, August 1999.

17. R. Fielding, J. Gettys, J. Mogul, H. Frystyk, L. Masinter, P. Leach and T. Berners-Lee. *The Hypertext Transfer Protocol – HTTP/1.1 (RFC 2616)*. http://www.w3.org/Protocols/rfc2616/rfc2616.html, June 1999.

18. S. Deering and R. Hinden. *RFC 2460, Internet Protocol, Version 6 (IPv6) Specification*. IETF, http://www.ietf.org/rfc/rfc2460.txt?number=2460, December 1998.

19. S. Goose and W. Hall. The Development of a Sound Viewer for an Open Hypermedia System. In *The New Review of Hypermedia and Multimedia*, volume 1, pages 213–231, 1995.

20. S. Pizzi and S. Church. Audio Webcasting Demystified. *Web Techniques*, pages 55–60, August 1997.

21. S. Reich, U. K. Wiil, P. J. Nürnberg, H. C. Davis, K. Grønbæk, K. M. Anderson, D. E. Millard, J. M. Haake. Addressing interoperability in open hypermedia: the design of the open hypermedia protocol. *The New Review of Hypermedia and Multimedia*, 5:207–248, 1999.
22. Synchronised Multimedia Working Group (SYMM-WG). *Synchronized Multimedia Integration Language (SMIL) 1.0 Specification*. W3C, `http://www.w3.org/TR/1998/REC-smil-19980615`, June 1998.
23. T. J. Berners-Lee, R. Fielding and L. Masinter. *Uniform Resource Identifiers (URI): Generic Syntax*. IETF, `http://www.ietf.org/rfc/rfc2396.txt?number=2396`, August 1998.
24. W. Hall. Ending the Tyranny of the Button. *IEEE Multimedia*, 1(1):60–68, Spring 1994.
25. W. Hall, I. Heath, G. J. Hill, H. C. Davis and R. J. Wilkins. The Design and Implementation of an Open Hypermedia System. Computer Science Technical Report 92-19, University of Southampton, Department of Electronics and Computer Science, UK, 1992.
26. XML Working Group. *Extensible Markup Language (XML)*. W3C, `http://www.w3.org/TR/1998/REC-xml-19980210`, February 1998.

Development Tools in Component-Based Structural Computing Environments

Uffe Kock Wiil

Department of Computer Science
Aalborg University Esbjerg
Niels Bohrs Vej 8, 6700 Esbjerg, Denmark
ukwiil@cs.aue.auc.dk

Abstract. The purpose of this paper is to present an overview of the development tools available in the Construct component-based structural computing environment. In particular, we focus on the most recent development tool that generates IDL specifications from UML diagrams (UML Tool). The development tools lower the entry barrier for service developers by allowing high level specification of new services in UML or IDL and by auto-generating much of the component source code based on well-defined design patterns and templates. The paper is organized into five parts: an introduction to the research area, a brief description of the Construct development environment, a brief overview of UML Tool, a detailed scenario using the development environment, and, finally, our conclusions.

1 Introduction

Open hypermedia systems have been around for more than a decade (e.g., [1, 5,6,9,17]). A recent trend in open hypermedia research and development is to develop systems as sets of services wrapped in separate service components. These component-based open hypermedia systems are more flexible, in particular with respect to developing and adding new services to the open hypermedia environment. Another recent trend is to provide different types of structure services (in addition to the standard navigational structure service) within the same environment. The term structural computing was coined to describe such environments [7]. In 1999 a workshop series was initiated to discuss important issues and advance the thinking about structural computing [8,12].

Construct [4,14] is a component-based structural computing environment developed as the common code base successor of the DHM [5], HOSS [9], and HyperDisco [17] open hypermedia systems. Construct is an attempt to take the best of the previous approaches and combine them into one environment. A strong part of HOSS was its development tools, the protocol definition compiler (PDC) and the generalized process template (GPT) [9]. The purpose of these tools was to assist the developer in creating new services for the environment. Following from this, an important point of focus in the Construct project is the provision of tools that can assist service developers in the process of developing new service components [16].

S. Reich, M.M. Tzagarakis, P.M.E. De Bra (Eds.): OHS/SC/AH 2001, LNCS 2266, pp. 82–93, 2002.
© Springer-Verlag Berlin Heidelberg 2002

Development of new functionality oftentimes requires expert knowledge of the target system. The goals with the Construct development environment is to lower the entry-barrier for developers by basing the environment on components that use well-defined design patterns and templates. The development tools take care of many of the complex design decisions and coding tasks. The developer does not need to know details of synchronization, multi-threaded programming, or remote method invocation. New service interfaces are defined in high-level specifications with the help of dedicated development tools. Only a moderate level of programming expertise is required to develop new service components in Construct.

The paper is organized into the following sections. Section 2 gives an overview of the Construct development environment. UML Tool is described in Section 3. Section 4 provides a development scenario and Section 5 concludes the paper.

2   Construct Development Environment

Figure 1 provides an overview of the development tools available in the Construct environment and the first few steps in the process in which they are deployed. The circle at the top represents the service developer using the development tools (represented by screen shots). The ovals at the bottom represent products at different stages in the development process.

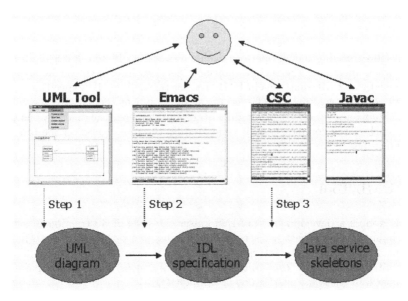

Fig. 1. The first few steps in the development process with the Construct development tools. The remaining steps in the development process are the classical tasks of coding and compilation. Emacs can also be used for those steps.

The overall steps in the development of new services in the Construct structural computing environment are:

1. UML Tool is used to create a UML diagram specifying the interface of the required service. When the diagram is ready, UML Tool can generate an IDL specification from the UML diagram. UML Tool is a client of the Construct navigational structure service. Both class names and field names can serve as endpoints of links.
2. Emacs is used to display and edit IDL specifications. If the developer prefers to write an IDL specification of the service interface directly (instead of starting with a UML diagram), then this step is the first step in the development process. Emacs is a client of the Construct navigational structure service as well as the Construct metadata service [13]. Arbitrary text strings can serve as endpoints of links. Each file in Emacs can have a metadata record attached. A metadata record consists of arbitrary key/value pairs.
3. The Construct Service Compiler (CSC) transforms the service interface specification in IDL into a Java skeleton service component. The CSC runs inside a shell tool (e.g., Emacs).
4. Emacs is used to edit the Java source code in the skeleton service. The developer creates the semantic parts (method bodies) of the operations defined in the service interface. When the semantic parts are added to the skeleton service, the service is fully developed.
5. The Java source code for the skeleton service is compiled into a Construct service component that automatically is operational in the Construct structural computing environment. The Java compiler (Javac) runs inside Emacs in its own shell.

As illustrated, the developer can decide to work at different levels of abstraction when specifying the service interface. Services interfaces can be specified graphically as UML diagrams in UML Tool or textually as IDL specifications in a text editor (e.g., Emacs). The use of the development tools makes the coding step (Step 4 above) easier. Many difficult design decisions are made by the tools and much of the complex code is generated by the tools based on the interface specifications.

3   UML Tool

UML Tool is a development tool that raises the level of abstraction in service development. New Construct service components can be specified in UML diagrams defining the service interfaces. UML Tool is described in detail in [3]. The user interface of UML Tool consists of a white canvas and several operations grouped into three menus (Figures 2 through 4).

The *File* menu provides operations to create a new UML diagram (*New*), to load an existing UML diagram from a file (*Load*), to save a diagram to a file (*Save as*), to translate a UML diagram into IDL and store it in a file (*Export in IDL*), and, finally, to exit UML Tool (*Exit*). The *Load, Save as,* and *Export in*

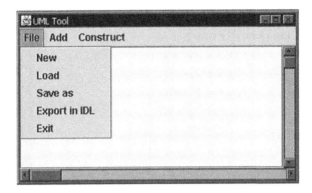

Fig. 2. The *File* menu in UML Tool

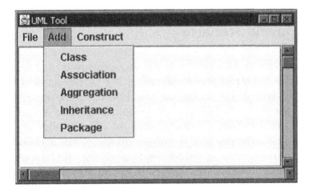

Fig. 3. The *Add* menu in UML Tool

IDL operations open standard file selector windows to specify/select files in the file system.

The *Add* menu allows the UML abstractions to be created. UML Tool supports packages, classes and different relationships between classes (association, aggregation, and inheritance). Classes can be grouped inside packages. Classes and relations that have been created can be manipulated (updated or deleted) by double-clicking or right clicking on them. Classes can be moved around on the canvas by clicking on them and dragging them to a new location.

The *Construct* menu provides the interface to the Construct navigational structure service with five basic operations to create, delete and traverse links. Links are created in the following sequence of operations: *Start link*, select endpoint (class or field name), *Create anchor*, select endpoint, *Create anchor*, and *End link*. The second endpoint can be either inside UML Tool or inside another client of the Construct navigational structure service (e.g., Emacs, Microsoft Word, or Netscape 6). Links are traversed by selecting an endpoint (anchors appear as blue, underlined text in UML Tool) and initiating the *Traverse link* operation.

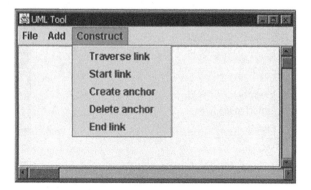

Fig. 4. The *Add* menu in UML Tool

4 Development Scenario

This following scenario shows some of the steps involved in the development of a simple navigational structure service using the Construct development tools. The focus of the scenario is on the specification of interfaces using UML Tool. The remaining stages in the Construct development process are described in [15], which contains details about the development of a file-based storage component.

Jakob is a graduate student at some university. He decides to follow the structural computing course given by the Department of Computer Science. As a part of the course, students are required to get hands-on experience in developing structure services. Jakob decides to develop a simple navigational structure service. Jakob has no prior knowledge of hypermedia or structural computing systems and decides to make use of the public domain Construct development tools to assist him in the development process. The first step is to make the overall design of the simple navigational structure service. Jakob decides that the service should support two types of structural abstractions: Anchor and Link. He finds this sufficient for his simple model. Jakob now uses UML Tool to assist him in the specification of the simple navigational component. He starts by defining a package named simplenav (Figure 5).

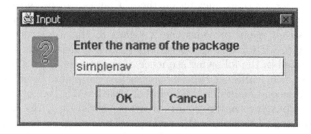

Fig. 5. The *Add Package* interface in UML Tool

Then, he creates the **Anchor** interface (Figures 6 through 8) and, subsequently, the Link interface. In Figure 6, Jakob has entered the name "Anchor" and has specified that Anchor is an interface.

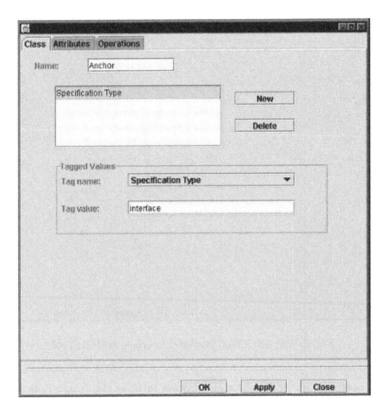

Fig. 6. The *Add Class* interface in UML Tool

In Figure 7, Jakob has added three attributes to the **Anchor** interface (*document, link,* and *value*). The attribute named *value* is private in scope, is of type String, and has the default value Null.

In Figure 8, Jakob has added four operations to the **Anchor** interface (*createAnchor, updateAnchor, deleteAnchor,* and *getDocumentAnchors*). The *createAnchor* operation is public in scope, is of type void, and has four parameters (*document, link, value,* and *anchor*). The *document* parameter is an input parameter (indicated by the direction In) of type URN.

Finally, Jakob creates an association between the **Anchor** and **Link** interfaces (Figure 9). He specifies that an anchor instance is part of 0 or 1 link instances, and that link instances connect 2 or more anchor instances.

The resulting UML diagram for the simple navigational structure service interface is shown in Figure 10.

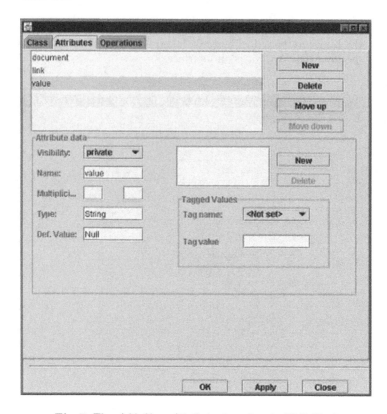

Fig. 7. The *Add Class Attributes* interface in UML Tool

The next step in the development process involves the translation from the UML diagram to an IDL specification. Jakob initiates the *Export in IDL* command and the IDL specification in Figure 11 is generated by UML Tool and saved in a separate file.

Jakob decides that he is happy with the interface specification and starts to document the design and the decisions leading to the specification. He creates a text file in Emacs (named navigational.txt) describing the interface. Then he creates a two-way link between the *Anchor* interface in the UML diagram (Figure 12) and the phrase "Anchor" in the text file in Emacs (Figure 13). He continues to document the design and creates links between the different types of development artifacts as part of the documentation of the simple navigational structure service interface.

In Figure 12, Jakob has started to create a link from the Anchor interface.

In Figure 13, Jakob has finalized the link from the **Anchor** interface in the UML diagram to the phrase "Anchor" in the text file in Emacs containing the documentation about the **Anchor** interface.

The remaining steps in the development process are to use the CSC to generate Java source code, to add the method bodies, and to compile the Java

Fig. 8. The *Add Class Operations* interface in UML Tool

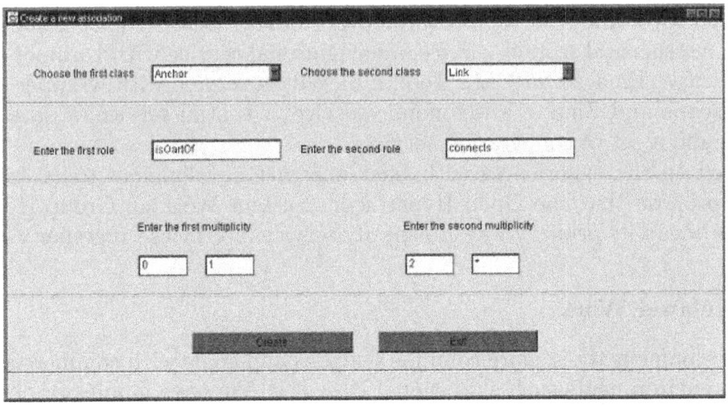

Fig. 9. The *Add Associations* interface in UML Tool

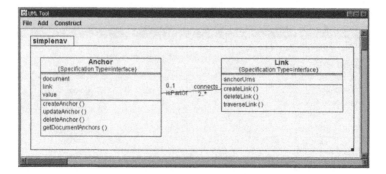

Fig. 10. The resulting UML diagram of the simple navigational service in UML Tool

source code. As mentioned above, [15] contains a detailed example of how the CSC works, what source code it generates, etc., based on the development of a file-based storage component.

5   Conclusions

The paper has examined how the development tools (in particular UML Tool) can assist service developers in developing services for the Construct component-based structural computing environment. We have demonstrated that the development tools lower the entry-barrier for structural computing service developers. New services can be specified as UML diagram or IDL specifications and many difficult design decisions relating to the coding process are automatically handled by the development tools.

We have over the past two years accumulated valuable development experiences. As of September 2001, well over 10 services have been developed (or are under active development) using the Construct development tools. The services developed cover different architectural layers and different structural domains including a structural storage service, a navigational service with wrapper services for Netscape, Emacs and UML Tool, a metadata service with wrapper services for Netscape and Emacs, a taxonomic service, a spatial service, a data mining service, and a set of cooperation services.

Based on the experiences with the Construct development tools, we would like to propose that the Open Hypermedia System Working Group [10] adopt UML as one of its primary ways to specify service interfaces - together with IDL.

5.1   Related Work

The development tools share common features and goals with commercial development environments such as Rational Rose [11]. We have found two noticeable differences between our approach and approaches like Rational Rose. First of all, the Construct software is publicly available free of charge (Construct is an open source project). Secondly, we have taken an open systems approach to the

```
module simplenav {

interface Anchor {
  attribute Urn document;
  attribute Urn link;
  attribute String value;
  void createAnchor(in Urn document, in Urn link, in String value, out Anchor anchor);
  void updateAnchor(in Urn anchor, in String value);
  void deleteAnchor(in Urn anchor);
  void getDocumentAnchors(in Urn document, out LinkedList anchors);
};

interface Link {
  attribute LinkedList anchorUrns;
  void createLink(in LinkedList anchorUrns, out Link link);
  void deleteLink(in Urn link);
  void traverseLink(in Urn anchor, out LinkedList anchors);
};

};
```

Fig. 11. The IDL specification generated by UML Tool

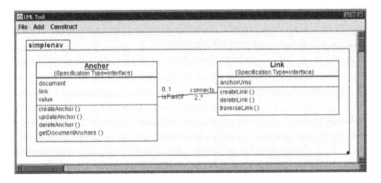

Fig. 12. A link endpoint created from the **Anchor** interface in UML Tool

development environment, which aims at re-using and integrating with existing applications, tools, and services in the computing environment.

ArgoUML is an object-oriented design tool with UML support [2]. ArgoUML is still under active development - the current stable version is v0.8.1a (as of September 2001). ArgoUML includes more features than the Construct UML Tool does. Like Construct, ArgoUML is an open source project.

5.2 Future Work

Our effort has resulted in a set of stand-alone tools that can be deployed in different phases of service development. In our future work, we plan to examine

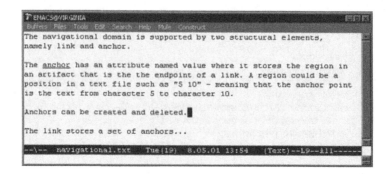

Fig. 13. The other link endpoint created from the phrase "Anchor" in the file "navigational.txt" managed by Emacs

ways to achieve a smoother integration of the development tools by deploying control integration techniques. A simple example of control integration is to have UML Tool initiate the CSC with the generated IDL specification. This will allow developers to generate the service component skeleton from the UML diagram in one step.

On a short term basis, we also plan to examine ArgoUML in detail and follow how the design tool evolves. Since we have no current plans for additional development of UML Tool, we will look closely into the possibility of integrating ArgoUML (or a similar tool) with Construct.

On a long term basis, we plan to investigate the relationships between the Construct component framework and other component frameworks (e.g., CORBA) as well as agent frameworks.

Acknowledgements. Several people have been involved in the development of Construct tools and services. Peter Nürnberg developed the Construct Service Compiler (CSC). Stéphane Blondin and Jérome Fahler, two Socrates exchange students from the University of Bretagne Occidentale in Brest, France, implemented the UML Tool during a three-month visit at the Department of Computer Science and Engineering, Aalborg University Esbjerg during the Summer of 2000.

References

1. Anderson, K. M., Taylor, R., and Whitehead, E. J. 1994. Chimera: Hypertext for heterogeneous software environments. In *Proceedings of the 1994 ACM European Conference on Hypertext*, (Edinburgh, Scotland, Sep.), 94-107. ACM Press.
2. ArgoUML. 2001. http://argouml.tigris.org.
3. Blondin, S., Fahler, J., Wiil, U. K., and Nürnberg, P. J. 2000. UML Tool: High-level Specification of Construct Services. Technical Report CSE-00-01, Department of Computer Science and Engineering, Aalborg University Esbjerg.
4. Construct. 2001. http://www.cs.aue.auc.dk/construct.

5. Grønbæk, K., and Trigg, R. 1999. From Web to Workplace - Designing Open Hypermedia Systems. MIT Press.
6. Hall, W., Davis, H., and Hutchings, G. 1996. Rethinking Hypermedia - The Microcosm Approach. Kluwer Academic Publishers.
7. Nürnberg, P. J., Leggett, J. J., and Schneider, E. R. 1997. As we should have thought. In *Proceedings of the 1997 ACM Hypertext Conference*, (Southampton, UK, Apr.), 96-101. ACM Press.
8. Nürnberg, P. J., Ed. 1999. Proceedings of the First Workshop on Structural Computing. Technical Report CS-99-04, Department of Computer Science, Aalborg University Esbjerg, Denmark.
9. Nürnberg, P. J., Leggett, J. J., Schneider, E., R., and Schnase, J. L. 1996. HOSS: A new paradigm for computing. In *Proceedings of the 1996 ACM Hypertext Conference*, (Washington, DC, Mar.), 194-202. ACM Press.
10. Open Hypermedia System Working Group. 2001. `http://www.ohswg.org`.
11. Rational Rose. 2001. `http://www.rational.com/rose`.
12. Reich, S., and Anderson, K. M. Eds. 2000. Open Hypermedia Systems and Structural Computing. Proceedings of the 6th Workshop on Open Hypermedia Systems and the 2nd Workshop on Structural Computing. Lecture Notes in Computer Science 1903, Springer Verlag.
13. Wiil, U. K., Hicks, D. L., and Nürnberg, P. J. 2001. Multiple open services: A new approach to service provision in open hypermedia systems, In *Proceedings of the 2001 ACM Conference on Hypertext*, (Aarhus, Denmark, August). ACM Press.
14. Wiil, U. K., Nürnberg, P. J., Hicks, D. L., and Reich, S. 2000. A development environment for building component-based open hypermedia systems. In *Proceedings of the 2000 ACM Hypertext Conference*, (San Antonio, TX, Jun.), 266-267. ACM Press.
15. Wiil, U. K. 2000. Using the Construct development environment to generate a file-based hypermedia storage service. In [12], 147-159.
16. Wiil, U. K., and Nürnberg, P. J. 1999. Evolving hypermedia middleware services: Lessons and observations. In *Proceedings of the 1999 ACM Symposium on Applied Computing*, (San Antonio, TX, Feb.), 427-436. ACM Press.
17. Wiil, U. K., and Leggett, J. J. 1997. Workspaces: The HyperDisco approach to Internet distribution. In *Proceedings of the 1997 ACM Hypertext Conference, (Southampton, UK, Apr.)*, 13-23. ACM Press.

Peer-Reviewed, Publishable Hypertexts: A First Look

Peter J. Nürnberg and David L. Hicks

Department of Computer Science, Aalborg University Esbjerg
Niels Bohrs Vej 8, DK-6700 Esbjerg, Denmark
{pnuern,hicks}@cs.aue.auc.dk
http://cs.aue.auc.dk/

Abstract. Despite the fact the hypermedia has long been discussed as a suitable format for academic research publications, the academic community has made little progress toward realizing hypermedia publishing. In this paper, we provide an initial framework for considering the problems facing any system designed for publishing academic hypertexts, and propose some first steps our community can take toward realizing this goal.

1 Introduction

Hypertext and hypermedia are now part of the everyday landscape. Generally, computer-literate people are familiar and even comfortable with hypermedia documents. Hypermedia is a mainstream technology. Furthermore, it is recognized by many people as the most appropriate medium for delivery of certain types of information. From help files to API documentation, many people have become accustomed to seeing certain highly interconnected types of information delivered as hypertext. Other forms of delivery for such information, such as printed manuals or online "flat" text files may be seen as inappropriate and impoverished.

Despite this, the academic community has not adopted a mechanism by which original research contributions may be submitted and published in hypertext form. Certainly, this is not due to the nature of the information. A hallmark of quality research is its positioning within the fields to which it contributes. This requires connections to be built among pieces of existing work and the research in question. Research contributions without such connections are at best difficult for others to reuse and at worst inaccurate and misleading. (When we speak of connections, we do not mean only references to other work, although this is certainly a very common and valuable type of connection to build. We also mean to include higher-level semantic connections – observations that tie together several existing research contributions for the purposes of comparison, contrast, support, refutation, extension, or other exegesis.)

Currently, the methods we use to mark connections among works in our research contributions (such as references or extended quotations) are often clumsy,

S. Reich, M.M. Tzagarakis, P.M.E. De Bra (Eds.): OHS/SC/AH 2001, LNCS 2266, pp. 94–103, 2002.
© Springer-Verlag Berlin Heidelberg 2002

prone to error, and difficult to use. At first glance, hypertext seems to be an ideal technology for the representation of these connections. Even the paper widely acknowledged to be the first in the hypertext research area, Bush's famous "As we may think" article of 1945 [2], envisioned the use of hypertext in academia as a means to convey accurately connections among existing work. Bush went so far as to describe an entire profession devoted to the generation of structure among already given data (trailblazers). However, we have yet to adopt any conventions for actually realizing these types of contributions.

In this paper, we take a first look at a mechanism by which hypertexts might be compiled, peer-reviewed, and published. We begin by listing some requirements we see as critical for any such mechanism, and discuss some of the technological issues and non-technological barriers in realizing a system that meets the requirements we generated. We close with an agenda that will help use move toward the goal of realizing peer-reviewed, publishable academic hypertexts.

2 Requirements

In this section, we examine some of the requirements for a hypertextual academic research publishing system (HARPS). Before we begin, we offer this initial working definition: a HARPS is a set of technologies and practices that enable the production and dissemination of academic research in hypertext form. That is, we are not only speaking of particular software (or hardware) systems, but also of guidelines for how people will interact with such computer systems, with one another, and with the generated artifacts. Clearly, a HARPS must reside within a larger system that enables production and dissemination of academic research in other, more traditional, forms, such as printed, non-hypertextual proceedings or journals.

We also point out that this discussion is meant only to seed further work. The set of requirements we present is by no means complete. However, we believe it represents a useful starting point for future work.

Broadly speaking, we can divide the requirements for a HARPS into two categories: infrastructure and frontend. Infrastructure requirements are largely technological. We offer them as axiomatic, but based within the framework of previous, related work. Frontend requirements are largely motivated by social and political factors. We divide our discussion of frontend requirements by addressing the motivations of various parties to the academic publishing process.

2.1 Infrastructure Requirements

From a systems perspective, the infrastructure requirements for a HARPS would seem to induce another OHSWG (Open Hypermedia Systems Working Group) scenario [7]. Traditionally, the OHSWG would begin work in this application domain by generating one or more scenarios of system use, which could then be analyzed for structural abstraction requirements. Before we begin this exercise, however, it may be worth asking whether we can reuse one or more existing

OHSWG scenarios. Have we discussed the problem of publishing hypertexts before?

In fact, although there is no existing OHSWG scenario that exactly describes a system used for the purpose of publishing hypertextual academic research, there have been a number of closely related discussions. As pointed out above, Bush [2] describes the production of academic research in hypertext form. Engelbart [4] describes hypertext support for generic knowledge workers. Nürnberg et al. [5] describe the production of taxonomies by botanical taxonomists. This discussion relies on the "navigational" and "taxonomic" structural abstractions identified by the OHSWG. In this field, such taxonomies comprise a significant portion of the academic product. Nürnberg et al. [6] also describe a scenario in which linguists generate various intermediate and final hypertextual products modeling language relationships. In addition to the "navigational" and "taxonomic" structural domains, this scenario also uses "spatial" and "issue-based" structural abstractions.

In fact, at a broad level, the potential types of structural abstractions used by academics to represent their work products comprise an unbounded set. This may be a rather bleak outcome for this inquiry. Supporting such a wide variety of structural abstractions may simply be impractical.

Although some might advocate proposing a generic structural computing or component-based open hypermedia system (CB-OHS) approach to handling this open and unbounded abstraction situation (approaches specifically designed to handle arbitrary co-existing structures), we would propose that we look for a simpler, if strictly less powerful, solution. Consider the current situation in academic publishing – despite the fact that work products come in many different forms (botanical taxonomies, linguistic relationships, etc.), the forms in which research is peer-reviewed, published, and disseminated are relatively constrained. Is this a result of a poor fit between how results are generated and how they are disseminated, driven by an inadequate technology (paper)?

Perhaps, but leaving aside how we arrived at our current model, there are some powerful reasons for "normalizing" dissemination products across fields. Such uncoupling of work product format from dissemination format allows academics trained in virtually any field at least to be able to read through the results in other fields. One need not be familiar with all the intricacies of botanical taxonomies to be able to read a journal paper on the subject (although such familiarity is obviously helpful) – it is sufficient (for certain limited purposes) simply to be trained to read and understand journal papers.

What can we take away from this analysis? We may be best served by choosing structural abstractions (a hypertextual dissemination format) for research results that is uncoupled from the structures used in the construction of those results. As a starting point, we propose using the abstractions identified by the OHSWG as "navigational" hypertext abstractions (see, e.g., [7] [8]). Although discussed at great length elsewhere, briefly, this structural domains allows for the creation, manipulation, and deletion of first-class, n-sided, optionally directional associations (links) between (whole or parts of) node content. Nodes wrap arbitrary (possibly third-party managed) content. Being first-class objects, associations themselves may associated, may be tagged with arbitrary attribute-value set pairs, may be subject to access, concurrency, and versioning control, etc.

Some may argue that a number of useful structural abstractions, such as transclusions or composites are missing from the base navigational model. Clearly, more abstractions lead to more powerful systems. However, they also lead to more complex systems. We feel that the base navigational model represents a good starting point. These abstractions support at least the final delivery format described in the aforementioned scenarios. Also, since navigational hypertext systems are by far the most common in use today, such systems presumably face a smaller acceptance threshold by users.

Another potential issue is how much "complex" functionality should be made available. Using the OHSWG "1+4" paradigm[1], how many (and to what degree) of the "4" additional services should be included. We see a clear need for versioning, since existing academic research products are also versioned, and we do not want a HARPS that is strictly less powerful than existing systems of publishing and dissemination. Access control is also clearly necessary, since copyright holders (and/or authors, if these are different) should be able to modify or delete structures, even if generic readers cannot. Concurrency and notification control, while useful in authoring, seem less so in dissemination systems, as long as systems support a many-read semantic on unlocked entities. Since versioning and access control in hypermedia are still open research areas, it is difficult to formulate the exact form of these additional services.

Finally, it should be clear that only an open systems solution can be considered here. There can be no justification for imposing a fixed (set of) interaction style(s) on all authors and readers anymore.

Several existing, freely distributable and licensable (CB-)OHS's currently under development (e.g., Callimachus [3] or Construct [9]) could be used to support basic navigational structures over an open set of applications. Thus, the basic front-end technological concerns may be reasonably expected to be handled by current technology. Continuing work by the OHSWG on standardizing structure interchange formats will fill in the remaining technological issues on this front. With respect to advanced functionality (versioning and access control), while these exist in both of the aforementioned systems, much work still lies ahead for the OHSWG on the standardization front before this area can be considered fully addressed.

To summarize, a HARPS must support:

---

[1] The "1+4" explanation of services was coined at OHS 3.5 in Århus, Denmark. The "1" refers to a base service, such as the "navigational" service. The "4" refers to versioning, access, concurrency, and notification control services that can be "layered" on top of the base service. The "1+4" formulation is meant to imply that the four "advanced" services are optional, since they may not be needed in many cases.

Req. 1.   an open set of applications (clients);

Req. 2.   the structural abstractions of the basic OHSWG navigational model;

Req. 3.   some (as yet to be fully specified) level of versioning support; and,

Req. 4.   some (as yet to be fully specified) level of access control.

We explicitly avoid more expressive possibilities, such as systems that support open sets of structural abstractions, due to their inherent complexity, and the fact that we see advantages in "normalized" representations for published academic research.

2.2   Frontend Requirements

There are a number of frontend requirements for any HARPS. Above all, there must be motivation and reward for using a HARPS over (or in conjunction with) traditional dissemination systems for the readers, the authors, and the reviewers. We treat each of these cases separately.

Reader motivated requirements. What advantages does a reader of hyper-textual research enjoy over a reader of research published with traditional media only? Clearly, however a particular HARPS is implemented, it must provide as many of the favorable aspects of traditional publishing systems as possible. A HARPS that lacks desirable features of traditional publishing systems certainly faces a much greater adoption challenge. Where possible, features of traditional systems should be augmented. Finally, there may be features of a HARPS not able to be easily reproduced in traditional systems.

One way in which to secure many positive features of traditional systems within a HARPS is to provide a method for hypertextual research to be rendered on paper. This requirement, though easy enough to state, is in fact quite challenging to meet. Hypertextual models such as the OHSWG navigational model admit arbitrarily complicated structures – links may be n-sided, may link to both nodes and other structural abstractions (and thus be nested to arbitrary levels), and may have associated traversal semantics that take the form of arbitrary computations (that, in turn, may generate traversal destinations dynamically, interact with the reader, check traversal state, etc.) How can such structures and behaviors be rendered on paper?

There are three basic types of approaches to this problem. The first type essentially attempts to define paper renderings for all types of structures and behaviors. We believe such types of approaches are doomed to failure, because even moderately complicated structures are likely to have such complex generic renderings as to make them unreadable. The second type of approach essentially disallows certain types of structures and behaviors, arbitrarily limiting authors to a simple, "renderable" set of abstractions. While this addresses the potential unreadability problem engendered by the first type of approach, we see this as unnecessarily limiting to authors. We do not yet know what kinds of structure and behaviors authors will find useful – deciding on limitations now is premature.

The third type of approach places the rendering requirement on the author, by forcing the author to define "paper rendering semantics" for all structures and behaviors used in a given hypertextual work (as is possible in KMS [1], which provides ways in which to affect the behavior of the "linear" program, which produces a paper renderable document from a KMS hypertext.) While this may be seen as a great burden to place on authors, we feel that the advantages of doing so are great enough to merit its requirement. Over time, we expect that communities would develop shorthand ways of describing common renderings, thus reducing the onus on authors.

What features of traditional publishing systems can a HARPS augment or improve; and, what totally new features can a HARPS offer? Certainly, HARPS software can render structures and behaviors in an active way, making structures traversable, computations executable, etc. This may take very simple forms (e.g., allowing references to be retrieved by a mouse click) or very complicated forms (e.g., allowing traversal between a set of data and multiple analyses carried out dynamically). Limited depth-first searches of hypertextual research products could be used as a way of building high-level overviews or "digest versions" of work. A HARPS could also offer annotation capabilities. Annotations could be linked into hypertextual documents, and themselves become a further research product that could be distributed, shared, and even published as further work. This simple scaling from informal annotation support to full peer-reviewed publishing could be a powerful benefit for readers who themselves become authors. Finally, a HARPS should offer readers the ability to select which structure/behaviors they wish to see/execute. The OHSWG model abstraction of context might be useful here.

To summarize, a HARPS must support:

Req. 5.   a method by which authors specify a "printable rendering" of their products;

Req. 6.   the ability to render structures and behaviors actively in software; and,

Req. 7.   tailorable and personalizable reading experiences.

Author motivated requirements. Why do authors of academic research publish? Certainly, the desire to disseminate results is one important factor. Inasmuch as this is true, advantages for readers of a HARPS are also by extension advantages for authors – if a HARPS offers benefits to readers of research work, this helps the author disseminate this work. More interesting are other motivations for authors. How can a HARPS appeal to these motivations?

An author of hypertextual research work must be able to use this work to help secure promotion, tenure, or other perquisites on the job. Traditional publishing is an important aspect of acquiring these job benefits. Work published within a HARPS must also confer these benefits to authors. Informally, we have noticed that any type of electronic publication is less likely to be weighted as highly by academic administration as traditional publications. To the degree that this is true, we must recognize that hypertextual publications will also tend to be discounted if delivered only in electronic form. We feel, however, that the requirement on authors of generating "paper rendering" directions may mitigate the problems faced by electronic-only publications. In the foreseeable future, an important component of any HARPS will be the traditional publication of these paper rendering, even if these rendering are not the primary means of consumption by other academics.

Perhaps the most difficult hurdle faced by a HARPS will be how hypertextual work is evaluated by other academics. What kinds of structures represent significant research contributions? What types of tradeoffs are there between quantity and quality of structures? How complex do structures (and the insights behind them) need to be to constitute a workshop position statement, a conference full paper, or a journal article? All of our experience points to the fact that building hypertextual works of any sort is difficult. Consider hypertext fiction, which by sheer word count is often much shorter than comparable conventional writing. We feel that academic communities will need to develop an appropriate weighting for the construction of complex hypertextual structures (when these structures are informative and insightful, of course). Stated another way, authors will need to be justly compensated (recognized) for their hypertextual work.

To summarize, a HARPS must support:

Req. 8. a major focus on the publication and distribution of author specified "printable renderings"; and,

Req. 9. a set of conventions for the judging the complexity and value of hypertextual structures and behaviors.

Reviewer motivated requirements. In many ways, reviewer motivations may be the easiest to dismiss if one superficially considers the problems facing a HARPS. However, we feel reviewers must be carefully considered if widespread adoption of hypertextual work is to become a reality. Reviewers most often agree to review work partly out of motivation for the "public good". The academic publishing system only works if there are reviewers who are willing to assess the appropriateness, originality, and overall value of contributions. Recognizing this, many academic feel duty-bound to review, at least occasionally. This motivation seems independent of the actual publication format, but it may not be independent of the submission format (which also takes hypertextual form in a HARPS). Therefore, any HARPS must support the needs of reviewers. Submissions must be able to be read on a wide-variety of platforms, etc. This, however, would seem to be addressed by the open systems requirement (Req. 1) described above. More importantly, there must be a way for reviewers to annotate the structures and behaviors of a submission, much in the same way that reviewers can markup a paper submission with a pen.

Some electronic journals provide a method by which reviewers can "co-publish" their reviews along with an article. A HARPS should of course accommodate this possibility. We feel, however, that it is worth pointing out that a HARPS would be especially able to support this practice quite easily. by linking reviews off of the reviewed article. Reviews might be modeled as separate contexts that are initially only viewable by a program committee, and then are made optionally available to wider audiences. More broadly, one can imagine an "open reviewer" model in which comments on articles form a second-level literature all their own. The line between "original contribution" and "review" may begin to blur.

To summarize, a HARPS must support:

Req. 10. annotations on content, structures, and behaviors; and,

Req. 11. a convenient way in which these annotations (reviews) can be linked from works, and made optionally available.

3   Agenda

An agenda to move forward toward the goal of realizing peer-reviewed, publishable academic hypertexts must consider both the infrastructure and frontend challenges faced by a HARPS. Addressing the category of infrastructure challenges will require further research focused on the lower (backend and middleware) levels within an open hypermedia environment, in that these challenges correspond to functional requirements that are most appropriately addressed at these levels. The frontend challenges are generated by the necessity to support specific user capabilities and work practices within a HARPS in order for it to succeed. Addressing this category of issues will require further work at higher levels within an open hypermedia environment, to ensure that applications provide the required functionalities for users, and that policies and guidelines are in place to ensure the required work practices are followed.

3.1   Infrastructure Issues

As mentioned earlier, several component based open hypermedia systems currently under development support basic navigational structures over an open set of applications. These systems are largely capable of handling the more basic technological issues raised earlier (Req. 1 and Req. 2). It is important, however, that along with the continued development of these systems that the standardization process of the OHSWG also progress so that the interchange of structures between systems is possible.

While some open hypermedia systems do provide support to address certain aspects of the more advance technological issues of versioning and access control (Req. 3 and Req. 4), more work is needed in these areas. A reasonable place to begin is with a detailed study and analysis of the versioning and access control requirements of a HARPS. First, an examination of the current procedures used for submitting, evaluating, and publishing academic research can be used to elucidate the requirements that are inherent in the process. In addition, existing (OHSWG) scenarios can be extended, and new ones can be created, that deal more directly with the peer review and publishing process to uncover ways in which versioning and access control functionality can be used in a HARPS to augment existing procedures. Once a more specific list of requirements has been generated, it can be used to analyze the facilities of existing systems. This can serve as a guide for researchers in extending their systems to accommodate the infrastructure support required by a HARPS.

An additional benefit of starting with an analysis of the infrastructure requirements of a HARPS is the targeted approach it promotes for coping with the issues that are involved. Versioning and access control are challenging capabilities to provide, especially in the general open hypermedia environment. Identifying and focusing on the specific subset of functionality from each of these areas required for a HARPS will enable solutions to be developed faster than attempting to address each issue comprehensively. At the same time, the targeted solutions developed to address these issues for a HARPS will be informative for researchers considering them within the broader general open hypermedia environment.

3.2 Frontend Issues

Critical to the success of a HARPS is the provision of the required capabilities at the user level as described earlier. A number of requirements from Section 2, especially the reader motivated and reviewer motivated ones (Reqs. 5, 6, 7, 10, and 11) identified specific functionality necessary in a HARPS environment. These all must be supported in order for a HARPS to succeed. Some of these capabilities, such as creating printable rendering of works and defining annotations, exist in various forms in current applications. Others can be built utilizing OHS infrastructure support, including the expanded access control and versioning facilities described above. Providing these capabilities will most likely involve a combination of modifying existing OHS applications and middleware components and perhaps creating new ones. Regardless of the strategy utilized, it will be important for standardization to take place, so that the solution will be an open systems one.

A number of the requirements from Section 2, especially the author motivated ones (Req. 8 and Req. 9) pertain to the work practices followed by those involved in the publication of academic works. Addressing these issues requires studying current practices and policies and developing from these a set of guidelines for HARPS users.

3.3 Call to Action

Can the OHSWG workshops (the Workshop on Open Hypermedia Systems and the Structural Computing workshops) be a testbed for hypermedia publishing? This is a tantalizing idea. In this paper, we've pointed to various areas that will require more study, but how best to carry out these studies? Perhaps the question should be, "how better than to try ourselves?" We propose that within the next 2 years, both workshops adopt a HARPS track which would allow authors to experiment with compiling and submitting hypertextual work, and would allow the community to evaluate the technologies and practices used to review and publish such work. This should be done in parallel to the calls for further study made above. One might argue that if this community cannot or will not adopt such a track, who else will?

References

1. Akscyn, Robert M., McCracken, D., Yoder, E.: KMS: A distributed hypermedia system for managing knowledge in organization. Communications of the ACM 31, 7 (Jul 1988), 820–835
2. Bush, Vannevar: As we may think. Atlantic Monthly 176, 1 (Jul 1945). 101-108
3. Christodoulakis, Dimitris, Vaitis, Michael, Papadopoulos, Athanasios, Tzagarakis, Manolis: The Callimachus approach to distributed hypermedia. Proceedings of Tenth ACM Conference on Hypertext and Hypermedia (HT '99) (Darmstadt, Germany, Feb). ACM Press, New York
4. Engelbart, Douglas C.: Augmenting human intellect: A conecptual framework. Stanford Research Institute Technical Report AFOSR-3223 Contract AF 49(638)-1024 (Oct 1962) Palo Alto, CA
5. Nürnberg, Peter J., Leggett, John J., Schneider, Erich R.: Designing digital libraries for the post-literate age. Journal of Universal Computer Science 2, 9 (Sep 1996)
6. Nürnberg, Peter J., Wiil, Uffe K., Leggett, John J.: Structuring facilities in digital libraries. Proceedings of the European Conference on DigitalLibraries 1998 (Crete, Greece, Sep)
7. OHSWG. 1997. Open Hypermedia Systems Working Group Home Page. Available at <http://www.ohswg.org/>
8. Reich, Sigfried, Wiil, Uffe K., Nürnberg, Peter J., Davis, Hugh C., Grønbæk, Kaj, Anderson, Kenneth M., Millard, David E., Haake, Jörg M.: Addressing interoperability in open hypermedia: the design of the Open Hypermedia Protocol. New Review of Hypermedia and Multimedia 5, 1 (1999)
9. Wiil, Uffe K., Nürnberg, Peter J.: Evolving hypermedia middleware services: Lessons and observations. Proceedings of ACM Symposium on Applied Computing 1999 (San Antonio, TX, Mar). ACM Press, New York

Because I Seek an Image, Not a Book

Moritz Neumüller

Wirtschaftsuniversität Wien
1090 Wien, Austria
mneumueller@ekno.com

Abstract. Drawing on a semiotic approach to hypermedia introduced at last year's OHS workshop, this paper presents a fresh look and new questions on the retrieval of – and navigation in – visual hypermedia.

1 Introduction

Searching and navigating visual hypermedia is a special case of the "exploratory, discovery-based, serendipitous form of search, typified by poorly defined goals – I'll know it when I see it – [which] has typically been contrasted with traditional goal oriented search as addressed by Information Retrieval" [11, p. 26]. In today's WWW, many efforts have been made to raise the capabilities and usability of search engines. This is a revolutionary increase of functionality especially at the beginning of a hypertext session. Yet, the results are often frustrating or just too numerous to be feasible for review. In this paper, I propose semiotic methodology for those theoretical issues that have to be taken into account – besides technological considerations – in a Web augmentation that is based on encouraging linkage [16].

2 Semiotic Basics

Many people will not even be aware of the fact that there is difference between the signifier /dog/ and its signified, our concept of the dog. Saussure takes this as reason enough to speak of the sign as their sum. From the experience that a child will automatically say "dog" whenever it sees a drawing of one, we can see that the process works in both directions, as depicted in Fig. 1. In the semiotic terminology, a sign is to be distinguished from what we often call a "sign" in colloquial language.[1]

Saussure had stressed that the signifier and the signified were as inseparable as the two sides of a piece of paper, they were intimately linked in the mind by an associative link, and wholly interdependent, neither pre-existing the other, cf. [41, p. 77]. Lacan was one of the main engineers in the conversion of the

---

[1] Hypertext theorists who ignore the key results of decades of semiotic investigations (whilst using the terms sign, text, communication, code, metaphors, etc.) risk failing to produce state of the art user-centered research.

S. Reich, M.M. Tzagarakis, P.M.E. De Bra (Eds.): OHS/SC/AH 2001, LNCS 2266, pp. 104–113, 2002.
© Springer-Verlag Berlin Heidelberg 2002

Fig. 1. The Saussurean sign model. Source: [41, p. 78]

Saussurean sign model, appropriating Saussure through Jakobson to Freud: He related metaphor to *Verdichtung* (condensation) and metonymy to *Verschiebung* (displacement), cf. [20]. Peirce offered a triadic relation between the representamen (R), the interpretant (I) and the object (O), see fig. 2. Nöth [35] has substituted these terms for more intuitive terminology: the sign vehicle, the sense and the reference object. Accordingly, signs might be considered in themselves, or in relationship to their object, or finally in relationship to their interpretants. These three considerations yield three trichotomies: a sign considered in itself might be a quality and thus a qualisign, an individual thing or event, thus a sinsign, or a law, hence a legisign; the relation of a sign to its object can be an iconic or indexical or symbolical; the relation of the sign to its interpretant is a rheme or dicent or argument, cf. [10, p. 132].

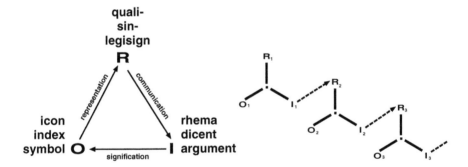

Fig. 2. Peircean sign classes and unlimited semiosis. Sources: Source: [31]; [28, p. 137]

This concept, of course, can be seen as going beyond Saussure's emphasis on the paradigmatic and syntagmatic value of a sign in its relation to other signs. To demonstrate the logics of the Peircean classification, Colapietro takes the example of a knock on the door.[2] The second trichotomy has been cited more than once in isolation from the two other trichotomies. An iconic relation

---

[2] "If there is a knock on the door announcing the arrival of guests, this rap is a sinsign. More accurately, it is a dicent, indexical sinsign. It is a dicent (or dicisign) since it in effect performs the function of an asserted proposition ('The guests have arrived'). It is indexical since there is an actual, physical connection between the sign vehicle and its object (the knocking sound and the guests announcing their arrival by means of knocking). Finally, it is a sinsign because the knocks as they are occurring here and now – the sounds in their individuality – serve as the sign vehicle" [10, p. 132].

is a mode in which the sign vehicle physically or perceptually resembles the reference object (e.g. a portrait, a scale-model, the sound of a gun in a computer game). A sign function in which a sign vehicle represents its object by virtue of a causal or physical connection is called indexical, cf. [10, p. 118]. This linkage can be observed or inferred (e.g. fingerprints revealing the identity of a thief or in biometrics, medical symptoms for certain illnesses, etc.). In a symbolic relation, the sign vehicle does not resemble the reference object but is arbitrary or purely conventional, like most words of our natural languages, road signs, an arrow on a Web page or the browser tool bar that points to the left for "back", etc. Naturally, different cultures show very different conventions, e.g. the arrow to the left in Arabic or Hebrew means "forward". Semiosis, a term borrowed from Peirce, is expanded by Umberto Eco to "unlimited semiosis" to refer to the way in which a series of successive Peircean interpretants lead to a (potentially) *ad infinitum* process, as any initial interpretation can be re-interpreted; cf. [37, 1.339, 2.303], [12]. Merrell [28, p. 137] illustrates this as Fig. 2b, an extension of his tripod model of the sign.

3   The Role of the Medium

Human experience is inherently multisensory, yet every representation of experience is subject to the constraints and affordances of the medium involved. Peirce's consideration of the medium instead of signs has often been revisited, reminding us that the study of the sign just like the study of the media is the study of the process of mediation between ourselves and the world outside, cf. [34, p. 3]. Every medium is constrained by the channels which it utilizes. While aural and visual signs seem to be privileged in current hypermedia systems, other channels are helpful for the reception of expressive signs. The visualization of the WWW is echoed by the evolution of interfaces from symbolic to iconic (in Brown's sense [7]). Semiotics will have to play a major role in the successful introduction of gustatory, olfactory and tactile data into hypermedia and the construction of indexical interfaces.[3]

4   Finding Images

As a picture says more than a 1000 words[4], many contemporary cultural theorists have remarked on the growth of the importance of visual media compared

---

[3] These sensual inputs are extremely interesting for the human understanding, learning and interpreting of data: for example, "odors, and even tastes [...] hardly know more than long-term memory" and "touch is sort of at the crossroads regarding sensory modes" [28, p. 151, 157]. Olfactory and gustatory sign vehicles have a strong indexical relation to the referent, which will influence future use in hypermedia environments: We can identify certain odors, even if their source has long left the place. These media will strongly enhance our comprehension, as we understand through the body, cf. [21].

[4] This is true for all non-verbal sensations, which belong to a certain kind of "archaic" thinking, as formulated in psychoanalytic terms by Ulrich: "Am Bild (wie am Ton,

with linguistic media in contemporary society and the associated shifts in the communicative functions of such media, cf. [9]. Verbal language must serve as a meta-language for visual signs because there is no meta-image to describe or analyze another image. Sign languages, such as the sign language for deaf people or the Braille notation for the blind, have to be learned just like verbal language and share its arbitrary character. Pictograms do not share this arbitrariness, and they can show abstract concepts only on "semiotic detours" [43], e.g. taking advantage of metonymic relations. Language can describe concepts in a compact manner, e.g. "your chance of winning is one to a thousand", as compared to a depiction of a sign for "you win" beside a thousand signs of "you loose", cf. [22]. Mathematical notation is explicitly tailored to show relationships such as $p = \frac{1}{1000}$. But when the formulae become too complicated and too many factors get involved, visualization is needed again: The endeavor to design better charts, maps and diagrams has lead to Neurath's "Wiener Methode der Bildstatistik" (later known as ISOTYPE), and also to Bertin's semiology of graphics, cf. [32, 5]. For Neurath, images have two major advantages: They are not dominated by the systematic fallacies of natural language and they can transgress cultural and language barriers. Of course, this "renaissance of the hieroglyph" faces problems quite similar to Wittgenstein's attempt to formalize language in the *Tractatus*, cf. [13]. Pictures on the computer screen can be classified into those recorded vs. those created in digital form. The first category consists of direct digital photographs and scans, the second of "synthetic or infographic images" [39, p. 121], such as CAD pictures, diagrams, bullets, arrows, graphs, etc. As these two categories are blurring, digital images loose their "authenticity". The authenticity of recorded material, in semiotical terms, is expressed as indexicality. Furthermore, digital images are infinitely reproducible by anybody, as there is no negative or mould and a total absence of any "aura of the original", cf. [3]. Besides general semiotic interest, these issues become important in connection with the construction of, and navigation in hypermedia: Content Based Retrieval (CBR) and Content Based Navigation (CBN). More precisely, linking (parts of) a picture to related pictures, be it by hand or automatically, draw on the same syntactic dimensions as Nöth's question "Can pictures lie?" [33, p. 137]. Since there are no words nor verbal propositions in pictures, Nöth proposes Peirce's more general semiotic terminology: rheme, as the more general semiotic equivalent of words, and dicent, as the general equivalent of propositions: "Can pictures function as autonomous dicentic signs, or do they only consist of rhematic signs? Do pictures only represent objects, or can they represent objects together with predications about these objects?" [33, p. 137]. Nöth tries to invalidate the logocentric arguments for a negative answer to these questions, as they are contextual incompleteness, non-segmentability, and dicentic vagueness. The first logocentric argument, contextual incompleteness, was first exposed by Gombrich [15] and reformulated by Muckenhaupt [30]. It implies that only when a picture is accompanied by a caption or label can the resulting text-picture message con-

---

Geruch, Geschmack, den taktilen Sensationen, dem Gleichgewichtssinn) arbeitet die Sprache sich ab und erreicht es nie ganz" [47, p. 104].

vey a true or false proposition. Nöth argues that "the function of pictures in text-picture combinations says nothing about the semiotic potential of pictures seen without labels or captions" [33, p. 138]. The second argument against pictures as autonomous dicentic signs, non-segmentability, is developed in Jerry A. Fodor's paper "Imagistic Representation" [14]. Fodor concludes that no pictorial language could exist because the linearization of arguments and predicates would prevent such pictorial words from being interpreted as a propositional whole.Nöth's counter-argument is that "Fodor commits the error of projecting the linearity of verbal language onto the visual domain where simultaneity is the structural principle relating the rhematic elements in question" [33, p. 139]. Here, of course, Nöth is in line with Langer's dichotomy of discursive linearity vs. presentational immediacy, cf. [22]. Neurath has mastered this problem with the "invention" of compound signs: The pictograph for "worker" combined with the pictograph for "miner's hammer" generates the "miner", cf. [13, p. 20]. Yet, Eschbach's semiotic analysis has shown other frontiers of the picture language, cf. [13]. The third syntactic argument against the possibility of assigning truth values to pictures is the argument of dicentic vagueness: "This argument claims that pictorial messages are so ambiguous, vague, and polysemous that they cannot serve to prove any truth or falseness" [33, p. 141]. Both Gombrich and Fodor have defended the point of view that we cannot express pictorially whether we mean 'the' cat (an individual) or 'a cat' (a member of a class). Nöth claims that this argument, which crucial for CBR/N, "is clearly logocentric".[5] Against Gombrich's and Fodor's view that pictorial polysemy prevents pictures from being vehicles of truth, Nöth argues that a message which conveys a plurality of facts about the world must not therefore be less true than a message that conveys only a single true statement: "Neither polysemy nor ambiguity can thus be accepted as general arguments against the truth potential of pictures" [33, p. 142].

Schmauks [43] has analyzed similar questions in connection with picture dictionaries, e.g. Langenscheidt's OhneWörterBuch [1]. She follows Baldinger [2] in stating that dictionaries follow a semasiologic order (they list words alphabetically), while picture dictionaries follow an onomasiologic strategy: They arrange the world in clusters or time-lines, cf. [2,42]. The same is true for hypermedia systems that are based on graphic navigation. Yet, in hypermedia, interconnected subjects and structures do not have to be flattened out into a sequential order. A symbol (especially in the strict sense of Peirce's terminology) should have as little connotations as possible in order to function as a sign.[6] But most "natural" symbols (such as animals, colors, etc.) are homonymous in different contexts and cultures. Think of or the color white as the symbol of joy (in Western cultures) vs. grief (in certain Asian cultures). Or, the eagle as a symbol for

---

[5] "It does not ask whether pictures can convey statements, but asks whether it can convey the same statement as a given sentence. The answer would be different if the picture were the point of departure in the comparison with verbal statements. A particular photograph of a cat on a mat, being an indexical sign, is certainly in the first place about an individual cat and not about a member of a class." [33, p. 141].

[6] "The power of the symbol lies in its scarcity and indifference" [22, p. 83].

freedom, strength, speed (Fig. 3a), but also as an emblem for institutions and countries (Fig. 3c). In the form of a spread eagle, the eagle appears as a heraldic emblem on flags and seals (Fig. 3b).

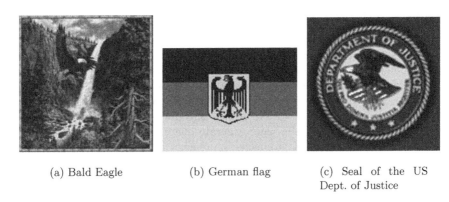

(a) Bald Eagle   (b) German flag   (c) Seal of the US
                                                     Dept. of Justice

Fig. 3. Depictions of eagles (See http://www.frankmillerfineart.com, http://www.fotw.ca/flags/, and http://www.usdoj.gov/)

Symbols for non-visual concepts tend to be *gestalts* that can be recognized at first sight (think of company logos and road signs), while pictures that trigger the ve-rediction mechanism invite the eye to travel through the picture space.[7]: When compared to the emblem of the German flag (fig. 3b), the print of the "Bald Eagle, Symbol of Freedom series" (fig. 3a) demonstrates this longing for expression: The heroic print is rich in narrative details.[8] The journey (or, navigation) through this kind of pictures is led by the composition of the picture, but always influenced by the direction of reading, i.e. left-to-right[9] in the Latin-based languages. These issues relate to the theoretical problem of human and artificial interpretation of visual information and the implementation into hypermedia, such as CBR/N. Chandler [9, Signs] equates unlimited semiosis with the process of browsing a dictionary. Bolter [6] and McGuire [27] expand the equation to hypertext navigation.

"Because I seek an image, not a book" says Ille in W.B. Yeats' poem *Ego Dominus Tuus* to Hic. And this is exactly what many users are doing in hyper-

[7] Caneparo/Caprettini mean by *verediction* – in accordance to Greimas – that the image points outwards "towards a certain reality, or rather, a certain concept of reality" [8, p. 148].

[8] The design of the German flag, however, follows the traditional heraldic notation for flags and emblems. Therefore, it can be described precisely in a specialized vocabulary. The seal of the US Department of Justice is a mixture of modes: It depicts heraldic elements in a illusionistic manner.

[9] This is especially likely where pictures are embedded in written text. "There is thus a potential sequential significance in the left-hand and right-hand elements of a visual image – a sense of 'before' and 'after'." [9, Syntagmatic Analysis]

media. At the time of writing this paper, the search engine Google implemented a beta version of an image searching tool on the WWW. A search for "eagle" in early August 2001 brought up 845 results that imply that the search mechanism looks for the requested term in the file name as well as in the context of the image on the Web page. Accordingly, the grade of usefulness of the retrieved images varies a lot, and the browsing of the 43 result pages can be quite tiresome. This result corresponds with the findings of Smolinar et al. [45] who have used Semiotics to formulate an authoring perspective to multimedia search. They point to the research of Gerald Edelman. They conclude that we have to accept that searching on such a query can only be viable if it yields a set of candidates, "some (if not many) of which may have nothing to do with the content we had in mind and many of which may only be valuable to the extent that they can help us formulate a more accurate query" [45, p. 5-6]. Half a decade later we have a number of promising approaches using CBR/N together with the Open Hypermedia paradigm, such as Miyabi, ARTISTE and MAVIS [17, 26,24]. The ARTISTE system includes algorithms for color, textile/fabric and shape matching for parts of, or entire images. MAVIS (the Multimedia Architecture for Video, Image and Sound) brings together techniques for CBR/CBN in different types of media, into a single hypermedia system, allowing cross-media navigation, concept navigation and retrieval via a multimedia thesaurus [46]. To overcome the inadequacies of the low level feature matching of images, Tansley et al. propose a mid-level extraction method for images based upon scale space matching and graph matching to achieve topological matching of images and object retrieval. Yet, in spite of significant progress in CBR, it is clear that "to achieve truly robust and versatile retrieval of images based on content will require a general solution to the recognition problem in image analysis and this is far from being achieved" [23]. In the process of building MAVIS2, Joyce et al. investigated the applicability of semiotic concepts and intelligent agents for integrating and navigating through multimedia representations of concepts [19]. First, they follow Smolinar et al. [45] in considering the Saussurian notion of signifier and signified as the focal concepts in multimedia data. But then they reject it because they "note that the 'user' is abstracted out of the Saussurian model" [19, p. 133]. They turn to Ogden/Richards' interpretation of Peirce's system as a semiotic triangle and Peirce's second trichotomy iconic/indexical/symbolic [36, 37]. Of course, this leads into the direction of Computational Semiotics, a field of research which applies and implements semiotic principles into Artificial Intelligence systems. As any thorough approach to these issues would by far go beyond the scope of this paper, I want to limit my commentaries on the following points of departure, which may serve as a basis for further work:

– The simplified model of a semiotic triangle promoted by Morris [29] and Ogden/Richards [36] has been criticized by many semioticians, e.g. Umberto Eco, Renzo Raggiunti and Mihai Nadin [12,38,31]. In his pansemiotic view, Peirce sees the whole world as a semiotic system, cf. [19], [35, p. 59ff.] which works by means of semiosis. This means that the user never gets to (i.e.

never uses, never means) the "real object" but he decodifies the sign as far as he needs it for the communication act.

- This unlimited semiotic chain is also inherent in the Saussurian model with its syntagmatic and paradigmatic axes (despite Derrida's critique, it can thus be described as multi-dimensional, cf. [48]). In my point of view, it is simplistic to say that Saussure's model "abstracts out" the user while Peirce's "includes" him/her. Especially extensions of the Signifier/Signified model (from Lacan and Jakobson to Kristeva) make it obvious that the user is not a closed entity that stands either inside or outside.
- In Peirce's own words, the sign is "something which stands to somebody for something in some respect or capacity" [37, vol. 2, p. 228]. Thus, the "meaning" of a sign depends on the context. In connection with CBR, Santini/Jain have tried to close the semantic gap by considering these different "meanings": "Context is essential for the determination of the meaning of an image and for the judgment of image similarity" [40]. They use an interaction model that seems very similar to the spatial hypermedia approach – although they do not explicitly refer to this approach, cf. [44].
- Peirce's other two trichotomies are often neglected, because they are a bit harder to grasp than the taxonomy iconic/indexical/symbolic. Yet, they can be just as vital to close the semantic gap.
- In Peircean terminology, Wexelblat's *footprint system* [49] can be interpreted as a system of indexical qualisigns. Social navigation could play a major role in this kind of CBR/N.

References

1. OhneWörterBuch. 500 Zeigebilder für Weltenbummler. Langenscheidt, Berlin & München, 1999.
2. Kurt Baldinger. Semasiology and Onomasiology. In Roland Posner, Klaus Robering, and Thomas A Sebeok, editors, *Semiotics. A Handbook on the Sign-Theoretic Foundations of Nature and Culture*, volume 2, pages 2118–2145. Mouton de Gruyter, New York, 1998.
3. Walter Benjamin. Das Kunstwerk im Zeitalter seiner technischen Reproduzierbarkeit. *Zeischrift für Sozialforschung*, (5), 1936.
4. Jeff Bernard and Gloria Withalm, editors. *Neurath. Zeichen*. S-Labor. ÖGS-ISSS, 1996.
5. Jacques Bertin. *Sémiologie graphique*. Editions Gauthier-Villars, Paris, 1967.
6. Jay David Bolter. *Writing Space; The Computer, Hypertext and the History of Writing*. Lawrence Erlbaum, Hillsdale, NJ, 1991.
7. Peter Brown. The Ethics and Aesthetics of the Image Interface. http://peirce.inf.puc-rio.br/chi2000ws6/ppapers/brown.htm, April 2000. Last visited: Jul. 30, 2001.
8. Luca Caneparo and Gian Paolo Caprettini. On the Semiotics of the Image and the Computer Image. In Nöth [34], pages 147–158.
9. Daniel Glen Joel Chandler. *Semiotics: The Basics*. Routhledge, London, 2001. Citations taken from WWW version, *Semiotics for Beginners*, http://www.aber.ac.uk/media/Documents/S4B/semiotic.html. Last visited: Jul. 18, 2001.

10. Vincent M. Colapietro. *Glossary of Semiotics*. Paragon House Glossaries for Research, Reading, and Writing. Paragon House, New York, 1993.
11. Daniel Cunliffe. Trailblazing: trends in hypermedia. *The New Review of Hypermedia and Multimedia*, 6:19–46, 2000.
12. Umberto Eco. *A Theory of Semiotics*. Macmillan, London, 1976.
13. Achim Eschbach. Bildsprache. ISOTYPE und die Grenzen. In Bernard and Withalm [4], pages 15–48.
14. Jerry A. Fodor. Imagistic Representation. MIT Press, Cambridge, MA, 1981.
15. Ernst Gombrich. *Art and Illusion*. Phaidon, London, 1960.
16. Wendy Hall. The Button Strikes Back. *The New Review of Hypermedia and Multimedia*, 6:5–17, 2000.
17. Kyoji Hirata, Hajime Takano, and Yoshinori Hara. Miyabi: A hypermedia database with media-based navigation. In *Proceedings of the 5th Conference on Hypertext*, pages 233–234, New York, NY, USA, November 1993. ACM Press.
18. Roman Jakobson. *Selected Writings*. Mouton, The Hague, 1971.
19. Dan W. Joyce, Paul H. Lewis, Robert H. Tansley, Mark. R. Dobie, and Wendy Hall. Semiotics and Agents for Integrating and Navigating through Multimedia Representations of Concepts. In *Proceedings of SPIE Vol. 3972, Storage and Retrieval for Media Databases 2000*, pages 132–143, 2000.
20. Jacques Lacan. *Écrits*. Éditions du Seuil, Paris, 1966.
21. G. Lakoff and M. Johnson. *Metaphors We Live By*. Univ. of Chicago Press, 1980.
22. Suzanne K. Langer. *Philosophy in a New Key*. Harvard Univ. Press, Cambridge, MA, 1942.
23. Paul Lewis. Trends in information technology: Notes usenet, www and hypermedia systems. http://www.ecs.soton.ac.uk/ phl/ctit/hyp98/hyp98.html, March 1998. Last visited: Jun. 23, 2001.
24. Paul H. Lewis, Hugh C. Davis, Steve R. Griffiths, Wendy Hall, and Rob J. Wilkins. Media-based navigation with generic links. In *Proceedings of the 7th ACM Conference on Hypertext*, pages 215–223. ACM Press, 1996.
25. Peter Lunefeld. *Snap to Grid. A User's Guide to Digital Arts, Media, and Cultures*. MIT Press, Cambridge/London, 2000.
26. Kirk Martinez. Outline of the ARTISTE Proposal. http://www.ecs.soton.ac.uk/ km/projs/artiste/proposal.html, 2000. Last visited: Jun. 22, 2001.
27. A. McGuire. Some Semiotic Aspects of Web Navigation. http://www.comfortableplace.demon.co.uk/semiotic1.html, 1999. Last visited: Apr. 28, 2001.
28. Floyd Merrell. *Sensing Semiosis. Toward the Possibility of Complementary Cultural "Logics"*. Semaphores and Signs. St. Martin's Press, New York, 1998.
29. Charles W. Morris. *Foundations of the Theory of Signs*. Chicago Univ. Press, 1938.
30. Manfred Muckenhaupt. *Text und Bild*. Narr, Thübingen, 1986.
31. Mihai Nadin. Semiotics for the HCI Community, 2001. http://www.code.uni-wuppertal.de/uk/hci/. Last visited Jul. 30, 2001.
32. Otto Neurath. *Gesammtelte bildpädagogische Schriften*. Verlag Hölder-Pichler-Tempsky, Wien, 1991.
33. Wilfried Nöth. Can pictures lie? [34], pages 133–146.
34. Wilfried Nöth, editor. *Semiotics of the Media: State of the Art, Projects and Perspectives*. Mouton de Gruyter, Berlin, 1997.
35. Wilfried Nöth. *Handbuch der Semiotik*. Metzler, Stuttgart, 2. edition, 2000.

36. C. K. Ogden and L. A. Richards. *The Meaning of Meaning.* Routledge, London, 2. edition, 1949.
37. Charles S. Peirce. *Collected Papers 1931-35.* Harvard Univ. Press, Cambridge, MA, 1935.
38. Renzo Raggiunti. *Philosophische Probleme in der Sprachtheorie Ferdinand de Saussures.* Alno, Aachen, 1990.
39. Lucia Santaella. The prephotographic, the photographic and the postphotographic image. In Nöth [34], pages 121–132.
40. Santini and Jain. Similarity measures. *IEEE Transactions on Pattern Analysis and Machine Intelligence,* 21, 1999.
41. Ferdinand de Saussure. *Grundfragen der allgemeinen Sprachwissenschaft.* Walter de Gruyter & Co., Berlin, 1967. Edited by Charles Bally and Albert Sechehaye.
42. Dagmar Schmauks. Wittgenstein kauft Gavagai: vom Nutzen sprachfreier Bildwörterbücher. *Semiotische Berichte,* 21:367–384, 1997.
43. Dagmar Schmauks. Book review of [1]. *Kodikas/Code,* 23:155–157, 2000.
44. Frank M. Shipman III and Catherine C. Marshall. Spatial hypertext: An Alternative to Navigational and Semantic Links. *ACM Computing Surveys,* 31(4es), December 1999.
45. Stephen W. Smoliar, James D. Baker, Takehiro Nakayama, and Lynn Wilcox. Multimedia search: An authoring perspective. In *Proceedings of the ISIS Workshop on Image Databases and Multimedia Search, Amsterdam, Netherlands,* 1996.
46. Robert Tansley, Colin Bird, Wendy Hall, Paul Lewis, and Mark Weal. Automating the linking of content and concept. In *Proceedings of the 8th International ACM Conference on Multimedia,* pages 442–444, N.Y., Oct 30–Nov 04 2000.
47. Anna Katharina Ulrich. Zwei Schwestern. Zum Verhältnis zwischen Bild und Sprache. *Riss – Zeitschrift für Psychoanalyse,* 15(48):99–120, 2000.
48. Eva Waniek. *Bedeutung? Beiträge zu einer transdisziplinären Semiotik.* Turia & Kant, Wien, 2000.
49. Alan Wexelblat and Pattie Maes. Footprints: Visualizing histories for web browsing. http://wex.www.media.mit.edu/people/wex/Footprints/footprints1.html, 1997. Last visited: Aug. 01, 2001.

The Third Workshop on Structural Computing (SC3)

Program Committee Members of SC3

The following people have served on the Program Committee of the Third Workshop on Structural Computing. Their support is gratefully acknowledged.

Peter J. Nürnberg, Aalborg University Esbjerg, DK
David L. Hicks, Aalborg University Esbjerg, DK
Monica M.C. Schraefel, University of Toronto, CA
Weigang Wang, Fraunhofer IPSI Darmstadt, DE
Sigi Reich, Salzburg Research, AT
Uffe K. Wiil, Aalborg University Esbjerg, DK
Michael Vaitis, University of the Aegean, GR
Athanasios Papadopoulos, University of Patras, GR
Manolis Tzagarakis, CTI, GR
Maria Kyriakopoulou, University of Patras, GR
Dimitris Avramidis, University of Patras, GR
Sofia Stamou, University of Patras, GR
Evangelia Kavakli, University of the Aegean, GR

List of Presentations at SC3

Manolis Tzagarakis "Introduction and Wrap Up"
Saul Shapiro "Writing the Holes; 'Structural' Reflections of a Visual Artist"
Dimitris Avramidis "Broadening Structural Computing towards Hypermedia Development"
Weigang Wang "A Graphical User Interface Integrating Features from Different Hypertext Domains"
Kenneth M. Anderson "Using Open Hypermedia to Support Information Integration"
Uffe K. Wiil "Providing Structural Computing Services on the World Wide Web"
Samir Tata "Cooperation Services in a Structural Computing Environment"
Peter J. Nürnberg "Structural Computing and Its Relationships to Other Fields"

List of Participants at SC3

Trond Aalberg, NO
Kenneth M. Anderson, University of Colorado, Boulder, US
Dimitris Avramidis, Computer Technology Institute, Patras, GR
Timothy Miles-Board, University of Southampton, UK
David L. Hicks, Aalborg University Esbjerg, DK
Peter J. Nürnberg, Aalborg University Esbjerg, DK
Saul Shapiro, Aarhus, Denmark
Sigi Reich, Salzburg Research, AT
Lloyd Rutledge, CWI, NL
Monica M.C. Schraefel, University of Toronto, CA
Samir Tata, Aalborg University Esbjerg, DK
Manolis Tzagarakis, Computer Technology Institute, Patras, GR
Weigang Wang, FhG-IPSI, Darmstadt, DE
Uffe K. Wiil, Aalborg University Esbjerg, DK

Introduction to SC3

Manolis M. Tzagarakis

Dept. of Computer Engineering and Informatics
University of Patras
Computer Technology Institute (CTI)
Riga Ferraiou 61,
GR-262 21, Patras, Greece
tzagara@cti.gr

Hypermedia has been used to support a wide variety of user tasks. These tasks range from Bush's association of information to more elaborate activities such as hyperfiction authoring and reading, information analysis and classification. Each of the tasks exemplifies how the human mind perceives structure in different problem domains. The identification of new problem domains is the main concern of *hypermedia domain research*. On the contrary, *Hypermedia system research* is focused on designing and building the computational foundations to support people working with structure concentrating especially on issues regarding openness. The Open Hypermedia movement originated from such an approach. Yet, the conceptual foundations of Open Hypermedia – its underlying structures and behaviors - have all focused on supporting one task: information navigation. As it has been shown, the abstractions provided by systems supporting information navigation cannot address issues in new domains (e.g. spatial and taxonomic) in a convenient and efficient way. These domains require conceptual foundations markedly different from those used to support navigational hypermedia manifesting, thus, a gap between hypermedia domain and system research. The need for delivering the tailored support required by different domains gave birth to Component Based Open Hypermedia Systems (CB-OHSs).

CB-OHSs are the realization of a philosophy called *structural computing* (SC). Structural computing asserts the "primacy of structure over data" [1, 3] shaping the theoretical and practical foundations upon which applications in new hypermedia domains can be developed. In achieving such a framework, structure-oriented models, as well as services that can be build on top of it, should be the primary research focus of the open hypermedia community. Structural computing attempts to change the way the invisible but important infrastructure of contemporary Open Hypermedia Systems (OHS) work in providing open structure-based services in heterogeneous environments. The current move of the hypermedia community in developing Component-Based Open Hypermedia Systems (CB-OHS) provides the vehicle for structural computing to become increasingly important and relevant to the hypermedia community in general.

SC3 was held in conjunction with is the 12th ACM Conference on Hypertext and Hypermedia. Like the previous workshops [2,4], SC3 solicited the submission of papers concerning requirements placed on structural computing by particular domains, application of structural computing principles to real problems as well as experimental structural computing environments. Moreover, viewing struc-

S. Reich, M.M. Tzagarakis, P.M.E. De Bra (Eds.): OHS/SC/AH 2001, LNCS 2266, pp. 118–119, 2002.
© Springer-Verlag Berlin Heidelberg 2002

tural computing as a school of thought, SC3 attempted also to lay down the foundations to consider structural computing a "first class" research thread.

The papers presented in this proceedings can be grouped into several topic areas. The first topic area entitled "Requirements for Structural Computing" includes papers that discuss requirements for structural computing from the perspective of a particular domain. Saul Shapiro focuses on the hypermedia art domain; Dimitris Avramidis addresses hypermedia development from a structural computing perspective; and Weigang Wang focuses on visualization and navigation aspects in structural computing systems. The second topic area entitled "Structural Computing Systems" includes papers on design/implementation issues of actual structural computing systems. Kenneth Anderson presents the design of infrastructure services based on structural computing principles; Uffe Wiil discusses structural computing services on the World Wide Web; and Samir Tata presents the cooperation services of the Construct structural computing environment. Finally, in the third topic area entitled "Introspection, Retrospection and Future", Peter Nürnberg compares structural computing to related fields in order to define a research agenda for structural computing.

References

1. Nürnberg, P. J. and Leggett, J. J.: A Vision for Open Hypermedia Systems. Journal Of Digital Information, 1 (2), Nov. 1997.
2. Nürnberg, P. J., (Editor): Proceedings of the First Workshop on Structural Computing. Technical Report CS-99-04, Department of Computer Science, Aalborg University Esbjerg, Denmark.
3. Nürnberg, P. J., Leggett, J. J. and Schneider E. R.: As We Should Have Thought. Proceedings of the 8th ACM Conference on Hypertext (Hypertext '97), Southampton, UK, April 6-11, 1997, 96-101.
4. Reich, S., and Anderson, K. M. (Editors): Open Hypermedia Systems and Structural Computing. Proceedings of the 6th Workshop on Open Hypermedia Systems and the 2nd Workshop on Structural Computing. Lecture Notes in Computer Science 1903, Springer Verlag.

Writing the Holes; "Structural" Reflections of a Visual Artist

Saul Shapiro

Magnoliavej 12
8260 Viby J., Denmark
shapiro@mail1.stofanet.dk

Abstract. The epistemology that can be found in structural computing holds promise as a foundation for digital visual art. The fields of literature and art criticism and reception and communication theory have parallels with structural computing's call for structure as a first class object. The concept of authoring structure can then be applied to the field of visual art. Using foundations taken from literary theory and theater montage, a theoretical scenario is proposed for constructing an authoring tool that can access and influence a changing, dynamic structure of a multimedia work of visual art. The "holes" of a multimedia presentation – its changing structure – can be added to the domain of the author.

1 Introduction

The following reflections are the professional of a visual artist. My point of departure is based on my own work as a photographer and artist and the accompanying concepts of temporality, memory and icon as the foundations for an exhibition space. I feel that these three are closely linked to the epistemology that can be described as *association-recall* – *"new proprioceptive situation"*, an alternative to node and link epistemology. The tool imagined at the end has not yet been built, but I have written a more detailed unpublished draft version of a possible authoring UI to help invoke and manipulate structure and emerging structure.

1.1 A La Recherche

. . . imagine if Proust had left it to us to decide if it was space or time we had lost.

2 Poetic – Position

Years ago, before the rise of digital media, I held an exhibition of black and white photography. Normally, captions and texts were put on the wall and "exhibited" along with the visual art. This time these texts were written as small, poetic reflections on the context that the act of photographing occurred in. Sometimes

S. Reich, M.M. Tzagarakis, P.M.E. De Bra (Eds.): OHS/SC/AH 2001, LNCS 2266, pp. 120–130, 2002.

they were decidedly factual; other times they were associative and wandering; but in all cases they were informative. Text and picture were separated and the visitor had to reassemble them.

Some visitors started in a typically "art exhibition" way. After a few seconds of overview almost everyone would be attracted to one of the photographs and make directly for it. Seeing the title as they got close, they would find it on the list and read the accompanying text, looking at the photo - and at the surrounding ones – now and then. They would then reorient themselves, being able to see an overview of some of the other walls, and start the process over again.

Other guests would start by standing in the doorway and leafing through the folder. Then they would often sit on the bench in the middle of the room, reading words and ignoring images. After a while they would get up and wander around the rooms *not* looking at photographs but rather trying to find *a* photograph. The photographs were arranged as described above, structured by a combination of physical necessity and formal visual association. The texts were arranged alphabetically.

This presentation design dictated an ease of "travelling" from photo to text. There was significance in the difficulty of travel in the other direction. The guest, in trying to find the photograph that fit the text, perused many other photos that were not randomly arranged on the walls. Perusal gave intuitive familiarity with the formal elements. This familiarity resulted in a sort of "alternating current" of concentration; now words, now photographs.

2.1   Writing the Holes

What could be called the archeological model of reading assumes that the reader is trying to uncover a truth, and that the work is "used up" once this truth is out [10]. Opposed to this is a more anthropological model - we "forage" for secrets and for information, while at the same time admitting that our activities effect the result. But we must not assume that an anthropological model can be couched in node and link terminology; we are not hunting for individual *lexia* (or whatever the name), nor are we hunting for the path to get there on. Anthropology is concerned with the changing social context and meaning of these lexia. We can therefore read of a tribe who has incorporated a new character in their traditional dances, the character of the anthropologist who *doesn't dance but takes notes while watching*, thus restructuring the entire concept of dance [13].

In dealing with the world of photographic visual art I would consider the term anthropology to be the evidence of a personal discourse which comprises the viewing of the work and consequent *judging*. Using the terminology of association-recall-new-proprioceptive-situation as descriptive for the act of experiencing a work of art, this discourse overlaps – or at least has a common edge – with what is linguistically its opposite, intuition, and it is this junction that we are concerned with.

"[O]n the edge of the text, neither inside nor outside, yet both inside and outside, what matters is *what ends up inside*, the inside that is always realigning itself and being realigned. This inside, this intratext, is, I would prefer to say, a process of accretion: painting on painting, text on text, fiction on fiction" [9]. Widened intratextuality includes the real world as well as other texts that the reader/viewer might sense. The minute that a work points beyond itself it is introducing (or rather, the reader is introducing) that *beyond* into its insides. It is this structure, this fact of bringing the outside inside, that is our new building block, our new set of choices, the new dimension from where we can see a new inside.

There is an assumption that can be found in hypertext theory that "nonlinearity is clearly not a trope, since it works on the level of words, not meaning" [1]. I find this at odds with a basic precept of art, that "symbol is not only a microcosmic reflection of something macrocosmic, not just a distillation. It is, as importantly, an irreducible thing, the smallest atomic unit of which the macrocosmic may be reduced" [13]. The image is in this sense the unit from which our personal view of the world **as a whole** flows. It is from the image and not from the atomic units of textuality that we structure the world.

There is a certain – ironic – similarity between the concepts of the "generic digital" and art theories dealing with minimal art of the 60's. It has often been proposed that the new digital media – the so-called multimedia systems – contain no inherent semantic structure above the digital base. "A computer [...] is a symbolic system from the ground up. Those pulses of electricity are symbols that [...] represent words or images, spreadsheets or e-mail messages" [11]; "the digital form [is] ultimately generic in the sense that it can be realized in any number of ways without any loss or damage to its essential nature, so to speak" [12]. This argument can be looked at in light of some of the theories of art that surfaced in the USA in the 60's (although they had probably existed since time immemorial). At this time art was questioned as to its being a "window onto another reality" [13], and was deemed to be something that was "true to its materials" [ibid.]. "The question, therefore, that must be asked is not What does truth to materials mean? but Why this focus on the character of materials at all? furthermore, what, in a metaphysical sense, is being suggested about who artists are in our culture by such a narrow and concrete focus on the material world?" [ibid.] This opposite face of this obsession with the material world finds expression as this "something" which *can be* realized in *any* physical form. But still the question remains, from whence comes symbolic value?

"The real question is: what do different languages do, not with these artificially isolated objects but with the flowing face of nature in its motion, color, and changing form; with clouds, beaches, and yonder flight of birds? For, as goes our segmentation of the face of nature, so goes our physics of the cosmos." [16].

The concepts of structural computing as applied to visual art seem to parallel the transformation in literary criticism from structuralism to so-called poststructuralism and beyond. The reader no longer works merely with the understanding of words and semantics but is faced with another level of work, constantly forced to change the structure of understanding within the work of art is placed. In 1964, Roland Barthes could say that "in every society various techniques are developed intended to *fix* the floating chain of signifieds in such a say as to counter the terror of uncertain signs" [3]. From this attempt, if you will, at understanding node-link organization, Barthes comes to welcome structural computing and what I would call proprioceptive reading; in 1970 he can speak of something beyond both informational levels and symbolic levels; the "third meaning, [which] appears to extend outside culture, knowledge, information" [4].

When the ordering of events in a work of art can be changed by the viewer, then the meaning to be extracted from this world always lies on another level of understanding demanding another dimension of overview. The technology of node-link interactivity seems in some way to be the literal realization of the cognitive acts described by Barthes. The movement from node-link philosophy to structural computing seems to promise a change of epistemology similar[1] to that experienced by Barthes above, and necessary in a field where change itself can become a carrier of meaning.

2.2   Communication and Montage

How do we understand messages in digital art systems when we are participants in both the setting and the restructuring of context? What does the inextricable combination of author and interactivity do to our ability to "jump" a level and define context? We are at the mercy of our ability to translate our new experiences of the world into a language that is supported by our previous state of knowledge. "Flatland" [2] is a description of a two dimension world inhabited by geometric figures. One day the "author", a square, is taken by a sphere to the third dimension where he for the first time is able to see an entire overview of his world – able to see the previously unthinkable "inside". Returning to his two dimensions, he is unable to point to this third dimension nor convey his experience of it, but can merely describe it symbolically as "upward, and yet not northward".

Gregory Bateson [5] defines concepts of learning (and communication) as having different levels. Each level brings changes in how we view and understand the world, and changes first the elements and later the sets of elements that we can choose from in our attempt to order the world and define *context*. Each new level says something *about* the previous level.

As in the theater, on the multimedia stage there are huge numbers of elements the viewer is aware of and impressions (how the viewer perceives the context of these impressions). Each image is comprised of elements that are happening simultaneously and understood together.

2.3   Partial Images and Montage

The viewer looks "through" the work at any one time, and forms a "partial image" out of the accessible elements. The montage of these partial images becomes

---

[1] Though perhaps best conceived as the negative; moving towards structure rather than towards deconstruction.

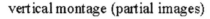

vertical montage (partial images)

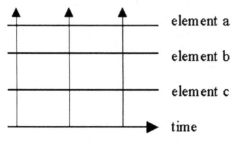

element a

element b

element c

time

horizontal montage (global images)

Fig. 1. Vertical and horizontal montage (adapted from [14])

in the viewer the "meta-image" of the work as a whole. The common factor is called context.

Two consecutive partial images can, in the viewer's understanding, be connected to two totally different contexts, depending upon how the viewer has chosen the elements of each partial image – and of course on the skill and purpose with which the author has placed these elements. The viewer has been able to change the structure that these images reside within. At the same time the addition of temporality in the construction of this understanding may risk becoming so paramount as to win the battle between object and completeness on one side and time and change on the other. Concepts of structure as first class object would seem useful in retaining, in a changing digital universe, the idea that "it is as though one's experience of [modernist painting and sculpture] *has no* duration – not because one *in fact* experiences [a picture or sculpture] in no time at all, but because *at every moment the work itself is wholly manifest*" [7].

We will now imagine the beginnings of a scenario permitting the technology behind interactive media to permit both the author and the viewer access to the realms of the expanded unconscious intratext.

3   The Flight Deck[2]

The simple question is: when the viewer queries a photo at an exhibition, what photo is then shown and where?

---

[2] "The part of an airplane accommodating the pilot, co pilot, engineer, navigator, etc."

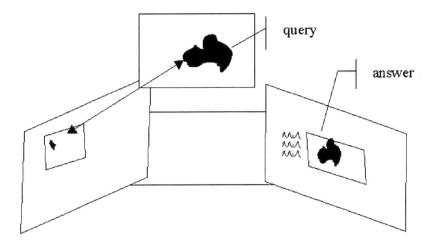

Fig. 2. A simple question

3.1   Introduction: "Life Is Like a Cinema of Stills[3]"

The flight deck is an attempt to imagine a system for structuring the backbone of interactivity for an electronic exhibition space. I am not proposing a general authoring system, but am dealing with a specific case of black and white photography where an author already has defined a body of work as an exhibition and wants to present it electronically in a physical space. The user will have a degree of control that for the purposes of this paper will remain undefined. The assumptions made are that action – behavior – on the part of the viewer, can as well as personal montage in time and space be considered as media types that can be used as both a form of generic link that makes the exhibition "happen" and as a bearer of meaning and thus a *part* of the exhibition.

I use the word "query" to describe an activity that can take place either with the author or the viewer of the exhibition. In the case of the viewer this means in some way interacting with the material in order to change both the properties of the object that is viewed and the structure that it is perceived within. This can be also seen as a general term to describe the fact that the person involved is trying to find out something about the "grammar" – the structure of the language – of what he or she is perceiving.

Although we will not deal directly with forms of interactivity between viewer and exhibition, we can briefly mention that for the viewer a query can be anything from a simple touch that activates an embedded link to more general behaviors such as looking at portions of a photograph while at the same time pointing to another area so that eye and finger and body position tracking over

---

[3] Attributed to Minor White (Am. photographer, 1908-1977).

time can determine – and directly manipulate – the viewer's experience of context.

Queries in this scenario are related to the way in which the author manipulates the formal elements of photography, but there are certainly other query structures imaginable.

4   Representation

A black and white photograph can be reduced in technical terms to a matrix of points, each with a gray scale value[4]. A query that defines a line (figure 3). From one point to another on the photograph: can be represented graphically in terms of the gray scale values that the line traverses, as in figure 4:

Fig. 3. A query

Fig. 4. Gray scale values traversed by the line in figure 3

When a user queries a photograph, the data that is graphically represented in figure 4 can be used to define congruence, similar areas in other parts of the same or other photographs. The author can predefine *congruence* or can build in changing definitions that can to a greater or lesser degree be accessed by the user.

Any photograph with a traverse that fits the restraints of congruence can be the next element of the exhibition. Changing definitions of congruence can be

---

[4] We could also include nominal values such as the names of objects, vectors which are tangents to borders between recognizable objects, texture of surfaces, focus ("circle of confusion").

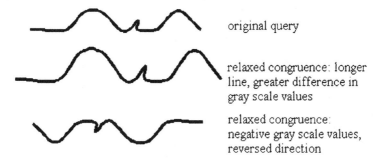

original query

relaxed congruence: longer line, greater difference in gray scale values

relaxed congruence: negative gray scale values, reversed direction

Fig. 5. Forms of congruence

used to restructure the entire exhibition both in time and in space, and are the domain of both author and reader.

The changing structure of congruence could be visualized in two ways. The first is a matrix of all of the photographs included in the exhibition, useful to the author in laying out the restraints on congruence. The second is what I would call a "radar" view, a graphical representation of the exhibition space.

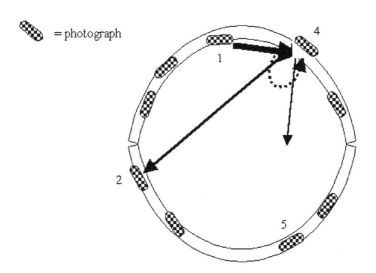

= photograph

Fig. 6. The radar view

This radar screen represents a schematic diagram of the exhibition space. The original series has already been reordered once, indicated by the thick line from photo 1 to photo 4. Right now the best congruence is the long unbroken line pointing from photo 4 to photo 2. The second best is represented by the unbroken, thinner line from photo 4 half-way to photo 5. There is a good match within photo 4 itself (dotted line circling back on photo 4).

Queries from both author in the production phase and from the user in runtime can address "hidden" structural characteristics of the work of art and their interrelationships. "Writing the holes" with the "Flight Deck" could offer a feeling of seamless presentation of query results, leaving the viewer (and permitting the author) a greater degree of freedom to define new categories of understanding gleaned through montage.

5   Possibilities

- States could be saved in order to be applied to real time interactivity with the viewer. The viewer could be allowed manipulation of the photographic hierarchy or grouping in ways that are not connected with the "backbone" of structure, but which creates arrangement that can be recognized as congruent with authored states. Thus the user can indirectly query the formal rules of congruence set up by the author.
- Temporal elements could also be included in the structure of congruence. For example: the computer takes measurable amounts of time to calculate congruence hierarchies from any given query; the viewer takes measurable amounts of time in perusal and querying.
- We could consider systems where the user also gets to add to the number of elements that are included in the exhibition. Here we could use congruence to author the structure that defines the elements and media types that the user can add at any time and state.
- The radar view could be linked to a textual mapping as in [15]. We could imagine exhibitions of visual art accompanied by text, where the textual mapping is congruent to a visual mapping in radar view.

6   Concluding Remarks

"But then what? Order or the illusion of order? Inside or outside? The text or the reader, or the peregrinations of forever moving in the space between?" [9].

Events in a work of interactive visual art can be considered a functions rather than links; $f(\text{object } 1) \rightarrow (\text{object or event } 2)$. The result of this transformation can be spatial, physical , or temporal. The function can be abstracted and restraints authored to it so that - all the while that it can take on new forms and new "end points" – the changes in this function become visible to the user.

There are two areas that we haven't touched upon at all. The first resides wholly within the realm of the author's vision. What must be produced that comprises the origins and end points of the viewer's sense of changing context and what if the production of "end points" is set free? The author's view of this issue will also decide the storage architecture of the flight deck; will information been stored "in the system" - or will some or all of it follow the photographs in a writeable "style sheet" which can come to define the author's artistic vision as it matures and the photographs become useable in a greater number of contexts?

The second is, as mentioned, the actual forms that interactivity is placed within. What does the digital technology register, and how does the viewer have to act to trigger events?

I share the assumption that "there is a class of fine artists who use modern and new technology in a deep and significant way" [8]. I have proposed a basis for this significance that lies in our human ability to discover and grasp changing context. While technology and interactive presentations can assist us by capturing contexts and augmenting our senses (and perhaps our powers of judgment), they do not *per se* change the rules of the game. The reader's (viewer's) interaction with works of art can be softly manipulated by the very technology of production to increase the possibility of the delight of *informed* surprise.

To be enthralled by a sense of change as a bearer of meaning is not to be ignorant of "nodes and links" that define the start and end of this change. Indeed, there can probably be no sense of change at all without such knowledge. Just as "a dangerous assumption of semantics and of those who profess the discipline is that meaning can exist apart from its ontogenesis as an analytical concept," [6] so is it dangerous to consider each case of change *per se* without considering its origins.

References

1. Aarseth, Espen J. "Nonlinearity and Literary Theory." In Landow, George P. (ed.): "Hyper/Text/Theory." The Johns Hopkins University Press, Baltimore, 1994, pp. 51-86.
2. Abbott, Edwin A.: "Flatland." Dover Publications, New York, 1952.
3. Barthes, Roland. "The Rhetoric of the Image." In "Image, Music, Text." Hill and Wang, New York, 1982, pp. 32-51.
4. Barthes, Roland. "The Third Meaning." In "Image, Music, Text." Hill and Wang, New York, 1982, pp. 52-68.
5. Bateson, Gregory. "The Logical Categories of Learning and Communication." In "Steps to an Ecology of Mind." Ballantine Books, New York 1972, pp. 279-308.
6. Darbyshire, A.E. "A Grammar of Style." Andre Deutsch Limited, London, 1971.
7. Fried, Michael. "Art and Objecthood". In Battcock, Gregory (ed.), "Minimal Art: A Critical Anthology." E.P. Dutton & Co., New York, 1968, pp. 116-147.
8. Gold, Rich. http://www.parc.xerox.com/red/members/richgold/PAIRTALK/HTML/slide4.html.
9. Grigely, Joseph. "Textualterity: Art, Theory, and Textual Criticism." The University of Michigan Press, Ann Arbor, 1995.
10. Iser, Wolfgang. "The Act of Reading." Johns Hopkins University Press, Baltimore, 1980. Ch. 1, pp. 3-19.
11. Johnson, Steven. "Interface Culture." Harper Edge, San Francisco, 1997, chapter 1.

12. Kitzmann, Andreas. "Paradigms of the Digital." Source unknown; printed in compendium "Elektronik Kultur II", MMA, Aarhus University, autumn 2000; reference to previously published version in "Convergence: the journal of Research in New Media Technologies." Autumn 1998.
13. Napier, A. David. "Foreign Bodies: Performance, Art, and Symbolic Anthropology." University of California Press, Berkeley, 1992.
14. Ruffini, Franco. "Horizontal and Vertical Montage in the Theatre." article 4 from NTQ, vol. II, no. 5, 1986.
15. Salton, Gerard; Allan, James; Buckley, Chris; Singhal, Amit. "Automatic Analysis, Theme Generation, and Summarization of Machine-Readable Texts." In Card, Stuart; Mackinlay, Jock; Shneiderman, Ben. "Readings in Information Visualization", Morgan Kaufmann Inc., San Francisco, 1999, pp. 413-418.
16. Whorf, Benjamin Lee. "Languages and Logic." In "Language, Thought & Reality", The M.I.T. Press, Cambridge, Mass. 1962, pp. 233-245.

Broadening Structural Computing towards Hypermedia Development

Maria Kyriakopoulou, Dimitris Avramidis, Michalis Vaitis,
Manolis M. Tzagarakis, and Dimitris Christodoulakis

Department of Computer Engineering and Informatics
University of Patras
GR-265 00, Rion Patras, Greece
Computer Technology Institute (CTI)
Riga Ferraiou 61,
GR-262 21, Patras, Greece
{kyriakop, avramidi, vaitis, tzagara, dxri}@cti.gr

Abstract. The success of structural computing depends heavily on the degree such systems can support structuring tasks that are well known within the hypermedia community. In this paper we outline issues of hypermedia development from a structural computing point of view. Although such issues are addressed for the navigational domain, the need for hypermedia modeling and design in other hypermedia domains is left open to discussion.

1 Introduction

Structural Computing asserts the primacy of structure over data [15], [14], shaping the foundations upon which applications in new hypermedia domains can be developed. The embodiment of this philosophy, Component-Based Open Hypermedia Systems (CB-OHS) – also referred to as structural computing systems – provide a common infrastructure and focus on the services layer to provide the structural abstractions required by hypermedia. In such systems, the structure layer is itself open, allowing new services to be inserted and thus support for new domains to be added.

Structural computing systems attempt to bridge the gab between hypermedia system and domain research. While hypermedia domain researchers investigate how humans use structure in diverse problem domains, system researchers have the task to build the appropriate tools and environments providing such usage with the ultimate goal to solve the issues arising in a *convenient* and *efficient* way.

Over the last years, a number of different hypermedia domains have been presented and are currently addressed from a structural computing perspective. Domains such as navigational and taxonomic have been successfully supported by structural computing systems. However, the set of all possible domains is still open and – more important – domains that already exist are only now approached from a structural computing perspective [7], [20].

S. Reich, M.M. Tzagarakis, P.M.E. De Bra (Eds.): OHS/SC/AH 2001, LNCS 2266, pp. 131–140, 2002.

In this paper we outline issues of hypermedia development from a structural computing point of view. In particular, requirements are presented enabling structural computing systems to reason about structure in a way suitable to support *Hypermedia Modeling and Design* of navigational applications – a core principle in hypermedia development. Although such design issues are proposed for the navigational domain, the need for hypermedia modeling and design in other hypermedia domains is left open to discussion.

2   Hypermedia Modeling

Hypermedia has been pointed out as a means to capture and organize the structure of complex subjects making them clear and accessible to the user [5]. Users, often referred to as *readers*, come across *hypermedia applications* that allow them to navigate through information by selecting paths to follow on the basis of interests emerging along the way [13]. Hypermedia applications offer rich navigational facilities to readers. *Hypermedia systems*, though, provide environments to facilitate the creation of hypermedia applications. Although readers are unaware of how hypermedia applications are created, two other user groups are very much concerned about that issue; namely, *hypermedia designers* and *authors*. Designers, as well as authors, use services provided by hypermedia systems to create hypermedia applications engaging in an activity called *hypermedia development*.

During hypermedia development the complex relations of subject specific information are captured in a clear and comprehensible way. Yet, hypermedia development is a complicated cognitive process that consists of recursive activities, like emergence of ideas, representation and structuring of ideas, evaluation and update [12], requiring a mental model of the target application domain. As it has been recognized, it is this complexity that roots the classic problems of cognitive overload and disorientation in hypermedia [12]. Thus, much effort has been given in the creation of sophisticated tools and methodologies that will assist developing hypermedia applications.

Towards the better support of activities related to hypermedia design, *systematic* and *structured* development of hypermedia applications have been proposed [9], [11], [5], [8], [19], [23]. These approaches differentiate between *authoring-in-the-large*, carried out by designers, aiming at the specification and design of global and structural aspects of a particular hypermedia application, and *authoring-in-the-small*, carried out by authors, referring to the development of the contents of the nodes [4]. With regard to authoring-in-the-large, they provide convenient environments within the hypermedia system for hypermedia development, offering a suitable data model helping articulate structural designs. A rich set of abstractions including *aggregation, generalization/specialization* and the notion of *constraints*, facilitates the process of conceptual tailoring. Furthermore in these approaches, a *hypermedia schema*[1] embodies structural designs leading to the notion of *hypermedia modeling*.

---

[1] A hypermedia schema is also known as a template of structure.

The above kind of modeling is useful to hypermedia development because it can help designers to avoid structural inconsistencies and mistakes, and applications developed according to a model will result in very consistent and predictable representation structures [5]. Flexibility in definition of hypertext semantics, schemas and authoring of specific documents, is an important prerequisite in order to support the authoring mental process and to avoid "premature organization" problems [17]. Additionally, hypermedia modeling provides a framework in which authors can develop hypermedia applications at a high level of abstraction. It helps them to conceptualize these applications via an instantiation of a schema without too much regard to structural details. In general, one of the major goals in hypermedia modeling is to provide authors with the ability to customize knowledge structures for their specific tasks.

In some cases, these hypertext schemas are only metaphors of designs on a piece of paper that should be followed by the designer. In other cases, a modeling environment provides mechanisms to capture formal type representations and associations between them[2] [Fig. 1 & Fig. 2]. It also helps designers draft, observe, edit and produce variations of a given navigational structure [12], regarding it as the software tool for managing hypertext schemas.

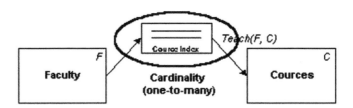

Fig. 1. Part of RMDM data model [8] indicating *Cardinality*

3   Literature Overview

Many researchers have proposed methodologies, models, and systems for hypertext authoring-in-the-large, i.e. creating a hypertext schema that expresses a number of constraints to be activated during the authoring of the instance hypertexts (authoring-in-the-small). Typical examples of such constraints are: limiting the types of nodes that a specific link type may associate; defining the directionality of a link type; or, describing the specific attributes a node type should include as its content. On the one hand, having constraints during authoring-in-the-small restricts the author' s linking freedom; but, on the other hand, it produces coherent hypertext documents that help eliminate the hypertext disorientation problem.

---

[2] There are even cases where CASE tools can be developed based on these representations.

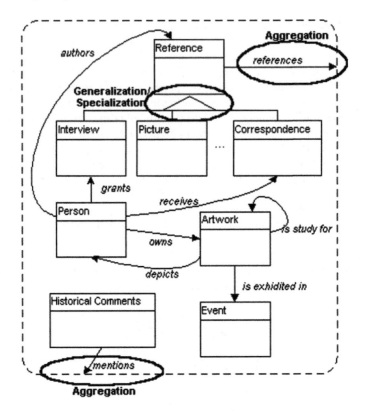

Fig. 2. Example schema of OOHDM [19]. Circles indicate abstractions provided such as *Aggregation* and *Generalization/Specialization*

Most methodologies and models concerning hypermedia modeling focus mainly on prescribed techniques to produce the design. Specifically, methodologies provide the authors with guidelines and a set of actions that must be followed in order to complete the design process of an application. Moreover, models, either relying on such methodologies or not, consist of diverse structural elements and associative relations. Therefore, the applications developed according to these models can be viewed as a combination of the aforementioned fundamental elements. To date, several approaches have tried to help designers generate navigational hypertext structures more easily and systematically.

Aquanet is one of the first approaches to modeling, and was designed "to provide users with the ability to customize knowledge structures for their specific tasks" [9]. According to the model, through the combination of specific basic objects and relations, one can create various schemas. That is, a schema describes the representation of the knowledge structure and acts as a framework for the creation of hypermedia applications. In the same way, HDM [5] uses schemas so as to define particular hypermedia applications, at a global level, through a collection of type definitions. Such type definitions are made of entities, components, units and links, and specify the characteristics that the applications can have. In accordance with the former use of "schemas" for creating applications, RMDM [8] introduces the notion of "data-model". Using the E-R diagram to represent the information domain of an application, a designer can easily create the paths that will enable hypertext navigation.

Respectively to the above models, there have been developed object-oriented ones trying to map an object-oriented structure to hypertext. MacWeb [11] is a model of such type that uses structure types to incorporate knowledge in hypertext. Typed chunks and links are its primitive objects that can be combined in order to create "webs". Therefore, an application derives from a web and is an instance of it. Similarly, OOHDM [19] describes, in a convenient and concise way, the design process of a hypermedia application, through the conceptual schema, using well-known object-oriented modeling principles. Nodes are defined as object-oriented views of conceptual classes, whereas links are defined as views on relationships in the conceptual schema. Eventually, a designer can create a hypermedia application specifying a navigational texture in the conceptual schema.

4   Hypermedia Modeling and Structural Computing

Hypermedia systems supporting the manipulation of hypermedia schemas view such schemas as networks of semantically rich entity and relationship types controlled by rules. Providing explicit abstractions, these systems reason about structure in a suitable way.

Table 1 presents the *hypermedia modeling* design pattern. Within the Callimachus [21], [22] project we adopted the use of "design patterns" to document problems in a particular context in addition to the "scenario" approach used by the OHSWG [16]. Design patterns – first introduced in [1] – represent a contemporary and popular approach to document problems as well as provide a solution within a particular context, and have been successfully used also in hypermedia [6].

The ability to reason about structure is the core objective of structural computing systems too. Yet, structural computing attempts to address an open set of structuring problems in a generic way. By specializing *generic structural abstractions*, contemporary structural computing systems such as Construct [3] and FOHM [10] provide convenient and efficient foundations to solve structuring problems in the navigational, taxonomic and spatial domain. Driven by the fact that hypermedia development is a popular user activity and commercial systems exist [2], the Callimachus projects started an attempt to support tasks related to hypermedia development within its (structural computing) environment; that is, to reason about schemas in a way suitable for hypermedia schema management (i.e. creation, modification and update). Although the navigational structure server in structural computing systems [18] is sufficient to support *hypermedia applications*, we believe that management of hypermedia schemas cannot be ad-

Table 1. Design pattern for Hypermedia Modeling

Name	Hypermedia Modeling.
Context	Development of navigational structures and ability to customize them for a specific target domain.
Problem	To provide navigational structuring facilities in order to describe them in a way conceptually close to the target domain.
Solution	Specify independently structural aspects of the target domain. Use abstractions to customize generic constructs of the hypermedia system incorporating structure in entities. Create relationships between entities specifying the type of participation based on the constraints of the target domain. Use a hypermedia schema to capture formally the outcome of the above design process. Provide mechanisms to store and reuse hypermedia schemas.
Examples	AquaNet, MacWeb, HDM, RMM, OOHDM, RICH.
Related Patterns	N/A.

dressed in a convenient way from existing structural computing systems due to lack of support of specific abstractions.

In the following we outline some requirements that structural computing systems need to address in order to enable manipulation of hypermedia schemas. These requirements also highlight the limitations of contemporary structural computing systems towards such a goal.

4.1 Support for Typing and Arbitrary Granularity of Structural Entities

Structural computing environments should support the management of typed structural entities. These typed entities should be building blocks of hypermedia schemas. Typing structural entities allow the objects of the real world to be represented within the system in a natural way. Moreover, they should be treated as first class objects by the system, meaning among others that their definition is stored within the system, can be searchable and might be (re)used in different schemas. For example, the creation of a node type called "Book" might appear in a university application as well as in a library application.

Designers should be able to create any typed entity they need. That is, while for one schema it may be convenient to treat a node as a whole, other schemas may require greater detail (i.e. granularity) such as attributes.

4.2   Using Aggregation to Express Complicated Structures

Through aggregation, a schema (or a part of a schema) can be viewed as a single entity and is treated in the same manner as any other entity. This approach for constructing complex entities is observed in all aforementioned systems. In particular, Aquanet exhibits inclusion [9] where an entire relation is included as a value of a slot in some other relation, while in OOHDM [19] new conceptual classes may be built using aggregation. For example, a node type "Borrowings" could contain the schema that describes the "Borrowers" and the "Books" they have borrowed.

Structural computing environments should support the composition of structural entities through aggregation. Although current constructs supported by navigational structure servers can be overloaded to create the feeling of aggregation (e.g. the attributes specifying node data), it is clearly not a convenient way.

4.3   Defining Associations between Structures through Cardinality

The concept of cardinality in hypermedia development came up when RMDM [8] used associative relationships (one-to-one or one-to-many) to limit quantitatively associations among entity types. The notions of anchor and endpoint are too complicated to express linking constraints among node types in a convenient way, so cardinality is essential. This can be obvious when a designer would like to denote that a "Book" cannot be lent to more than one (1) "Borrower" at a time.

Cardinality is not a mean to express constraints between structures but is an intrinsic feature of links[3]. Thus, support for cardinality is eminent in current systems enabling manipulation of schemas.

4.4   Union and Inheritance via Generalization/Specialization

Specialization and generalization define a containment relationship between a higher-level[4] entity set and one or more lower-level entity sets. Specialization is the result of taking a subset of a higher-level entity set to form a lower-level entity set. Generalization is the result of taking the union of two or more disjoint (lower-level) entity sets to produce a higher-level entity set (i.e. HDM using anchor types [5]). Owing to an object-oriented approach, MacWeb [11] and OOHDM [19] can build classes using generalization/specialization hierarchies. Thus, lower-level objects (entity sets) inherit attributes of higher-level ones. The node type "Book" for example can contain either a "Novel" or a "Scientific Book".

High-level concept structures (like generalization/specialization) are difficult to model. Hypermedia modeling should support such structures and provide an independent abstraction mechanism for expressing semantics.

---

[3] This feature is independent of the type of link.

[4] "Level" is the degree of correspondence between entities and real world odjects. Due to closure, this also applies to entity sets.

4.5   Using Constraints to Make Designs Conceptually Coherent

Constraints play a key role in hypermedia schemas since they provide the rules that make the design conceptually coherent. In many application areas, complex rules exist that should be able to be represented. For example, constraints such as a "Borrower" cannot borrow more than five (5) "Books" at a time should be able to be expressed in a convenient way. While these constraints may be viewed as behaviors in structural computing systems, management of hypermedia schemas requires them to be accessible by designers. Moreover, targeting convenience as well as efficiency, they should be able to be expressed with the use of a high-level declaration language.

Since the structural computing paradigm adopts a generic approach to structure reasoning, the presence of a constraint declaration language would also imply the existence of a constraint engine within its infrastructure interpreting and executing such expressions.

5   Conclusions

The success of structural computing depends heavily on the degree such systems can support structuring tasks that are well known within the hypermedia community. We view hypermedia development as one of such task. In this paper we have proposed the broadening of structural computing systems in order to support the management of hypermedia schemas, a core concept in the area of hypermedia development. For this reason, new requirements were presented outlining the specifications a structural computing system should follow. Although the analysis is not thorough and many issues are still open, we believe that the level of awareness of contemporary structural computing systems needs to be raised to support the process of hypermedia development.

The tailoring of a domain according to a specific problem offers a high level of abstraction improving the consistency of hypermedia applications. In general, modeling is a way to form knowledge structures referring to an application conceptually close to a particular domain. Thus, there is a need for hypermedia systems to support modeling mechanisms in order to develop applications of various domains (navigational, spatial, taxonomic, etc.). Thorough research is required to define the reification of generic structural elements to modeling entities.

References

1. Alexander, C.: Notes on the Synthesis of Form. Cambridge, Mass.: Harvard University Press, 1964.
2. Christodoulou, S., Styliaras, G., and Papatheodorou, T.: Evaluation of Hypermedia Application Development and Management Systems. Proceedings of the 9th ACM Conference on Hypertext and Hypermedia (Hypertext '98). Pittsburgh, PA, June 20-24, 1998, pp. 1-10.

3. Construct, `http://www.cs.aue.auc.dk/construct`.
4. Garzotto, F., Paolini, P., Schwabe, D., and Bernstein, M.: Tools for designer. Hypertext/Hypermedia Handbook, E. Berk and J. Devlin Eds. McGraw Hill, 1991, pp. 179-207.
5. Garzotto, F., Paolini, P., and Schwabe, D.: HDM – A Model-Based Approach to Hypertext Application Design. ACM Transactions on Information Systems, vol. 11, no. 1, January 1993, pp. 1-26.
6. Grønbæk, K., and Trigg, R.: From Web to Workplace: Designing Open Hypermedia System. MIT Press, 1999.
7. Haake, J. M.: Structural Computing in the Collaborative Work Domain? Proceedings of the 2nd International Workshop on Structural Computing. San Antonio, Texas, June 2000, pp. 108-118.
8. Isakowitz, T., Stohr, E. A., and Balasubramanian, P.: RMM: A Methodology for Structured Hypermedia Design. Communications of the ACM, vol. 38, no. 8, August 1995, pp. 34-44.
9. Marshall, C. C., Halasz, F. G., Rogers, R. A., and Janssen Jr. W. C.: Aquanet: A Hypertext Tool to Hold your Knowledge in Place. Proceedings of the 3rd ACM Conference on Hypertext (Hypertext '91). San Antonio, Texas, December 15-18, 1991, pp. 261-275.
10. Millard, D. E., Moreau, L., David, H. C., and Reich, S.: FOHM: A fundamental open hypertext model for investigating interoperability between hypertext domains. Proceedings of the 11th ACM Conference on Hypertext (Hypertext 2000). San Antonio, Texas, June 2000, pp. 93-102.
11. Nanard, J., and Nanard, M.: Using Structured Types to Incorporate Knowledge in Hypertext. Proceedings of the 3rd ACM Conference on Hypertext (Hypertext '91). San Antonio, Texas, December 15-18, 1991, pp. 329-344.
12. Nanard, J., and Nanard, M.: Hypertext Design Environments and the Hypertext Design Process. Communications of the ACM, vol. 38, no. 8, August 1995, 49-56.
13. Nielsen, J.: Hypertext and Hypermedia. Academic Press, San Diego, Calif., 1990.
14. Nürnberg, P. J., and Leggett, J. J.: A Vision for Open Hypermedia Systems. Journal Of Digital Information, vol. 1, no. 2, November 1997.
15. Nürnberg, P. J., Leggett, J. J., and Schneider E. R.: As We Should Have Thought. Proceedings of the 8th ACM Conference on Hypertext (Hypertext '97). Southampton, UK, April 6-11, 1997, pp. 96-101.
16. Open Hypermedia Systems Working Group, `http://www.csdl.tamu.edu/ohs/scenarios`.
17. Papadopoulos A., Vaitis M., Tzagarakis M., and Christodoulakis D.: A Methodology for Flexible Authoring of Structured Hypertext Applications. ED-MEDIA/ED-TELECOM '98, Freiburg, Germany.
18. Reich, S., Wiil, U. K., Nürnberg, P. J., Davis, H. C., Grønbæk, K., Anderson, K. M., Millard, D. E., and Haake, J. M.: Addressing Interoperability in Open Hypermedia: The Design of the Open Hypermedia Protocol. The New Review of Hypermedia and Multimedia, vol. 5, 1999, pp. 207-248.
19. Schwabe, D., Rossi, G., and Barbosa, S. D. J.: Systematic Hypermedia Application Design with OOHDM. Proceedings of the 7th ACM Conference on Hypertext (Hypertext '96). Washington, DC, March 16-20, 1996, pp. 116-128.
20. Shum, B. S., Dominigue, J. and Motta, E.: Scholarly Discourse as Computable Structure. Proceedings of the 2nd International Workshop on Structural Computing. San Antonio, Texas, 2000, pp. 120-128.

21. Tzagarakis, M., Vaitis, M., Papadopoulos, A., and Christodoulakis, D.: The Callimachus approach to distributed hypermedia. Proceedings of the 10th ACM Conference on Hypertext (Hypertext '99). Darmstadt, Germany, February 1999, pp. 47-48.
22. Vaitis, M., Papadopoulos, A., Tzagarakis, M., and Christodoulakis, D.: Towards Structure Specification for Open Hypermedia Systems. Proceedings of the 2nd International Workshop on Structural Computing. San Antonio, Texas, June 2000, pp. 160-169.
23. Wang, W., and Rada, R.: Structured Hypertext with Domain Semantics. ACM Transactions on Information Systems, vol. 16, no. 4, October 1998, pp. 372-412.

A Graphical User Interface Integrating Features from Different Hypertext Domains

Weigang Wang and Alejandro Fernández

FhG-IPSI
Dolivostrasse 15
D-64293 Darmstadt, Germany
{wwang, casco}@ipsi.fhg.de

Abstract. Integration of different hypertext domains is a relatively new concern to the hypertext community. This paper presents an integrative design of graphical user interfaces of hypermedia systems. This design embraces features from navigational, spatial, taxonomic, and workflow hypertexts. The result is a visual hypertext with a rich set of visual components and user interface mechanisms.

1 Introduction

One of the most important aspects that make hypertext popular is its intuitive appeal for users to browse information following explicitly indicated (visible) relationships or structures. Different flavors of hypertext are currently emerging with the goal of covering the specific needs of various application domains. Navigational, spatial, taxonomic, and workflow hypertexts are some examples. In the research community of open hypertext systems (OHS) much effort is being invested towards achieving interoperability between these hypertext domains. For instance, a component-based architecture has been developed to extend and utilize hypertext components from different hypertext domain in an open hypertext system [1]. In addition, a common data model has been developed for navigational, spatial, and taxonomic hypertexts [2]. Work has been already done mainly aiming at interpreting hypermedia belonging to one domain with the goal of visualizing it in some other [2]. However, how to integrate the user interface features found in these hypertext domains or how to meaningfully combine the look-and-feel of these flavors is still an open issue.

The rest of the paper is organized as follows: section 2 provides an introduction to different hypertext flavors of four well-known hypertext domains. Section 3 de-scribes the motivation for the co-existence of the user interface features found in different hypertext domains. Section 4 presents an integrated design of a visual hypertext that embraces selected user interface features of different hypertext flavors. Section 5 discusses related work and the contribution of this work to the literature. Section 6 concludes the paper.

S. Reich, M.M. Tzagarakis, P.M.E. De Bra (Eds.): OHS/SC/AH 2001, LNCS 2266, pp. 141–150, 2002.
© Springer-Verlag Berlin Heidelberg 2002

2   Hypertext Flavors

Following, we provide a brief description for each of the previously mentioned hypertext flavors. Emphasis is not placed on their underlying models, but on their look-and-feel, i.e. the visualization and navigation aspects that this paper tries to integrate:

1. Set-based, *Taxonomic Hypertext* [3]: In this domain, relationships are indicated by nested, composition structures. Navigation in a taxonomy hypertext is to move up and down within its hierarchically nested structure (by closing or opening a composition structure at different levels).
2. Layout-based *Spatial Hypertext* [4]: In this domain, relationship is indicated by spatial layout and visual characters of composition structures. Navigation within nested structures in spatial hypertext is similar to that of taxonomic hypertext. The difference lies in the fact that the graphical layout of the components at each level reveals the relationships between these components. For instance, related elements are placed near to each other or grouped in a composite. To navigate among components at the same level of a composition structure is to move from one component to the other mentally, based on the visual clues or to zoom or scroll in a content pane manually.
3. Graph-based, *Navigational hypertext*: This is the classical hypertext model, which is based on nodes and links [5]. In navigational hypertext, relationships are indicated by embedded and/or explicit links. Nodes of navigational hypertext are normally presented as multimedia documents with embedded links (as in the case of web documents). Activating an embedded link has as a result the target node being displayed. Navigational hypertexts are also commonly presented as maps (i.e. as graphs of nodes and links). Opening a node in a map leads to the display of such node as in the previous case. When opening a node from a docu-ment or a map, the same or a new window can be used. Link representations (e.g. lines) in a map are often purely visual relationship indications.
4. Automata-based, *Workflow Hypertext* [6,7]: Workflow hypertext is hypertext with application domain specific computational semantics. The computational behavior attached to nodes and links can support process enactment, for instance, to cause data or control to flow along the explicit workflow links. The control flow semantics can be used for process animation, which can serve as a mecha-nism for the implementation of guided tours.

3   Co-existence of Different Hypertext Flavors

In our experience of constructing holistic process centric enterprise models using hypermedia based visual languages, we have found the need for combining display mechanisms from the various hypertext domains into a single interface representation. For instance, while explicit link representations (e.g. as arrows) are good for expressing that an Actor has been assigned to a task, proximity is

better to express that the Actor belongs to a given team. We use composition
structures to express the way complex task are composed by simpler ones. However, we use proximity to indicate teams of Actors and explicit representation of
links (arrows) to indicate dependencies between tasks. Figure 1 shows another
example where the visual and layout based spatial hypertext and graph based
navigational hypertext co-exist. In Figure 1, a list of pie chart images are placed
together representing Market Segments. The Business Partner (as an image of
shaking hands) and the Business Competitor (as an image of wrestling hands)
are placed near to each other with images of the same background. Explicit
links (represented as arrow lines) are used to indicate that some of the market
segments are in the scope of the business partners and that others are in the
scope of the business competitors. Here the navigational (semantic network map)
metaphor is used together with the spatial and visual metaphors to enrich the
expressiveness of spatial hypertext.

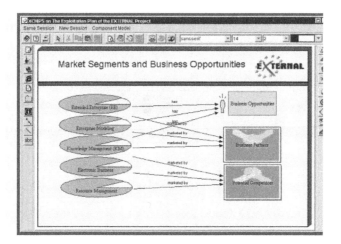

Fig. 1. Co-existence of different hypertext flavors

Although we realize that not all combinations will make sense, we are motivated by the previous examples to look for an integrative model for the construction of the user interface of a hybrid hypertext. In this paper we discuss
a group of hybrid features that, we believe, will lead us to such an integrative
design.

4   An Integrative Interface Design for Visual Hypertext

The design we are presenting assumes that hypertext is presented in a graphical
hypertext browser. A graphical representation of a hypertext is a view of its
underlying model (instance). It is composed of the representations of the objects

(nodes) and relationships (links, containment, and visual layout) in the model. For the remainder of this paper, the graphical element used to represent a node is called *node representation*. Likewise, the graphical element used to represent a link is called *link representation*. It is possible to have more that one representation for a node or link. In this case, all of them are kept consistently up-to-date with the model. The following sub-sections outline the key points in the model.

4.1 Graphic Elements, Their Layout, and Other Visual Properties

Building up on spatial hypermedia, nodes and links are represented by graphic elements. These elements can be moved and scaled. Some visual characteristics of graphic elements may relate to the attribute values of a node or a link. In this way, nodes are represented using shapes containing detailed information on type images, its content and attributes (see Figure 1). Lines in different styles are used as representations of explicit links between nodes (see Figure 1).

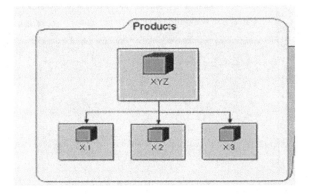

Fig. 2. Node and link layout in a composite node

In addition to the explicit links, the layout (e.g. positions and visual properties) of the nodes can also indicate relationships. For instance, for a composite node presenting the structure of an organization, the contained representations of nodes and links can be laid out as an organization chart – a top down hierarchical structure whose links are lines with rectangular corners (see Figure 2). A representation of a composite node can be provided with a layout manager to automatically layout its components. Visual properties related menu operations can be activated (on the visual component) for users to change the foreground and background colors or patterns, the label text, the size, the orientation, the shape, and the Z-ordering of the visual component. For manually handled free layout, positions, bounds and other visual properties should be persistently stored so as to assure a stable spatial and visual relationship representation.

4.2   Graphical Structure Unfolding in Its Original Context

When a composite node is opened (for example through a double-click in the mouse button), its content is unfolded within the bounds and location of the composite node (see Figure 3 and Figure 4).

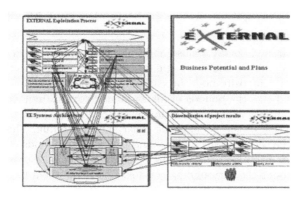

Fig. 3. Node at upper right corner is closed

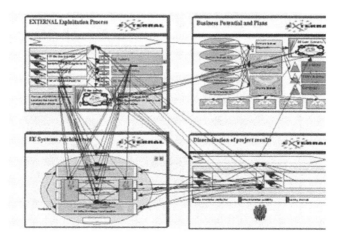

Fig. 4. Node at upper right corner is opened in its original context

Opening a composite node may also make visible all the links connected from other nodes to its components (see Figure 4). The original bounds of the composite node are still visible (in light color or as surrounding outline) at the background to make moving and scaling possible. When the composite node is closed (for example through a menu operation), its graphical representation (for its closed view) will cover all its bounding area, and consequently hide (or fold) its internal structure (see Figure 3). If a user is only interested in having a local view of the composite structure, he or she can also open the composite node in a new window.

4.3 Spatial Navigation in Nested Structures and Along Explicit Links

Users can select and open (or close) multiple composite nodes in one operation. When many composite nodes are opened, users can zoom in/out the boundary of an unfolded composite node by clicking on any place within its bounds or its back-ground (i.e. the bounds of its containing composite node) respectively. Clicking on the representation of a link leads the browser to scroll and zoom to the representation of the node at the other end of the link. This node then is displayed at the center of the window and parts of the bounds of its containing composite node can also be seen. The background elements provide users with information about the surrounding con-text and allow them to click and zoom out. Users can click and hold down the left/right mouse button to repeatedly zoom in/out. This navigation mechanism re-quires "browsing" to be independent from "editing" where mouse actions already have a special meaning. In editing mode, users can use menu operations or short cut keys for spatial navigation.

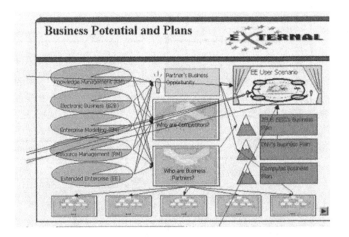

Fig. 5. Spatial traversal along links

4.4 Filtered Views

The display of explicit links can be switched off to make a view less crowded and to allow users to navigate spatially in a graphical world (see Figure 5, which is a filtered view of the node at the upper right corner in Figure 4). Users can have a filtered view in which only selected types of explicit links are visible. They can also select a group of nodes to see its neighborhood (i.e. all the selected nodes and all the nodes that are connected to the selected nodes, again with/without all the explicit links between them displayed). Filtered views can be shown in separate tabbed panes in the graphical hypertext browser and users can switch between these views by selecting different tabs of the tabbed panes.

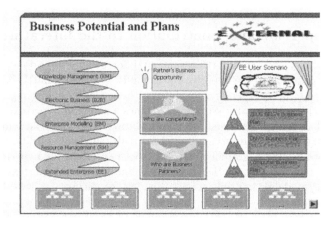

Fig. 6. A filtered view of a composite node

Filtered views can also be use to filter-out spatial relations. That means that in a view where spatial relations have been left out, the proximity of some objects may not indicate that they are related. It must be noted that we are removing "implicit" relations, which cause an extra problem. Let's say we decide to leave out only the spatial relation that express participation in a given team; we would be able to freely move all members of this team. However, for other teams, proximity would still imply participation. In this case it is necessary to make it clear that some relation has been filtered out while other stays (like in the case of explicit links). For instance, when moving a node representation, the positions of other representations of the node is kept unchanged in all its other views.

4.5   Spatial Tour Along Workflow Links

Process animation along workflow links can be used as a guided tour mechanism. Built on the spatial traversal feature described in Section 4.3, such a guided tour would resemble a spatial tour within and across composite structures. Support for process enactment can also be used for coordinating multimedia presentations (through triggering the audio/video applications by the task nodes containing or referencing the multimedia contents).

4.6   Views of Non-composite Nodes

Similar to composite nodes, non-composite nodes can also be visualized with a closed view and an opened view. The symbol of a closed view normally indicates the type of a node; while the opened view presents the content of the node (in its original bounds). Opening a non-composite node would display the information object contained in or referenced by the node in the same window in its original bounds, or in a separate window if the content is handled by an external application (e.g. MS Word).

5   Comparison and Contribution to the Literature

Interoperability and "cross fertilization" of different hypertext domains are relatively new concerns to the hypertext community [1,2]. Work in [1] allows users to add and use structural services for different hypertext domains, e.g. one service for (clients in) one domain. Work in [2] defines a common hypertext data model of selected domains and develops different browsers to view the same model in different flavors (i.e. one service/model for multiple clients of different flavors). This paper specifies a graphical hypertext user interface for hypertexts with a mixture of navigational, spatial, taxonomic, and workflow hypertext flavors (i.e. one service/model or multiple services/models for clients of a hybrid flavor).

Many graphical hypermedia interfaces use small icons to represent nodes. This design uses full size, scalable graphics to represent nodes. This makes a graphical hypertext presentation a real picture of art. Pure spatial hypertext normally does not present explicit links (i.e. lines) for relationship. In this design, by adding explicit links and their layout to spatial hypertext, we have enriched its relationship expressiveness.

SuperBook [8] can fold/unfold sub-headings in the "table of content" part of an electronic book. Guide [9] can fold/unfold sub-headings plus their underlying content in their original context. This design allows a sub-graphical structure of a composite node or the content of a base node to be folded/unfolded in its original context (i.e. in its surroundings universe of nodes and links).

Spatial hypertext supports zoom-based navigation in a flat or nested structure [4]. By integrating explicit links, this design allows users to navigate (or zoom in) from one graphical component to the other by following the additional explicit links.

For people who want a pure spatial hypertext view, they can choose not to create explicit links, or to filter out such links for a tidy image of spatial hypertext. Unlike the filtered view mechanisms developed in each individual hypertext domains, in this design, it allows people to show a single hypertext flavor or a mixture of many flavors. It also allows people to create new persistent views of the underlying hypertext.

By incorporating process-related computational semantics to hypertext nodes and links, this design provides a guided tour mechanism for hypertext navigation or hypermedia presentation. Such a guide tour results in an automatic zooming-based traversal (i.e. a visual tour) in a spatial hypertext. Before activating such navigation, users can filter out the explicit links from display for a better spatial hypertext view. This kind feature is not possible in a pure spatial hypertext system.

Visual enterprise modeling tools (e.g. METIS [5] and System Architecture 2001 [10]) allow users to create and browse various diagrams of visual enterprise models. Such visual enterprise models resemble the visual hypertext this work wants to offer. Actually, the look-and-feel of the visual enterprise models in such visual enterprise modeling tools (especially the METIS system [5]) has inspired this work. However, most of such visual modeling tools are or have their root in diagramming or drawing tools, rather than hypermedia systems. They do not have all the integrated user inter-face features as described in this paper, since these features are made possible by their underlying hypermedia structures derived from various hypertext domains.

6   Conclusions

Integration of different hypertext domains is a relatively new concern to the hypertext community. This paper presents an integrative design of graphical hypertext user interfaces. This design embraces features from navigational, spatial, taxonomic, and workflow hypertexts. The multiple hypertext structures and their visual relation-ship indications (e.g., explicit links, nested structures, their graphical layout and visual clues such as position, size, color, shape, pattern and orientation) provide rich expressiveness of a *visual hypertext*. Consequently, the hypertext model underlying such a visual hypertext should be a generic structure based one that has structural constructs and properties for the variety of structures and relationship representations. The component-based system architecture [1] for structural computing has provided a basis for implementing clients using the user interface design presented in this paper. The structural services for the clients can be separated services for each of the hyper-text domains or an integrated service based on an integrated data model of these hypertext domains.

Among the user interface mechanisms presented in this paper, the structure un-folding unifies the presentation of nested and flat graphical structures. The spatial traversal and the spatial tour along explicit links provide a new link traversal method in a visual hypertext space. This kind of user interface allows users to see a visual hypertext structure at various levels of granularity, from holistic to detailed. The design has been partly implemented in a cooperative hypermedia browser of the XCHIPS system [11] (see `http://www.darmstadt.gmd.de/concert/xchips.html` for details). Currently, we are using such visual hypertext to externalize and manage various knowledge models, such as process-centric, holistic enterprise models. We expect that the general availability of a shared visual enterprise model and the various ways to navigate in the visual hypertext space will cut training time and confusion of (virtual) enterprise partners and customers.

Acknowledgements. The authors thank Jörg M. Haake for his very helpful comments on an earlier version of the paper.

References

1. Peter Nürnberg, Kaj Grønbæk, D. Bucka-Lassen, C. A. Pedersen, and O. A. Reinert component-based open hypermedia approach to integrating structure services. New Review of Hypermedia and Multimedia (1999), vol 5, pp. 179- 205.
2. David E. Millard, Luc Moreau, Hugh C. Davis, and Siegfried Reich, FOHM: a fundamental open hypertext model for investigating interoperability between hypertext do-mains. In proc. of ACM Hypertext'00, pp. 93-102.
3. H. Van Dyke Parunak: Don't Link Me In: Set Based Hypermedia for Taxonomic Reasoning. In proc. of ACM Hypertext'91, pp.233-242
4. Catherine C. Marshal and Frank M. Shipman III: Spatial Hypertext and the Practice of Information Triage. In proc. of ACM Hypertext'97, pp : 124-133
5. Frank Lillehagen, Dag Karlsen, Visual Extended Enterprise Engineering and Operation embedding Knowledge Management and Work Execution, Computas, METIS Whitepaper, Bekkajordet, N-3194 Horten, Norway
6. P.D. Stotts and R. Furuta Programmable browsing semantics in trellis. In Proceedings Hypertext '89. 27-42.
7. Weigang Wang and Jörg M. Haake "Supporting Workflow Using the Open Hypermedia Approach", Proceedings of the 1st Workshop on Structure Computing, June 22, 1999
8. D. E. Egan, J. R. Remde, L. M. Gomez, T. K. Landauer, J. Eberhardt, and C. C. Lochbaum "Formative Design-evaluation of 'SuperBook'," ACM Transactions on Information Systems, 7, 1, pp. 30-57, 1989.
9. Peter J. Brown, "Turning Ideas into Products: The Guide System," ACM Hypertext'87, pp. 33-40, University of North Carolina, Chapel Hill, North Carolina, November 13-15, 1987.
10. Popkin Software, System Architect 2001 - Heralds a New Era in Enterprise Modeling, http://www.popkin2001.com
11. Weigang Wang, Jörg M. Haake, Jessica Rubart "The Cooperative Hypermedia Approach to Collaborative Engineering and Operation of Virtual Enterprises", in Proceedings of IEEE CRIWG2001, the Seventh International Workshop on Groupware, pp. 58-67, September 6-8, 2001, Darmstadt, Germany

Using Structural Computing to Support Information Integration

Kenneth M. Anderson and Susanne A. Sherba

Department of Computer Science
University of Colorado, Boulder
430 UCB
Boulder CO 80309-0430
{kena, sherba}@cs.colorado.edu
http://www.cs.colorado.edu/users/{kena, sherba}

Abstract. Software engineers face a difficult task in managing the many different types of relationships that exist between the documents of a software development project. We refer to this task as *information integration,* since establishing a relationship between two documents typically means that some part of the information in each document is semantically related. A key challenge in information integration is providing techniques and tools that manage and evolve these relationships over time. The structural computing domain provides a set of principles to derive new techniques and tools to help with these tasks of relationship management and evolution. We present a prototype information integration environment, InfiniTe, and describe how we are exploiting structural computing principles in the design of its infrastructure services.

1 Introduction

Software development projects produce a wide variety of software artifacts, including requirements and design documents and source code. A key challenge in software development is managing the relationships that exist between these documents. For instance, software engineers need to know how a particular source code file relates to the modules and subsystems defined in the project's design document, and how these elements relate to the project's requirements. A benefit of having this information is the ability to perform change impact analysis, (e.g. if I change the interface to this subsystem, how does that impact its ability to meet its requirements, and what source code files need to change?) We refer to this relationship management task as *information integration,* since establishing a relationship between two documents typically means that some part of the information in each document is semantically related.

We are designing and developing an information integration environment, InfiniTe [5] (pronounced "infinity"), to provide tools to software engineers that increase their ability to discover, manage, and evolve the relationships that exist between their software artifacts. Managing and evolving relationships is a particularly important aspect of this work, since the creation and/or discovery of

S. Reich, M.M. Tzagarakis, P.M.E. De Bra (Eds.): OHS/SC/AH 2001, LNCS 2266, pp. 151–159, 2002.

relationships in a software development project is typically only the "tip of the iceberg" of the relationship management problem facing software engineers. The initial requirements and design stages of a large, complex software system represents only 25% of the total lifetime of a software system. That is, large software systems spend most of their time being used, maintained, and evolved, and a key maintenance challenge is keeping a deployed software system consistent with the software artifacts that represent its documentation.

Structural computing is an emerging field of research exploring a new paradigm of computation based on structure as opposed to data. Peter Nürnberg emphasizes this point of view by stating that structural computing "asserts the primacy of structure over data" and that computing should be performed on entities that are intrinsically structured [10]. Stated another way, the "atoms" of structural computing should have the ability to both contain (structured) information and participate in arbitrary structural relationships. We believe that structural computing can provide critical design guidance to the infrastructure of an information integration environment, especially with respect to this notion of a structural "atom."

In the past, we have argued that structural computing can be usefully applied to the domain of software engineering [2]. This paper represents an initial attempt to apply structural computing principals to the software engineering problem of information integration. The rest of this paper is organized as follows. We briefly present the InfiniTe architecture. Then, we discuss the structural computing issues surrounding the design of InfiniTe's infrastructure services. Next, we briefly discuss related work, and then offer a few conclusions.

2   InfiniTe Information Integration Environment

Fig. 1 presents a model of the conceptual elements of the information integration environment. The model consists of users, data sources, integrators, translators, contexts, a repository, and an open hypermedia layer. The basic idea is that information is brought into the information integration environment by invoking a *translator*. The translator retrieves information from a *data source* and stores it in a *repository*. The repository consists of multiple *contexts*; contexts store information (using XML [6]) along with attributes, which serve to provide meta-data on the information. Contexts can contain sub-contexts. In addition, the documents of a context can be linked together in arbitrary relationships; relationships can span multiple contexts and can have type information associated with them (e.g. a requirements traceability link, a consistency relationship, etc.). Relationships can be stored as XLinks [8] or within the open hypermedia layer.

Integrators aid users in finding, creating, maintaining, and evolving *relationships* within the repository. While our main focus is on relationship management, integrators are free to create new contexts and to store information within them while performing their tasks. For instance, an integrator that searches documents for particular keywords, may store the location of discovered keywords in

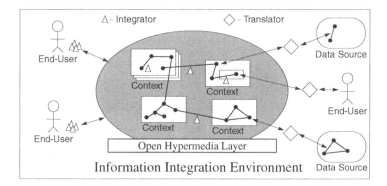

Fig. 1. InfiniTe's Conceptual Model

a document separate from the documents being searched. It may then create a new context and include pointers to the searched documents plus the document that it created.

Finally, the relationships that are generated by integrators can be imported into the open hypermedia layer and then made available to the original data source using its native editing tools. This feature allows software engineers to submit a set of artifacts to the repository, make use of integrators to discover relationships contained in those artifacts, and then view the generated relationships within the native editing environment of the original artifacts. This capability is critical to enabling the adoption of the information integration environment, and is discussed in more detail below; while it is true that our approach requires the use of a new environment to perform information integration tasks, the results of those operations can be made available to the software engineers within their own tools. Software engineers, thus, gain access to tools and techniques to perform information integration tasks, but they are not required to give up the tools they already use to gain these capabilities.

We have implemented a proof-of-concept prototype of InfiniTe to explore a variety of research issues (See Figure 2). The implementation makes use of a set of Java Servlets that can invoke integrators and translators on XML documents stored in the repository. XSLT [7], the transformation component of the XML Stylesheet Language, is used to translate repository information from XML into HTML for presentation in a Web browser. In addition, repository relationships can be extracted from the environment as a set of XLinks that can then be imported into an open hypermedia system for display in the documents of integrated third-party applications.

3   Structural Computing Issues

Our use of XML as a means for storing documents and relationships in InfiniTe's repository enabled the rapid creation of a prototype system to explore informa-

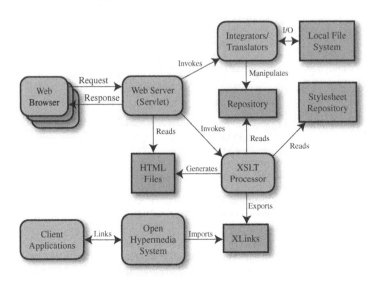

Fig. 2. InfiniTe's Prototype Architecture

tion integration research issues directly. However, it is currently not clear that XML will prove to be the right choice with respect to its ability to scale to modern software development projects, or its ability to flexibly specify heterogeneous types of relationships.

As we have reported in previous work [1], modern software development projects can quickly test the scalability of software tools. In that particular project, our open hypermedia system, Chimera [4], had to support the creation of hyperwebs containing hundreds of thousands of relationships, and indicated that true industrial support would require hypermedia technology that can scale to hyperwebs containing millions of relationships. With respect to the problem of defining heterogeneous sets of relationships, XLink [8] is certainly a step in the right direction. XLink provides the ability to specify relationships external from the documents they relate and has the ability to assign types to links to help distinguish between different XLink instances. However, XLink is a relatively new standard with sparse tool support and its typing mechanisms relies on XML Namespaces, which is a somewhat difficult-to-use standard that has generated significant controversy in the XML community [9].

As such, we are designing an implementation of the repository for InfiniTe that is based upon structural computing principals. We believe the use of structure servers [10] and a carefully-designed set of structural abstractions can address both of the potential problems raised above, and provide a flexible platform for adding new information integration capabilities and strengthening our integration with open hypermedia technology. We now describe our design of the structural computing-based repository and our plans for implementing and evaluating it.

3.1   Structural Abstractions

Our design for InfiniTe's repository, using structural computing principals, is centered around the concept of a *file*. In InfiniTe, a file will be the structural atom, upon which all other structures are based. As defined by Nürnberg, a file will have the ability to contain structured information as well as participate in structural relationships. The repository will be accessed via two structure servers. One server will provide access to structural abstractions within a file (known as the repository file server), while the other server will provide access to structural abstractions between files (known as the repository structure server). These servers will be hosted on top of a database (most likely a relational database, although XML databases will be evaluated) to help address our scalability concerns.

The repository file server is used to create and access files within the repository. Translators will be the primary user of the repository file server, either storing new files into the repository or extracting files from the repository to a (local or remote) file system. Integrators will also access this server when they are examining the contents of a file looking for relationship instances. This server will provide operations to create files and define their internal structure. Internal structure in the current implementation is provided by the structural aspects of XML. The current repository does not impose a canonical XML format to which all files must conform. Instead, it allows any XML document to be stored in the repository. The tradeoff associated with this design choice is that some translators/integrators may not be able to interact with a particular file if it does not understand its XML structure. The use of a structure server should help to alleviate this problem since a structure server will provide reflection methods that will enable a translator or integrator to query and search the structure of a file dynamically, trying to discover substructures that it can understand and manipulate. Methods for defining the structure of a file will initially support the creation of tree structures but will eventually support matrix and directed graph structures as well. The final set of methods provided by the repository file server concern the creation and manipulation of anchors. Anchors are created by integrators when they discover a structure in a file that they can classify. These anchors can then be used by the repository structure server to establish relationships between files. Note that anchors can be assigned types and queries can be made against those types, e.g. retrieve all anchors of type A from document B.

The repository structure server is used to establish and access the relationships between files in the repository. The primary users of this server will be integrators, who need these services in order to perform their primary duty of finding and manipulating InfiniTe relationships. The repository structure server treats files as atoms, not caring about their internal structure. Instead, files can be grouped in *contexts* and linked with *relationships*. Operations will be provided to create, edit, query, link, and destroy contexts. Contexts can have relationships established between them: For instance versioning relationships, that express that one context is an earlier or subsequent version of some other context. Operations will also be provided to create, type, edit, query, and destroy relationships. Relationships require anchor points to link files with each other (although both a file and context can serve as its own anchor point). In addition, relationships can be typed, which can constrain both the number and type of anchors that can be related by a particular relationship. With these operations, integrators can be given a starting context or file as input, and use the repository structure server to access other files, either by querying the context, or retrieving a set of relationships from the input file and traversing them to reach related files.

3.2   Structural Transformation

In response to our previous work on structural transformations [3], we have identified the need for structural transformation services in the InfiniTe environment. In particular, in software development projects, relationships between software artifacts may change in both structure and purpose over time. For instance, a subsystem may always maintain a relationship between itself and the most recent version of a particular module. As that module is changed, new versions are created, and the subsystem relationship must be modified to point to the new version automatically. Another example involves the changing of a relationship's type. For instance, a relationship that is used to perform change impact analysis in a maintenance context, may need to serve the role of a requirements traceability link in a software understanding context. As such, the same instance of a relationship needs to be viewed as different types depending on the context from which it is accessed.

In order to support these scenarios, our structure servers will provide operations for defining temporary sets of relationships, known as change sets, to which type transformations can be applied. This will support scenarios such as retrieve all change impact relationships from context A and reify them as requirements traceability relationships in context B. In addition, operations will be provided to associate computations with relationships to handle scenarios like the versioning scenario described above. Essentially this capability requires that behaviors that return anchors can be treated as anchors themselves. When such an anchor is accessed, the computation is triggered which retrieves and returns the anchor which is to be used in that instance. This technique is, of course, borrowed from the open hypermedia domain [11] where many systems provide this dynamic linking capability.

3.3   Implementation and Evaluation Plans

The work described in this paper is at a preliminary stage. The initial XML-based prototype of the InfiniTe environment has just been completed. This prototype allows us to explore interesting information integration issues now, while the design and implementation of the structural computing-based repository takes place. We intend to integrate the two identified structure servers incrementally, starting with basic support to store and retrieve files and then adding services such as organizing files into contexts, adding anchors to files and establishing relationships between anchors.

We intend to evaluate our work by applying the information integration environment to several open source projects. Open source projects provide a wealth of software artifacts to analyze, including all artifacts of all previous versions of an open source system. Such projects will allow us to test InfiniTe's scalability as well as its ability to track and transform complex relationships between a heterogenous set of software artifacts.

4   Related Work

We now briefly review two related systems. The GeoWorlds environment [13] is an information analysis environment that allows users to retrieve documents off the Web, organize them into collections, and apply a variety of analyses upon them. GeoWorlds is strictly focused on the World Wide Web and can only import information from Web-based data sources. We intend to support both remote and local information sources, with particular attention to supporting legacy, third-party, data formats. This will allow our environment to be applied to both existing and new software development projects. In addition, GeoWorlds services are focused more on information analysis while our focus will be on relationship management. Our environment will thus have greater capabilities for discovering, viewing, and manipulating relationships than what is found in the GeoWorlds environment.

The second related system is xlinkit [12]. It is a link generation engine that allows consistency relationships to be specified over software artifacts. The basic idea is that a software engineer writes consistency rules for a set of documents and then submits those rules along with a set of documents. (Documents must be converted to XML before the link generation engine can process them.) The link generation engine then checks the documents to see if they follow the submitted consistency rules. As output, the engine generates a report that displays the results of the analysis: instances of the rules are highlighted and information is provided to show, for each instance, if the rule was followed or violated. Our environment can be used to check consistency relationships over software artifacts, but it is also intended to support a broader spectrum of relationship types. For instance, we intend to build integrators that can aid the process of generating requirements traceability links, similar to the results we achieved with Northrop Grumman using only the Chimera open hypermedia system [1]. Rather than providing a rule-based language for a single relationship type, our environment will provide APIs to software engineers that will allow them to construct their own translators and integrators to manage the relationships relevant to their software development projects. This does not mean that rule-based languages are not helpful in automatic link generation; indeed the experience with xlinkit demonstrates the benefits of this technique. In fact, we plan to leverage the results of the xlinkit experience, along with other work in hypermedia link generation, to create a generic rule-based integrator that can support various rule sets via a plug-in mechanism. In addition, our use of open hypermedia will allow the relationships discovered in the environment to be viewable within the native editing context of the original software artifacts. Thus, while both of these systems require a translation step into XML, our approach will allow information to flow back to the original artifacts.

5   Summary

We believe that structural computing principals can be applied to the design of infrastructure services for an environment designed to help software engineers with the problem of information integration. We outlined a design for two structure servers to serve as the repository for the InfiniTe information integration environment centered around a file as the key structural abstraction. We have described the need for structural transformation services in this environment and have provided insight into our implementation and evaluation plans. Although this work is still at a preliminary stage, we believe the design presented in this paper provides utility to structural computing developers as an example of the type of applications that can be addressed by the domain of structural computing.

References

1. Anderson, K. M. (1999). Issues of Data Scalability in Open Hypermedia Systems. *The New Review of Hypermedia and Multimedia*, 5: 151-178.
2. Anderson, K. M. (1999). Software Engineering Requirements for Structural Computing. In *Proceedings of the First International Workshop on Structural Computing*. Darmstadt, Germany. February 21, 1999.
   http://www.cs.colorado.edu/users/kena/papers/workshops/sc1.html.
3. Anderson, K. M. (2000). Structural Computing Requirements for the Transformation of Structures and Behaviors. In *Proceedings of the Second International Workshop on Structural Computing*. San Antonio, TX, USA.
4. Anderson, K. M., Taylor, R. N., and Whitehead, E. J., Jr. (2000). Chimera: Hypermedia for Heterogeneous Software Development Environments. *ACM Transactions on Information Systems*, 18(3): 211-245.
5. Anderson, K. M., and Sherba, S. A. (2001). Using XML to support Information Integration. In *Proceedings of the 2001 International Workshop on XML Technologies and Software Engineering (XSE 2001)*. Co-located with the 2001 International Conference on Software Engineering. Toronto, Ontario, Canada. May 15, 2001.
6. Bray, T., Paoli, J., and Sperberg-McQueen, C. M. (1998). Extensible Markup Language (XML) 1.0, W3C Recommendation, 10-February-1998.
   http://www.w3.org/TR/REC-xml.
7. Clark, J. (1999). XSL Transformations (XSLT) Version 1.0 W3C Recommendation, 16 November 1999. http://www.w3.org/TR/xslt.html.
8. DeRose, S., Orchard, D., and Trafford, B. (1999). XML Linking Language (XLINK). http://www.w3.org/TR/xlink/.
9. Dumbill, E. (1999). Eight Greats of XML.com 1999.
   http://www.xml.com/pub/a/1999/12/bestof/index.html.

10. Nürnberg, P. J., Leggett, J. J., and Schneider, E. R. (1997). As We Should Have Thought. In *Proceedings of the Eighth ACM Conference on Hypertext*, pp. 96-101. Southampton, UK. April 6-11, 1997.
11. Østerbye, K., and Wiil, U. K. (1996). The Flag Taxonomy of Open Hypermedia Systems. In *Proceedings of the Seventh ACM Conference on Hypertext*, pp. 129-139. Washington DC, USA. March 16-20, 1996.
12. `http://www.xlinkit.com/`.
13. Yao, K., Ko, I., Eleish, R., and Neches, R. (2000). Asynchronous Information Space Analysis Architecture Using Content and Structure-Based Service Brokering. In *Proceedings of the 2000 ACM Conference on Digital Libraries*. San Antonio, TX, USA.

Providing Structural Computing Services on the World Wide Web

Uffe Kock Wiil and David L. Hicks

Department of Computer Science
Aalborg University Esbjerg
Niels Bohrs Vej 8, 6700 Esbjerg, Denmark
{ukwiil,hicks}@cs.aue.auc.dk

Abstract. The World Wide Web is one of the most successful software systems. The web provides a simple, extensible, and standardized hypermedia platform with millions of users that have access to millions of servers holding billions of documents. Hence, an increasing number of researchers and developers are making their systems and services available on the web. In conformance with this trend, this paper describes the first important results in the ongoing effort to provide the Construct structural computing services on the web. The paper is organized into five parts: an introduction to the research area, a brief overview of the Construct structural computing environment, a detailed description of the completed development effort to provide the Construct metadata services on the web, a quick overview of ongoing and future work in this area, and finally, our conclusions.

1 Introduction

The World Wide Web, one of the most successful software systems, can be viewed as a large digital collection. However, data alone is oftentimes not enough. Many work practices require different types of structuring mechanisms (e.g., links and metadata) to be carried out in an efficient manner. Scholarly work is an example of a common work practice among researchers and students that requires a broad range of structuring mechanisms [21]. Structural computing research is targeted at providing support for different types of structures over existing data.

Structural computing research grew out of the research on open hypermedia systems. The open hypermedia research community has been active for more than a decade. A series of workshops on open hypermedia systems was started in 1994 [16,24,25,27,28,29]. In 1996 the open hypermedia community formed the Open Hypermedia System Working Group [15] as an instrument to address the important issues of standardization and interoperability [4,17]. Prominent open hypermedia systems include Chimera [1], Microcosm [8], DHM [7], HOSS [14], and HyperDisco [26]. Open hypermedia technologies have matured over the years and, as a result, some research systems have been commercialized (e.g., Microcosm and DHM). Another important result of open hypermedia research is that some research systems have been integrated successfully into the web (e.g.,

S. Reich, M.M. Tzagarakis, P.M.E. De Bra (Eds.): OHS/SC/AH 2001, LNCS 2266, pp. 160–171, 2002.
© Springer-Verlag Berlin Heidelberg 2002

Arakne [2], Chimera, Microcosm, and DHM) and made available to the millions of web users either on a public domain or commercial basis.

The term *structural computing* was coined in 1997 [13]. A structural computing environment can be characterized as an open hypermedia platform that provides different types of structure services within the same environment (e.g., navigational, spatial, and taxonomic). In 1999 a workshop series on structural computing was initiated [12,16]. Development of the first structural computing environments is now well underway (e.g., FOHM [10], Callimachus [18], and Construct [3]).

Construct is a component-based structural computing environment developed as the common code base successor of the DHM [7], HOSS [14], and HyperDisco [26] open hypermedia systems. Construct has been under development since 1997 and provides an increasing number of structural computing services. The current set of services includes navigational, metadata, taxonomic, spatial, cooperation, and data mining services.

This paper describes the first important results in the ongoing effort to provide the Construct structural computing services on the web. Providing structuring services on the web is not a new thing. Many open hypermedia systems have been integrated with the web to add external linking capabilities (e.g., DHM [7], Microcosm [8], and Chimera [1]). The techniques involved in integrating applications such as web browsers have also been discussed extensively in the open hypermedia literature (e.g., by Davis et al. [4], Whitehead [18], and Bouvin [2]). While these approaches have mostly focused on navigational structures (links), Construct aims at providing a wide variety of structuring mechanisms on the web including navigational, metadata, taxonomic, spatial, etc.

The first Construct structural computing service to be provided on the web was the metadata service. In a narrow perspective, this can be seen as a step towards the semantic web where users can maintain a metadata record for each document on the web. A metadata record consists of an open set of key/value pairs containing data about the document – for example, the Dublin Core initiative [6] suggests 15 types of keys for library materials. The metadata can be used to perform advanced queries. In a broader perspective, the provision of the metadata service on the web can be seen as a first step towards providing an open set of structuring mechanisms on the web. Once in place, this will enable several new work practices (involving working with structure over data) to be performed in standard web browsers using the existing data on the web.

The paper is organized in the following way. Section 2 provides a brief overview of the Construct structural computing environment. In Section 3, we describe the development effort to integrate the Construct metadata services into Netscape 6. Section 4 describes our ongoing and future work (including open research issues) towards providing structural computing services on the web. Section 5 concludes the paper.

2   The Construct Structural Computing Environment

The activities in the Construct project have taken many different directions.
First of all, different categories of services have been developed as part of the
Construct structural computing environment: foundation services, structure
(middleware) services, infrastructure services, and wrapper services. Secondly,
a number of development tools have been developed to assist in the process of
generating new services. Thirdly, a set of end-user tools (applications) has been
developed to make use of the structure services. Finally, a number of existing
applications have been integrated with Construct – mostly by the use of wrapper
services.

In the following, we will provide a brief overview of Construct structure
services, end user tools, and integrated applications. The overview will be given
from an end user perspective. Additional details about Construct can be found
in [20], [21], [22], and [23].

The structure services are at different stages in their development. A navigational hypermedia service and a metadata service have been operational for
a while and have reached a high level of maturity. The metadata service allows users to add arbitrary metadata (consisting of key-value pairs) to all types
of documents. The navigational structure service allows users to add arbitrary
associations (links) between all types of documents.

Figure 1 shows a screen shot of Emacs when using both the navigational and
metadata services. The buffer in the top part of the screen displays the file named
navigational.txt overlaid with navigational structure. Anchors are displayed on
screen as blue, underlined text. The buffer in the lower part of the screen displays
the metadata record for the file named *navigational.txt*.

A taxonomic service and a spatial service are under development. They are
both operational with basic capabilities. The spatial structure service allows
users to organize documents on a desktop using a spatial metaphor (similar
to organizing documents on a table). The taxonomic structure service allows
users to organize (classify) documents in classification trees according to certain
criteria. Fully featured versions of these two services are expected to be ready
by the end of 2001.

Figure 2 shows a screen shot of the Construct taxonomic tool. In the upper
part of the tax tool, a user has organized open hypermedia systems in a classification structure. The lower part of the tax tool displays an HTML file attached
to the DHM object in the classification tree.

Figure 3 shows a screen shot of the Construct spatial tool. A user is in the
process of organizing an information space. The space displays twelve objects
each representing an open hypermedia research issue. At this point, the user has
managed to group some of the objects into clusters of related issues by placing
them next to each other. For instance, the user has indicated that the issues
Foundation services, *Access control*, and *Version control* belong together.

A suite of cooperation services and a data mining service are under development. The cooperation services will consist of three parts: a service to manage
shared sessions, a service and a tool to support awareness among multiple users

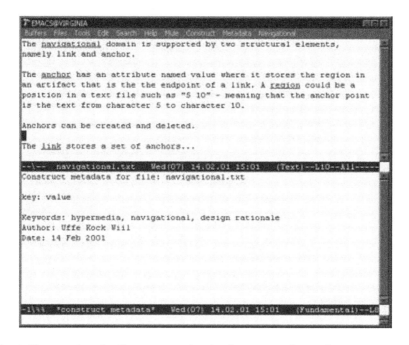

Fig. 1. Emacs using the Construct navigational service and metadata service on the same file at the same time (from [20])

(loosely coupled mode), and a formal cooperation service supporting synchronous collaborative work (tightly coupled mode). The data mining service will allow users to discover automatically different types of relations among documents, based on different input criteria. For example, the data mining service can produce a classification of documents based on their metadata keys and values. The first versions of all of these services are expected during the Fall of 2001.

The remainder of the paper describes past, present, and future work targeted at providing the Construct structural computing services on the web.

3   Providing Metadata Services on the World Wide Web

The focus in the first phase of the integration work described in this section was to provide a proof of concept implementation. Many important issues relating to user interface design and usability studies were left open for future work (see Section 4).

The success criteria and overall goals of the first phase of the metadata integration project were to make the Construct metadata services available as an integral part of Netscape 6 and at the same time to produce a general integration platform (code base) in Netscape 6 that can be used for integration of other

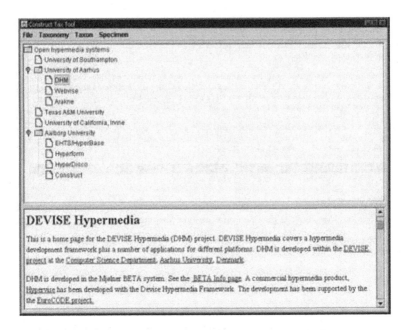

Fig. 2. The Construct taxonomic tool (from [21])

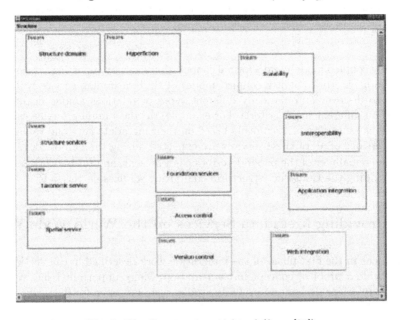

Fig. 3. The Construct spatial tool (from [21])

Construct services. Netscape 6 was selected due to its open standards, its publicly available source code, and its availability on most platforms.

The Construct metadata services has been made available through a Java applet running in a panel in *My Sidebar* in Netscape 6. This section will walk through the different parts of the user interface of the integration. The technical details of the analysis, design, and implementation of the integration are documented in [11].

3.1   Launching the Metadata Services

The *My Sidebar* item in the *View* menu must be activated to launch the metadata services sidebar in Netscape 6 (Figure 4).

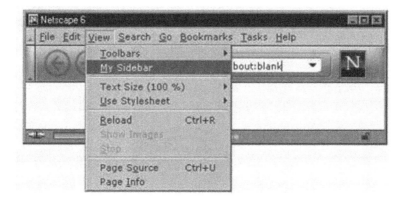

Fig. 4. Getting Netscape 6 to display *My Sidebar*

My Sidebar will then appear on the left hand side of the browser (Figure 5). The *Metadata service* item can now be selected in the *Tabs* menu. This will display the user interface of the metadata services applet in *My Sidebar*.

3.2   Using the Metadata Services

The metadata services applet that runs inside the panel works just like any other application inside *My Sidebar*. The applet provides three different tabs (*Main, Enlarged*, and *Preferences*), which can be selected at the top of the panel (Figure 6). The *Main* panel is the default one. It is separated into three different parts: the *Display* area, the *Metadata* area, and the *Current URL* area.

The *Display* area allows users to decide if they want the applet to retrieve metadata each time they load a new web page. If they check the *Auto-Update* button, metadata will be retrieved automatically when a new web page is loaded. Otherwise, the user will have to use the *Refresh* button to retrieve metadata for a newly loaded web page.

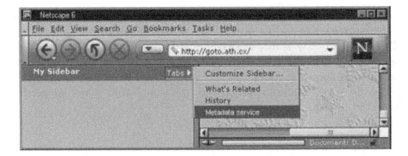

Fig. 5. Getting Netscape 6 to display the Construct metadata service in *My Sidebar*

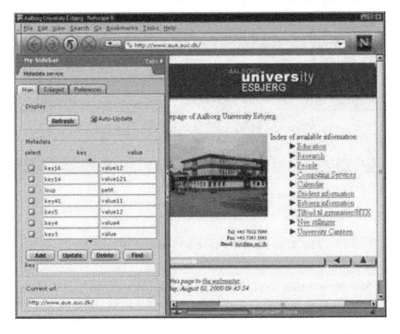

Fig. 6. The *Main* panel of the metadata services in *My Sidebar*

The *Metadata* area displays all metadata keys and values for a given web page. If there are too many keys (and values) to see them all in the limited metadata area, a scroll bar will appear and allow the user to scroll up and down the list of metadata keys and values. Four metadata operations are provided: *Add, Update, Delete,* and *Find*.

- **Add a key**. If the user wants to add a key, she enters the name of the new key in the *key* field and presses the *Add* button. The applet will then switch to the *Enlarged* panel where the user can enter the value of the key.

- **Update a key**. A key can be updated by selecting it (by checking the *select* button to the left of the key name) or by entering its name in the *key* field. When the *Update* button is activated, the key value is displayed in the *Enlarged* panel. The user can now modify the value of the key.
- **Delete one or more key(s)**. The user can delete one or more keys by checking their *select* button and pressing the *Delete* button. Alternatively, the user can enter the name of the key in the *key* field and press *Delete*.
- **Find or enlarge the display of a key value**. The *Main* panel displays all the metadata keys and values of a given web page. The limited screen real estate available for the metadata display area can easily result in lack of overview. Even with a relatively small number of metadata keys and values, it is not possible to see them all. Also, even with relatively small key values (with respect to number of characters), it is impossible to see the entire value of the key. The *Find* operation is included to help the user to deal with these problems. If the user selects a key or enters its name and presses the *Find* button, then the key and its value will be displayed in the *Enlarged* panel and it will be easy to read the value of this key.

Finally, the *Current URL* area reminds the user of the URL of the document corresponding to the displayed metadata. If the *Auto-Update* button is checked the *Current URL* field will change automatically when a new web page is loaded.

The *Enlarged* panel also has three parts: the *Key* area, the *Value* area, and the *Url* area (Figure 7). It essentially allows the user to perform the same operations as the *Main* panel does.

The user can directly add or update a key by entering its name and its value in the *Key* and *Value* fields (and pressing the *Add* or *Update* button, respectively). The user is also able to find the value of a key or delete a key by typing in its name in the *Key* field (and pressing the *Find* or *Delete* button, respectively). The URL of the document to which the currently displayed metadata refers is shown at the bottom of the interface, like in the *Main* panel.

The *Preferences* panel allows the user to choose what Construct metadata service to use (Figure 8). To select a service, the user must enter the *server address* and the *port number* of an active (running) Construct metadata service into the two corresponding fields (and press the *Apply* button). The default connection parameters (localhost port 16000) can be restored by pressing the *Default* button.

If the user does not need to consult any web pages while performing metadata operations, the Java applet can also run as a standalone application (called the Construct Metadata Viewer) that can be used to work with (display, edit, delete, etc.) metadata records [11].

4   Ongoing and Future Work

We plan to make all Construct structure services available on the web by integrating them into Netscape 6 (or some other web browser). Section 3 explained

Fig. 7. The *Enlarged* panel of the metadata services in *My Sidebar*

how the metadata service was integrated into Netscape 6. Following the integration of the metadata service, we have integrated the navigational structure service into Netscape 6 using the general integration platform developed in connection with the metadata integration [9].

In the future, additional Construct structure services will be provided on the web whenever they are ready to be used by a wider audience. As mentioned earlier, several new structure services and tools are under development including a spatial structure service and a space tool (Figure 3), a taxonomic structure service and a tax tool (Figure 2), a data mining service and tool, and a set of cooperation services and tools. We have plans to start development of additional structure services and tools as part of our future work including tools and services for workflow and argumentation support.

The provision and deployment of a broad range of structuring mechanisms in large digital collections such as the web, poses several new research issues. The issues regarding interoperability of structure services and re-use of structures across structural domains is a new area wide open to future research [20]. We have started to deploy our structure services in a large digital library that is

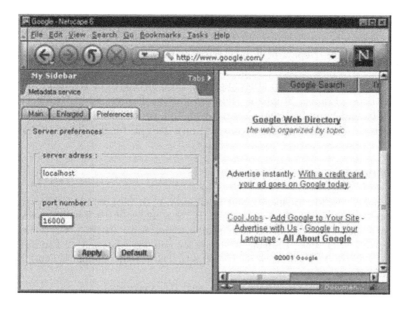

Fig. 8. The *Preferences* panel of the metadata services in *My Sidebar*

accessible through standard web browsers. This is a pre-requisite to investigating interoperability issues.

Also, the user interface and other issues involved in managing multiple structure services inside applications deserves much attention. In fact, we have recently initiated the development of a framework for evaluating web service user interfaces. The purpose of the framework is to provide an overview of the important aspects involved in providing and subsequently evaluating structural computing services on the web.

5   Conclusions

We think that the first phases of the Netscape 6 metadata integration project has been a great success for a number of reasons. First of all, the Construct metadata services are now available on the World Wide Web as an integral part of Netscape 6. Secondly, it is a first important step towards providing all the Construct structural computing services on the World Wide Web. Additional Construct services will be integrated as they become ready for it. Finally, the Netscape 6 integration software has been developed in a general way that will allow additional Construct structure services to be made available on the web in the future using the general code base developed in this project. In fact, we are have recently completed an integration of the Construct navigational structure service using the same integration platform.

Acknowledgments. Several people have been involved in the development of Construct tools and services. In particular, we wish to acknowledge our three colleagues in the Department of Computer Science and Engineering, Aalborg University Esbjerg, Peter J. Nürnberg, Samir Tata, and Dragos Arotaritei and the five Socrates exchange students from the University of Bretagne Occidentale in Brest, France, Stephane Blondin, Jerome Fahler, Yann Neveu, Youenn Guervilly, and Yann Le Doare. Yann Neveu and Youenn Guervilly were responsible for the Netscape 6 metadata integration – see [11] for details on this project.

References

1. Anderson, K. M., Taylor, R., and Whitehead, E. J. 1994. Chimera: Hypertext for heterogeneous software environments. In Proceedings of the 1994 ACM European Conference on Hypertext, (Edinburgh, Scotland, Sep.), 94-107. ACM Press.
2. Bouvin, N. O. 1999. Unifying strategies for web augmentation. In Proceedings of the 1999 ACM Conference on Hypertext, (Darmstadt, Germany, Feb.), 91-100. ACM Press.
3. Construct. 2001. http://www.cs.aue.auc.dk/construct.
4. Davis, H. C., Millard, D. E., Reich, S., Bouvin, N. O., Gronbæk, K., Nürnberg, P. J., Sloth, L., Wiil, U. K., and Anderson, K. M. 1999. Interoperability between hypermedia systems: The standardisation work of the OHSWG. In Proceedings of the 1999 ACM Conference on Hypertext, (Darmstadt, Germany, Feb.), 201-202. ACM Press.
5. Davis, H. C., Knight, S., and Hall, W. 1994. Light hypermedia link services: A study of third party application integration. In Proceedings of the 1994 ACM European Hypertext Conference, (Edinburgh, Scotland, Sep.), 41-50. ACM Press.
6. Dublin Core. 2001. http://www.dublincore.org.
7. Gronbæk, K., and Trigg, R. 1999. From Web to Workplace – Designing Open Hypermedia Systems. MIT Press.
8. Hall, W., Davis, H., and Hutchings, G. 1996. Rethinking Hypermedia – The Microcosm Approach. Kluwer Academic Publishers.
9. Le Doare, Y., Wiil, U. K., and Hicks, D. 2001. Providing external links on the World Wide Web. Technical Report CSE-01-02, Department of Computer Science and Engineering, Aalborg University Esbjerg.
10. Millard, D. E., Moreau, L., David, H.C., and Reich, S. 2000. FOHM: A fundamental open hypertext model for investigating interoperability between hypertext domains. In Proceedings of the 2000 ACM Conference on Hypertext, (San Antonio, TX, Jun.), 93-102. ACM Press.
11. Neveu, Y., Guervilly, Y., Wiil, U. K., and Hicks, D. L. 2001. Providing metadata services on the World Wide Web. Technical Report CSE-01-01, Department of Computer Science and Engineering, Aalborg University Esbjerg. http://www.cs.aue.auc.dk/~kock/Publications/Construct/aue-cse-01-01.pdf
12. Nürnberg, P. J., Ed. 1999. Proceedings of the First Workshop on Structural Computing. Technical Report CS-99-04, Department of Computer Science, Aalborg University Esbjerg, Denmark.
13. Nürnberg, P. J., Leggett, J. J., and Schneider, E. R. 1997. As we should have thought. In Proceedings of the 1997 ACM Hypertext Conference, (Southampton, UK, Apr.), 96-101. ACM Press.

14. Nürnberg, P. J., Leggett, J. J., Schneider, E., R., and Schnase, J. L. 1996. HOSS: A new paradigm for computing. In Proceedings of the 1996 ACM Hypertext Conference, (Washington, DC, Mar.), 194-202. ACM Press.
15. Open Hypermedia System Working Group. 2001. http://www.ohswg.org.
16. Reich, S., and Anderson, K. M. Eds. 2000. Open Hypermedia Systems and Structural Computing. Proceedings of the 6th Workshop on Open Hypermedia Systems and the 2nd Workshop on Structural Computing. Lecture Notes in Computer Science 1903, Springer Verlag.
17. Reich, S., Wiil, U. K., Nürnberg, P. J., Davis, H. C., Gronbæk, K., Anderson, K. M., Millard, D. E., and Haake, J. M. 1999. Addressing interoperability in open hypermedia: The design of the open hypermedia protocol. Special Issue on Open Hypermedia, The New Review of Hypermedia and Multimedia, 5, 207-248.
18. Tzagarakis, M., Vaitis, M., Papadopoulos, A., and Christodoulakis, D. 1999. The Callimachus approach to distributed hypermedia. In Proceedings of the 1999 ACM Conference on Hypertext, (Darmstadt, Germany, Feb.), 47-48. ACM Press.
19. Whitehead, E. J. 1997. An architectural model for application integration in open hypermedia environments. In Proceedings of the 1997 ACM Hypertext Conference, (Southampton, UK, Apr), ACM Press, 1-12.
20. Wiil, U. K., Hicks, D. L., and Nürnberg, P. J. 2001. Multiple open services: A new approach to service provision in open hypermedia systems, In Proceedings of the 2001 ACM Conference on Hypertext, (Arhus, Denmark, Aug.), 83-92. ACM Press.
21. Wiil, U. K., and Hicks, D. L. 2001. Tools and services for knowledge discovery, management and structuring in digital libraries. In Proceedings of the Eighth ISPE International Conference on Concurrent Engineering: Research and Applications, (Anaheim, CA, Jul.), 580-589.
22. Wiil, U. K., Nürnberg, P. J., Hicks, D. L., and Reich, S. 2000. A development environment for building component-based open hypermedia systems. In Proceedings of the 2000 ACM Hypertext Conference, (San Antonio, TX, Jun.), 266-267. ACM Press.
23. Wiil, U. K., and Nürnberg, P. J. 1999. Evolving hypermedia middleware services: Lessons and observations. In Proceedings of the 1999 ACM Symposium on Applied Computing, (San Antonio, TX, Feb.), 427-436. ACM Press.
24. Wiil, U. K., Ed. 1999. Proceedings of the 5th Workshop on Open Hypermedia Systems. Technical Report CS-99-01, Aalborg University Esbjerg.
25. Wiil, U. K., Ed. 1998. Proceedings of the 4th Workshop on Open Hypermedia Systems. Technical Report CS-98-01, Aalborg University Esbjerg.
26. Wiil, U. K., and Leggett, J. J. 1997. Workspaces: The HyperDisco approach to Internet distribution. In Proceedings of the 1997 ACM Hypertext Conference, (Southampton, UK, Apr.), 13-23. ACM Press.
27. Wiil, U. K. Ed. 1997. Proceedings of the 3rd Workshop on Open Hypermedia Systems. Scientific Report 97-01, The Danish National Centre for IT Research.
28. Wiil, U. K., and Demeyer, S., Eds. 1996. Proceedings of the 2nd Workshop on Open Hypermedia Systems. UCI-ICS Technical Report 96-10, Department of Information and Computer Science, University of California, Irvine.
29. Wiil, U. K., and Osterbye, K., Eds. 1994. Proceedings of the ECHT '94 Workshop on Open Hypermedia Systems. Technical Report R-94-2038, Department of Computer Science, Aalborg University.

Cooperation Services in a Structural Computing Environment

Samir Tata, David L. Hicks, and Uffe Kock Wiil

Department of Computer Science
Aalborg University Esbjerg
Niels Bohrs Vej 8, 6700 Esbjerg, Denmark
{tata, hicks, ukwiil}@cs.aue.auc.dk

Abstract. Environments for structural computing have seen significant recent development. Generally, they provide several hypermedia facilities involving several applications. Users within these environments may perform activities involving several applications and handle several types of hypermedia data. In this context, they need within the structural computing environment some cooperation facilities that help them to coordinate their activities and manage their roles in cooperation. This paper proposes to integrate some cooperation services into the Construct structural computing environment.

1 Introduction

The cooperative applications have seen, in the last few years, significant development and a real improvement of their underlying technologies. Among others, the particular class of cooperative applications dedicated to support project-based organizations is actually emerging. Our work is concerned with this particular class of cooperative applications, which aggregate several partners around a common project. Cooperation in these applications occurs in the more common case through the sharing of objects: the products of the project. Shared objects in developed cooperation environments are considered as atomic without structure and isolated without dependencies. These aspects are more subjects of research in the structural computing field. This field aims at the development of environments that provide different types of structure services (*e.g.* navigational, metadata, data mining, etc.)

Tools and frameworks for cooperative applications have been developed without real support for hypermedia facilities (*e.g.* metadata management). And environments for structural computing lack facilities to support cooperation. We think that it is important to combine computer-supported cooperative work (CSCW) and the structural computing fields [9]. The potential synergism they hold for each other can be very effective in supporting projects involving several cooperating partners and handling structural data.

The combination of the CSCW and the structural computing fields can be seen under several points of view. We can develop research in the CSCW

S. Reich, M.M. Tzagarakis, P.M.E. De Bra (Eds.): OHS/SC/AH 2001, LNCS 2266, pp. 172–182, 2002.
© Springer-Verlag Berlin Heidelberg 2002

field by using results in the structural computing field and support cooperation on hypermedia documents. In this context, Haake and Wilson propose an approach based on the technologies of hypertext systems, computer networks, and database management systems to support collaborative writing of hyperdocuments in SEPIA[8]. We can also develop the CSCW domain as an application of the structural computing field. For example Haake proposes in [7] to model coordination task with a structural computing approach. In addition, we can develop the hypermedia field by using results in the CSCW field and support cooperation in open hypermedia systems. This work takes place in this context. Indeed, we aim to combine the CSCW field and the structural computing field by supporting cooperation services in open hypermedia systems and developing a proof-of-concept implementation of theses services in The Construct System [14]. This position paper constitutes a first step toward this target. We propose here some services to support mainly asynchronous and informal cooperation in a structural computing environment.

This paper proposes a session management service and an awareness service within the Construct structural computing environment. The paper proceeds with an overview of the Construct system in the following section. In Section 3, a scenario of cooperative interaction in an architectural design project is presented. This scenario is used in order to identify the need for supporting cooperation services in the Construct system. The integration of the cooperation services into the Construct system is discussed in Section 4. We present also in this section the design of the cooperation services and we provide their IDL interfaces. Section 5 concludes this paper and presents a brief summary of the future work.

2   The Construct System

The Construct system is a structural computing environment based on previous open hypermedia system research efforts that focused on the provision of infrastructure services. In the Construct system, services are decomposed into chunks that can be used independently of one another [14]. Figure 1 presents the architecture of this system. Mainly, we distinguish three layers: applications layer, structure services layer, and foundation services layer. Services belong to a layer depending on the type of service they provide. The system is designed in order to allow each layer to be open to new services. It consists of different categories of software components: Applications, Wrapper services, Structure services, and Foundation services.

The application category includes desktop applications (*e.g.*, Netscape, MS Word, and Emacs). These applications are integrated (modified, extended, or wrapped) in the Construct environment. Integrated applications can make use of different types of structure services to organize data located in data stores. Each type of structure service provides a different set of structural abstractions (*e.g.*, navigational, metadata, taxonomic, and argumentation) that support different application domains. The structure services depend on the very basic services provided by the foundation services.

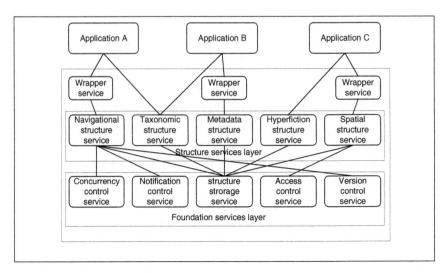

Fig. 1. Conceptual overview of the Construct system

3   Scenario

An important application area to which the Construct system can be applied is the support of CSCW applications. Indeed, the system approach to provide infrastructure services is well suited to the provision of facilities to support cooperation. In addition, the system supports the integration of information across several applications and hypermedia domain boundaries, which constitutes a good foundation for data sharing and cooperation. To find out the capabilities of the Construct system to support cooperation, we analyze in the following a case study from the domain of architectural design and building construction. This case study has been done in a research project involving France Télécom, the ECOO[1] research team and the CRAI[2] research team.

Assume that in a given architectural design project there are three cooperating partners: an architect, an engineer, and an economist. The architect is the person responsible for the production of the final plan of the building and all of the related documents. However, the engineer can be in charge of some parts of this plan or of some technical details. All along the design process, the economist produces cost estimations corresponding to the current version of the plan. The architect reads these cost estimations in order to check the compatibility of the project with the budget conditions.

---

[1] Environments for COOperation, see http://www.loria.fr/equipes/ecoo/english/ for more detail.

[2] Research Center in Architecture and Engineering (Centre de Recherche en Architecture et Ingénierie), for more detail see
http://www.crai.archi.fr/Cadres/_Presentation.html.

In Figure 2, we present an example of a cooperative interaction scenario, within a UML interaction diagram, involving the architect, the engineer, and the economist within the Construct system. First of all, the architect creates the plan using the store service (a foundation service). After that, s/he creates metadata using the metadata service (a structure service) for this plan that will later be used by the engineer to perform her/his work. Indeed, this metadata may represent some rules (representing some technique choices or the sketch of the plan) established by the architect (the person responsible for the plan design) that will be followed by the engineer in her/his work.

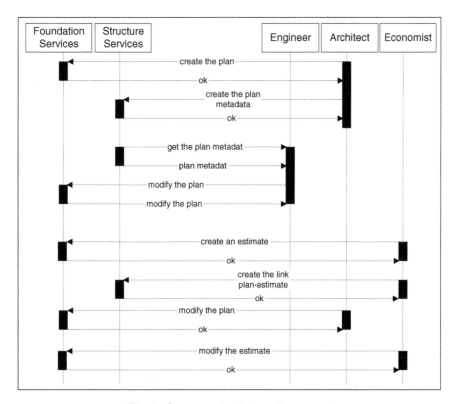

Fig. 2. A cooperative interaction scenario

During the process of the plan design, the economist has to produce estimates of the building construction cost corresponding to the current plan. For this reason, s/he has first to create the estimate using the store service and after s/he has to link this estimation to the plan. She/He uses for that the navigational structure service.

By analyzing this scenario, we have found mainly two insufficiencies in the Construct services in supporting cooperation.

- When the architect or the engineer changes the plan, the economist has to (must) be made aware about this modification in order to update her/his estimate. So the Construct system needs for that an awareness service, which allows the different cooperating partners to be aware of the current status and the activity of others. This service will act as an integrating mechanism by allowing cooperating partners to talk to each other, discuss, show results and update them.
- The architect and the economist on one hand and the architect and the engineer on the other hand constitute two cooperating groups with different relationships and goals. So the Construct system needs for that a session service, which allows the separation of the cooperation into two cooperation types in two cooperation contexts (i.e. two sessions). The session service will create and manage sessions and allow cooperating partners to start, stop, join, leave, and browse them.

In the following, we present the design of the session and awareness services that we call cooperation services.

4   Cooperation Services Design

To support the type of cooperation examined in this paper, we have found the need of services to manage cooperative sessions and group awareness. In addition, we think that the Construct system needs also a service that provides naming facilities. Indeed, this service will associate construct components with names. The naming facilities are necessary especially in cooperation situations, which can involve several applications and consequently several services. When, for instance a new service is added to the system, without hard coding this service can subscribe within the naming service and can be used by applications.

4.1   Cooperation Services Integration

Depending on the type of service they provide, new Construct services are integrated in the structure services layer or in the foundation services layer. To integrate cooperation services into the Construct system, a question arises: should these new services be integrated into the foundation or the structure services layer or do we need a new layer for them?

We can integrate cooperation services into the foundation services. This eventuality enforces the openness criterion of the Construct system. Indeed, if the cooperation services are foundation services, each time that we integrate a new structure service, it can be used in a cooperative application that uses the existing service without altering or changing any service. Nevertheless, the Construct service cannot support in this case the cooperation within one service. For example, to support cooperative applications using the navigational service, this later have to used by several cooperations actors and consequently have to be used by the cooperation services. If the cooperation services are in an underlying layer the Construct system can not the cooperation within one service.

Although it is clear that cooperation services are not of the foundation services type, it is not clear that they are of the structure services type.

We can integrate cooperation services into the structure services layer considering the facts that they use the foundation services. For instance:

- The session service uses the store service to save objects representing session information (session name, online users, etc.) and uses the access control service to control whenever a user can join a session.
- The awareness service uses the notification control service to get and set events representing the activities that the cooperating users perform.

We can also create a new layer (cooperation services layer, see Figure 3) considering the fact that cooperation services use the structure services and so have to be in a higher layer. Indeed, in cooperation, users work together on shared objects and use for that several services within a session. In this context the session service can use all structure services. Although the question of the integration position of cooperation services in the Construct system still remains, we present in the following the design and the IDL specifications of the naming, the session management and the awareness services.

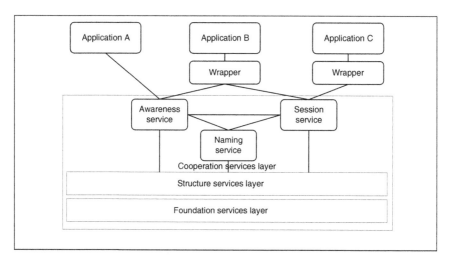

Fig. 3. Construct conceptual architecture with cooperation services layer

4.2 Naming Service

The Construct naming service allows services to locate other construct components by a user definable name. The system allows associating an object (i.e. a user, a group, a structural service, a foundation service) with a name. Once the name is associated with the object, any Construct service or application can access the object through the name.

The naming service is both very simple and very useful. It is simple because it just maps Construct object references and abstract names. New services can be registered with the naming service and so can be used by Construct services and applications.

The IDL specification of this service is given below.

```
interface Naming{
        void register(in Namingable object);
        void remove(in string name);
        Namingable lookup(in string name);
};

interface Namingable{
        string getName();
};
```

4.3   Session Management Service

A session is a context allowing cooperative users to start, stop, join, leave, and browse collaborative situations across the network [10]. Within a session, users can connect from various locations to the structural computing environment in order to work together on shared artifacts such as a white board and use multimedia conferencing tools to communicate. The context of a text document being edited within a shared editor and a video conference among a number of participants are examples of sessions.

In order to create sessions and allow users to work within sessions, the structural computing environment needs a service to manage sessions. A session management service determines the way in which the users of a cooperative application join together into a collaborative endeavor [2]. The major functions of this service are the session information management and the command management. In the following, we describe broadly these functions and we give their IDL specifications. We describe, after that, the interaction of the session management service with other Construct services.

Session Information Management. The session information management function creates sessions and updates information within active sessions. A simplified IDL specification of this function is given below. Among other things, the session information management manages the list of online users working in a given session: adds/removes users to/from a given session

```
interface SessionInformationManager{
        attribute string name;
        attribute Vector onlineUsers;
        string getName();
```

```
        void setName(in string newname);
        void addOnlineUser(in string name);
        void removeOnlineUser(in string name);
        Vector getOnlineUsers(in string group);
        Vector getAllOnlineUsers();
        void close();
};
```

Command Management. The command management function opens and closes sessions. It allows users to log in and log out and provides to the logged in users facilities to execute commands on shared data using any structural service in the Construct system. The IDL specification of this function is given below.

```
interface CommandManager{
    string create();
    void close(in string name);
    void login(in string name,in string password,
               in string group, in string session);
    void logout(in string name, in string session);
    void handle(in Command cmd, in string session);
};
```

Interacting Services. The session management service depends on some services within the structural computing environment.

Foundation services: Like almost all Construct services, the session management service depends on the store service. In fact, the store service is used to save objects representing session information (session names, online users, etc.) and Construct services, which are used to execute users' commands. In addition, the session service may use the store service to keep user preferences, personal data, application defaults, etc. In order to control session accesses, the session management service uses the access control service. In fact, it controls whenever a user has the permission to create or join sessions, to issue commands or to get the online users in a given session.

Naming service: The session management service depends on the naming service. This later is used to select users and groups and to select and to locate Construct services (that the session service may use to execute users' commands).

Other Construct services: To allow users to work together on shared objects using several Construct services, the session management service interacts with all structural services. It sends commands that will be handled by these services.

4.4   Awareness Management Service

In cooperative systems, users can be distributed in space, in time, and even over organizations. To interact effectively they need means that allow them to be aware of others: who is doing what? Coworkers need to be aware of the current status and the activity of others. For them, the awareness acts as an "integrating framework" by allowing them to talk to each other, discuss, show results and update them. The need of supporting awareness in cooperative applications has been identified in several works. Some applications that support awareness include Quilt [5] and GROVE [4] that are summarized in [1].

The term awareness has a common usage to indicate mindfulness, or being conscious of surroundings, situations, or other people. Since the literature has not set a technical definition of the term awareness, we can, like in [3], present a definition based on separating the concept into two components, which have been investigated in the literature:

- Presence and location of coworkers
- Previous and current tasks

To detect the presence and the location of coworkers and determine the previous and the current tasks, we propose here a Construct service based on the naming, session, and notification Construct services. For instance, using the naming service and the operation getOnlineUsers of the session service the Construct awareness service can locate the online users. In addition using the notification Construct service, the awareness service can get the posted messages reflecting the activity of coworkers.

The IDL specification of this service is given below.

```
interface awareness{
      attribute java::util::Vector members;
      attribute java::util::Vector memberLevels;
      int getMemberLevel(in string member);
      void setMemberLevel(in string member, in int level);
      void postEvent(in string initiatorMember, in int prefix,
                       in string message, in int memberlevel);
      Vector getLoggedEventsPrefix(in int prefix);
      Vector getLoggedEventsMember(in string initiatormember);
      Vector getLoggedEventsLevel(in int level);
   };
```

5   Conclusion and Future Work

We have proposed in this paper a session management service and an awareness service and we have integrated them in the Construct structural computing environment. We think that this constitutes a first step toward the development of cooperation services and consequently toward supporting cooperation within the Construct system.

At present, we have implemented the awareness service as well as an awareness tool allowing each user to see, according to her/his awareness level, the services other users are using and events about operations they are performing.

The user can also set her/his awareness level and get events about operations that other users have performed before her/his login. The user can in addition send/receive messages to/from other users. We think that this allows cooperating users to maintain awareness of each other.

The session management and the awareness services can support a large number of cooperation types, especially those based on social protocol cooperation. Nevertheless, we need to extend this work in order to support more formal cooperation, allowing users to specify their roles and cooperation policies [12]. This is important especially in cooperation involving a large number of users and handling a large amount of data. It is also useful in this case to establish constraints for the cooperation to guide it to the common users' goal. To do that, we plan to integrate into the Construct structural computing environment a cooperation policy service based on the access control foundation service to support users' roles and also based on a synchronization foundation service to support cooperation constraints.

References

1. P. Dourish and V. Bellotti. Awareness and coordination in shared work space. In *Proceedings of the ACM Conference on Computer Supported Cooperative Work*, pages 51–58, Toronto, Canada, November 1992.

2. W. K. Edwards. Session management in collaborative applications. In *Proceedings of the ACM Conference on Computer Supported Cooperative Work*, pages 332–330, Chapel Hill, October 1994.

3. W. K. Edwards. *Coordination Infrastructure in Collaborative Systems*. PhD thesis, Georgia Institute of Technology, College of Computing, Atlanta, GA, December 1995.

4. C. A Ellis, A. Gibbs, and G. Rein. Groupware: some issues and experiences. *Communications of the ACM*, 34(1):38–58, 1994.

5. R. S. Fish, R. E. Kraut, , and M. P. Leland. Quilt: A collaborative tool for cooperative writing. In *Proceedings of the Conference on Office Automation Systems, Collaborative Work*, pages 30–37, 1988.

6. K. Gronbek, J. A. Hem, O. L. Madsen, and L. Sloth. Cooperative hyper-media systems: A dexter-based architecture. *Communications of the ACM*, 37(2):64–74, February 1994.

7. J. M. Haake. Structural computing in the collaborative work domain. In *Proceedings of the 2nd International Workshop on Structural computing*, San Antonio, Texas, USA, May/June 2000.

8. J. M. Haake and B. Wilson. Supporting collaborative writing of hyperdocuments in sepia. In *Proceedings of the ACM Conference on Computer Supported Cooperative Work*, pages 138–146, Toronto, Canada, October 1992.

9. D. L. Hicks and U. K. Wiil. Towards collaborative design in an open hypermedia environment. In *Proceedings of the Sixth International Conference on CSCW in Design*, London, Ontario, Canada, July 2001.

10. R. D. Hill, T. Brink, F. Patterson, S. L. Rohall, and Winter.W. T. The rendezvous language and architecture. *Communication of the ACM*, 36(1):62–67, January 1993.

11. P. J. Nurnberg, J. J. Leggett, E. Schneider, and J. Schnase. Hoss: A new paradigm for computing. In *Proceedings of the 2001 ACM Conference on Hypertext*, Washington, DC, March 1996.

12. S. Tata, G. Canals, and C. Godart. Specifying interactions in cooperative applications. In *Proceedings of the 11th International Conference on Software Engineering and Knowledge Engineering*, Kaiserslautern, Germany, June 199.

13. U. K. Wiil and J. J. Leggett. The hyperdisco approach to internet distribution. In *the 1997 ACM Hypertext Conference*, pages 13–23, Southampton, UK, April 1997.

14. U. K. Wiil, D. L. Hicks, and P. J. Nurnberg. Multiple open services: A new approach to service provision in open hypermedia systems. In *Proceedings of the 2001 ACM Conference on Hypertext*, Arhus, Denmark, August 2001.

Structural Computing and Its Relationships to Other Fields

Peter J. Nürnberg[1] and Monica M.C. Schraefel[2]

[1] Department of Computer Science, Aalborg University Esbjerg
Niels Bohrs Vej 8, DK-6700 Esbjerg, Denmark
pnuern@cs.aue.auc.dk
http://cs.aue.auc.dk/
[2] Department of Computer Science, University of Toronto
Toronto, ON, Canada M5S 3G4
mc@dgp.toronto.edu
http://cs.toronto.edu/

Abstract. We briefly describe the field of structural computing as it relates to a number of other pursuits. By doing this, we identify issues that are under- or misrepresented in other research areas – issues that we feel may form the beginnings of a core research agenda for structural computing. We also feel this exercise points to natural academic allies of the structural computing field – people and ideas who can inform our work, and with whom we may be able to share our ideas.

1 Introduction

Structural computing still feels like a new field. In fact, though, it's been four years since the term first appeared in print. There have been two previous workshops on the topic, each motivating many more papers on the subject. The field still feels young partly because there is as of yet no unifying vision or research agenda to tie together the disparate work done under the label "structural computing".

In this paper, we make a first attempt at defining such a research agenda. We do so by comparing structural computing against a number of other pursuits, trying to help "negatively define" our field by pointing out the ways in which it differs from more established or better known areas. Specifically, below, we differentiate structural computing from a more traditional notion of hypertext, the recent W3C "semantic web" initiative, Will et al.'s notion of multiple open services, and structuralism. We use this to "stake a claim" to important questions that we feel are underrepresented in other areas, and use these as seed material for our own research agenda. We hope that this exercise can help bring together structural computing work, and point out synergies that have so far remained untapped. Also, along the way, we raise issues concerning our community and how to further our goals.

S. Reich, M.M. Tzagarakis, P.M.E. De Bra (Eds.): OHS/SC/AH 2001, LNCS 2266, pp. 183–193, 2002.
© Springer-Verlag Berlin Heidelberg 2002

2   Structural Computing and Hypertext

Structural computing has most often been closely associated to hypertext[1] by most people, and with good reason. Structural computing was first billed as a "generalization" of hypertext – a bringing together of various applications of hypertext under one umbrella.

As has already been discussed at length at the SC1 and SC2 workshops, this has greater implications than simply accommodating various structural models. Structural computing environments require more flexible and generic infrastructure to support an open set of models. Whereas hypertext environments can (and often do) offer highly specific and optimized infrastructure functionality (e.g., database tables optimized for link resolution), structural computing environments have not yet been able to do so. The optimizations possible in hypertext environments seem to limit the generality of their infrastructure.

Another important idea is that hypertext, for wide-ranging reasons, has become popularized. This is not necessarily a bad thing, but it does have consequences. Hypertext is a term that has been appropriated (or misappropriated) by many different people with many different agendas. This means the term itself has become increasingly blurry. Its popular usage may not correspond to any traditional usages. In fact, the meaning of the word may be changed by others as they seek to carry out particular programs. This is most clear on the critical theory front, in which hypertext has been appropriated by critics seeking an embodiment of modern critical thought. Hypertext as postmodern technology is a siren song to many theorists, even though recent discussions at ACM Hypertext conferences by less programmatic (and younger) critics have questioned this idea. Nonetheless, hypertext, for better or worse, is seen by many as affiliated with a set of particular theoretical programs. Structural computing, conversely, is not yet popularized. We still have our pick of allies. (We visit some of these potential allies in sections below.)

2.1   What Is the Generic Structural Abstraction?

This question was posed very early on in the structural computing line of work, but has not since been addressed. If structural computing infrastructure should support an open set of structural abstractions, what abstraction(s) should be made available by the infrastructure? A related issue concerns the relationship between data and structure. Is structure a "superclass" of data, or just a peer? Structural computing has asserted the former, but how can we show this to be true (or untrue)? Is this even demonstrable? We examine some of the philosophical implications of generic abstractions (as fundamental) below.

---

[1] We understand the terms "hypertext" and "hypermedia" to be interchangeable.

2.2   How Can Infrastructure Performance Be Optimized with Generic Abstractions?

If structural computing infrastructures support generic abstractions, how can they achieve efficiencies similar to the highly optimized infrastructures of modern hypertext environments? At first, this seems to be impossible – optimizations based on semantics of structural elements (something of which the infrastructure is not normally aware) would seem to violate the layering of typical structural computing architectures? Are there other approaches? Wiil and Hicks have recently begun to discuss alternatives to layered architectures [personal communication]. Can other such architectures help structural computing architects to deliver efficient infrastructure services?

2.3   How Can Interoperability Be Supported?

Interoperability has meanings specific to structural computing environments. Since open sets of structural abstractions may exist within such environments, "mapping strategies" for interoperability that may be appropriate in more limited hypertext environments may fail for us. Interoperability is not simply a desirable trait for structural computing environments – it is a necessary characteristic. By this, we mean not only inter-system interoperability (supporting a plug-and-play metaphor, whereby services from one environment can interact with services and applications from another), but also intra-system interoperability (supporting a way structures and behaviors from one service can be used by another service). Anderson has presented intriguing work in this direction [2]. Tzagarakis has recently begun to discuss specialized structure-oriented dynamic service discovery [personal communication]. Can this be a starting point for general structural interoperability? Have we even begun to think about interoperating behaviors?

2.4   How Do We Make Connections to Other Academics in Related Fields?

Many of the challenges we discuss above are difficult. However, we may be able to benefit from work in such fields as operating systems, programming language design, middleware and client/server systems, and distributed computing. How can we benefit from this related work? How can we draw in people from these other fields? For instance, similar work on multiple structures can be found in the Intensional Programming Language community, which proposes an intensional approach, to the practical problems of software version control [21] and hypertext version control [23]. Do we reach out specifically to these researchers and ask them to engage with us in our key questions? If so, do we provide a forum (at the next workshop) specifically for these replies?

2.5 Should We Move the Venue for the Workshop?

Despite the fact that structural computing was "born" in the hypertext community, we may want to consider moving the venue of future SC workshops. The hypertext research community has, broadly speaking, moved in different directions, away from embracing open structural computing environments and opening dialogs with a variety of other fields (technical and non-technical) towards narrowly Web-focused applications and further elucidation of hypertext's connection to postmodern critical theory. Is this the best community for us?

3 Structural Computing and the Semantic Web

A semantic web (as described by Nelson, and recapped in the W3C's use of his Scientific America article [5]) proposes to let web pages continue to be web pages – that is to appear semi-structured in database terms, but to be at least tagged structurally behind the scenes. Such tagging will allow dynamic structures to be built across a heterogeneous web space in order to address complex user queries, such as "where did David get his PhD." The glue for such queries across multiple, heterogeneous sites consists of ontologies. An example of an ontological system for a semantic web can be found at [17].

It may be tempting to view the relation between semantic webs and structural computing as a special case of the relationship between information retrieval and hypertext. Information retrieval is geared to automatic processing, whereas hypertext is geared to structures authored and browsed by people. Structural computing was born of hypertext work, whereas semantic webs, with their focus on ontological support, may be seen as a descendent of information retrieval. And yet, the semantic web work claims still to be positioned as a hypertext. However, we see the the semantic web view of hypertext as impoverished and, ultimately, tied to popular notions of hypertext that do not reflect the technology or approach traditionally associated with hypertext. Rather than retrieving a single answer, a semantic web may retrieve a possible hypertext that can be refined, argued with, contain links for further discovery. And yet, in the semantic web work, the emphasis has been on retrieving the "one effective answer" to complex queries, rather than constructions of hypertexts. We see this as a very "data first" approach in which the web becomes structurable source material for the ontologically stitched-together query across heterogeneous data spaces.

In any event, this view may be overly simplistic. While structural computing was indeed born of hypertext, it has gone farther in discussing general structure. While we have often understood this to mean "general hypertext structure", there is no reason why we should limit ourselves in this way. Nürnberg et al. [18] point to a variety of non-hypertext structural possibilities (e.g., conceptualizing "make" or "cron" as structure services, building structure-aware kernels, etc.) Structural computing may most properly be viewed as being just as concerned with automatic, machine-processable structures (e.g., the ontologies of semantic webs) as with hypertext structures.

3.1 Can Structural Computing Environments Support Semantic Webs, Information Retrieval, and/or Other "Machine-Processable" Structures?

Is a semantic web most properly seen as a potential application (and/or set of middleware services) for structural computing environments? Are our environments able to provide specialized support for semantic web work? How about other structures from fields like information retrieval or databases. There appear to be recent developments in these directions. Arotaritei et al. have begun discussing using Construct to support data mining services [personal communication]. Wiil et al. [25] describe using Construct to support traditional metadata services. Can we build upon these early ideas? These issues are probably tightly bound to the efficiency issues described above (see Sec. 2).

3.2 How Should We Repackage Our Work as More General Infrastructure?

We have been ineffective in selling the structural computing work outside of the hypertext and digital libraries communities. How can we begin to disseminate our work outside of these limited areas? Should we as a workshop community form a plan for which communities to target next? Anderson [1] has discussed exporting structural computing technologies to the software engineering communities extensively. Wang and Haake [24] have described connections between structural computing and computer supported collaborative work. How can we leverage these footholds? Also, how can we draw in people from these fields to our workshop to help inform our work?

4 Structural Computing and Multiple Open Services

Wiil [26] posed a challenge to the structural computing community at the very first SC workshop – is structural computing simply a special case of the multiple open service approach to service provision? Discussions at that workshop did not resolve this challenge. Here, we look more closely at the relationship between these endeavors.

The primary determining architectural characteristic of structural computing environments versus traditional hypertext environments was the radical middleware layer openness – an architectural axiom that structural abstractions comprise an unbounded set, and so, therefore, do structural services. Wiil claimed that multiple open services generalizes structural computing. In what way can this be understood?

One possible interpretation is that multiple open services stresses openness at the infrastructure layer as well as the middleware (and client) layer(s). This objection seems reasonable, at least inasmuch as openness at this level is in fact not stressed in structural computing work (although it clearly is a part of existing structural computing systems, such as Callimachus [8] or Construct [27].

Indeed, in [25], Construct is used to illustrate the multiple open services concept.) Nonetheless, the multiple open services approach does make more explicit its radical infrastructure openness. Also, there is explicit mention of integration of development tools into the environments they help develop – a "bootstrapping" focus not explicitly present in structural computing work to this point.

However, we believe the intended objection goes to the heart of seeing services that are unspecified (as they are in the multiple open services conceptualization) as a generalization of services that are structural. Stated in this way, the point seems to be axiomatic. This, we believe, is the crux of the claim made by Wiil.

The error in this conceptualization, however, is in this very seemingly axiomatic formulation. Structural services are not a subset of services in general, as, in principle, they are not concrete instances of services per se, but conceptualizations of services in general. The structural computing theoretical argument is that *any* service is better seen (and treated) as a structural services regardless of implementation. Thus, any service admitted by a multiple open services environment (or any service in general) is also admitted by an structural computing environment. It is this reconceptualization that is at the heart of structural computing.

4.1   Are There Examples of Truly Non-structural Services?

The gauntlet has been thrown down. The claim that all services, regardless of implementation, are better viewed as structural services, is now on the table. Is this true? Or, are there in fact services that suffer from a structural recasting? Disproving the hypothesis should be straightforward enough, provided we can define what it means to "reconceptualize" a service in structural terms. This issue is intimately related to the nature of the "generic" structural abstraction discussed above (see Sec. 2).

4.2   How Do We Leverage the Multiple Open Service Insights?

How can we take (co-opt?) the work at the lowest levels of architectures stressed in the multiple open service work? Although not discussed in [25], one could argue that a multiple open service environment is more naturally modeled with a non-layered architecture. (In fact, the notion of layer is rather muddled in the current multiple open service literature – this may point to the fact that it may be largely unnecessary or even harmful.) If multiple open service work does break the layer model, can adopting the multiple open service approach to infrastructure and development tools, with its architectural implications, inform our previously mentioned inquiry into infrastructure optimization?

5   Structural Computing and Structuralism

In previous work [19], the potential relation of Structuralism to structural computing was touched upon. The question was raised as to whether or not structural computing should be reframed as structuralist computing. We would like to say "No" for the time being, due to the rationalization for the structuralist project across linguistics, psychology, philosophy, narratology or any other discipline that claims a structuralist approach. That is, structuralism is in pursuit, as mentioned in [20], of "laws" or foundational structures through which understanding can be known and discovered. These laws take the form of discovered structures or "transformations ... inherent in the object" [14] which can refer to an innate or even genetic source through which we can understand ourselves. Even Chomsky's transformational grammars refer back to a Cartesian "innate rationality." As such, structuralism seems, to put it over-simply, rather deterministic. This innate determinism is something with which the existentialists, contemporaries of high structuralists, took great issue.[2]

5.1   Look for the Irony

We, too, take issue with this determinism, if for different reasons than the existentialists. It does not seem that the goal of SC (at least at this point, and perhaps at no point) is to attempt to claim that we can, through the experimental Structure First model of SC, and its investigation of the way we build computational architectures, determine an innate understanding of Who We Are, fundamentally, as a species (or how we are, Structuralism might suggest, programmed to be). Let us suppose, however, that the models we choose do tell us something about ourselves here and now, rather than ultimately. We would therefore suggest that, perhaps rather than Structuralism, our project is better aligned with Irony as conceptualized in Donna Haraway's "Cyborg Manifesto" [12]. Haraway suggests that the Cyborg knows that its identity is constructed socially, physically and temporally rather than "naturally." There is a (potentially dark) ironic ambiguity in the awareness between what is constructed in the Cyborg and what is assumed to be natural or historical. By challenging the primacy of Data in the Data/Structure pair, we introduce this kind of irony that allows us to question the implications, beyond architecture, of designing architectures from this perspective.

5.2   What Was the Question?

Structural computing's willingness to foreground the relation of structure to data creates a place to discuss the philosophy of computation or the political science of computational models. (We use the term "science" with respect to its Latin origins as "knowledge", not as objectivity or absolutism.) Some may suggest that these discussions have taken place in hypertext for some time. We would like to suggest that they have, but have been geared to a particular audience and from a particular audience – namely, literary critics who have found the pleasure of the

---

[2] The reader is invited to look at the history of philosophy with respect to the ongoing antagonism and animosity between Levi-Strauss and Lacan's Structuralism and Sartre and de Beauvoir's Existentialism. For a cogent discussion and critique of these relations, see [7] and [16].

(hyper)text [4] in a mainly post-modern way, and, understandably, at the surface of the media, in its textual presentation and interaction rhetoric. The Structure and Data pairing, however, also raise distinct questions at the architectural and system level. These questions are interesting to consider from an engineering context and are raised by structural computing's attempts to shift the focus of computing from Data to Structure. What are the implications for computing (and beyond) from such a shift? Why are they worth considering?

Marx proposed a consideration of work and work relations to capital as the site of profound social investigation [15] (see also [22], e.g. pp. 443-465)[3]. We propose that the philosophical consideration of structural computing may also act as a site of, if not profound social investigation, at least a more foregrounded investigation into our own practices, assumptions and their consequences, once we consider that engineering is not innocent (not distinct from other cultural practices), nor our approaches absolute. What are the biases and beliefs that both inform our technology and are created by that technology? Ursala Franklin, a renowned metallurgist, defined technology as "Practice," as a "Way of Doing Things" [11]; and, that we are identified as belonging or not to a particular group based on our technology, on how we do things.

Structural computing suggests a new practice with respect to the relation of structure and data, and in Franklin's sense, therefore, proposes a new technology. We are fortunate that while in the process of creating that technology, we are reflecting on the implications of its definition. The questions we can ask, therefore, concern why we think that the shift to Structure First will be "better" than the Data First approach. We do not have proof yet that such is the case, but we have experiments we wish to try to demonstrate the value of this approach at least in certain contexts. However, we should not dismiss the potential profundity that such a shift may imply at the more general levels of our technology, our practice, in pursuing such an approach. We don't pretend to have yet worked out all the implications of this shift, but we would like to mention one in particular for further consideration: the relation of structural computing to Structuralism. We will then get more practical, in terms of how this approach might be applied for its functional efficacy to be evaluated.

5.3   What Is Implicit in the Structure/Data Pair?

So let us put the question again, perhaps in a more deconstructionist[4] way: what happens when we challenge the primacy of Data over Structure by inverting the

---

[3] Marx is also frequently considered part of the Structuralist way, since his work is often seen to remove human action (and history) from impact on the system. This determinism, however, is a site of regular controversy among branches of Marxist thought, such as Marxist Feminism and the Frankfurt school. A valuable overview of Marxism is available in [6].

[4] It seems relevant if beyond the scope of the paper to dwell on the differences between post-structuralism and deconstruction. Again, to oversimplify, post-structuralism, as embodied in Barthes *S/Z* [3] foregrounds how one can continue to define not one but multiple structures from any proposed ultimate structure. Deconstruction, on

pair to say structure should lead, or at least become on the same level as data? That data does not determine structure, but structure data? Are we making structure data-like, or data a lower class form of structure? Or something else? And if any of these, therefore what are the costs to the model of computer science that foregrounds Data rather than Structure? A more Marxist-informed question about the shift may ask, whose interests are being served by redefining these relations?

In the interim, one practical, lower level effect may be to provide a rationale to eliminate fixed markup in a hypertext. In a sense, the semantic web is heading in this direction in terms of data-based queries across heterogeneous sites, where markup's role is semantic rather than presentational. Structural computing suggests that even semantic markup needs to be considered as contextual, to be determined by the structure to represent that data at any time.

The shift from Data to Structure problematizes models of representation and perhaps notions of originality, so germane to discussions of intellectual property in the digital domain. That is, in the Structure First model, does data become seen as a kind of neutral receptor of multiple structures (and therefore, sampling and recontextualization are where the IP is, rather than in any single contextualization of the data), rather than something that is simply inseparable from structure? If the former, it would seem then that data becomes almost atomistic, pre-existing structure, and therefore primary again (a sort of structural linguistics-like position). If the latter, then at least we recognize that data and structure are toujours deja implicated in each other. As such, if data becomes the "simpler case" of dealing with structure in a computational model, the corollary of this means that structure is always present. Data is not structure neutral, not atomistic. This constant implied relation of structure and data is as close as structural computing may come to a Structuralist perspective of the system informing relations within the system. We resist the next step which would suggest that the structures we discover or models we build are fundamental. After all, the relation of structure and data is itself a constructed relation and we are just as interested in the implications of that construction as the effects of its inversion.

6   Conclusions

In the above sections, we have attempted to suggest what we are about by at least delineating some of what we are not. Within these anti-definitions, we have also postulated where we can look for near-future application challenges (a standard research agenda). We have also considered how we might meet those challenges by establishing clearer ties with related approaches (a meta-agenda).

---

the other hand, as reflected in Derrida's *Of Grammatology* [9], or more briefly in his article "Structure, Sign, Play," [10] is focused on oppositions proposed by any approach – Good/Evil; Speech/Writing – and uses those to undo the assumptions which hold one part of the pair in primacy over the other. In our case this would be Data/Structure.

Structural computing has echoes in other areas of computing and philosophy, only some of which are touched upon above. Part of our goal of course should be not to reinvent the wheel. Therefore, we need to be interdisciplinary in our approach to develop structural computing as school of thought and as technology. Part of our mandate must be to reach out beyond our group to research (and researchers) in these other domains to critique, inform and enrich our practice. We deliberately seek consultation and collaboration with these other areas. By this, we make our practice potentially more deliberately socially constructed.

Similarly, we are aware that at this point we seem to have more questions than answers, but we believe that the questions are valuable and have the potential to create both effective models for improved computational delivery of information and potentially new ways of interpreting computational practice.

References

1. Anderson, Kenneth M.: Software engineering requirements for structural computing. Proceedings of the Workshop on Structural Computing (SC1) (Darmstadt, Germany, Feb 1999). Available in technical report AUE-CS-99-04 (Aalborg University Esbjerg, Denmark) at `http://cs.aue.auc.dk/publications/`
2. Anderson, Kenneth M.: Structural computing requirements for the transformation of structures and behaviors. Proceeding of the Second workshop on Structural Computing (SC2) (San Antonio, TX, May 2000). Lecture Notes in Computer Science vol. 1903. Springer-Verlag, Berlin
3. Barthes, Roland: S/Z. (trans. Richard Miller). Hill and Wang, New York (1974)
4. Barthes, Roland: The Pleasure of the Text. Hill and Wang, New York (1975)
5. Berners-Lee, Tim, Hendler James, Lassila, Ora: The Semantic Web. Scientific American (May 2001). Available at `http://www.scientificamerican.com/2001/0501issue/0501berners-lee.html`
6. Bottomore, Tom (ed.): A Dictionary of Marxist thought (2nd ed.) Blackwell, Oxford, Cambridge (1991)
7. Brodribb, Somer: Nothing Mat(t)ers: a Feminist Critique of Postmodernism. Spinifex Press, North Melbourne (1992)
8. Christodoulakis, Dimitris, Vaitis, Michael, Papadopoulos, Athanasios, Tzagarakis, Manolis: The Callimachus approach to distributed hypermedia. Proceedings of Tenth ACM Conference on Hypertext and Hypermedia (HT '99) (Darmstadt, Germany, Feb). ACM Press, New York
9. Derrida, Jacques: Of Grammatology. (trans. Gayatri Spivak). Johns Hopkins University Press, Baltimore (1976)
10. Derrida, Jacques: Structure Sign and Play. Writing and Difference. University of Chicago Press, Chicago (1978)
11. Franklin, Ursala: The Real World of Technology. CBC Massey Lectures Series. (Revised Edition) Anasasi Press, Toronto (1999)
12. Haraway, Donna: A cyborg manifesto: science, technology, and socialist-feminism in the late twentieth century. In Simians, Cyborgs and Women: The Reinvention of Nature. Routledge, New York (1991) 149-181
13. Innes, Paul: Structuralism. A Dictionary of Cultural and Critical Theory. (ed. Michael Payne). Blackwell Publishing, Oxford (1997) 513-517
14. Lévi-Strauss, Claude: Structural Anthropology. Basic Books (1963)

15. Marx, Karl: Das Kapital. (vol. 1 – A Critique of Political Economy). (trans. Ben Fowkes). Penguin/New Left Review, London (1990)
16. Moi, Toril: Simone de Beauvoir: The Making of an Intellectual Woman. Blackwell, Oxford Cambridge (1994)
17. Miles-Board, Timothy, Kampa, Simon, Carr, Leslie, Hall, Wendy: Hypertext in the Semantic Web. Proceedings of the Twelfth ACM Conference on Hypertext and Hypermedia (HT '01) (Århus, Denmark, Aug). ACM Press, New York
18. Nürnberg, Peter J., Leggett, John J., Schneider, Erich R.: HOSS: A new paradigm for computing. Proceedings of Seventh ACM Conference on Hypertext and Hypermedia (HT '96) (Washington, DC, Mar). ACM Press, New York
19. Nürnberg, Peter J.: Repositioning structural computing. Proceedings of the Second Workshop on Structural Computing (SC2) (San Antonio, TX, May 2001). Lecture Notes in Computer Science vol. 1903. Springer-Verlag, Berlin
20. Piaget, Jean: Le Structuralisme. Que sais je. Onzième édition. Presse Universitaires de France, Paris (1996)
21. Plaice, J., Wadge, W. W.: A new approach to version control. IEEE Transactions on Software Engineering (Mar 1993) 268-276
22. Tucker, Robert C. (ed.): The Marx-Engels Reader. Norton, New York (1978)
23. Wadge, W. W., Brown, G., schraefel, m. c., Yildirim, T.: Intensional HTML. Proceedings of the 4th International Workshop (PODDP '98). Lecture Notes in Computer Science vol. 1481. Springer Verlag, Berlin 128-139
24. Wang, Weigang, Haake, Jörg M.: Supporting workflow using the open hypermedia approach. Proceedings of the Workshop on Structural Computing (SC1) (Darmstadt, Germany, Feb 1999). Available in technical report AUE-CS-99-04 (Aalborg University Esbjerg, Denmark) at http://cs.aue.auc.dk/publications/
25. Wiil, Uffe K., Hicks, David L., Nürnberg, Peter J.: Multiple open services: A new approach to service provision in open hypermedia systems. Proceedings of the Twelfth ACM Conference on Hypertext and Hypermedia (HT '01) (Århus, Denmark, Aug). ACM Press, New York
26. Wiil, Uffe K.: Multiple open services in a structural computing environment. Proceedings of the Workshop on Structural Computing (SC1) (Darmstadt, Germany, Feb 1999). Available in technical report AUE-CS-99-04 (Aalborg University Esbjerg, Denmark) at http://cs.aue.auc.dk/publications/
27. Wiil, Uffe K., Nürnberg, Peter J.: Evolving hypermedia middleware services: Lessons and observations. Proceedings of the ACM Symposium on Applied Computing (SAC '99) (San Antonio, TX, Mar). ACM Press, New York

The Third Workshop on Adaptive Hypermedia (AH3)

Program Committee Members of AH3

The following people have served on the Program Committee of the AH3 Workshop. Their support is gratefully acknowledged.

Paul De Bra, Eindhoven University of Technology, NL
Peter Brusilovsky, University of Pittsburgh, US
Alfred Kobsa, University of California at Irvine, US
Liliana Ardissono, University of Turin, IT
Licia Calvi, Eindhoven University of Technology, NL
Wendy Hall, University of Southampton, UK
Lynda Hardman, Centrum voor Wiskunde en Informatica, NL
Paul Maglio, IBM Almaden Research Center, US
Barry Smyth, ChangingWorlds Ltd, IE
Marcus Specht, GMD, DE
Carlo Strapparava, IRST Trento, IT

List of Presentations at AH3

Paul De Bra "Introduction and Wrap Up"
Kalina Bontcheva "The Impact of Empirical Studies on the Design of an Adaptive Hypertext Generation System"
Berardina De Carolis, Fiorella de Rosis "User-Adapted Image Descriptions from Annotated Knowledge Sources"
Kyparisia A. Papanikolauou, Maria Grigoriadou, Harry Kornilakis, George D. Magoulas "INSPIRE: An INtelligent System for Personalized Instruction in a Remote Environment"
Gerhard Weber, Hans-Christian Kuhl, Stephan Weibelzahl "Developing Adaptive Internet Based Courses with the Authoring System NetCoach"
Christopher Bailey, Samhaa R. El-Beltagy, Wendy Hall "Link Augmentation: A Context-Based Approach to Support Adaptive Hypermedia"
Mario Cannataro, Andrea Pugliese "XAHM: an XML-based Adaptive Hypermedia Model and its Implementation"
Sébastien Iksal, Serge Garlatti "Revisiting and Versioning in Virtual Special Reports"
Liliana Ardissono, A. Goy, G. Petrone, M. Segnan, P. Torasso "Tailoring the Recommendation of Tourist Information to Heterogeneous User Groups"
Guntram Graef, Christian Schaefer "Application of ART2 Networks and Self-organizing Maps to Collaborative Filtering"

David Bueno, Ricardo Conejo, Amos A. David "METIOREW: An Objective Oriented Content Based and Collaborative Recommending System"
Paolo Buono, Maria Francesca Costabile, Stefano Guida, Antonio Piccinno "Integrating User Data and Collaborative Filtering in a Web Recommendation System"
Yoshinori Hijikata, Tetsuya Yoshida, Shogo Nishida "Adaptive Hypermedia System for Supporting Information Providers in Directing Users through Hyperspace"
W.W. Wadge, M.C. Schraefel "A Complementary Approach for Adaptive and Adaptable Hypermedia: Intensional Hypertext"

List of Participants at AH3

AH3 consisted of two sessions: one at the 8th International Conference on User Modeling (UM 2001, Sonthofen, Germany) and one at the 12th ACM Conference on Hypertext and Hypermedia (HT 2001, Aarhus, Denmark). Some people attended both sessions, others only one session. We only provide a list of participants who where on the program committee, presented a paper, or contributed a poster or position paper.

Dimitris Avramidis, Computer Technology Institute, Patras, GR
Toni Alatalo, University of Oulu, FI
Martin Alberink, Telematica Institute, Enschede, NL
Christopher Bailey, University of Southampton, UK
Kalina Bontcheva, University of Sheffield, UK
Paul De Bra, Eindhoven University of Technology, NL
Peter Brusilovsky, University of Pittsburgh, US
David Bueno, University of Málaga, ES
Licia Calvi, Eindhoven University of Technology, NL
Rosa M. Carro, University of Madrid, ES
Berardina De Carolis, University of Bari, IT
Maria Francesca Costabile, University of Bari, IT
Anna Goy, University of Turin, IT
Guntram Graef, University of Karlsruhe, DE
Wendy Hall, University of Southampton, UK
Yoshinori Hijikata, Osaka University, JP
Sébastien Iksal, ENST Bretagne, FR
Alfred Kobsa, University of California at Irvine, US
Nora Koch, Ludwig-Maximilians University of Munich, DE
Muan H. Ng, University of Southampton, UK
Kyparisia Papanikolaou, University of Athens, GR
Andrea Pugliese, University of Calabria, IT

Monica M. C. Schraefel, University of Toronto, CA
Patrick Sinclair, University of Southampton, UK
Carlo Strapparava, IRST Trento, IT
Mettina Veenstra, Telematica Institute, Enschede, NL
Gerhard Weber, Pedagogical University Freiburg, DE
Hongjing Wu, Eindhoven University of Technology, NL

Introduction to AH3

Paul M.E. De Bra

Eindhoven University of Technology
Department of Computer Science
PO Box 513 NL 5600 MB Eindhoven, The Netherlands
debra@win.tue.nl

In an increasing number of application areas, including but not limited to education, e-business, culture, tourism and news, the need for automated personalization is being acknowledged. The navigational freedom in conventional hypermedia leads to comprehension and orientation problems. As a result, users are not finding the information they need. Starting in the early 1990's, several research teams began to investigate ways of modeling features of individual users and groups of users to create hypermedia systems for a variety of information systems applications that would adapt to these different features. This has led to a number of interesting adaptation techniques and adaptive hypermedia systems, both Web-based and not Web-based. Adaptation is done both to the information content and to the link structure.

Adaptive hypermedia is a direction of research on the crossroads of hypertext (hypermedia) and user modeling, with an overall goal of improving the usability of hypermedia. Adaptive hypermedia has been the topic of a number of workshops, some emphasizing the hypermedia aspects, and some emphasizing the user modeling aspects. These workshops include, in chronological order:

- Workshop on Adaptive Hypertext and Hypermedia, held in conjunction with the Fourth International Conference on User Modeling (UM'94);
- Workshop on User Modeling for Information Filtering on the World Wide Web, held in conjunction with the Fifth International Conference on User Modeling (UM'96);
- Flexible Hypertext Workshop, held at the Eighth ACM International Hypertext Conference (Hypertext'97) ;
- Intelligent educational systems on the World-Wide Web, held in conjunction with the 8th World Conference on Artificial Intelligence in Education (AI-ED'97);
- Workshop on Adaptive Systems and User Modeling on the World Wide Web, held in conjunction with the Sixth International Conference on User Modeling (UM'97);
- Second Workshop on Adaptive Hypertext and Hypermedia, held in conjunction with the Ninth ACM Conference on Hypertext and Hypermedia (Hypertext'98);
- Second Workshop on Adaptive Systems and User Modeling on the World Wide Web (ASUM99), held in conjunction with the Eight International World Wide Web Conference and the Seventh International Conference on User Modeling.

S. Reich, M.M. Tzagarakis, P.M.E. De Bra (Eds.): OHS/SC/AH 2001, LNCS 2266, pp. 199–200, 2002.
© Springer-Verlag Berlin Heidelberg 2002

The expanding research area of adaptive hypermedia has also led to the start of a series of International Conferences on Adaptive Hypermedia and Adaptive Web-based Systems. The first conference was held in Trento, Italy, in August 2000. Proceedings are available from Springer (LNCS 1892). The second conference will be held in May 2002, at the University of Málaga, Spain. Its proceedings will also appear in Springer's LNCS series. The Third Workshop on Adaptive Hypertext and Hypermedia provided researchers in the field of Adaptive Hypermedia to present their new adaptive hyp;ermedia techniques and applications, and evaluations thereof. Eleven distinguished members of the adaptive hypermedia community, both from academia and from industry, selected 9 long and 4 short presentations for inclusion in the workshop and proceedings, along with six posters (that are not included here). Thus, although the chosen format was that of a workshop, associated with a main conference, a rigorous refereeing process has lead to the selection of the papers that are included in this volume.

In order to provide researchers with a main interest in either hypermedia or user modeling a possibility to attend the workshop in conjunction with a "main" conference on these topics, the workshop was split into two sessions: one at the Eight International Conference on User Modeling (UM2001, Sonthofen, Germany) and one at the Twelfth ACM Conference on Hypertext and Hypermedia (HT'01 Aarhus, Denmark). The joint proceedings enable those who attended only one of the sessions to also learn about the research presented at the other sessions. The workshop's website http://wwwis.win.tue.nl/ah2001/ shows which papers belonged to which session. It contains preliminary versions of the papers (and also short papers for the presented posters). Authors were given the opportunity to produce final versions for the LNCS proceedings, taking into account the comments and questions from the workshop sessions.

The Impact of Empirical Studies on the Design of an Adaptive Hypertext Generation System

Kalina Bontcheva

University of Sheffield, Regent Court, 211 Portobello St.
Sheffield S1 4DP, UK
kalina@dcs.shef.ac.uk

Abstract. This paper presents two empirical usability studies based on techniques from Human-Computer Interaction (HCI) and software engineering, which were used to elicit requirements for the design of a hypertext generation system. Here we will discuss the findings of these studies, which were used to motivate the choice of adaptivity techniques. The results showed dependencies between different ways to adapt the explanation content and the document length and formatting. Therefore, the system's architecture had to be modified to cope with this requirement. In addition, the system had to be made adaptable, in addition to being adaptive, in order to satisfy the elicited users' preferences.

1 Introduction

The aim of our research was to design and implement an adaptive hypertext generation system, HYLITE+, which generates factual explanations of domain terminology. The corpus analysis of online encyclopaedia and previous empirical studies (e.g., [16,5]) have shown the positive effect of additional information – e.g., definition of key vocabulary, less technical content, supply of background information and illustrations – on the subjects' reading comprehension and reading behaviour. On the other hand, hypertext usability studies [14] have shown that hypertext needs to be concise with formatting that facilitates skimming. Therefore, we performed empirical studies to test users' preferences and their perception of several adaptivity techniques. The results were used to establish a set of requirements for HYLITE+ and influenced the choice of adaptivity techniques adopted in the implementation.

For instance, the experiment showed that users prefer different additional clarifying information depending on the chosen formatting and desired explanation length. Another, somewhat unexpected, result was the strong desire of users to control the personalisation techniques applied by the system. Consequently, HYLITE+ was designed to be **adaptable**, in addition to being *adaptive*.

The main difference between our approach and other existing adaptive hypertext generation systems (e.g., [10,12]) is the use of results from hypertext usability studies, user trials with similar software products, mockups and walkthroughs during system design. The use of these techniques, together with corpus

S. Reich, M.M. Tzagarakis, P.M.E. De Bra (Eds.): OHS/SC/AH 2001, LNCS 2266, pp. 201–214, 2002.

analysis, which is traditionally used in the design of language generation systems [17], enabled the choice of adaptivity techniques, tailored to and by the user.

When compared to adaptive hypertext systems, not just generation-based ones, this work shares most similarities with the MetaDoc system [5], which is an intelligent document reading system. Apart from providing definitions of key vocabulary, it also facilitates readers' comprehension by offering less technical versions and background information. The evaluation results of MetaDoc confirmed the benefit of vocabulary definitions, which has been shown also in earlier studies [16], and together with our corpus analysis, motivated us to choose parenthetical definitions as one of the adaptivity methods to be explored. The main difference between the two systems is that the focus in HYLITE+ is on how to generate the definitions automatically and integrate them appropriately in the explanation. Also, our system is Web-based and produces conventional hypertext, instead of the stretchtext used in MetaDoc.

2   The Empirical Studies

Hypertext readability studies [14] have shown that people read 25% slower on the screen and dislike scrolling. Therefore, unlike printed material, people prefer hypertext with concise, objective content and scannable layout, i.e., the length and formatting of the hypertext are very important. For our system these requirements translate as:

- *brevity* – do not exceed one or, if a more detailed explanation is needed, two pages;
- *structuring* – use formatting that makes it easy to pick out the important information while skimming the text, e.g., bullet lists.

2.1   The First User Experiment

Research in usability engineering [13] has shown that empirical user tests on existing similar products are a productive way to elicit user requirements and facilitate system design. Therefore we performed a limited user trial with an existing electronic encyclopaedia: The Encyclopaedia Britannica CD-ROM [6]. The goal of the experiment was to gain insight into the ways users browse encyclopaedic hypertext, the types of information they prefer, and the best ways to present it.

8 subjects (4 male and 4 female) were asked to find and browse articles related to dispersion (physics sense) and computer memory[1]. The subjects were asked to think aloud and were also interviewed at the end of the session. Their path through hyperspace was logged using software that intercepts the Web browser, and the sessions were also recorded on audio tapes.

---

[1] In this research we followed the discount usability engineering practices [13] which have shown that a small number of expert users is sufficient for this task.

The subjects were not given a strict time limit because the idea was to let them decide when they had got enough information since encyclopaedia browsing often does not have a well-defined goal and different people might have different strategies depending on their personalities and interests (e.g., skimming versus in-depth reading of all relevant articles)[2].

The interviews and transcript analysis showed a set of problems which was consistent among the users:

1. The multimedia software did not always show visited links in a different colour, so sometimes users could not recognise easily whether they have already followed a link.
2. Links need to be informative in order to help users decide whether they want to follow them or not.
3. Users do not like following long sequences of links away from the page they are reading since they feel distracted from the main topic.
4. Most users first skim a page to assess whether it is relevant and only afterwards read in detail the parts they are interested in. Consequently, they prefer formatting which facilitates skimming, not the usual mostly textual pages. Most users also decide which links to follow only after skimming the entire article first.
5. Most users found the articles too detailed and expressed a preference for having unimportant information on separate pages connected with links.

In addition, users with background or interest in the subject area (i.e., more familiar with the terminology) found it much easier to navigate through the hyperspace and looked at less pages since they ignored links to already known terms and also judged better whether a link is likely to lead to relevant material. Unlike them, novice users had problem navigating because most links contained unfamiliar specialised terms. They also showed a preference towards examples and figures which help them understand dry, abstract domains (physics, computers).

2.2   The System Mockup Experiment

The user study, the analysis of encyclopaedic texts[3] and previous research in dynamic hypertext (e.g., [10,12]) suggested various ways for adapting the generated explanations:

1. Provide the user with *definitions of* important *unknown terms* in brackets (used in encyclopaedias to facilitate users' text comprehension; our study suggests it might also improve users' navigation);

---

[2] Previous studies of hypertext usability have already established that most users fall into two broad categories – skimmers (79%) and word-for-word readers [14, p.104].
[3] We analysed a corpus that included texts from Encyclopaedia Britannica Online (www.eb.com), Microsoft Encarta (encarta.msn.com), and Harcourt Academic Press Dictionary of Science and Technology (http://www.harcourt.com/dictionary).

2. Provide the user with a *familiar superconcept* in brackets to clarify unknown terms (same as above);

3. *Omit already known information*, e.g., omit mentioning computer parts when describing a computer if the user knows them already;

4. Contextualise the explanation by *referring to previously seen material*. For example, use phrases like 'As already mentioned' at the beginning of an already visited page or an already seen fact.

5. Use syntactic structures that refer explicitly to *previously seen material* when it is part of a sentence (e.g., 'Besides dispersion, other characteristics ...');

6. When a user is returning to an already visited page, modify its content to take into account what was seen in the mean time;

7. Include *links to other related material* or if there is space, include this material on the page (e.g., information about the subtypes of the explained concept).

Before implementing these features in HYLITE+, we decided to test the user perception of their usefulness, that of adaptivity in particular, because many were derived from research on text/dialogue generation and might not fit well with the user expectations about encyclopaedic hypertext. Some of these alternatives have been explored in previous work on dynamic hypertext (e.g. [10, 12]). In particular, these systems explored the notion of hypertext as a dialogue between the system and the user. Therefore, the content and presentation of the hypertext pages, including those previously visited, were generated by taking into account the interaction history and the user model. Empirical evaluation, in the context of museum browsing [9], has shown that the participants did not report problems with the changing nature of previously visited pages. However, these results were obtained in a mixed-initiative application, which is different from the user-controlled interaction typical for information systems like ours.

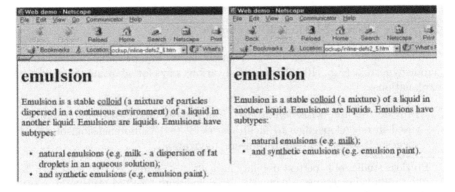

Fig. 1. The preferred version with the clarifying definition (left) and the one with a familiar supertype (right)

Research in Human-Computer Interaction has shown that one fast, yet effective, way to test alternative designs is by using *predictive evaluation* techniques [15], which involve a small number of users that test a set of scenarios, realised as paper mockups and walkthroughs.

We created paper mockups for several user interaction scenarios which were used to test users' preference of different adaptivity techniques. Each scenario consisted of one or more set(s) of hypertext pages which presented approximately the same information in alternative ways (see Figure 1 for an example of two such alternatives (out of 6 in total for this scenario)). The scenarios which tested different ways to adapt the presentation depending on previously seen material consisted of a sequence of pages which were given to users one after another as they pretended to follow a given link. The scenarios were designed so that they only focus on one ot two adaptivity techniques at a time.

The participants from the previous study were asked to rank the different page versions according to their own preferences and explain the reasons for their choice[4]. All subjects were experts in hypertext and Web browsers and have already interacted with a similar online system, so they could successfully simulate computer interaction using the paper mockups. Again, we used two domains – chemistry and computer science, so the same users were both novices in the former and experts in the latter domain.

The mockup consisted of screen shots of the hypertext alternatives displayed in Netscape. The subjects were asked initially to customise the window and font size according to their preference and then the mockup material was produced to look exactly as it would on their screens. This was particularly important because, e.g., visually-impaired users use much larger fonts and their page ranking might have been affected if the experiment conditions did not match their everyday use.

The mockup experiment had to be performed on paper, because for most subjects it was not possible to show on the computer screen more than 2 windows in parallel. Most scenarios consisted of at least 4 alternatives, so we used a big table where the alternatives could be viewed simultaneously and compared. The order in which the alternatives were arranged was changed at random between the subjects.

The experiment differentiated two types of users with respect to content: those who always preferred the most *concise texts* with links which they can explore further; and those who rated higher texts with *additional information* which might even lead them to material they did not initially intend to read. These preferences were consistent in all scenarios.

Due to space constraints, here we will only discuss the three scenarios which tested users' attitudes towards clarifying information (e.g., definitions of important unknown terms and familiar supertypes); a detailed discussion of the scenarios on adapting previously visited pages and presentation of previously seen material is available in [2].

---

[4] We chose to use the same subjects since they already had some experience with the electronic encyclopaedias and were familiar with the problems of using such systems.

One scenario tested the use of *clarifying information inside definitions*; the second tested its use in descriptions of *object parts*; the third one covered descriptions of *object subtypes*. All scenarios covered several alternatives:

1. provide *only a link* to the term (concise);
2. provide *a familiar supertype* in brackets and a link to the term;
3. provide *a definition* of the unknown term in brackets and a link to the term;
4. include a familiar supertype and no link to the term;
5. include the definition and no link to the term.

In all scenarios users always preferred to have the links included, because otherwise they would have to perform a search if they wanted to find further details about the term. Also, somewhat surprisingly, the experiments showed a connection between formatting and preferred alternatives. For example, definitions are acceptable when they are not too long (about 10 words), i.e., do not interfere with the flow of the main explanation. In parts and subtypes descriptions, definitions are preferred when list formatting is used because it makes it easier to ignore them when skimming the page (see the generated example in Figure 2).

For the first scenario, half of the experts preferred the text with the definition in brackets (Figure 1, left), whereas the other half rated the one with the familiar supertype best (right). The difference comes from overall personal preference for concise versus more informative texts but there is also a connection with the user's familiarity with the words used in the definition.

For the second and third scenarios the most preferred version was the one that used lists to enumerate all the parts/subtypes and provided short definitions of them (see the generated example in Figure 2). For terms where the system had further information (e.g., properties), links were also provided. The preference for definitions is not dependent on users' expertise in the domain, because the definitions can be easily ignored while skimming. In fact, one of the experts said she would rather have the short definitions there, rather than follow the link only to discover that the page contains just this information (i.e., is of no interest to her).

3   Summary

To summarise, all users exhibited strong preference for well-formatted, concise explanations, where further detail and additional information can be obtained from links and the form interface.

The scenarios which tested different ways of providing clarifying material showed that some users always preferred the shortest text with links to further detail, while others always chose relatively concise, but more informative, explanations. Therefore the system interface was designed to allow easy selection of different levels of explanation detail with further finer-grained tuning available from the user preferences page.

The results from these scenarios and those on adaptation of previously seen material showed that the participants had widely different opinions. For example,

Table 1. Adaptivity techniques summarised

Type of adaptivity	Default behaviour	User choices
Links to related pages	after the explanation grouped as **More general, More specific, Similar**	disable
Return to a visited page - using **Back** - using a link	show same page modify page opening	disable modification customise the page opening phrase
Already seen material	include with a cue phrase	disable
Clarify unknown terms - short, to-the-point text - more informative text	known superconcept in brackets and short definitions of parts/subtypes short definitions	switch to links only switch to definitions switch to superconcepts
Related information	only as a link to a related page	include as section in current page

one of the users found phrases like **as you have already seen** and **as you probably remember** too patronising and would want to disable their use, although she liked the other adaptivity ideas. The fact that none of the other users disliked these phrases shows how individual these preferences can be.

Therefore, the polarity in the user preferences motivated us to adopt a more individualistic approach, where users can customise the system adaptivity behaviour. The adaptivity techniques preferred by the majority of the mockup users are enabled by default in our implementation and the interface allows users to change them easily, including disabling all personalisation.

The users also expressed a desire to have control over the personalisation techniques applied by the system, i.e., customise the system behaviour with respect to both adaptivity and language use. Consequently, the system was designed and implemented to be adaptable in addition to being adaptive. In order to help users customise the system without interrupting the interaction, only adaptivity alternatives relevant to the current page are made available at the bottom of each generated page, with the full set of choices available from a separate preference page. For example, if the system has used definitions of unknown terms and links to related pages, only options related to these techniques (e.g., disable related links, switch to known superconcepts, disable all adaptivity) are displayed. This interface is based on HTML forms with check boxes and radio buttons for ease of use. These preferences are also stored in the user's model, so they can be retrieved and used in future sessions.

Finally, one must be aware of the possible discrepancies between user preferences regarding some system features and the impact of these features on users' performance. Therefore, when choosing the default system configuration or behaviour, it is also important to consider relevant results from existing task-based experiments. For example, the disabling parenthetical definitions for unfamiliar terms might lead to a decreased reading comprehension, because previous studies have shown their benefit [5]. On the other hand, denying users the possibility to change the system behaviour according to their liking could damage their acceptance of the adaptivity, because, as shown in our empirical evaluation (see Section 6), users want to have the option to change system features they do not like.

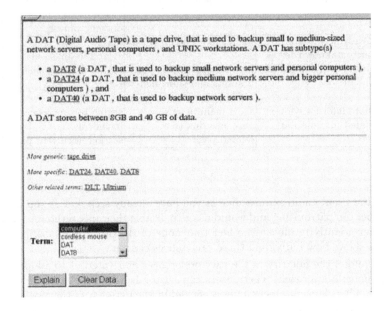

Fig. 2. An automatically generated text with added definitions and links to related material

4   The Implemented System

Based on these results, we implemented an adaptive hypertext system which, similar to [12,10,1], uses Natural Language Generation (NLG) techniques to create dynamically the hypertext nodes and links. HYLITE+ generates factual explanations of domain terminology which have been developed and evaluated in the domains of chemistry and computer hardware. The need for such explanations, for example in e-commerce, has been proven in practice by the increasing number of online computer shops that provide reference guides and tutorials (see e.g. www.action.co.uk). Computer magazines like 'What laptop' and 'What PC' also have terminological glossaries, as part of their buyer's guides.

Following the distinctions made in [7], HYLITE can be classified as an *on-line information system* which provides *referential* information, without having educational goals as do, for example, intelligent tutoring environments. The information is requested by users with different knowledge and interests and typically each hypertext node corresponds to a domain concept.

The user interacts with the system in an ordinary Web browser (e.g., Netscape, Internet Explorer) by specifying a term she wants to look up. Further information about subtypes, parts, and other related concepts is obtained by following hypertext links or specifying another query.

Similar to all Web applications, HYLITE+ needed to *(i)* respond in *real-time*, i.e., avoid algorithms with associated high computational cost; and *(ii)* be *robust*, i.e., always produce a response. Consequently the system uses some efficient and well-established applied NLG techniques such as text schemas and a phrasal lexicon (see [17,12,10]).

The system consists of several modules organised in two main stages: *(i)* content organisation, which includes *content selection, text organisation* and *semantic aggregation*; and *(ii)* surface realisation modules [3,4]. The adaptivity is implemented on the basis of a user and a discourse models. The user model is updated dynamically, based on the user's interaction with the system. When a user registers with the system for the first time, her model is initialised from a set of stereotypes. The system determines which stereotypes apply on the basis of information provided by the user herself. If no such information is provided, the system assumes a novice user.

Unlike previous NLG systems which have their own, application-specific user models, our adaptive hypertext system has re-used a generic agent modelling framework (ViewGen) instead [3]. Apart from avoiding the deloployment costs of a new model, this also enabled a more modular and extendable system architecture. As argued by [8], such modularity and re-use are much desired in adaptive hypertext systems and one way of achieving that is by using generic user models, such as BGP-MS [11] and ViewGen.

The user model is used to determine which concepts are unknown, so clarifying information can be provided if appropriate (e.g., parenthetical definitions for parts/subtypes). An example of a hypertext explanation generated by the adaptive system appears in Figure 2. In this example, the user model did not contain these concepts as known, so all three types of DAT drive are explained briefly in parenthesis. More detailed information about each one of them is available by following the hypertext links provided.

The model is also used to detect misconceptions, which might come either from a user stereotype or individual's beliefs. An example of a generated explanation addressing a common misconception follows:

Emulsion is a stable <u>colloid</u> (a mixture of disperse phases in a continuous environment) of a liquid in another liquid. Emulsion has subtypes natural emulsion (e.g. milk) and synthetic emulsion (e.g. emulsion paint).

Typically people believe that photographic emulsion is emulsion, whereas in fact, photographic emulsion is gel.

4.1 Design Impact 1: Adaptability

As discussed above, the mockup experiment revealed a lot of variation in user preferences which motivated us to adopt an individualistic approach, where users can customise the system's adaptive behaviour.

At present, the user has control over the user model and the adaptivity features, some of which are listed below. Table 1 showed the adaptivity features which are enabled by default.

- User modelling:
  - whether or not the system *updates their* VIEWGEN *model*;
  - whether or not the system *uses their* VIEWGEN *model*;
  - whether or not the system provides *information inherited* from more generic concepts;
  - whether or not the system uses *stereotypes*;
- Adaptivity features
  - whether or not the system generates *parenthetical definitions*;
  - whether or not the system presents *familiar supertypes* in brackets;
  - whether or not the system provides *links to related material*;
  - whether or not the system uses *contextualising phrases* like besides.
- *Disable all* adaptivity and user modelling.

When an adaptivity feature is disabled, this affects the generation algorithms. For example, if parenthetical definitions are disabled, but familiar supertypes are still enabled, then only the latter will be generated for unfamiliar terms, because the rules for the generation of the former will not fire.

The adaptability also proved useful during the development and testing of the generation algorithms, because it offered control over the corresponding functionality. In this way it was possible to examine the influence of each of these features on the generated hypertext (a kind of ablation experiment).

4.2 Design Impact 2: Recursive Architecture

As shown by our studies, there are several ways to provide additional information about unknown terms in generated encyclopedic entity descriptions. When such information is needed, the most appropriate clarification needs to be chosen depending on formatting, user knowledge and constraints (e.g., concise versus detailed pages). Each alternative requires different text content to be selected at the start of the generation process but the choice of alternative can only happen after the content and formatting for the main description have already been determined. Therefore, the typically used pipeline NLG architecture was extended to allow some module feedback. In the resulting *recursive architecture* additional content can be requested in later stages of the generation process, only if necessary. Below we provide an example to demonstrate how the recursion operates. A more detailed NLG-oriented description of the architecture is given in [4].

5   Generation Example

Let us assume a user who has looked up computer programs and then followed a link to personal computer; the user has not specified preferences for types of clarifying information, so definitions can be provided where appropriate. Following this request, the content organisation stage passes the following facts for realisation as text (the fact listing all parts is truncated here[5]):
[PC] <– (ISA) <– [MICRO_COMP *fs(um_state:unknown)*].

[PC] <– (PART_OF) <– [CPU *fs(um_state:unknown)*]
  – (PART_OF) <– [MEMORY *fs(um_state:explained)*]
  – (PART_OF) <– [HDD *fs(um_state:unknown)*]
  – (PART_OF) <– [DISPLAY]...

First the realisation component determines the document formatting; in this case a bullet list is chosen to enumerate all parts. Then it starts generating text for the first graph. Because the introduced supertype is unknown, but important for the understanding of the text, the generator decides to provide clarifying information in parenthesis. Since it is not always appropriate to include parenthetical information, e.g., because the user has disabled this feature or because she has requested very short texts, such clarifications are generated recursively, only if they are appropriate.

An example of a recursively generated definition is shown in Figure 3: "a small computer that uses a microprocessor as its central processing unit". Similarly definitions are generated recursively for all unknown parts of the PC.

The only exception here is computer memory, because it has already been explained in a previous page (um_state:explained). In this case, the generator uses the discourse history to determine whether memory is recently explained. If so, additional information is not needed, so no recursive calls need to be made and the final text will only contain the term and a hypertext link, in case the user wants further detail.

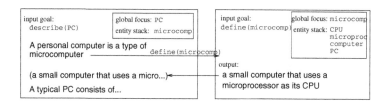

Fig. 3. An example of recursively generated parenthetical information

---

[5] The facts are encoded as conceptual graphs, a type of semantic network, where concepts are written in square brackets and relations in round ones. Extra information (e.g., whether a concept is familiar to the user, as determined on the basis of the user model) can be associated with concepts and graphs as feature structures.

6   Evaluation

The acceptability and utility of the adaptive features were evaluated by users who interacted with two versions of the system: a baseline one, with the user model and adaptivity disabled, and the default adaptive version (see Table 3). Since the goal was to evaluate the adequacy of the adaptivity methods, a small-scale formative evaluation was chosen, where the participants provided detailed feedback through questionnaires and semi-structured interviews. In this way, it was possible to gather qualitative results, which would help improving the system. Quantitative data was also gathered and analysed, but due to the small user sample (8 users), it was not possible to obtain statistically significant results.

The qualitative results showed that users prefer adapted explanations to the neutral version where information about unknown terms is not automatically provided but has to be accessed by following a link. If relevant to their task, the additional information provided by the adaptive system was also used by the participants to minimise the number of visited irrelevant pages. As stated by one of the users in their interview: "They [parenthetical definitions and examples] helped me to determine which pages are more relevant to me. In the non-adaptive system I had no choice but to visit them all." In addition, the users' subjective opinion showed that the adaptive system was easy to use and did not confuse them. Finally, 75% agreed that working with the adaptive system was more enjoyable than with the non-adaptive one, while only 12.5% disagreed.

The evaluation also showed that the acceptability of the adaptive system can be improved even further if its interface provided users with a way of changing the default system behaviour. For example, one of the users did not like the links to related information, included at the bottom of the page, while she liked the rest of the system. These results validated the conclusion from the mockup experiment, that people have different preferences, so the system needs to provide users with a way of controlling the default adaptive behaviour. Since the adaptability has already been implemented, it only remains to evaluate it by comparison with the default adaptive system, which does not allow user control.

Finally, probably the most important outcome of this formative evaluation was that it showed the need to control not just for user's prior knowledge (e.g., novice, medium, advanced), but also for reading style. Although previous studies of people browsing hypertext (e.g., [14]) have distinguished two types: *skimmers* and *readers*, in this experiment we did not control for that, because the tasks were concerned with locating information, not browsing. Still, the results obtained showed the need to control for this variable, regardless of the task type, because reading style influences some of the quantitative measures (e.g., task performance, mean time per task, number of visited pages, use of browser navigation buttons). Due to space constraints, we will refer the reader to [2] for details on the evaluation experiment, including the exact quantitative results obtained.

7   Conclusion

The paper presented the *empirical studies* which were used to design the dynamic hypertext generation system HYLITE+. The results influenced two main aspects: (i) adaptable adaptivity: giving control to the users, so they can control the system's default behaviour; (ii) recursive architecture, which allows additional information to be generated only when necessary.

The formative evaluation of the implemented system showed that the adaptivity techniques designed on the basis of our empirical studies, were found acceptable and useful by the users.

While the empirical results on preferred adaptive behaviour are probably not applicable to applications other than intelligent online information systems, the low-overhead HCI techniques used in these emprical studies have shown their effectiveness and could be easily applied to facilitate the design of other adaptive hypertext applications. Meeting user expectations and designing the system with users in mind is particularly important for Web-based systems because users have strong preferences and if a Web site does not live up to their expectations, they can often go to other sites instead.

Acknowledgements. We wish to thank Yorick Wilks, Hamish Cunningham, Peter Brusilovsky, and the anonymous reviewers for their helpful comments and suggestions.

References

1. Liliana Ardissono and Anna Goy. Dynamic generation of adaptive web catalogs. In Peter Brusilovsky, Oliviero Stock, and Carlo Strapparava, editors, *Adaptive Hypermedia and Adaptive Web-Based Systems*, number 1892 in Lecture Notes in Computer Science, pages 5—16, Berlin Heidelberg, 2000. Springer Verlag.
2. Kalina Bontcheva. *Generating Adaptive Hypertext Explanations with a Nested Agent Model*. PhD thesis, University of Sheffield, 2001.
3. Kalina Bontcheva and Yorick Wilks. Generation of adaptive (hyper)text explanations with an agent model. In *Proceedings of the European Workshop on Natural Language Generation (EWNLG'99)*, pages 67 – 76, Toulouse, France, May 1999.
4. Kalina Bontcheva and Yorick Wilks. Dealing with dependencies between content planning and surface realisation in a pipeline generation architecture. In *Proceedings of the International Joint Conference in Artificial Intelligence (IJCAI'2001)*, Seattle, USA, August 2001. To appear.
5. Craig Boyle and Antonio O. Encarnaçion. Metadoc: An adaptive hypertext reading system. *User Modelling and User-Adapted Interaction*, 4(1):1 – 19, 1994.
6. Britannica Inc. *Encyclopaedia Britannica CD'99*. 1999. Multimedia Edition.
7. Peter Brusilovsky. Methods and techniques of adaptive hypermedia. *User Modelling and User-Adapted Interaction*, 6(2-3):87–129, 1996. Special issue on Adaptive Hypertext and Hypermedia.
8. Peter Brusilovsky. Adaptive hypermedia. *User Modelling and User-Adapted Interaction*, 11(1–2):87–110, 2001.

9. Richard Cox, Mick O'Donnell, and Jon Oberlander. Dynamic versus static hypermedia in museum education: an evaluation of ILEX, the intelligent labelling explorer. In S.P. Lajoie and M. Vivet, editors, *Artificial Intelligence in Education: Open Learning Environment: New Computational Technologies to Support Learning, Exploration and Collaboration*, pages 181–188. IOS Press, Amsterdam, 1999.

10. Alistair Knott, Chris Mellish, Jon Oberlander, and Mick O'Donnell. Sources of flexibility in dynamic hypertext generation. In *Proceedings of the 8th International Workshop on Natural Language Generation (INLG'96)*, pages 151 – 160, 1996.

11. Alfred Kobsa, Andreas Nill, and J. Fink. Hypertext and hypermedia clients of the user modelling system BGP-MS. In Mark Maybury, editor, *Intelligent Multimedia Information Retrieval*. MIT Press, 1997.

12. Maria Milosavljevic, Adrian Tulloch, and Robert Dale. Text generation in a dynamic hypertext environment. In *Proceedings of the 19th Australian Computer Science Conference*, Melbourne, 1996.

13. Jakob Nielsen. *Usability Engineering*. Morgan Kaufman, CA, 1993.

14. Jakob Nielsen. *Designing Web Usability: The Practice of Simplicity*. New Riders Publishing, 2000.

15. Jenny Preece, Yvonne Rogers, Helen Sharp, David Benyon, Simon Holland, and Tom Carey. *Human-Computer Interaction*. Addison-Wesley, Reading, MA, 1994.

16. David Reinking and Robert Schreiner. The effects of computer-mediated text on measures of reading comprehension and reading behaviour. *Reading Research Quarterly*, Fall:536—551, 1985.

17. Ehud Reiter and Robert Dale. *Building Natural Language Generation Systems*. Cambridge University Press, Cambridge, England, 2000.

INSPIRE: An INtelligent System for Personalized Instruction in a Remote Environment

Kyparisia A. Papanikolaou[1], Maria Grigoriadou[1], Harry Kornilakis[1], and George D. Magoulas[2]

[1] Department of Informatics & Telecommunications
University of Athens, Panepistimiopolis
GR-15784 Athens, Greece
{spap, gregor, harryk}@di.uoa.gr
[2] Department of Information Systems and Computing
Brunel University
West London, UB8 3PH
George.Magoulas@brunel.ac.uk

Abstract. In this paper we present the architecture of an Adaptive Educational Hypermedia System, named INSPIRE. This particular system, throughout its interaction with the learner, dynamically generates lessons that gradually lead to the accomplishment of the learning goals selected by the learner. The lessons are generated according to the learner's knowledge level, learning style and follow his/her progress. The adaptive behavior of the system, the functionality of the various modules and the opportunities offered to learners for intervention are presented.

1 Introduction

Adaptive Educational Hypermedia Systems (AEHS) [3,2], extend the benefits derived from the instructional use of the Web by incorporating the idea of offering learners personalized support and/or instruction in a distance learning setting. The adaptive characteristics of an Educational Hypermedia System usually aim to both *usability* and *learning*. Thus, the educational implications are very important and should be considered during the design and development stages of the system. Although many questions are still open in the area of Instructional Design about instruction / learning and how it is efficiently provided / attained [17], it is important to consider adaptation within the framework of current learning theories and models, and thoroughly plan the sharing of the task of adaptation between the learner and the system.

We have developed an AEHS, named INSPIRE. Based on the learning goal that the learner selects, INSPIRE generates lessons that correspond to specific learning outcomes accommodating learner's knowledge level and learning style. Thus, aiming at individualizing instruction, the system generates lesson plans tailored to the needs, preferences and knowledge level of each individual learner

S. Reich, M.M. Tzagarakis, P.M.E. De Bra (Eds.): OHS/SC/AH 2001, LNCS 2266, pp. 215–225, 2002.

by making use of information about the learner gathered through their interaction. Furthermore, the system provides learners with the option to intervene, expressing their perspective about their own characteristics, or about the lesson contents, and accordingly formulate their interaction with the system, in an attempt to engage learners in the learning process.

2 INSPIRE's Adaptive Functionality

The proposed system aims to facilitate distance learners during their study, adopting a pedagogical framework inspired by theories of the area of Instructional Design and Adult Learning. In the beginning of the interaction, the domain knowledge presented to the learner is restricted and gradually it is enriched, following the internal structure of the domain (*curriculum sequencing technique*), while a navigation route is pro-posed based on learner's progress (*adaptive navigation technique*).

The main instructional outcomes of the generated lessons on learners' level of performance are to: understand and remember the most important instances and generalities associated with the learning goal they study (*Remember*); be able to apply them to specific cases (*Use*); and be able to generate new generalities (*Find*) [13]. The presentation of the educational material provided for each different level of performance, i.e. Remember, Use and Find, is mainly determined by the learning style of the learner (*adaptive presentation technique*). Thus, learners' preferences that usually guide systems' adaptation [3], are determined based on their learning style. Following the theory of learning styles [4, 9,12], how much individuals learn, i.e. the effectiveness of instructional manipulations, is mainly influenced by the educational experiences geared toward their particular style of learning. This approach to learning emphasizes the fact that individuals perceive and process information in very different ways. In this paper we propose a framework for the system's adaptive behavior that exploits the information of the learning style. The learning style model that we adopted in the current implementation of the system is that of [8], where Honey and Mumford, based on Kolb's theory of experiential learning [9], suggested four types of learners: *Activists, Pragmatists, Reflectors and Theorists*.

The proposed system also supports end-learner modifiability offering opportunities to the learners to intervene in different stages of the lesson generation process, as well as on the construction of their learner model. Thus, learners have the option to activate or deactivate the lesson generation process of the system. In case of activation, they have the option to guide system's instructional decisions by updating accordingly their characteristics on their model, i.e. their knowledge level on the different concepts of the learning goal and their learning style. The externalization of the model to the learners is implemented in a manner that allows it to be understandable, transferable and usable [7].

3   The Architecture of INSPIRE

INSPIRE's architecture has been designed so as to facilitate knowledge communication between the learner and the system and support its adaptive functionality. INSPIRE is comprised of five different modules (see Fig. 1): (i) the *Interaction Monitoring Module* that monitors and handles learner's responses during his/her interaction with the system, (ii) the *Learner's Diagnostic Module*, which processes data recorded about the learner and decides on how to classify the learner's knowledge, (iii) the *Lesson Generation Module* that generates the lesson contents according to learner's knowledge goals and knowledge level, (iv) the *Presentation Module* that generates the educational material pages sent to the learner, and (v) the *Data Storage*, which holds the *Domain knowledge* and the *Learner's Model*.

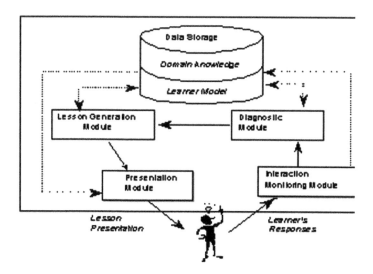

Fig. 1. INSPIRE's components and the interactions with the learner

3.1   Representing Knowledge about the Domain and the Learner: *Data Storage*

The domain knowledge of the system is structured in three hierarchical levels of knowledge abstraction: *learning goals, concepts* and *educational material* [15]. Every learning goal is associated with a subset of concepts. Assigning qualitative characterizations provides interrelation among the different concepts of a learning goal, i.e. *outcome concepts, prerequisite concepts* and *related concepts*. Note that the prerequisites and related concepts are linked to specific outcome concepts. The outcome concepts of a learning goal are further organized in a layered structure, i.e. the outcome concepts of the ith layer should be presented before the outcome concepts of the next, i+1, layer.

The educational material related to each outcome concept consists of *knowledge modules*, developed according to three levels of performance: *Remember, Use* and *Find*, as proposed in [13]. Each level of performance is associated with a different combination of multiple types of knowledge modules aiming at increasing the learning efficiency: (i) the *Remember* level of performance includes information necessary to present the concept, i.e. expository and inquisitory theory presentations and/or examples plus images and/or questions and self-estimation tests, assessment tests, (ii) the *Use* level of performance includes information necessary to apply the concept to specific cases, i.e. hints from the theory and/or examples and/or exercises and/or activities based on computer simulations, self-estimation tests, assessment tests, and (iii) the *Find* level of performance aims to the ability of the learner to find a new concept, principle, procedure, and thus the educational material provided includes activities on simulations, exploration activities, case studies. The representation of the educational material pages in the database is based on the ARIADNE recommendation for educational metadata [1]. Metadata specify the attributes that fully and adequately describe the knowledge modules of the educational material.

The learner model. The learner model is the system's representation of the learner. It supports learner's communication with the system and reflects some of his/her features. It describes the learner (general information, learning style) and his/her "current state" (knowledge level on the different concepts and learning goals, performance on assessment tests, number, type and order of resources s/he has accessed etc.).

The knowledge level of the learner on a certain concept is assigned one of the characterizations I, RS, AS, S = Insufficient, Rather Sufficient, Almost Sufficient, Sufficient. This assignment is made based on learners' answers to assessment questions of different types. The diagnostic module uses the approach described in [10] for multicriterial decision-making in order to assess learner's knowledge level on each particular concept of a learning goal.

Currently, the dominant learning style of the learner, which is stored in his/her profile, is initialized by means of a Honey & Mumford questionnaire [8], which the learner fills in the first time s/he logs on the system. Alternatively, the learner is provided with the option to directly select his/her dominant learning style, based on information provided by the system about the general characteristics of the different learning style categories.

3.2   Monitoring the Learner: *Interaction Monitoring Module*

The function of the Interaction-Monitoring Module is to log the requests made by the learner, as part of his/her HTTP request, and update the learner's model with the newly acquired information. Since the interaction-monitoring module is the only part of INSPIRE that receives direct input from the learner, it is responsible for collecting data concerning the learners' observable behavior and for notifying the other modules about their actions; examples of such actions are: the inspection or modification of his/her model, the selection of a learning goal and the activation/deactivation of the lesson generation process.

3.3 Planning the Lesson's Contents: *Lesson Generation Module*

The Lesson Generation Module realizes the lesson generation process, which plans the content and the delivery of each lesson. The outcome concepts of a learning goal are presented gradually according to the priority of the layer they belong to. The lesson generation process determines which one of the layers of the outcome concepts (as described in Sect. 3.1 about the structure of the domain knowledge) should be proposed to the learner (see in Fig.4 the lesson contents in the Navigational Area). This decision is mainly guided by learner's knowledge level on the outcome concepts of the previous layers.

Every outcome concept of the selected layer is accompanied by its prerequisites and related ones. In the proposed approach we use different strategies for planning the content of a lesson in each particular layer. This process takes into account the relative importance of each concept on the learning goal as well as the knowledge level of the learner on those concepts. For example:

1. If the knowledge level of the learner has been evaluated as {Insufficient} on a number of outcome concepts. Then, s/he has to study the educational material of the *Remember* level on these outcome concepts and their entire prerequisite ones.
2. If the knowledge level of the learner has been evaluated as {Rather Sufficient} on a number of outcome concepts and {Sufficient} on several prerequisite concepts. Then, s/he has to study the educational material of the *Use* level on these outcome concepts and the rest of the prerequisite ones of the outcome.

The relative importance of the concepts included in a lesson determines the extent of their presentation. Thus, the generated lesson includes: (i) complete presentation of the outcome concepts (according to the three levels of performance), (ii) links to brief presentations of the prerequisite concepts, focusing on their relation to the outcome if necessary and (iii) links to the definition of the related concepts in a glossary. The educational material associated to each of the concepts is predefined, and its presentation to the learner is tailored to his/her learning style. Furthermore, the results of the lesson generation process on the contents and the delivery of the generated lessons are reflected on the navigational route that the system proposes to the learner (this will be described in more detail below).

3.4 Presenting the Lesson: *Presentation Module*

The Presentation Module is responsible for the presentation of the lesson to the learner. After the lesson contents have been specified by the Lesson Generation

Module using information on the knowledge level of the learner, the Presentation Module takes over to reflect these contents as a navigation route in the domain and to decide on the presentation of the educational material based on information on the learning style of the learner.

Adaptive Presentation. Learners with different learning styles view different presentations of the educational material. The main objective is to support learners, following their preferred way of studying. To this end we exploit the information of their learning style in order to guide decisions on the instructional approach proposed to each individual learner.

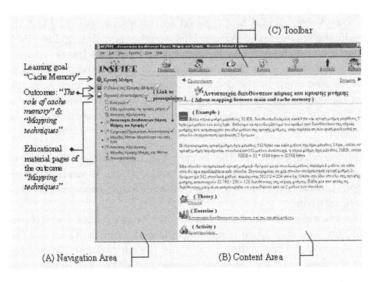

Fig. 2. INSPIRE's main screen presenting the educational material page "Address mapping between main and cache memory" of the outcome concept "Mapping Techniques" of the learning goal "Cache Memory". The screen is divided into three areas: (A) Navigation Area, which includes the contents of the lesson in a hypertext form as links (for clarity purposes the colored icons are denoted by a bullet), (B) Content Area, which presents the contents of the page that the learner selects from the Navigation Area, and (C) Toolbar, which includes several tools that offer learners *easy access* to various facilities. In the Content Area, different knowledge modules comprising the page of educational material as viewed by Reflectors. *Example*: description of an application example; *Theory*: link to hints from the theory; *Exercise*: link to an exercise; *Activity*: link to an activity based on a computer simulation.

According to the proposed framework, the multiple external representations of the outcome concepts (expository and inquisitory presentations, examples, exercises, activities based on computer simulations) constitute different instructional primitives [11], which are combined to formulate alternative instructional strategies for the presentation of the educational material. The selection of the appropriate instructional strategy for each learning style category reflects some tendencies of the category in approaching information and is in accordance to related work proposed in the literature [6,16]. Furthermore, empirical investigations on the learning preferences of learners have been realized during the first stages of the formative evaluation of INSPIRE aiming at providing direct information about learners attitudes towards the instructional material while studying [14].

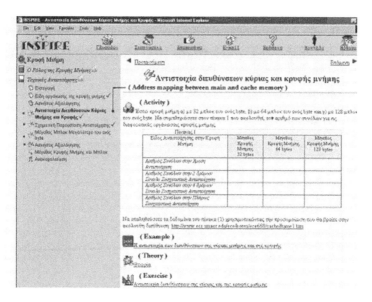

Fig. 3. Different knowledge modules comprising the educational material page "Address mapping between main and cache memory" of the outcome concept "Mapping Techniques" of the learning goal "Cache Memory" as viewed by Activists. *Activity*: description of an activity in a computer simulation; *Example*: link to application examples; *Theory*: link to hints from the theory; and *Exercise*: link to an exercise.

Although all learners are provided with the same knowledge modules, the method and order of their presentation on each page is adapted, implementing multiple instructional strategies that focus on different perspectives of the concepts. This way, we attempt to maximize the benefit gained from style awareness [8,9]. Learners are motivated to pass through all the provided educational material exploiting their own capabilities and developing new ones. Consequently, for Reflectors who tend to collect and analyze data before taking action, an *example-oriented strategy* (see Fig.2) proposes him/her to start reading the example, continue with a brief theory presentation and then try to solve an exercise. Accordingly, for the presentation of material to Activists, who are more motivated by experimentation and attracted by challenge, the instructional strategy adopted is *activity-oriented* (see Fig.3) and suggests to him/her to start experimenting with an activity designed for a computer simulation and provides him/her with the necessary information (example & theory).

Thus, with regards to the implementation of the adopted instructional strategy, if it is example-oriented then the knowledge module "Example" will be presented on the top of the page while the rest of the modules will appear next as links in a specified order (see Fig. 2); if the instructional strategy is activity-oriented then the knowledge module "Activity" will be presented on the top of the page while the rest of the modules will appear next as links in a specified order (see Fig. 3).

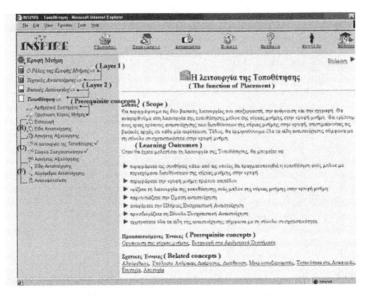

Fig. 4. INSPIRE's main screen presenting the initial page of the outcome concept "Placement". In the Navigation Area note that: the coloured icons are denoted by bullets; (R), (U), (F): educational material pages associated with the *Remember*, *Use*, *Find* levels of performance accordingly.

The approach of using multiple representations (knowledge modules) in the different instructional strategies that INSPIRE adopts, formulating alternative presentations of the educational material, alleviates the problem of rewriting the same content tailored to each learning style category. The different knowledge modules are either embedded in the page or appear as links in a specified order depending on the learning style of the learner. Thus, through the adaptive presentation technique, the same knowledge modules can be reused in different instructional strategies.

Adaptive Navigation Support. The system supports learner's navigation and orientation in the lesson contents by annotating the links that appear in the Navigation Area. Additional information is provided to the learner through the use of icons next to the names of concepts and the educational material. Different icons are used to distinguish between the outcome and the prerequisite concepts, as well as the educational material provided for each level of performance (notice in Fig.4, the different icons in the Navigation Area). Especially on the outcome concepts, the filling of a measuring cup is used as a metaphor denoting learner's progress.

Furthermore, two state icons accompany the prerequisite concepts and the educational material of the outcomes reflecting the instructional decisions of the lesson generation process on the educational material that the learner should study next. Thus, colored icons accompany the links that lead to the material that the system proposes the learner to study next, while black and white icons appear next to the rest of the links (see in Fig.4 the icons in the Navigation Area - the colored ones are denoted by a bullet).

Finally, a history-based mechanism has been developed so that, as each page is visited, a check mark appears next to its link in the Navigation Area (see Fig. 4 - Navigation Area).

4   Implementation Issues

INSPIRE is currently used to support an introductory course on Computer Architecture. In particular, educational material referring to the learning goal "What is the role of cache memory and its basic operations" has been developed based on the chapter *Computer Memory* of the module "Computer Architecture" [5] developed at the Department of Informatics and Telecommunications of the University of Athens. The current implementation of the system is using an IIS web server running on Windows NT, which processes the requests made by the learners. The learner model and the educational metadata describing the educational material [1], are stored in a SQL Server database that communicates with the web server through use of the ActiveX Data Objects (ADO) technology. The education material itself is stored in the file system pages. We are making use of the Active Server Pages (ASP) technology developed by Microsoft, which allows the dynamic generation of HTML page, in order to implement the adaptive presentation technique.

5   Conclusions and Further Research

INSPIRE is an adaptive system that monitors learner's activity and dynamically adapts the generated lessons to accommodate diversity in learners' knowledge state and learning style. An experiment focusing on the evaluation of the instructional design of the system has been conducted with students of the Department of Informatics and Telecommunication, who attend the course on Computer Architecture, and with participants of a seminar on the "Usability of Educational Software". The initial reactions towards the system have been encouraging while students' comments inspired several improvements on system's interface.

The system is both adaptive and adaptable, as it allows the learner to control system's adaptation. The learner model of the system provides a complete description of the current state of the learner; it is open to the learner to make changes, and, in this way, allows him/her to intervene in the lesson generation process, supporting "end-learner modifiability". Further processing of the information stored in the learner model can be exploited by: (i) the system for the learner diagnosis process, (ii) the learner in order to be informed on system's decisions and intervene accordingly, and (iii) the tutor for the evaluation of the provided material and for monitoring learners' progress and study attitude. From the various statistics stored in the learner model the tutor can have a quantitative estimation of the learners' preferences on the educational material, in the sense of the time they spent on it, their performance, their attitude while studying, their progress, their requests to the system for help on specific pages etc.

The knowledge level and the learning style of the learner are used for the appropriate selection of the lesson contents and the presentation of the educational material. The domain structure is comprised by independent elements, i.e. concepts, educational material modules. These elements are reused in different learning goals and support multiple instructional strategies so that the different learners' educational needs and preferences can be fulfilled. In the current implementation of the system, the preferences of each individual learner are approached through his/her learning style, which is recognized through the submission of the appropriate questionnaire or defined by the learner. Further research is on progress concerning the estimation of the way each learner uses the educational material in order to identify inconsistencies in the association of the learning style of the learner (which has been detected by the system or specified by the learner) with the different types of educational material. For example, it is expected that the Activist will spent most of his/her time on activities and exercises, while the Reflector on theory presentations and examples. The way a learner uses the educational material in conjunction with his/her progress is valuable information denoting how successful is the selection of particular type of educational material for the particular learner. Furthermore, this information can also be used for the dynamic adaptation of the instructional strategy adopted for presentation of the educational material during learner's interaction with the system.

Acknowledgement. This work was partially supported by the Greek General Secretariat for Research and Technology of the Greek Ministry of Industry under a PENED99 grant No 99ED234.

References

1. ARIADNE project. Available at http://ariadne.unil.ch
2. Brusilovsky, P.: Adaptive and Intelligent Technologies for Web-based Education. In: Rollinger, C., Peylo, C. (eds.) Künstliche Intelligenz, Special Issue on Intelligent Systems and Teleteaching (1999)

3. Brusilovsky, P.: Methods and Techniques of Adaptive Hypermedia. Learner Modeling and Learner-Adapted Interaction, Vol. 6. Kluwer Academic Publ., Netherlands (1996)
4. Entwistle, N.J.: Styles of Learning and Teaching. David Fulton, London (1988)
5. Grigoriadou M., Papanikolaou K., Cotronis Y., Velentzas Ch., Filokyprou G.: Designing and Implementing a Web-based course. In: Proc. of Int. Conf. of Computer Based Learning In Science, Enschede, Netherlands (1999) H5
6. Groat, A., Musson, T.: Learning Styles: individualising computer-based learning envi-ronments. ALT - Journal 3 (2) (1995) 53–62
7. Hartley, R., Paiva, A., Self J.: Externalizing Learner Models. In: Greer, J. (ed.): Proc. of Int. Conf. on Artificial Intelligence in Education. AACE, Washington (1995) 509–516
8. Honey, P., Mumford, A.: The manual of Learning Styles. Peter Honey Maidenhead (1992)
9. Kolb, D. A.: Experiential learning. Englewood Cliffs, Prentice-Hall, NJ (1984)
10. Magoulas, G.D., Papanikolaou, K.A., Grigoriadou, M.: Neuro-fuzzy Synergism for Planning the Content in a Web-based Course. Informatica 25 (1) (2001) 39–48
11. Marcke, V.: A Generic Task Model for Instruction. Instructional models for Computer-based Learning Environments. Nato ASI Series F, Vol. 104. Springer-Verlag, Berlin Heidelberg New York (1992)
12. McLoughlin, C.: The implications of the research literature on learning styles for the design of instructional material. Australian J. of Educational Technology 15 (3) (1999)
13. Merril, M.D.: Component Display Theory. In: Reigeluth, C.M. (ed.): Instructional design theories and models: An overview of their current status. Lawrence Elrbaum Association, Hillsdale NJ (1983)
14. Papanikolaou, K.A., Grigoriadou, M., Kornilakis, H., Magoulas, G.D.: Towards New Forms of Knowledge Communication: An INtelligent System for Personalised Instruction in a Remote Environment (INSPIRE) (Submitted)
15. Papanikolaou, K.A., Magoulas, G.D., Grigoriadou, M.: A Connectionist Approach for Supporting Personalized Learning in a Web-based Learning Environment. In: Brusilovsky, P., Stock, O., Strapparava, C. (eds.): Adaptive Hypermedia and Adaptive Web-based Systems. Lecture Notes in Computer Science, Vol. 1892. Springer-Verlag, Berlin Heidel-berg New York (2000) 189–201
16. Stoyanov, S., Aroyo, L., Kommers, P.: Intelligent Agents Instructional Design Tools for a Hypermedia Design Course. In: Lajoie, S.P., Vivet, M. (eds.): Artificial Intelligence in Education. IOS Press (1999)
17. Vosniadou, S.: Towards a revised cognitive psychology for new advances in learning and instruction. Learning and Instruction 6(2) (1996) 95–109

Developing Adaptive Internet Based Courses with the Authoring System NetCoach

Gerhard Weber, Hans-Christian Kuhl, and Stephan Weibelzahl

Pedagogical University Freiburg, Germany
{weber,kuhl,weibelza}@ph-freiburg.de

Abstract. Developing adaptive internet based learning courses usually requires a lot of programming efforts to provide session management, keeping track of the learners current state, and adapting the interface layout to specific requirements. NetCoach is designed to enable authors to develop adaptive learning courses without programming knowledge. In this paper, we describe the adaptive, the adaptable, the interactive, and the communicative features of NetCoach. Both authors and tutors are supported in many ways to develop and manage courses via an online interface. Experiences with NetCoach courses in different domains and settings have shown that learners profit from the adaptive features.

1 Introduction

Internet based instruction has grown strongly during the last years. While in the beginning most internet based courses consisted only of a collection of static HTML-pages (mostly simple translations of already existing scripts and papers), a lot of sophisticated internet based learning systems emerged in recent time. The former systems could be easily created by authors using simple authoring tools, but these systems were not much more than copies of textbooks and lacked any adaptivity and guidance that would be needed to support learners when learning a new topic on their own. On the other hand, most current more sophisticated learning systems are proprietary solutions and can only be built by experienced programmers and skilled web-based instruction authors.

This puts high demands on authoring tools to create adaptive internet based instruction courses. In this paper, we will introduce NetCoach, an authoring system that meets the needs to create adaptive learning courses in the internet. Creating adaptive courses with NetCoach is very easy and can be done without being a skilled programmer. NetCoach is derived from ELM-ART[1], one of the first and by now most comprehensive adaptive web-based educational systems [10].

---

[1] http://cogpsy.uni-trier.de/projects/ELM/elmart.html

S. Reich, M.M. Tzagarakis, P.M.E. De Bra (Eds.): OHS/SC/AH 2001, LNCS 2266, pp. 226–238, 2002.

2   Features and Adaptivity in NetCoach-Courses

NetCoach is an authoring-system which allows to create adaptive and individual course modules without programming-knowledge. This section describes four characteristics that are common to all courses that have been developed with NetCoach: the courses are adaptive, interactive, adaptable, and communicative.

2.1   Adaptive Elements in NetCoach Courses

According to [1], adaptive learning systems may adapt to the learners experience, knowledge, goals, or preferences. NetCoach adapts to the last three aspects of the user. This information can be used either to adapt the presentation of the content or to support the navigation [1]. NetCoach implements two adaptive navigation techniques: *curriculum sequencing* and *adaptive annotation of links*. The goal of *curriculum sequencing* is to provide the student with the most suitable, individually planned sequence of knowledge units to learn and the sequence of learning tasks (examples, questions, problems, etc.) to work with. In other words, it helps the student to find an "optimal path" through the learning material. The goal of *adaptive annotation of links* is to support the student in hyperspace orientation and navigation by changing the appearance of visible links.

These adaptation techniques require a content specific knowledge-base and a user model that allows the system for responding individually to learners' interactions with the system.

The Knowledge-Base as Basis for Adaptive Behavior. In NetCoach, the knowledge base of a course consists of concepts. These concepts are internal representations of pages that will be presented to the learner. In many domains the different concepts are related in many ways. To build up this knowledge-base, which is the basis for adaptive navigation support, the author can create many content-specific relations for every concept. However, the author is not forced to specify any relation. Default values that retain the sequential order of the concepts will be applied otherwise. Note, that specifying the concept relations is a simple procedure (as will be shown in Section 3) and is basically a content-specific task.

Normally the contents of a domain are related and interdependent. There are two relations between concepts: prerequisites and inferences.

First, the author can decide which other concepts are required to be learned to understand the current concept. These prerequisites can be chosen in the concept-list as shown in Figure 1 (*a*).

The system will guide learners to theses prerequisite pages before suggesting the current concept. Because prerequisite concepts might have prerequisite concepts themselves there are also indirect prerequisites (*b*). In our example-course the system will recommend the following sequential order of concepts in case *Chapter-2-1-2* is the current learning goal: *Chapter-1* (indirect prerequisite), *Chapter 1-2*, *Chapter-2* (prerequisites), and finally *Chapter-2-1-2*.

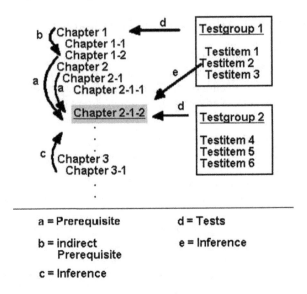

Fig. 1. Example of the relations of concept *Chapter-2-1-2*.

Second, the inferences (*c*) of a concept are in some way the opposite of prerequisites. Perhaps an user wants to learn *Chapter-3-1* first and solves the test items correctly. Because *Chapter-2-1-2* is marked as inferred by *Chapter-3-1*, the system will assume that the user already knows *Chapter-2-1-2* as soon as *Chapter-3-1* has been worked at successfully. Note that prerequisites and inferences are related but not equal. E.g., knowing A might be required to understand B, but if one knows B this does not necessarily imply that A is known.

In addition to these relations between concepts the knowledge base contains relations between test items and concepts. Sets of test items (so called test groups) assess the user's current learning state of a concept (*d*). However, test items may not only test one concept but also assess aspects of other concepts. Thus, it is possible to quantify the inference of test items to other concepts. If the learner solves *testitem 2* in Figure 1 correctly (*e*), she has understood some important aspects of *Chapter-2-1-2*. A concept is supposed to be learned if one has reached a critical value. If there are already some inferences from test items of other concepts, the learner is closer to this critical value and has to solve less test items in *Testgroup 2* correctly.

The User Model. Based on the descriptions in the concepts, all pages are computed individually with respect to the learner's user model. The user model used in NetCoach is a multi-layered overlay model [9]. Individual information about each learner is stored with respect to the concepts of the course's knowledge base (as described in the previous section). The first layer describes whether the user has already visited a page corresponding to a concept. The second layer

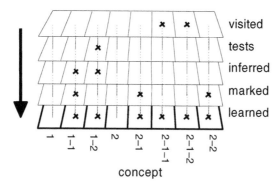

concept

Fig. 2. Example of a student's overlay model. NetCoach infers the student's current learning state from four independently updated layers. Concepts without tests are treated as learned if they have been visited.

contains information on which exercises or test items related to this particular concept the user has worked at and whether he or she has successfully worked on the test items up to a certain criterion. The third layer describes whether a concept could be inferred as known via inference links from more advanced concepts the user has already worked on successfully. Finally, the fourth layer describes whether a user has marked a concept as already known. That is, the user model can be inspected and edited [3]. Sometimes, this is called a cooperative user model [6]. Information in the different layers is updated independently. This leads to the fact that information from each different source does not overwrite others. E.g., if a student unmarks a concept because she realized that she has not enough pre-knowledge about it, the information about tests on this concept is still available.

See Figure 2 for an example of a student's overlay model. A concept is assumed to be learned if it is either tested to be known, inferred from other learned concepts, or marked by the user. In case no test group is available the concept is assumed to be learned if it has been visited. I.e., the visited layer and the test layer are applied alternatively.

Curriculum Sequencing and Link Annotation. The multi-layered overlay model supports both the adaptive annotation of links and individual curriculum sequencing. Links that are shown in an overview on each page or in the table of contents are visually annotated in correspondence to the user's current learning state. Individual curriculum sequencing means that the system's suggestion which page is best to be visited next is computed dynamically according to the general learning goal and the user's learning state of the concepts. Users get a warning if they visit a page with missing prerequisites. However, access to that page is not restricted and the warnings can be turned off. See Figure 3 for an example of a warning due to unfulfilled prerequisites, the corresponding page suggestion, and the link annotation in the overview frame on the lefthand side.

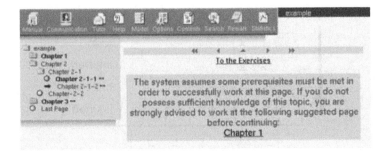

Fig. 3. Snapshot of the adaptive learning environment including curriculum sequencing and link annotation.

Learning Goals. In addition, NetCoach supports the specification of learning goals. A goal consists of a set of concepts that have to be successfully worked on by the learner. All (direct and indirect) prerequisites are computed automatically and corresponding pages are suggested. Thus, learning goals are especially useful for learners that do not want to complete the whole course. E.g., the goal "I want to get an introduction on this topic" might include the introductory chapters only, while the second goal "I am familiar with ..., but I want to know more about ..." would leave out the first chapter and suggest to go to the advanced sections directly.

2.2   Interactive Elements in NetCoach Courses

Online-presented and evaluated exercises and tests are central features of interactive courses. NetCoach provides the possibility to present exercises and tests in different formats. These are multiple choice, forced choice, gap filling tests, open questions and e-mail-questions. While the e-mail-questions will be evaluated individually by human tutors, open questions have an example-answer as feedback, so that the learners can compare their solution by themselves. The feedback for the remaining item formats consists of a hint which answer is correct and an explanation why the answer was false or correct. Moreover, it is possible to give at first a hint only, before the correct answer is given.

NetCoach courses can be additionally shaped highly interactive by connecting animations (e.g., flash-animations). These interactive animations can be contained like in every normal web-page. Animations can provide interactive work in simulated scenarios with multiple interactive mouse-events.

A glossary and a page with references can be accessed by the users with direct links in the text or a button. Finally, a search-tool and a notice-board are available.

2.3 Adaptable Elements in NetCoach Courses

Web-based courses are used by users with very different knowledge and different computer skills. Because of that it is useful if learners can adapt the learning environment to their own needs.

Not only the developed courses adapt to the user, but also the users themselves can adjust many features for their own preferences. Especially the kind of presentation, warnings and recommendations can be changed or switched off. The model behind the adaptive functions is not incomprehensible but can be investigated and changed by the learners themselves. The manner of annotation and the feedback can be adjusted, too.

2.4 Communicative Elements in NetCoach Courses

Courses developed with NetCoach provide different syncronous and asyncronous communication tools. Questions, proposals, etc. can be sent via e-mail to human tutors. A chat module provides direct communication between students. Besides, there is a possibility to discuss the contents in different discussion lists where the learners can exchange opinions and ask questions. It is also possible for every learner to exchange documents (e.g., word documents or pdf) with other learners.

All these communicative features enable lectures and teachers to organize complete virtual courses where students can interact with each other, but are still free to learn at their individual speed.

3 The NetCoach Authoring System

The NetCoach authoring-system bases on a LISP-server (CL-HTTP[2]) / web-browser-client technology. NetCoach[3] is available for Windows, Apple, and Linux operating-systems. Learners, tutors and even authors just need a standard-web-browser to work with the corresponding interfaces.

The goal of developing NetCoach was to provide authors with a tool to create highly adaptive courses without being required to program user models or interactive tests. The NetCoach authoring tool supports the complete developing process of adaptive web-based courses which includes authoring the learning material (e.g., texts, pictures), composing tests, defining learning goals, and adapting the layout and behavior of the interface. Figure 4 shows a snapshot of NetCoach's online-interface for authors.

In the concept editor, the concepts of the learning course (corresponding to pages presented in a browser) are described. Concepts may be arranged hierarchically similar to chapters and subchapters in a book. Authors may simply type in plain text, paste code from a HTML-editor, or even import an already existing HTML-file. In addition, animations that are created with Java, JavaScript or common plug-ins (e.g., flash animations) are supported as well.

---

[2] http://www.ai.mit.edu/projects/iiip/doc/cl-http/home-page.html
[3] http://www.net-coach.de

Fig. 4. Snapshot of the online-interface for authors

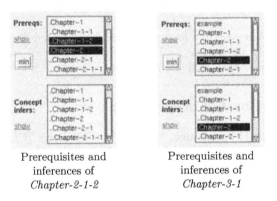

Prerequisites and
inferences of
Chapter-2-1-2

Prerequisites and
inferences of
Chapter-3-1

Fig. 5. Snapshot of a the author interface for specifying the prerequisites and the inferences of the concepts *Chapter-2-1-2* and *Chapter-3-1*.

The prerequisites on a concept and the inferences that can be drawn from successfully learning a concept are described by selecting the corresponding concepts from a table. See Figure 5 for a snapshot of how an author specifies the prerequisites and inferences of the concept *Chapter-2-1* which has been described in Section 2.1.

To achieve perfect adaptivity effects authors have to define these concept relations very carefully in dependence of the domain structure.

In the test editor, test items can be defined and tested. The test editor offers templates for all test types, so authors are not required to program complicated cgi- or Java-scripts. In fact, NetCoach presents the test-questions, evaluates the answers, and observes the learning state of each user automatically, while the author can focus on the contents of the test items. Each item consists of three parts: First, the question that will be presented to the user. Second, the correct answers that have to be filled in by the user (gap filling, free input) or that have to be marked (forced choice, multiple choice). Third, authors can provide an explanation for the solution to help learners in understanding why they were wrong. Some of our courses include item pools of more than a thousand items.

Test items are collected in test groups that are assigned to concepts. These test groups can be used as exercises or as introductory and final questionnaires. The learner's success on working on these test items is used to compute the user's learning state in the multi-layered learner model as described above.

Finally, a course might implement different learning goals. A learning goal consists of a set of concepts that has to be completed. Learners who decide not to work on the complete course but to fulfill a subgoal will receive individual recommendations which concept to visit next to complete this goal. The author has just to specify the concepts that are necessary to complete a goal. The prerequisites are computed automatically based on the hypertext model (see Section 2.1).

NetCoach not only is highly flexible in presenting different contents but also in adapting the course layout. Many optional parameters specify which buttons are presented how and where, which services are available (e.g., communication, search, or manual), and which components are adaptable by the user. This flexibility makes it easy to meet the requirements of different settings and even experimental studies. Moreover, NetCoach supports multiple languages, so courses can be developed in different target languages at the same time.

The NetCoach editors work in direct interaction with the NetCoach server so that it is possible to see effects of changing parameter settings, concepts, or test items directly in the course under development. This makes the creation of very sophisticated courses easy without requiring programming knowledge. A short tutorial on creating courses with NetCoach is described at
http://art.ph-freiburg.de/NetCoach-Tutorial.

4   Tutors in NetCoach Courses

Courses created with NetCoach are guided by tutors that aid users on help requests, inspect user data, edit discussion lists, send messages to users, and manage user accounts and user groups. This is done via an online-interface which is shown in Figure 6.

Authors of a course can register tutors via the main course editor. Tutors have their own access rights and are able to inspect the course and users in the course.

First, tutors can get into contact with users. In a tutor help window, users can ask questions to tutors or give remarks on the course. The text directly typed into the tutor help window is sent by the server to the tutor (or to several tutors) by e-mail. Tutors can respond by e-mail in case the user has provided his or her e-mail address or send a message that is stored with the learner's user

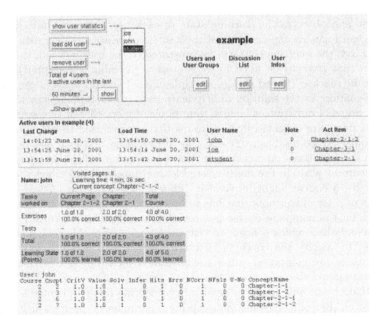

Fig. 6. Snapshot of the online-interface for tutors

model and will be displayed to the user with the next page the user opens in the course.

Second, tutors can observe users in the course. They get a list of all currently active users and have access to all users in the course. Tutors can inspect the current learning state of a user. That is, they can see how long users have been working at the course, which messages they have sent to tutors, which concepts they have worked at, how many errors they have made, and some more interesting information that may help a tutor to understand the difficulties learners have with the course in order to help these learners.

Third, tutors can manage a discussion list. They can provide new topics in the discussion list, change trees of contributions to the discussion list to a new topic, and remove parts of the discussion list. In the discussion lists, learners can place statements that can be read by all other learners from the same course or make remarks on those statements. Tutors can watch these discussion lists and remove contributions that are not related to the topics of the course.

Fourth, tutors can put information messages to all users of a course or to members of a user group. These messages have an expiration date so that messages that remind of an important date, for example, will be removed automatically after expiration. These information messages will be displayed to a user when he or she (re-)enters a course or even during working at the course.

Fifth, tutors have to manage user accounts and user groups. In case of closed courses (that is, the courses are restricted to users that have access rights), tutors can add new users or remove users, give access rights to users and assign users to working groups. Users assigned to working groups can exchange documents via the server. Additionally, users communicate directly with other members of the group via e-mail or chat.

5   Comparison with Other Authoring Systems

5.1   General Features of Authoring Systems

Presently there are many authoring systems to create virtual learning environments. Most of them are non-adaptive or just adaptable like WebCT. In the following, NetCoach will be compared to the well distributed authoring systems WebCT [5], Learning-Space[4], and TopClass[5]. These three authoring-systems where chosen because they are also based on a server/Web-Browser-Client technology and are already in use. In Section 5.2 we will compare NetCoach to other authoring systems that are designed to deliver adaptive hypermedia courses.

WebCT can be used flexibly to create entire online courses, or to publish materials that supplement existing courses. All interaction with WebCT takes place through a web browser. Essentially a WebCT course consists of a series of linked HTML pages that define a path or "road-map" through the course material. The course content is supplemented by WebCT tools which can be built into the course design by simply dragging the appropriate tool icon onto the web page.

TopClass courses are constructed of Units of Learning Material (ULMs). These ULMs can consist of pages, exercises, or further ULMs themselves. ULMs can be freely exported and imported from course to course. In addition to course management, TopClass also manages student progress, user-tracking, and access to course materials.

Learning Space is based on Lotus Notes and uses Notes Server technology to provide a secure environment with a rich set of tools. Learning space includes tools for browsing the web and inserting multimedia material into learning space documents. Links can be defined from Learning Space to multimedia content on the web. Additionally resources and other content may be exchanged via the Media Center. Completed courses may be archived by the instructor for future use. A Portfolio is contained in every participant's Profile. This is a secure area for returned assignments and assessments which can only be viewed by the participant and the tutor.

As shown in Table 1 there is much conformity comparing NetCoach and the other authoring-systems described above regarding the functionality for authors, tutors and learners. Authors can import contents or contain multimedia elements. Tutors can investigate, add or delete user data and provide discussion lists. Learners can use different asynchronous and synchronous communication tools like e-mail, discussion-lists, file-exchange, and chat. Whitebord, video conferences and homepage-authoring are not implemented in all systems and as well not in NetCoach. A web browsing tool only exists in Learning Space.

---

[4] http://www.lotus.com
[5] http://www.wbtsystems.com

Table 1. Comparison of authoring systems for web-based training

	NetCoach	WebCT	TopClass	Learning Space
Author Tools				
adaptive guiding	yes			
adaptive link annotation	yes			
creating / importing content	yes	yes	yes	yes
add / play multimedia content	yes	yes	yes	yes
Tutor Tools				
store & view learner data	yes	yes	yes	yes
add / remove learners	yes	yes	yes	yes
performing assessments	yes	yes	yes	yes
create discussion groups	yes	yes	yes	yes
Student Tools				
adaptable preferences	yes	by tutor	yes	yes
web browsing				yes
creating / importing content		yes		yes
store bookmarks		yes	yes	yes
play multimedia	yes	yes	yes	yes
homepage authoring		yes	yes	yes
calendar tool		yes		yes
searchable resource archive		yes		yes
Communication				
e-mail	yes	yes	yes	yes
noticeboard	yes	yes	yes	yes
file exchange	yes	yes	yes	yes
asynchronous discussions	yes	yes	yes	yes
chat	yes	yes	Add. module	yes
whiteboard		yes		yes
video conferencing			Add. module	yes
Technology				
server/web-browser-client	yes	yes	yes	yes

The main differences are the adaptive possibilities in course-development with NetCoach. These features like curriculum-sequencing and dynamic link-annotation are described in section 2.1. The course-management (e.g. registration, examinations, calendar) which is more central in the other systems is less important in NetCoach. NetCoach is mainly a system to develop entire, adaptive courses. For this reason, NetCoach will be compared with other intelligent systems in the following section.

Table 2. Comparison of authoring systems for adaptive hypermedia courses in reference to the user's features that the systems adapt to and the methods that are used for adaptation.

	Net-Coach	AHA	ECSAI-Web	Inter-book	Meta-Links
user features: to what?					
goals	yes		yes		yes
navigation history	yes	yes	yes	yes	yes
tested knowledge	yes		yes		
preferences	yes		yes		yes
methods: how?					
adaptive guidance	yes	yes	yes	yes	yes
adaptive annotation	yes	yes	yes	yes	yes
adaptive hiding of links		yes			
adaptive navigation maps					yes
adaptive text presentation		yes			yes

5.2 Adaptivity Features of Authoring Systems

Several other authoring systems aim at delivering adaptive web-based courses. We selected four of them to highlight the strengths and weaknesses of adaptivity in NetCoach: AHA [4], ECSAIWeb [8], Interbook [2], and MetaLinks [7].

See Table 2 for a comparison of the user's features that the systems adapt to and the methods that are used for adaptation. The comparison is based on the categorization of adaptive hypermedia systems introduced by [1].

NetCoach implements most commonly used adaptive features, but does not adapt the text presentation (as e.g., AHA) and refrains from hiding links. We argue that the student should have full freedom of navigation and content access while the adaptive system should provide hints and suggestions only. However, NetCoach's adaptations are based on a diversity of user data. Especially knowledge assessment with tests is only found in ECSAIWeb and NetCoach. The overlay model in ECSAIWeb is slightly less sophisticated as it does currently not consider the inference relation (section 2.1) for adaptation purposes.

6 Conclusion

Several courses have been developed with NetCoach. They are used at different universities in Germany and in some companies. Up to now, most courses are written in German, though some are written in English, French, Spanish, or Italian. Because NetCoach does not require any programming knowledge, many different authors from many disciplines developed courses in different domains including programming, spelling rules, cognitive and pedagogical psychology, medicine, and product presentation. At the Pedagogical University in Freiburg, students develop simple courses on their own and test these courses with pupils in secondary schools. NetCoach has been used for "learning on demand" settings, as well as for supplementing courses at universities and adult education. E.g., several courses on pedagogical psychology are used by students to prepare lessons and exams, while two courses on programming LISP and HTML are available world-wide for training purposes. Accordingly, the courses differ widely in structure and features to suit the specific settings. Experiences with these courses show that users can learn easily and successfully. Results of several investigations support the usefulness of the adaptive features of NetCoach ([10]; [11]).

References

1. Brusilovsky, P. Methods and techniques for adaptive hypermedia. *User Modeling and User-Adapted Interaction*, (1996) *6*(2-3), 87–129.
2. Brusilovsky, P., Eklund, J., Schwarz, E. Web-based education for all: A tool for developing adaptive courseware. In *Computer Networks and ISDN Systems. Proceedings of Seventh International World Wide Web Conference, 14-18 April 1998* (30, 291–300).
3. Bull, S., Pain, H. "Did I say what I think I said, and do you agree with me?" Inspecting and questioning the student model. In J. Greer *Artificial Intelligence in Education, Proceedings of AI-ED'95, 7th World Conference on Artificial Intelligence in Education, 16-19 August 1995. Washington, DC, AACE* (501–508). 1995.
4. De Bra, P., Calvi, L. AHA! An open adaptive hypermedia architecture. *The New Review of Hypermedia and Multimedia*, *4*, 115–139. 1998.
5. Goldberg, M. W., Salari, S., Swoboda, P. World Wide Web - course tool: An environment for building WWW-based courses. *Journal of Computer Networks and ISDN Systems*, *28*(7-11), 1219–1231. 1996.
6. Kay, J. The UM toolkit for cooperative user models. *User Models and User Adapted Interaction*, *4*(3), 149–196, 1995.
7. Murray, T., Shen, T., Piemonte, J., Condit, C., Thibedeau, J. Adaptivity in the MetaLinks hyper-book authoring framework. In *Workshop Proceedings of Adaptive and Intelligent Web-Based Education Systems workshop at ITS 2000*.
8. Sanrach, C., Grandbastien, M. ECSAIWeb: A web-based authoring system to create adaptive learning systems. In P. Brusilovsky, O. Stock, C. Strapparava *Adaptive Hypermedia and Adaptive Web-Based Systems. International Conference, AH 2000* (214–226). Berlin: Springer.
9. Weber, G. Adaptive learning systems in the World Wide Web. In J. Kay *User modeling: Proceedings of the Seventh International Conference, UM99* (371–378). Vienna: Springer.
10. Weber, G., Specht, M. User modeling and adaptive navigation support in WWW-based tutoring systems. In A. Jameson, C. Tasso *User Modeling: Proceedings of the Sixth International Conference, UM97* (289–300). Vienna: Springer.
11. Weibelzahl, S. Evaluation of adaptive systems. In M. Bauer, P. J. Gmytrasiewicz, J. Vassileva *User Modeling: Proceedings of the Eighth International Conference, UM2001* (292–294). Berlin: Springer.

Link Augmentation: A Context-Based Approach to Support Adaptive Hypermedia

Christopher Bailey, Samhaa R. El-Beltagy, and Wendy Hall

Intelligence, Agents, Multimedia,
Department of Electronics & Computer Science
University of Southampton, SO17 1BJ, UK
{cpb99r,seb,wh}@ecs.soton.ac.uk

Abstract. In today's adaptive hypermedia systems, adaptivity is provided based on accumulative data gained from observing the user. User modelling, the capturing of information about the user such as their knowledge, tasks, attitudes, interests etc., is only a small part of the global context in which the user is working. At Southampton University we have formed a model of one particular aspect of context that can be applied in different ways to the problem of linking in context. This paper describes how that context model has been used to provide link augmentation. Link augmentation is an existing open hypermedia technique, which has a direct application in adaptive hypermedia systems. This paper presents a technique for cross-domain adaptive navigational support by combining link augmentation with a model of the user's spatial context.

1 Introduction

One of the main goals of any adaptive hypermedia (AH) system is to increase user efficiency. This efficiency is usually measured either in the time spent searching for information or increasing the amount of information absorbed by the user. The work presented in this paper is built around the philosophy of providing the user with greater access to information through link augmentation - a technique whereby external links are inserted directly into the body of a document. There are already several proxy-based systems that provide link augmentation such as Microcosm [9], Personal WebWatcher [18], and WBI [17], but they base their insertion algorithms on individual keywords or phrases in the document. However because the English language contains multiple uses for individual words, a simple augmentation algorithm like this can lead to out-of-place or irrelevant links and in addition to being frustrating, this can also lower a user's confidence in the system.

Out of place links are added when the component that adds those links fails to recognize a document's context. Such contextual information can be obtained by analysing the text in a document and comparing it against previously visited documents. This information can then act as a filter to remove or ignore those links that fail to match the current context.

S. Reich, M.M. Tzagarakis, P.M.E. De Bra (Eds.): OHS/SC/AH 2001, LNCS 2266, pp. 239–251, 2002.

While user modelling involves capturing some contextual information such as a user's knowledge in a particular area, their tasks, goals and interests etc., this information is often obtained using explicit feedback which can distract the user away from their original task [15]. One advantage of the technique used in this paper is the lack of explicit user feedback required. All information about the user is obtained implicitly from the user's trail and the contents of each page the user views. This removes the need to question the user and although not exploited in this paper, this data can be employed in other user modelling environments to infer details such as user interests, hobbies, skills and tasks.

Another advantage of this system is that it works without making any pre-defined assumptions about its users, thereby removing the need to bootstrap the system with user data. Additionally, since the trail capturing component is located on the end user's machine, adaptive link augmentation can also be provided across any hypermedia web page that the user visits.

This paper focuses on the extraction and analysis of a user's spatial context through a non-proxy agent-based architecture. Spatial context has been referred to elsewhere as the browsing context [16]. A method is presented for obtaining this information and using it as the basis of a linkbase-filtering algorithm. A linkbase is simply a database of links and the filter results in a single 'active' linkbase that contains a set of context dependent links. These links can be dynamically inserted into the current document. A new linkbase will be activated whenever the system determines that the user has entered a new context (providing the system has an associated linkbase). Link augmentation as a technique, has been shown to provide users with a viable means of decreasing search times [12], an combining this with the concept of spatial context, will benefit users and provide a new research area for adaptive systems.

2   Background

The role of linking has long been established in the hypermedia community where its primary use has been as a mechanism for navigation. Since the early days of adaptive hypermedia systems, links have been employed in many systems as a means of adaptive navigational support [5,10,18], and adaptive presentation [13].

The importance of links was reinforced in Brusilovsky's seminal 1996 paper [4] where he defined several subcategories of adaptive navigational support: direct guidance, link sorting, link hiding, link annotation and map adaptation. While today these categories remain more or less unchanged, it seems that an additional category can be added - (adaptive) link augmentation - which we define as the process of dynamically inserting additional links into existing web page. This differs from link annotation, which concerns the visible properties of hyperlinks, although these techniques can be combined to provide annotated, augmented links. The advantage of augmented linking is that the underlining navigational structure of the web page remains unaffected as all the original hyperlinks remain intact. However, the danger lies in information overload, which results when too many links are added, possibly leading to the situation where 'every word becomes a link'.

While there are several link augmentation systems, the earliest occurrence was seen in Microcosm [14,9], which was first developed in 1990 as a distributed open hypermedia environment that provided the user with dynamic, cross-application hyperlinks on the fly. These links were inserted (augmented) into the user's existing application and selecting one of these links issued a request to the Microcosm link service. This link service maintained a set of link databases (linkbases) and each link had one of three start point types: generic, specific or local. Specific links originate from an object at a specific point in the source document; local links originate from an object at any point in a specific document, and generic links, link from an object at any position in any document. Microcosm also provided text retrieval links where the user could highlight any text and ask the system to supply a set of related links.

One of the follow up projects to Microcosm, the DLS (Distributed Link Service) [7], is a link delivery system that operates in an open hypermedia environment. The DLS was aimed at bringing the concepts from the open hypermedia community to the Web. It acts as a link service providing other applications with hyperlinks on demand. These links are stored in multiple linkbases maintained by the DLS. However, by removing the need for hard-coded hyperlinks, the responsibility of determining link context fell on the shoulders of the user. So the major limitation of the system is in its inability to automatically switch between linkbases depending on the context of documents [11].

Today, many of the features found in both Microcosm and the DLS can be seen in Active Navigation's Portal Maximiser[1]. Essentially a web site server engine, Portal Maximiser provides many features such as document recommendations, contextual and relevance ranked search results, document categorization and theme-based dynamic (augmented) linking.

Another link augmentation system, WBI (WeB Intermediaries) [17], has been written as a web proxy that adds intermediary functions to the World Wide Web (WWW). WBI sits between the user and the outside WWW, analysing every page a user visits. It has a set of knowledge bases (KB's) hand authored for a specific subject. When the user views a related page, it replaces any known word or phrase with a hyperlink from the KB. If the user clicks on this hyperlink, a further information dialog box pops up on the client's machine offering additional resources (like word definitions or links to external web pages).

The PWW system [16] offers an approach to implicit (zero-input) personalization that is similar to the one taken in this paper. The system described by Kushmerick et al. is a server side system that offers recommendations to pages in the web site based on the URL and/or content of the referring page. User evaluations of PWW indicate the performance of the system reaches 9.3%, giving a value 77 times more effective then random guesswork. Our approach significantly differs from PWW by moving the architecture away from server side scripting

---

[1] http://www.activenavigation.com/PortalMax/default.htm

thus allowing the system to gain a context of the user that extends across their entire browsing history and not just the referring page.

More recently, the Web, aided by improvements in browser technology, has seen the development of knowledge delivery systems that implement features similar to AH systems. While such system lack any formal user modelling component, knowledge delivery systems, such as Flyswat[2], Zapper[3] and Atomica[4], provide resources such as link augmentation, keyword lookup, recommender functionality and shopping facilities to provide additional information to their users.

The current systems that employ link augmentation do so on the basis of the individual text of each word or phrase. If there is a match with a known link, then the word is replaced with the corresponding link. However this causes a problem when words have different meanings in different contexts. For example, the word 'java' may refer to the programming language Java, the country or the coffee bean and it is only by analysing the context in which the word is used that it is possible to distinguish between these meanings.

3   Context

Context is an important concept that has been examined in many different fields and for various tasks. It is also an involved issue, as it depends on the task at hand and the available variables that can be modelled in relation to that task. In the case of 'linking' the primary entities involved in this particular task, are those of the user and the document. There are many factors that can affect the context of the user. These include the user's role in an organisation/group/etc, their physical location, level of expertise in various topics, browsing history, interests, tasks, etc. Many of these user features are already captured in existing user models. The context of a document can be defined in many different ways such as by its content, its format (html, pdf, gif, etc), its purpose, the date it was created, the server on which it resides on, its download speed, etc. [11] and it's relationship with other documents. One particularly relevant system to the work presented in this paper and which has addressed the issue of 'linking in context' is the QuIC system.

3.1   QuIC

The work in this paper has drawn on work undertaken for a project called QuIC (Queries in Context). QuIC is a multi-agent system that was developed at the University of Southampton with the overall goal of utilizing concepts from the open hypermedia community to help users with their navigation and information finding activities. One of the issues addressed by the QuIC system is the use of linking in context as a way of assisting users in their information

---

[2] http://www.flyswat.com/
[3] http://www.zapper.com/
[4] http://www.atomica.com/

finding activities. This specifically targets a failing associated with traditional information retrieval models which is attributed to the isolation of these systems from the context in which queries are made [6].

3.2   The QuIC Approach to Context

The model used by the QuIC project defines two factors for context: the interests of a user, and the contents of the document within which the links are to be rendered. A number of methods have been developed for using the content of unstructured information resources for inferring user interests for the purpose of constructing user or filtering models. In these models, the capture of user context or document context for the achievement of a specific task, is one of the goals. Depending on the specific task at hand, a number of techniques have been employed to build such models or profiles. Examples of techniques employed by Web agents to learn or capture a document or user profile include Decision trees, Neural Nets, Bayesian classifiers, Nearest Neighbour and TF-IDF (Term Frequency, Inverse Document Frequency) [19].

The decision was made to adopt a technique that would be capable of accurately capturing document context. TF-IDF is a very well studied and widely used information retrieval technique [22]. The technique is used to derive weights for terms in a way that would reflect their importance in a given document. TF-IDF is based on the vector space model where a vector is used to represent a document or a query. The cosine angle between different document vectors is a measure of how similar the documents are, and is used as a similarity function. Used in conjunction with a similarity function and other text processing techniques such as stop word removal and stemming, TF-IDF can be employed to distinguish between documents. The model has been used successfully for document ranking, document filtering, document clustering, and as the basis for relevance feedback [1]. One of the advantages of using the TF-IDF method is that unlike many other machine learning algorithms, it does not require large training data sets in order to distinguish between various documents. By representing a document through a vector space model computed via TF-IDF, comparing a document to other documents or queries is simply achieved through the application of a similarity function. The technique has therefore been employed by a large number of Web assistants, examples of which are: FAB [3], WebMate [8], and Margin Notes [21]. To further increase the accuracy of this method in distinguishing between different contexts, heuristics, as described in [12], have been introduced to the conditions of the context match to enable better determination of context.

The work resulting from the QuIC project has obvious applications for adaptive hypermedia systems, specifically adaptive navigational support such as link annotation and augmentation. To this end, the idea of context has been extended within this work to include the concept of a user's spatial context within an information domain.

4   Spatial Context

The goal of this work is to use the context technology described above to introduce the concept of spatial context into adaptive hypermedia systems. Such a system would work alongside existing user models providing another level of contextual information for the modelling component to draw upon.

A document's spatial context represents its location within the surrounding information domain. This spatial context is refined further by a user's path through the hyperspace before arriving at the current document. By doing this, a user is effectively selecting one path out of many other possibilities. In a hypermedia environment like the Web, the number of possible paths to a web page is continually changing, making it impossible for page designers to cater for the needs of all possible visitors. As a result, hard coded hyperlinks tend to cater for the 'average' user who has followed the most logical path to arrive at the current document.

4.1   Spatial Context in an Example Situation

Figure 1 shows three separate paths (starting from documents labelled 1,2&3) taken to reach the central document (shaded grey). The black arrows represent the traversed navigational hyperlinks, while the grey lines represent alternative hyperlinks. In a real-world scenario, the central document might be a review of an XML book in an online bookstore such as Amazon[5]. Trail 1 would be a single link from one XML book review to other similar books. Trail 2 could represent a direct link from the author's external homepage to the current book, while trail 3 might be traversed by a user interested in Computer Science technologies, who visits the bookstore and searches through reviews of Network and Programming language books before finally arriving at the XML book review.

Each of these three trails represents a different context. If link augmentation were to be provided, each user would require a different set of hyperlinks. Situation 1 would require links to other XML books, the user in trail 2 should be presented with links to books by the same author, while in the third example, the augmented links should point the user to books on a wide range of computer science subjects. It is this issue of knowing when to activate these 'dynamic linkbases' that can be overcome by understanding the user's spatial context when arriving at the current document.

The following system uses the contextual component of QuIC to provide a means of capturing a user's spatial context and, using this information, select and apply a dynamic linkbase.

5   System Architecture

The spatial context analyser has been implemented within an agent-based system built on top of the agent framework developed at Southampton University

---

[5] http://www.amazon.com/

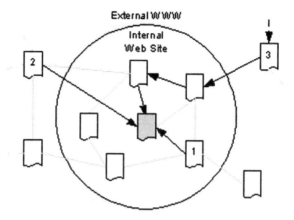

Fig. 1. Examples of a document's spatial context

called SoFAR (Southampton Framework for Agent Research) [20]. SoFAR is a Java implemented framework designed as a test bed for agent research. So-FAR provides performatives for communication between agents, and ontologies for defining the contents of these communications. The decision for building an agent system arose due to the modular nature of the system's components, which are well suited to an agent environment [2] and the desire to distribute the linking mechanism (which is essentially a DLS).

The network structure, as shown in Fig. 2, has been designed as a client-server approach. The agents (which run within the SoFAR framework) and user data all reside on a single server. In contrast to this, and in following with the architecture of the DLS, the linkbases used by the Linkbase Agent are fully distributed and can reside on any web server.

The client user interface is packaged as a downloadable Perl application and executed on the user's machine. This interface communicates with the agent server through the use of sockets and also hooks into the client's Internet Explorer Web browser through the Microsoft OLE (Object Linking and Embedding) automation feature that has been encapsulated as an ActiveX WebBrowser control. This allows the system to receive browser events such as OnLoad, DownloadComplete and DocumentComplete. However as a result, the system has been restricted to machines running Microsoft Windows with Internet Explorer 5.0 or later.

The system is triggered every time the Perl application receives a DocumentComplete event. The browser fires this event when it has finished loading both the text and images of a web page. For each new page the user views, the following steps are executed.

1. The Perl program first captures the URL of the current page and forwards this information onto the context agent.

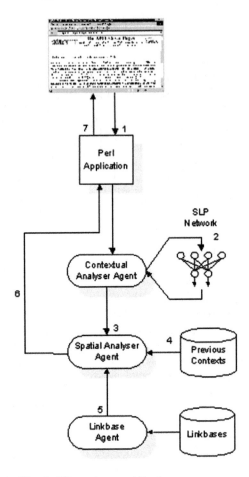

Fig. 2. The system architecture

2. An important issue for the context agent is that it needs to be aware that not every page is a possible candidate for context analysis. While some pages, such as Shockwave Flash sites, will produce empty context sets when processed which the system will ignore, others will produce misleading information, such as the '404 Not found' and '301 Document Moved' pages created automatically from broken hyperlinks. In order to identify these pages, the context agent employs a Single Layer Perceptron network (SLP) to extract the key features from the page and apply a set of weights to these features. These features include identifying phrases like 'Document Moved', the amount of text in the page, the number of hyperlinks and the frequency of keywords like 'broken', 'error' and '404'. The SLP produces a probability, which determines its confidence in the page belonging to the 'Page Not Found' category. If this is high, the page is ignored; otherwise the context

agent applies the TFIDF algorithm to the page and produces a 'context model' for this document.

3. This model is then passed to the spatial context analyser to determine the context of the current user. Here there are three possible outcomes: the user is in the existing context, the user has returned to a previous context or the user has entered a new context. Firstly, this agent compares the new context model against the current model using a cosine similarity function. If a match is found, then the system moves onto step 5, otherwise step 4 occurs.

4. The spatial analyser agent compares the current context model against the entire set of previous context's that the user has experienced in the current browsing session. This comparison uses the same similarity function. If the highest match exceeds a given threshold then the system assumes that the user has returned to a previous context. This could occur for a number of reasons. For instance, the user could press the back button after arriving at an irrelevant page or the user has finished following a search thread and is returning to an old topic, this could also occur if the user has several browser windows open and is switching between them. If no match is found, then the current document's context forms the start of the user's new browsing context (and a record of it is stored in the 'Previous Contexts' database).

5. When the system has calculated the current context of the user, a request is sent to the linkbase agent for matching linkbases. This agent searches through each known linkbase to find the highest similarity match with the context. The linkbase agent returns the highest matching linkbase (or null if no match is found).

6. The system passes all the links from the matching linkbase onto the Perl application.

7. The last job of the Perl program is to extract the text from the web, page search through it and replace all the matching words with a hyperlink. Matches are found through simple string/word comparison. The text extraction is achieved through an ActiveX call to the browser's Document Object Model requesting all the text in the current web page. This request ignores the page type giving the link augmentation process the ability to operate on any type of web page including dynamically generated pages such as ASP, JS, CGI, PHP and SHTML. The resulting augmented page is reinserted back into the browser window using the properties of dynamic HTML.

This whole process is executed in real time and the user will see the requested web page displayed, and then a split-second later, the new links will appear. Because the page is held in memory, there is no visible refresh; all that is apparent is that certain words are instantly transformed into hyperlinks. Often there is no visible delay between loading the page and inserting the links.

This context-based technique works due to the property that all the augmented links reside in the same linkbase and each linkbase has been hand-crafted to contain relevant links on specific subjects. For instance, a linkbase on the subject of XML might contain individual links to:

- W3C XML specification
- XML parsers
- XML technologies
- XML books

The authors of these linkbases have the freedom to make each linkbase as detailed as desired, so for example, there could be separate linkbases for each of the above sub-topics or even linkbases of each sub-sub-topic.

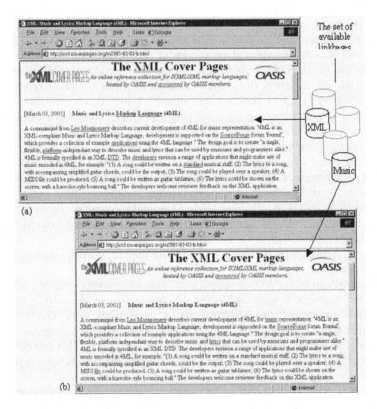

Fig. 3. An example link augmented page as viewed from an 'XML' and a 'Music' context

Fig. 3 shows the system in operation. It shows the same page is viewed from two different spatial contexts[6]. Page (a) appears as viewed by a user who has been reading articles about XML before arriving at the current document. In this instance, the system has determined that the user's spatial context best matches

---

[6] In these screen shots, the original document contains the hyperlinks: 'sponsored', 'Leo Montgomery' and 'SoundForge'.

the 'XML' linkbase and so links from the keywords 'XML', 'DTD', 'standard' and 'developer' have been inserted. Although it appears that this page exists in a predominately XML context, the user viewing page (b) has previously been looking at music related sites and therefore their spatial context best matches the 'Music' linkbase and so the page has been augmented with the links 'lyrics' and 'music'.

6   Linkbases and Cross-Domain Support

By abstracting the links and storing them in a set of linkbase, the system gains cross-domain support 'for free'. This one-size-fits-all approach will provide link augmentation to any information domain contained within the linkbases. However the system relies heavily on both the quality and quantity of these linkbases. Absent linkbases will simply lead to a lack of augmented links for that domain, however badly authored linkbases can lead to unhelpful or irrelevant links. While the current linkbases have all been hand authored, it is desirable to find an automated link extraction algorithm that could be used to create linkbases to cover a variety of topics.

7   Future Work

The work introduced in this paper describes one way of capturing the user's spatial context within an hypermedia system like the WWW, and then applying hyperlinks based on this context. However there are several major hurdles that need to be overcome before such a system can have any practical benefits. Firstly, the system relies heavily on hand-authored linkbases and without these the system is useless. This can be overcome with a link generation mechanism as used in both Portal Maximiser and QuIC. Providing the system could produce links of a high enough quality, this would remove the need for human 'experts' that would currently have to spend many man-hours manually creating each linkbase.

A second issue that arises is the question of multiple active linkbases. Currently, only one linkbase is ever 'activated' at any one time. However it is often possible for the user to exist in several different contexts simultaneously and in such a situation it would be beneficial to activate multiple linkbases. If this is the case, then care must be taken to avoid causing the user to suffer from information overload and as a result, further investigation is needed to see whether there is such a demand for this service.

One important area for further research would be to investigate the level of intelligence required when inserting links into a document. The current link augmentation algorithm matches document keywords words against the set of context-filtered links. If a match exists then the corresponding link is inserted. This can cause problems due to the disregard of the surrounding text - the paragraph context of the word. This is part of a bigger issue that concerns contextual scooping. Scooping examines the level at which contextual analysis is conducted. By analysing not only the document but also each paragraph and sentence, link insertion could become even more accurate.

Finally, while the system does indeed produce real-time context-dependent augmented links, there has yet to be any formal evaluation of the system. When the improvements stated above have been introduced, the final stage will need to involve a system evaluation.

8   Conclusions

While link augmentation is not a new technique and has been used in many systems before, applying context analysis as a means of filtering out irrelevant links is entirely new. The work here shows that link augmentation, when applied to a document's spatial context, is a highly significant area for further exploratory study. To support this claim, user evaluations of the QuIC project (as reported in [12]) and PWW [16] already show that link augmentation and recommendation are viable means of enriching the existing hypermedia domain with effective user-centric information which can be used as a means of decreasing search times.

The flexible design of the system allows link augmentation to be provided across a variety of information domains, dependent only on the availability of linkbases. In addition to this, the authors feel that adaptive link augmentation, when implemented with care, is a worthy addition to Peter Brusilovsky's list of adaptive navigation technologies and warrants further research.

Acknowledgements. The work presented in this paper has been supported by the QuIC project, ESPRC grant GR/M77086.

References

1. Baeza-Yates, R. and Ribeiro-Neto, B. (1999). "Modern Information Retrieval". Addison-Wesley/ACM Press.
2. Bailey, C and Hall, W. (2000) "An Agent-Based approach to Adaptive Hypermedia using a link service". P. Brusilovsky, O. Stock, C. Strapparava (Eds.): Adaptive Hypermedia and Adaptive Web-Based Systems International Conference, AH 2000, Trento, Italy, August 2000, pp. 260-263.
3. Balabanovic, M. and Shoham, Y. (1997). "Fab: content-based, collaborative recommendation". Communications of the ACM, 40(3), pp. 66-72.
4. Brusilovsky, P. (1996). "Methods and Techniques of Adaptive Hypermedia". Journal of User Modelling and User-Adaptive Interaction, UMUAI6.
5. Brusilovsky, P., Eklund, J. and Schwarz, E. (1998). "Web-based education for all: A tool for developing adaptive courseware". Computer Networks and ISDN Systems. Proceedings of Seventh International World Wide Web Conference, 14-18 April 1998, 30 (1-7), pp. 291-300.
6. Budzik, J. (2000). "User Interactions with Everyday Applications as Context for Just-in-time information Access". In Proceedings of Intelligent User Interfaces (IUI), ACM, New Orleans, LA USA, pp. 44-51.
7. Carr, L., De Roure, D., Hall, W. and Hill, G. (1995). "The Distributed Link Service: A Tool for Publishers, Authors and Readers". World Wide Web Journal 1(1), O'Reilly & Associates (1995). pp 647-656.

8. Chen, L. and Sycara, K. (1998). "Webmate: A Personal Agent for Browsing and Searching". In Proceedings of the Second International Conference on Autonomous Agents, ACM, Minneapolis, pp. 132–139.

9. Davis, H.C., Hall, W., Heath, I., Hill, G. and Wilkins, R.J. (1992) "Towards an Integrated Information Environment with Open Hypermedia Systems" In Proceedings of ECHT'92, ACM Press, pp. 181 – 190.

10. De Bra, P. and Calvi, L. (1998). "AHA: a Generic Adaptive Hypermedia System". In Proceedings of the 2nd Workshop on Adaptive Hypertext and Hypermedia, HYPERTEXT'98, Pittsburgh, USA, June 20-24, 1998.

11. El-Beltagy, S. (2001). "An Agent Based Framework for Navigation Assistance and Information Finding in Context". PhD thesis. University of Southampton, 2001.

12. El-Beltagy, S., Hall, W., De Roure, D. and Carr, L. (2001). "Linking in Context". To appear in the Twelfth ACM Conference on Hypertext and Hypermedia (HT'01), Denmark, 2001.

13. Espinoza, F. and Hö"ok, K. (1997). "A WWW Interface to an Adaptive Hypermedia System". Presented at PAAM (Practical Applications of Agent Methodology), April 1996, London.
http://www.sics.se/~espinoza/pages/PAAM_submission.html.

14. Fountain, A., Hall, W., Heath, I. and Davis, H. C. (1990) "Microcosm: an open model with dynamic linking". In Hypertext: Concepts, Systems and Applications (A. Rizk, N. Strietz, and J. Andre, eds.), (France), pp. 298–311, European Conference on Hypertext, INRIA, November 1990.

15. Kim, J., Oard, D. W., and Romanik, K. (2000) "Using implicit feedback for user modeling in Internet and Intranet searching". Technical Report, College of Library and Information Services, University of Marylandat College Park.

16. Kushmerick, N., McKee, J. and Toolan, F. (2000). "Towards Zero-Input Personalization: Referrer-Based Page Prediction". P. Brusilovsky, O. Stock, C. Strapparava (Eds.): Adaptive Hypermedia and Adaptive Web-Based Systems International Conference, AH 2000, Trento, Italy, August 2000, pp. 133–143.

17. Maglio, P., P. and Farrell, S. (2000). "LiveInfo: Adapting web experience by customization and annotation". In Proceedings of the First International Conference on Adaptive Hypermedia and Adaptive Web-based Systems (AH 2000). LNCS Series, Springer-Verlag.

18. Mladenic, D., (1996). "Personal WebWatcher: Implementation and Design". Technical Report IJS-DP-7472, Department of Intelligent Systems, J.Stefan Institute, Slovenia.

19. Mladenic, D. (1999). "Text-Learning and Related Intelligent Agents: A Survey". IEEE Intelligent Systems, 14(4), pp. 44-54.

20. Moreau, L., Gibbins, N., De Roure, D., El-Beltagy, S., Hall, W., Hughes, G., Joyce, D., Kim, S., Michaelides, D., Millard, D., Reich, S., Tansley, R. and Weal, M. (2000). "An Agent Framework for Distributed Information Management". In The Fifth International Conference and Exhibition on The Practical Application of Intelligent Agents and Multi-Agents, Manchester, UK.

21. Rhodes, B. J. (2000) "Margin Notes: Building a Contextually Aware Associative Memory". In Proceedings of Intelligent User Interfaces (IUI '00), ACM, New Orleans, LA USA, pp. 219-224.

22. Salton, G. and McGill, M. J. (1983). "Introduction to Modern Information Retrieval". McGraw Hill, New York.

XAHM: An XML-Based Adaptive Hypermedia Model and Its Implementation

Mario Cannataro[1] and Andrea Pugliese[1,2]

[1]ISI-CNR, Via P. Bucci, 87036 Rende, Italy
[2]D.E.I.S., University of Calabria, Italy
{cannataro, apugliese}@si.deis.unical.it

Abstract. This paper presents an XML-based Adaptive Hypermedia Model (XAHM) and a modular architecture, for modeling and supporting Adaptive Hypermedia Systems. We propose a graph-based layered model for the description of the logical structure of the hypermedia, and XML-based models for the description of *i)* metadata about basic information fragments and *ii)* "neutral" pages to be adapted. Furthermore, we describe a modular architecture, which allows the design of the hypermedia and its run-time support. We introduce a multidimensional approach to model different aspects of the adaptation process, which is based on three different "adaptivity dimensions": user's behavior (preferences and browsing activity), technology (network and user's terminal) and external environment (time, location, language, socio-political issues, etc.). An Adaptive Hypermedia is modeled with respect to such dimensions, and a view over it corresponds to each potential position of the user in the "adaptation space".

1 Introduction

In hypertext-based multimedia systems, the personalization of presentations and content (i.e. their adaptation to user's requirements and goals) is becoming a major requirement. Application fields where contents personalization can be useful are manifold; they comprise on-line advertising, direct web marketing, electronic commerce, on-line learning and teaching, etc.

The need for adaptation arises from different aspects of the interaction between users and hypermedia systems. Users' classes to deal with are increasingly heterogeneous due to different interests and goals, worldwide deployment of services, etc. Hypermedia systems should be made accessible from different user's terminals, which can differ not only at the software level (browsing and elaboration capabilities) but also in terms of ergonomic interfaces (scroll buttons, voice commands, etc.). Different kinds of network (e.g. wired or wireless) and other network-related conditions, both static (e.g. available bandwidth) and dynamic (per user bandwidth, latency, error rate, etc.), should be considered to obtain a comfortable and useful interaction. Finally, taking into account the spatio-temporal position of the user and other "environmental" conditions can lead to a more effective interaction.

S. Reich, M.M. Tzagarakis, P.M.E. De Bra (Eds.): OHS/SC/AH 2001, LNCS 2266, pp. 252-263, 2002.

To face some of these problems, in the last years the concepts of user model-based adaptive systems and hypermedia systems have come together in the *Adaptive Hypermedia* (*AH*) research theme [1, 4, 5, 6, 10].

The basic components of Adaptive Hypermedia Systems are the *Application Domain Model*, the *User Model* and the *Adaptation Model*. The Application Domain Model is used to describe the hypermedia basic contents and their organization to depict more abstract concepts. In addition to traditional models, such as those developed in the Human-Computer Interaction and Database fields, the modeling of AH must consider the different sources that affect the adaptation process. In our belief, a promising approach for modeling the Application domain is data-centric, and many researches employ well-known database modeling techniques [9]. The adaptation of content presented to the user can be generally distinguished into *adaptive presentation,* i.e. a manipulation of information fragments, and *adaptive navigation support*, i.e. a manipulation of the links presented to the user [4].

Due to the complexity of user models that usually try to capture user's needs, the adaptation process results in a complex task; it is even more demanding when considering dynamic conditions. To efficiently allow the realization of user-adaptable presentations, a modular and scalable approach to describe and support the adaptation process should be adopted. In particular *(i)* the adaptive hypermedia model and the adaptation process must allow describing the hypermedia in such a way it is easy to find all the system variables that need to be supported in an adaptive way; *(ii)* the User Model must capture not only the user's explicit behavior (e.g. browsing activity), but also other implicit aspects regarding his/her environment and its dynamic constraints; *(iii)* the architecture must easily and efficiently support the adaptation process. It should be noted that the architecture should also be flexible with respect to the kind of adaptivity sources (i.e. it should be easy to add new terminals or new kind of networks to the set of supported ones).

In this paper, we present a model for the description of Adaptive Hypermedia, named *XML Adaptive Hypermedia Model* (*XAHM*). XAHM allows describing:

- the logical structure and contents of an Adaptive Hypermedia, emphasizing the different parts of the hypermedia that should be adapted during the adaptation process (the *what*);
- the logic of the adaptation process, distinguishing adaptation driven by technological constraints and adaptation driven by user needs (the *how*).

The logical structure and the contents of an Adaptive Hypermedia are described along different logical levels; upper (abstract) layers are organized as weighted directed graphs of concepts whereas lower (physical) layers are composed of XML documents describing individual pages of the hypermedia. Such pages include basic multimedia fragments extracted from different data sources and described by XML metadata.

The adaptation scheme uses a multidimensional approach. Each part of the Adaptive Hypermedia is described along three different "adaptivity dimensions": *user's behavior* (preferences and browsing activity); *technology* (network and user's terminal), *external environment* (time, location, language, socio-political issues, etc.). A view over the Application Domain corresponds to each possible position of the user in the "adaptation space".

The rest of the paper is organized as follows: in Section 2 we describe XAHM and detail the different phases of the construction of an adaptive hypermedia; in Section 3 we propose an algorithm to classify users on the basis of their behavior; in Section 4 we show a modular multi-tier architecture for modeling and supporting AHS, which is entirely based on XAHM; Section 5 outlines conclusions and future work.

2 Adaptive Hypermedia Modeling

This Section presents XAHM, our approach to the modeling of Adaptive Hypermedia. We first introduce our proposed multidimensional adaptation scheme, and then we show a graph-based layered model for the Application Domain and a probabilistic interpretation of the hypermedia structure. XAHM adopts XML essentially because of its flexibility and data-centric orientation; in fact, it makes it possible to elegantly describe data access and dynamic data composition functions, allowing the use of pre-existing multimedia basic data and the description of contents in a terminal-independent way.

2.1 Adaptation Space

In general, user's goals and/or requirements can be captured analyzing the behaviour of the current user or of classes of users; for example, using data about user's browsing activity, or data mining techniques (e.g. clustering) to discover new knowledge about users can help to reveal latent wishes. On the other hand, monitoring user's location, terminal or available network bandwidth can allow satisfying response-time requirements. Many of these conditions can be considered orthogonal; others are correlated.

In the proposed architecture, the Application Domain can be viewed along three abstract orthogonal adaptivity dimensions (Fig. 1):

- *User's behavior* (browsing activity, preferences etc.);
- *External environment* (time-spatial location, language, socio-political issues, status of external web sites, etc.);
- *Technology* (kind of network, bandwidth, Quality of Service, user's terminal, etc).

The position of the user in the adaptation space (Fig.1) is denoted by a tuple of the form $[B, E, T]$. Each of the values B, E and T varies over a finite alphabet of symbols. The B value, related to the User's Behavior dimension, captures the group the user belongs to (i.e. his/her stereotype profile); the E and T values respectively identify environmental conditions and used technologies. As an example, B could vary over {*novice, expert*}, E over {*summer, autumn, winter, spring*} and T over {*HTML-low, HTML-high, WML*}. A personalized view over the Application Domain corresponds to each point of the adaptation space, e.g. [*expert, winter, HTML-high*].

The AHS monitors the different possible sources that can affect the position of the user in the adaptation space, collecting a set of values, called *User, Technology* and *External Variables*. The position of the user along the T axis, in the case of n Technology Variables, each having an associated domain V_i ($i=1, ..., n$) consisting of a finite alphabet of labels, could be identified by a simple mapping function $f: V_1 \times V_2 \times ... \times V_n \rightarrow T$ (where T can have $|V_1|*|V_2|*...*|V_n|$ values at maximum). Instead, the mapping from the User Variables to the user profile is carried out by an algorithm that makes use of a probabilistic interpretation of the link structure of the hypermedia (see Section 3).

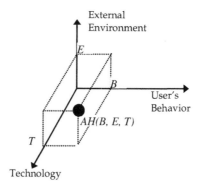

Fig. 1. Adaptation space and adaptivity dimensions

The Application Domain model remains abstract with respect to the alphabets of labels of dimension variables' domains; this feature is significant for the extensibility of the model, i.e. when an author needs to make the dimension variables feasible for a particular domain. For example, referring to the technology dimension, the author could freely split the point *WML* in two distinct points *WML-high* and *WML-low*; in the next Section, it will be shown how such extensions are reflected in new views over the Application Domain, obtained considering further parameters and modeling presentations subsequently.

2.2 A Layered Model for the Logical Structure of the Hypermedia

The proposed Application Domain Model uses a layered data model for describing the logical structure of the hypermedia.; it comprises the following abstract levels:

0. *Information Fragments (IF)* or *atomic concepts*, like texts, sounds, images, videos, etc. at the lowest level. The information fragments are stored in databases, file systems or in general everywhere in the Web. Data can be structured, semi-structured or unstructured and can be provided by different sources (e.g. external or local databases, XML and HTML documents, texts, files and so on). The IFs are described by metadata represented by XML documents.
1. *Presentation Descriptions (PD)*, XML documents constrained by a fixed DTD, which capture the so-called *Page Concepts*. They comprise multimedia contents, presentation layout and format, etc. Page elements are parameterized with respect to the technology, external variables and to the user profile, so they can be associated to a portion of the adaptation space. Included basic multimedia fragments are referenced by means of the XML metadata describing them. The

final pages composed of actual fragments, also called *Presentation Units* (*PU*), are dynamically generated at run time in a target language (XML, HTML, WML, VoiceXML, synthesized speech etc.) and delivered.

2. *Elementary Abstract Concepts* (*EAC*) representing larger units of information. An Elementary Abstract Concept is composed by one or more Presentation Descriptions organized in a digraph, whose links are annotated by a weight. Arcs represent relationships between elementary concepts or navigation requirements (e.g. a sequence of elementary concepts to be learned before learning an abstract concept), while weights represent their relevance with respect to each other. The linking structure of EACs is differentiated with respect to the user's behavior adaptivity dimension; an EAC is represented as a digraph as there can be more arcs between the same two nodes, each of which associated to a different user's profile.

3. *Adaptive Hypermedia*. Finally, an Adaptive Hypermedia is composed by a set of Elementary Abstract Concepts organized in a digraph. Arcs represent relationships between EACs; they are differentiated with respect to the user's behavior adaptivity dimension, but their weight is "null" since they are used only for describing relationships, and the user cannot perform any choice on them.

2.3 Probabilistic Interpretation of the Adaptive Hypermedia Structure

In the layered model presented in Section 2.2, we introduced a weight in the graphs representing Elementary Abstract Concepts to express links' relevance with respect to each other. In this Section, we detail our probabilistic interpretation of arcs' weight, which is used also for the classification of users based on their behavior (see Section 3).

We consider the overall Adaptive Hypermedia as a weighted digraph of Presentation Descriptions, i.e. a "plain" version of the AD, obtained from the layered one. Formally, an AD with M different profiles is a set N of Presentation Descriptions where the generic description $i \in N$ contains, for each profile $k=1, ..., M$, a set of weighted outgoing links (i, j, k) where j is the destination node. It can be mapped in a weighted digraph $G = (N, E)$ where each node corresponds to a description and each directed arc to an outgoing link; the digraph G can also be referred to as the set of the weighted graphs G_k, $k=1,...,M$, obtained extracting from G the nodes and arcs associated to each profile. Each G_k is named *Logical Navigation Graph*. Our probabilistic interpretation assumes that the weight $W_k(i,j)$ of the arc (i, j, k) is the probability that a user associated to the profile k follows the link to the j node having already reached the i node, i.e. $W_k(i, j) = P(j|k,i)$. $P(i|k,i)$ is considered to be always zero, as it is impossible a link from a node to itself. We define a path S in G as the ordered set of arcs $S = \{ (S_j, S_{j+1}, profile_j) \mid (S_j, S_{j+1}, profile_j) \in E, j=0, ..., l\text{-}1 \}$, where $profile_j \in \{1, ..., M\}$ represents the group the user belongs to when he/she reaches the node S_j. It should be noted that paths involving arcs associated to different profiles are allowed, since a user can be moved within different groups during his/her browsing activity.

The probability that a user belonging to the k–th group follows the S path is

$$P_S^k = \prod_{j=0..l-1} W_k(S_j, S_{j+1}), \text{ i.e. } P_S^k \text{ is the product of the probabilities associated to the}$$

arcs belonging to the S path, while the "shortest" path $\widetilde{S}_{ij}^{\,k}$ between two nodes i and j for a given profile k is the path with the maximum joint probability given as $\widetilde{P}_{ij}^{k} = \max_{S_{ij}^{k}} (P_{S_{ij}^{k}}^{k})$, where S_{ij}^{k} is the generic path between the nodes i and j through arcs belonging to the profile k.

3   User Classification

The probabilistic interpretation of the hypermedia structure is used essentially to characterize "latent" properties of the user's behavior, which can be captured by tracking his/her browsing activity. Such properties, related to the user's behavior adaptivity dimension, are expressed by means of an association of the user to a stereotype model. In this Section we describe our approach to such classification task.

The proposed algorithm builds a discrete probability density function (*PDF*) $A(k)$, with $k=1, \ldots, M$, measuring the "belonging probability" of the user to each group (i.e. how much each profile fits him/her). While the user browses, the system updates $A(k)$ and the user's profile is changed accordingly. In other words, on the basis of the user's behavior, the system dynamically attempts to assign the user to the best-fitting group.

First, some *static (intrinsic) properties* of the hypermedia structure are considered by constructing three PDF:

- $\mu(k)$, for each profile k, proportional to the mean value of the probability of the "shortest" paths in G_k; high values of this PDF indicate the existence of highly natural paths in the hypermedia.
- $p(k)$, for each profile k, proportional to the mean value of the length of the "shortest" paths in G_k; high values of this term mean longer natural paths in the hypermedia, which could be an advantage in the overall personalization process.
- $n(k)$, for each profile k, proportional to the number of nodes belonging to the profile.

A weighted mean $s(k)$ of such functions, expressing the "intrinsic relevance" of the profiles is computed. It should be noted that the values of $s(k)$ could change over time: the hypermedia structure can dynamically be updated (adding or removing nodes, arcs or their weight) e.g. on the basis of semi-automatic observation of the behavior of many users or on the basis of an increased knowledge of the Application Domain by the author.

Browsing starts from the presentation unit associated to a starting node. If the user is already registered, the last $A(k)$ is set as current. Otherwise, he/she is assigned to a generic profile, or to one calculated on the basis of a questionnaire (see [3] for an interesting way to interpret results in a probabilistic way); the initial value of $A(k)$ is called $A_0(k)$. When a user who is visiting the node R_{r-1} requests to follow a link, the system computes the new PDF $A'(k)$, on the basis of the User Behavior Variables and of $s(k)$, then it decides the (new) group to be assigned to the user. To avoid continuous profile changing it is possible to keep a profile for a given duration (i.e. the number of traversed links), evaluating the $A'(k)$ distribution at fixed intervals only.

The user's behavior is stored as a set of User Behavior Variables:

- The recently followed path $R = \{R_1, ..., R_{r-1}, R_r\}$, which contains the last visited nodes, where R_{r-1} is the current node and R_r is the next node.
- The time spent on recent nodes, $t(R_1), ..., t(R_{r-1})$.

On this basis, the system constructs three PDFs:

- $c(k)$, proportional for each profile k to the probability P_R^k of having followed the R path through arcs belonging to the profile k; a high value of P_R^k indicates that the visited nodes in R are relevant for the profile k as the actual path is "natural" for the profile k.
- $r(k)$, proportional for each profile k to the reachability $\tilde{P}_{R_1,R_r}^k$ of the next node R_r from the first node R_1, through arcs belonging to the profile k. This term takes into account the way the user *could have reached* the next node R_r; in fact, a high value means that there exists a very "natural" way to reach it through links of the profile k.
- $t(k)$, proportional for each profile k to the distribution $D'[k]$ of the visited nodes from R_1 to R_{r-1}, weighted with the time spent on each of them, with respect to the profile k. For example, let $\{n_1, n_2, n_3\}$ be the recently visited nodes and $\{t_1, t_2, t_3\}$ the time units spent on each of them: if node n_1 belongs to profiles k_1 and k_2, node n_2 belongs to k_2 and k_3 and node n_3 belongs to k_1 and k_4, the distribution is evaluated as $D'[k] = [\ (k_1, t_1+t_3), (k_2, t_1+t_2), (k_3, t_2), (k_4, t_3)\ ]$. $D'[k]$ shows how the time spent on visited nodes is distributed with respect to profiles, and we consider it as an indicator of the interest the user has shown with respect to them. The visiting times should be accurate; we believe that an interesting approach is to normalize the time units both "horizontally" and "vertically", e.g. with respect to the time spent on the same node by other users and to the time spent on other nodes by the same user.

Temporary deviations that do not move the user's interests can be taken into account trading off the effects of $c(k)$ and $r(k)$ on $A(k)$. The former takes into account the actual path so it aims to move towards profiles corresponding to local preferences, whereas the latter aims to disregard local choices, as the "shortest" paths do not necessarily involve the visited nodes between R_1 and R_r. Only the most recently followed $r-1$ links (r nodes) are considered, to avoid an "infinite memory" effect. In fact, considering R from the initial node, the probability P_R^k of having followed R in the profile k would be zero if the user visited just one node not associated to the profile k (obviously, we consider $W_k(i, j) = 0$ if $(i, j, k) \notin E$). Finally, a PDF $d(k)$ expressing the "dynamic relevance" of the profiles is computed by evaluating the weighted mean of $c(k)$, $r(k)$ and $t(k)$, called $d(k)$.

The algorithm that computes the new PDF $A'(k)$ takes as input the discrete PDFs $A(k)$, $A_0(k)$ and $s(k)$, and the user behavior variables. It computes the new $d(k)$ and applies the formula

$$A'(k) = \frac{\gamma_0 A_0(k) + \gamma_1 A(k) + \gamma_2 d(k) + \Delta\gamma_3 s(k)}{\gamma_0 + \gamma_1 + \gamma_2 + \Delta\gamma_3}, \text{ where } \Delta = \begin{cases} 1, \text{ if } s(k) \text{ has changed} \\ 0, \qquad\qquad \text{otherwise} \end{cases}$$

It should be noted here that the algorithm combines the user's dynamic behavior, synthesized in the term $d(k)$, with the structural properties of the hypermedia scheme, mainly depending on its topology, synthesized in the term $s(k)$. The new $A'(k)$ is also computed as a weighted mean of four terms, also considering the initial user's choices and the story of the interaction. A more detailed explanation of the algorithm can be found in [8].

4 System Architecture

In this Section we present the architecture for the construction and the run-time support of XAHM-based systems. After a description of our use of XML and XML-related technologies, we show the run-time support of the system and a set of authoring tools for the design and test of the AH.

4.1 XML Metadata and Presentation Descriptions

In XAHM both pages and metadata are described by using XML. Each data source is "wrapped" by an XML meta-description, and each Presentation Description is a XML document as well. The use of "pure" XML instead of more widespread formalisms for metadata, such as the *Resource Description Framework* [11] is due to the fact that it allows a simpler and more direct support to the proposed multidimensional approach, and that the *RDF* is well-suited essentially for metadata which is available on the Web. The use of metadata is a key aspect in order to accomplish the multidimensional adaptation task; for example, an image could be represented using different levels of detail, formats or points of view (shots), whereas a text could be organized as a hierarchy of fragments, represented using different languages, or an XML document could be differentiated along different "detail levels" [7]. Furthermore, by means of meta-descriptions, data fragments of the same kind can be treated in an integrated way, regardless of their actual sources: in the construction of pages the author refers to metadata, also avoiding too low-level access to fragments. A number of *Document Type Definitions* [11] for the XML meta-descriptions have been designed. They comprise descriptions of *text*, hierarchically organized, object-relational *database tables*, *queries versus object-relational databases*, *queries versus XML data* (expressed in *XQuery* [11]), *images* and *video sequences, XML documents, HTML documents* etc.

The Presentation Descriptions are XML documents whose key parts are the *content, fragment* and *embedded-code* elements. The *content* element is used to include text in the page. The *fragment* element is useful for including multimedia fragments referenced by their aliases. Finally, the *embedded-code* element increases flexibility allowing the insertion of terminal-dependent code (e.g. WML, HTML) in the page, thus allowing reusing of existing web hypermedia.

Each part of the PD is therefore organized as a sequence of elements; each of them can be associated to a portion of the adaptation space by means of the *dimension-parameters*, i.e. dimension variables interpreted here as parameters. Before storing the Presentation Descriptions, the system actually transforms them into *XSP* pages [2], containing portions of high-level code to be executed at run-time in order to instantiate them.

4.2 The Run-Time System

The run-time system supporting XAHM has a *three-tier* architecture (Fig. 2), comprising the *Presentation,* the *Application* and the *Data* layers.

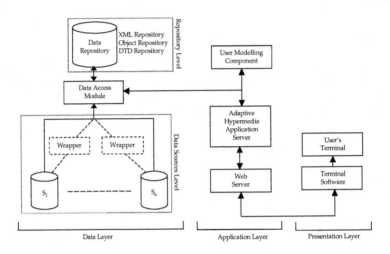

Fig. 2. Run-time system architecture

The Presentation layer receives final pages to be presented and eventually scripts or applets to be executed; these scripts are useful for detecting the *user context,* e.g. local time, physical location, available bandwidth or the time spent on pages.

The Application Layer is the core of the system: it observes the user behavior and characteristics and implements the adaptation process. Its two main modules are the *Adaptive Hypermedia Application Server (AHAS)* and the *User Modeling Component (UMC).* The UMC stores the most recent actions of the user and executes the algorithm for the evaluation of the user's profile. After a user has selected the next page and the system has determined his/her user's position in the Adaptation Space, the AHAS extracts from the XML repository the Presentation Description to be transformed and executes the application logic contained in it; the logic comprises the extraction and composition of basic data fragments from the data sources on the basis of the known user position. The final page is obtained applying the terminal-dependent XSL stylesheet, and returned to the Web server.

Finally, the Data Layer stores persistent data and offers efficient access primitives. It comprises the *Data Sources Level,* the *Repository Level* and a *Data Access Module.* The Data Sources Level is an abstraction of the different kinds of data sources used to build the hypermedia. Each data source is also accessed by a *Wrapper* software component, which generates in a semi-automatic way the XML metadata describing the data fragments stored in it. The Repository Level is a common repository storing data provided by the Data Source Level or produced by the author. It stores *(i)* XML documents into a *XML Repository,* including source Presentation Descriptions, generated XSP Presentation Descriptions, XSL stylesheets and XML metadata; *(ii)* persistent objects into an *Object Repository*, which represent graphs and data about registered users; *(iii)* the XAHM DTDs used to validate XML documents. Finally, the Data Access Module implements an abstract interface for accessing the Data Sources and the Repository levels.

4.3 The Java Adaptive Hypermedia Suite (JAHS)

According to the described architecture, we have designed and implemented a set of Java-based tools allowing the design, the simulation and the validation of an Adaptive Hypermedia based on XAHM, through an iterative and interactive process. Using a *RAD (Rapid Application Development)* approach, the author first defines the overall structure of the hypermedia, then simulates the behavior of the system on the basis of different classes of users and adjusts the hypermedia structure accordingly. Then, the author can complete the hypermedia construction providing the contents of the PDs.

4.3.1 Multidimensional Adaptive Hypermedia Authoring
In the construction of an Adaptive Hypermedia the following main phases can be identified, directly related to the layered model of Section 2.2.

High-Level Structure Definition
The high-level structure of an adaptive hypermedia is modeled by means of the first two layers of the graph-based model described in Section 2.2. The author first defines the set of stereotype user profiles representing users' groups. Subsequently, he/she describes the overall Adaptive Hypermedia as a digraph of EACs using the *Hypermedia Modeler*, a tool that allows designing EACs in a visual way. Finally, the author describes each EAC, specifying sets of PDs, differentiating links with respect to user profiles and adding to them the probabilistic weights. Notice that in this phase it is not necessary to specify the PD's content, but only their link structure. The Hypermedia Modeler provides some hints about typical graph structures and offers a set of utilities regarding the overall probabilistic structure of the hypermedia (shortest paths, minimum spanning tree, etc.). The structure of the hypermedia is stored by means of persistent objects, and it allows reusing parts of the hypermedia: after having been validated and stored, (part of) objects can be imported by the Hypermedia Modeler to design new EACs.

Semi-automatic Metadata Creation
Since basic multimedia information fragments are always accessed by means of metadata associated to them, a fundamental step is concerned with the creation of such metadata. The *Fragments Browser/Composer* allows browsing the information fragments provided by the Data Sources Level, using Wrapper software components, and extracting some explicit metadata. Moreover, the author can add information based on his/her domain knowledge. As an example, the Fragments Browser/Composer is able to connect to local or remote DBMS and automatically extract the structure of relational or object-oriented tables; or it can explore local or remote file systems and extract metadata about stored files of known types. The author of the hypermedia is allowed to integrate such metadata (e.g. with human-readable explanations) or to create new ones.

Presentation Descriptions Construction

The last (and typically longest) phase of the AH design is the construction of the Presentation Descriptions. Here, the author composes basic information fragments, referencing their metadata, and associates them to specific portions of the adaptation space by means of parameters regarding the adaptivity dimensions. This phase is performed by using a *PD Editor*, which allows editing XML Presentation Descriptions in the form of pure text or graphically (as pure trees, or in a "visual" way). It is possible to create new documents and to edit pre-existing ones; the PD editor also allows a "preview" of the final pages.

4.3.2 Simulation and Validation of the Adaptive Hypermedia

Generally, it is fundamental for an author to validate the high-level link structure of the hypermedia with respect to the mechanisms that drive the profile assignment decision. This is especially true in the proposed system, where links are weighted by probabilities. Therefore, the system provides a *Simulation Tool* that permits the author of the hypermedia to:

1. Analyze the intrinsic properties of the hypermedia (see Section 3), calculated from its structure.
2. Define a set of *Classes* of typical users by means of the *User Class Modeler*, and simulate their behavior to validate the response of the system; clearly, behaviors modeled by means of User Classes comprise random visiting times or choice of arcs.
3. Run the simulation by means of the *AHS Simulator*, which is a multithreaded machine that generates requests of a number of users to the AHAS, and presents the resulting logs in a graphical way.
4. Analyze the profile assignment decision (i.e. the response of the UMC) with respect to the User Classes.
5. Eventually (e.g. in the case of many *oscillations* of resulting PDFs), *(i)* tune the parameters used in the algorithm, as the length of the sliding temporal window or the values of the parameters used to weight the PDFs, or *(ii)* adjust the hypermedia structure.

5 Concluding Remarks and Future Work

In this paper we presented XAHM, an XML-based model for Adaptive Hypermedia Systems. XAHM models an Adaptive Hypermedia considering a three-dimensional adaptation space, comprising the user's behavior, technology, and external environment dimensions. The adaptation process is performed finding the proper position of the user in the adaptation space, and applying to "neutral" XML pages some constraints bound to that position.

We believe that the main contributions of this paper are *(i)* a new model to describe Adaptive Hypermedia allowing a flexible and effective support of the adaptation process; *(ii)* a probabilistic model of the user's behavior, and a classification algorithm that attempts to accomplish the profiling task in an effective and non-invasive way; *(iii)* a flexible and modular architecture for the design and the run-time support of Adaptive Hypermedia Systems.

Future work will concern the completion of the implementation and the test of the UMC response with respect to some canonical hypermedia structure and typical users' behavior. Moreover, we will introduce Data Mining techniques, to let the author examine the actual behavior of a number of users and fine-tune the probabilities accordingly.

References

1. Adaptive Hypertext and Hypermedia Home Page, http://wwwis.win.tue.nl/ah/.
2. Apache Software Foundation Home Page, http://www.apache.org.
3. L. Ardissono, A. Goy, "Tailoring the Interaction With Users in Web Stores", in *User Modeling and User-Adapted Interaction*, 10(4), Kluwer Academic Publishers, 2000.
4. P. Brusilovsky, "Methods and techniques of adaptive hypermedia", in *User Modeling and User Adapted Interaction*, v.6, n.2-3, 1996.
5. P. Brusilovsky, A. Kobsa, J. Vassileva, *Adaptive Hypertext and Hypermedia*, Kluwer Academic Publishers, 1998.
6. P. Brusilovsky, O. Stock, C. Strapparava (eds.), *Adaptive Hypermedia and Adaptive Web-based Systems*, proceedings of the AH International Conference, 2000.
7. M. Cannataro, G. Carelli, A. Pugliese, D. Saccà, "Semantic lossy compression of XML data", *8th Int. Workshop on Knowledge Representation meets Databases*, 2001.
8. M. Cannataro, A. Cuzzocrea, A. Pugliese, "A probabilistic approach to model adaptive hypermedia systems", in *Proceedings of the International Workshop on Web Dynamics*, 2001.
9. S. Ceri, P. Fraternali, A. Bongio, "Web Modelling Language (WebML): a modelling language for designing web sites", WWW9 Conference, 2000.
10. H. Wu, E. De Kort, P. De Bra, "Design issues for general-purpose adaptive hypermedia systems", in *Proceedings of the ACM Conference on Hypertext and Hypermedia*, 2001.
11. World Wide Web Consortium Home Page, http://www.w3.org.

Revisiting and Versioning in Virtual Special Reports

Sébastien Iksal and Serge Garlatti

Department of Artificial Intelligence and Cognitive Sciences
ENST Bretagne Technopôle de Brest Iroise
B.P. 832, 29285 Brest Cedex, FR
{sebastien.iksal,serge.garlatti}@enst-bretagne.fr

Abstract. Adaptation/personalization is one of the main issues for web applications and require large repositories. Creating adaptive web applications from these repositories requires to have methods to facilitate web application creation and management and to ensure reuse, sharing and exchange of data through the internet/intranet. Virtual documents deal with these issues. In our framework, we are interested in adaptive virtual documents for author-oriented web applications providing several reading strategies to readers. These applications have the following characteristics: authors have know-how which enables them to choose document contents and to organize them in one or more consistent ways. A reading strategy and the corresponding content are semantically coherent and convey a particular meaning to the readers. Such author's know-how can be represented at knowledge level and then be used for generating web documents dynamically, for ensuring reader comprehension and for sharing and reuse. Then an adaptive virtual document can be computed on the fly by means of a semantic composition engine using: i) an overall document structure - for instance a narrative structure - representing a reading strategy for which node contents are linked at run time, according to user's needs for adaptation, ii) an intelligent search engine and semantic metadata relying on semantic web initiative, and iv) a user model. In this paper, we focus on a semantic composition engine enabling us to compute on the fly adaptive/personalized web documents in the ICCARS project. Its main goal is to assist the journalist in building adaptive special reports. In such a framework, adaptation, personalization and reusability are central issues for delivering adaptive special reports.

1 Introduction

Numerous applications are available on the Web today and their size and volume are increasing. For instance, portals, e-learning, problem solving systems, decision support systems, digital libraries, on-line information systems, virtual museums, e-business and digital newspapers are current applications. On the World Wide Web, we have large distributed information repositories which convey large amounts of knowledge for internet users as well as for companies which

S. Reich, M.M. Tzagarakis, P.M.E. De Bra (Eds.): OHS/SC/AH 2001, LNCS 2266, pp. 264–279, 2002.

are the owners of this knowledge. Adaptation/personalization is one of the main issues for web applications. Adaptive web applications have the ability to deal with different users' needs for enhancing usability and comprehension and for dealing with large repositories. Indeed, adaptive web applications - also often called Adaptive Hypermedia Systems - can provide different kinds of information, different layouts, different navigation tools according to users' needs [1]. Creating adaptive web applications from these repositories requires the following features: i) methods to facilitate web application creation and management and ii) reuse, sharing and exchange of data through the internet/intranet.

The notion of flexible hypermedia and more particularly of virtual documents can lead to methods facilitating web application design and maintenance. According to Watters, "A virtual document is a document for which no persistent state exists and for which some or all each instance is generated at run time" [2]. Virtual documents have grown out of a need for interactivity and individualization of documents, particularly on the web. Virtual document and adaptive hypermedia are closely related - they can be viewed as the two faces of the same coin. Reuse, sharing and exchange through the internet/intranet require to have a precise search engine. Indeed, it is well known that keyword-based information access presents severe limitations concerning precision and recall. On the contrary, intelligent search engines, relying on semantic web initiative [3] and semantic metadata, overcome these limitations [4, 5].

In our framework, we are interested in adaptive virtual documents for author-oriented web applications providing several reading strategies to readers. These applications have the following characteristics: authors have know-how which enables them to choose document contents and to organize them in one or more consistent ways - author reading strategies. Content and organizations are "semantically" related to ensure reader's comprehension. In this paper, we focus on organizations called narrative structure. The reader has the ability to recognize - sometimes unconsciously - these structures. For instance, scientific papers, courseware, report, special report in journalism, etc., have each of them a distinct narrative structure. At present, the narrative structure is implicit in printed document, but also in digital one. Such author's know-how and skills can be represented at knowledge level and then be shared and reused among authors, used for generating web documents dynamically and for enhancing reader comprehension. A narrative structure provides an overall document structure which is a declarative description of web documents. Then, a web document can be computed on the fly by means of a semantic composition engine using: i) an overall document structure - for instance a narrative structure - representing a reading strategy for which node contents are substituted at run time, according to user's needs for adaptation, ii) an intelligent search engine, iii) semantic metadata, and iv) a user model. Each document is computed when it is necessary, we don't store each delivered document. An authoring tool is provided for creating narrative structures, specifying their content and associating metadata.

Numerous web sites offer tools to users for personalizing their information space and the presentation. Two projects aims at supplying personalized news on a Web site. Sistemi Telematici Adattativi [6] is a project which aims at filtering and displaying news and advertisement according to users' preferences and characteristics. The system selects a relevant set of news according to the reader's interests via probabilities. Then, some rules are applied for choosing the relevant presentation for a single news (abstract or full text, image or video, etc.). Personalization is done by a filtering process on news and a presentation selection. KMI Planet [7] is a kind of private on-line newspaper where all readers and writers are in a same group - university. It collects news through e-mail, processes them and sends the result to the most interested readers. The tool is able to order articles for filling in gaps, and after to inform the reader when the news is available. It supplies with an advanced interface for searching documents. Each news is annotated via an academic ontology, and then the query interface uses the same ontology for writing queries. The system uses the annotations and all queries given by a user to find out the most relevant news. Personalization mainly consists of a filtering process based on user queries and ontology annotations. In this two projects, personalization is mainly based on a filtering process using user's preferences for selecting the most relevant news.

Our project aims at delivering adapted special reports to news readers. They consist of a set of news - selected by authors - and several semantic structures organizing them. These semantic structures provide different reading strategies to the readers. A reading strategy and the corresponding news collection are semantically coherent and convey a particular meaning to the readers. This meaning can be viewed as a viewpoint on this collection. Some reading strategies are created by authors and others by the system. The reading strategies and their content may be adapted to users' needs. According to C. Watters, revisiting, versioning and reusability are some of the main issues for virtual documents. In this paper, we focus on a semantic composition engine enabling us to compute on the fly adaptive/personalized special reports in the ICCARS project. Its main goal is to assist the journalist in building adaptive special reports. In such a framework, adaptation, personalization and reusability are central issues for delivering adapted/personalized special reports.

Firstly, we present the context of our approach: journalism and reporting on the web via the ICCARS Project. Next, we will give a summary of the architecture of our semantic composition engine. We will present how we will manage revisiting and versioning of dynamic documents according to our context and our composition engine. Then, our adaptation policies is presented. Finally, some directions for the future will be proposed.

2   ICCARS Project

ICCARS is the acronym for INTEGRATED AND COOPERATIVE COMPUTER ASSISTED REPORTING SYSTEM. It is a joined project between the IASC Laboratory, a SME called Atlantide and a regional daily newspaper called Le Télégramme. It is funded by Brittany Regional Council. The ICCARS prototype will be a computer assisted reporting system. Its main goal is to assist the journalist in creating adaptive special reports. These documents are able to include audio and video material, links, and they are no longer limited in size.

Due to internet features, numerous web sites are offering news. Then, It is not sufficient to filter news. We need to go beyond a news delivery service and to provide new services around information. Special reports seem to be the most representative journalists' task. A special report offers news as well as analysis, debate, synthesis and/or development. It can be viewed as an organized collection of articles offering a viewpoint on events. It is a matter of journalist know-how for creating such type of document.

2.1   The Digital Special Report

A special report is a synthesis made by one or more journalists on a particular topic, for instance a yachting race. We consider a special report as a collection of articles with a given narrative structure. In a paper version, there is a single organization which appears through the sequence of pages and the page layout. A digital special report may naturally offer different narrative structures.

New Features. Digital special reports can provide new services to the reader. We present some of them: such as various reading strategies for a single special report, enrichment, reusability and adaptation. It is important to notice that as in the printed version, the journalist chooses the set of articles belonging to a special report. That is to say, in a digital special report we can find only the articles that the journalist wants to provide his readers with.

The Notion of Reading Strategy. In a special report, a set of articles can be read in different ways, according to a reader's or author's viewpoints. We call a particular sequence of articles a reading strategy. We distinguish two kinds of reading strategies:

1. An author strategy: This is a narrative structure designed by a writer for presenting a particular angle on a set of articles. One of the main roles of journalists is to analyse events and report them in a consistent and synthetic way. A narrative structure is composed of nodes and semantic relationships. Nodes are spans of texts. Relationships belong to those analyzed by Rhetorical Structure Theory (RST) [8]. RST defines relations between spans of text, each span have a role inside the relation (nucleus and satellite). Each relation is defined by some constraints on the nucleus, the satellite, the combination of the nucleus and the satellite, and an effect to the reader. Among these relations, we can find are antithesis, restatement, summary, interpretation and so on.
2. A reader strategy: This is an overall document structure computed from a reader's goals. For instance, it can be based on geographic, history or topic criteria - a domain model - organizing the access to articles. The structure delivered is computed on the fly and controlled by the computer according to a generic structure. Nevertheless, journalists are aware of such structures because they associate metadata with articles and special reports for these services.

Special Report Views. In a digital document, three different views coexist: semantic, logical and layout/presentation [9]. For each view we have a specific structure. The semantic structure of a document conveys the organization of the meaning of the content of a document. This view fits the semantic level of the semantic web architecture. Indeed, it can be represented by ontologies. Ontologies are used to model types of fragment as well as their relationships. For instance, "The fragment A which is an *interview* is the *volitional cause* of the fragment B which is an *analysis*", the underlying relationship cannot be represented by a syntactic structure [10]. Interview and analysis are types of fragment. The interview is the satellite and the analysis is the nucleus of this rhetorical relation. This relation is oriented and encode a particular reading guide. In this case, the fragment B will be better understood if the fragment A is read before. It could be interesting to show the type of relation to the reader as explanations or for increasing the comprehension.

The logical structure reflects the syntactic organization of a document. A document (for example books and magazines) can be broken down into components (chapters and articles). These can also be broken down into components (titles, paragraphs, figures and so forth). It turns out that just about every document can be viewed this way. The logical view fits the syntactic level of the semantic web architecture. A logical structure can be encoded in XML [11]. The layout/presentation view describes how the documents appear on a device and a physical structure describes it, (eg. the size and colour of headings, texts, etc). The layout/presentation view may be processed by an XSLT processor [12] for transforming an XML document into an HTML document that can be viewed by any web browser. It can also be processed by a java engine able to compute an XML document for presenting by a web browser.

In a printed document, these three views are intertwined and are not separable. There is no straightforward mapping between the semantic and the logical structure, that is to say, for instance, a paragraph does not correspond to a particular content's meaning. On the other hand, the logical and physical structure are closely related. Indeed, the physical structure encodes the logical structure. For instance, each section element has a particular presentation - font, size, colour, etc. The semantic structure is implicit and so it can be analyzed and/or recognized by a reader. Moreover, it is a key issue for reader comprehension. In a digital document, these three views may be represented and managed.

Reusability. It is very important for journalists to be able to reuse at least an article or a part of a special report in more than one special report and why not in the same report. Indeed, an article and a part of a special report generally concern more than one topic. Watters [2] as well as the Semantic Web Community argues that allowing reusability of fragments - articles, special report parts - leads to associate metadata with fragments. Moreover, narrative structures can also be reused for new special reports.

Enrichment. A special report can be updated. The journalist may add a new article in his base and modify the organization in order to insert this new article. A journalist can organize a subset of articles in order to develop various viewpoints (economic, ecological, for example.). Enrichment is a very important possibility with digital documents, but in order to not disturb the reader, the system must be able to rebuild the same special report, that is to say, the same version of the report. Enrichment leads to the management of versioning in special reports.

Adaptation/Personalization. The digital special report as a particular type of web site is a good candidate for adaptation. As a digital document may be managed at three different levels: semantic, syntactic and layout/presentation, adaptation can take place on each level. For instance, the content and the overall document structure may be adapted to the reader's preferences, knowledge and goals. At a syntactic level, different logical structures may be chosen to fit user needs. At a layout level, the presentation may be adapted to the current device and/or the user stereotype.

Moreover, we have to deal with versioning purposes due to enrichment purposes. Then, personalization involves annotating the documents already read, or those which have been added since the last visit.

2.2 Virtual Document for Special Reports

A journalist organizes a set of articles according to one or more reading strategies, but it is necessary to prepare the special report which is relevant to a particular reader and a specific device. First of all, we give a definition of a virtual document in our framework:

An adaptive/personalized virtual document consists of a set of information fragments, ontologies and a semantic composition engine which is able to select the relevant information fragments, to assemble and to organize them according to an author's strategy or user's goals by adapting various visible aspects of the document delivered to the user.

Fragments can be atomic or abstract information units. The latter are composed of atomic and abstract information units. In ICCARS, fragments are articles - atomic - , special reports and sub-reports - abstract. A special report and corresponding reading strategies are modelled as follows in figure 1.

In order to facilitate comprehension, we prefix all the elements of the special report model with the I of ICCARS. An I-SubReport is composed of a set of articles selected by the author - explicitly associated with it in order to define its relevant information space -, and one or more narrative structures - Reading strategies - between these elements. When a journalist considers that a particular I-SubReport is relevant enough to be a special report, an I-PublishedReport is created and gives a user access to this I-SubReport, that is to say, a document ready to be delivered to readers.

An I-SubReport can be organized according to one or more I-Structures - Reading strategies. An I-Structure is a collection of I-Components among which one is the root of the I-Structure. An I-Component is an abstract object, which exists only inside a particular I-Structure. An I-Component is linked to others through a semantic relation belonging to those of RST. This relationship gives the organization of the I-Structure. That is to say, each I-Component in the structure which is the source of a relationship, is a nucleus in RST and the corresponding destination (an I-Component also) is a satellite. So, we use RST as a basis to build a narrative structure in which nodes are different categories of fragments. If RST is very far from the journalists viewpoint, we will use journalists' relations in the future. The set composed of I-Components and the relationships is one narrative structure of the special report. An I-Component is a kind of information retrieval service which uses a description given by the author according to metadata, in order to send a query to the intelligent information broker. It is able to use the user model to filter the small set of answers. So the I-Component is able to deliver the most relevant articles or sub-reports. Then, the I-SubReport is a graph where the nodes are I-Components and the vertices are relations between I-Components. Several special reports can be generalized to provide special report templates. So, reusability concerns these templates as well as all the instances of the special report model. For instance, in the case of the wreck of the Erika, the structure can be reused for other wrecks - super tanker oil slick - (Tanyo, Amoco Cadiz, etc.).

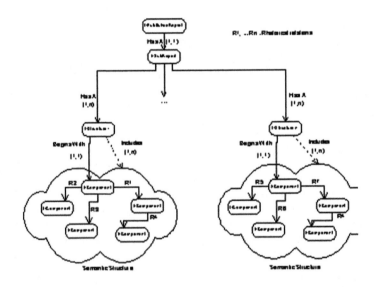

Fig. 1. Model for a Special Report

This special report model is an input for the semantic composition engine which computes an adaptive/personalized special report for a given reader.

3   Semantic Composition Engine Architecture

Our semantic composition engine relies on OntoBroker for ontology management and intelligent search engine. OntoBroker is a knowledge management engine which is useful for filtering and information retrieval in a large amount of data as well as in the model specification - ontologies [5, 13, 14]. OntoBroker contains four ontologies and facts closely related to them. These ontologies are: a domain ontology for representing contents, a metadata ontology at the information level which describes the indexing structure of fragments, a user ontology which may define different stereotypes and individual features and a special report ontology which represents the author's competences and know-how for creating special reports. The domain ontology defines a shared vocabulary used in the metadata schema for the content description of data. It will also be used by the semantic composition engine as an overall document structure, by the user as an information retrieval tool because the user often has difficulty in defining his/her interests, and it is easier for him/her to recognize required information in a domain model than to specify it.

According to the three views of a document, our semantic composition engine architecture is described below (cf. fig. 2).

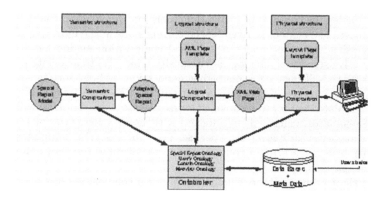

Fig. 2. The Semantic Composition Engine Architecture

One of the main ideas behind the notion of semantic composition engine is to declare as much as possible all the user's tasks and interactions. The semantic composition engine is composed of three different stages: a semantic composition which manages the semantic structure of a special report model for defining a user adapted special report and selects its contents, a logical composition which computes an XML web page from the user adapted special report and a physical composition which computes the current web page layout from the XML structure[1]. This architecture is based on two different studies: ICCARS Project and CANDLE Project (Collaborative and Network Distributed Learning Environment) which is an European project.

Semantic Composition: for an author's reading strategy, the main role of the semantic composition is to define the special report content and to adapt

---

[1] A logical structure is associated with one web page and not with the entire document - it cannot be relevant in such a framework.

the chosen I-Structure to user needs. Indeed, each I-Component has only a specification of the content. From this specification, one or more fragments may be selected from the relevant set of articles associated to the considered special report. Indeed, only a subset of metadata entries are used for content specification by the authoring tool. The others are used for defining variants of fragments - according to adaptation policies. The special report structure may also be adapted: an I-Fragment or an I-SubReport may be hidden according to reader's needs, that is to say topics, its professional activity and/or expertise level. Articles may be dedicated to specific professional activities and/or to some levels of knowledge. The semantic composition produces a user adaptive special report — user document — in which all I-components have contents according to their specification and to the user model.

Logical Composition: the logical composition aims at computing an XML page with a content and navigation tools for accessing the different fragments of a special report, by means of a template. A web page, represented as an XML structure [11], is generated from a particular template. A template describes the logical structure of a web page but without any content or navigation tools. It has queries for computing navigation tools and for loading the content via OntoBroker. The content is given by the current node in the narrative structure. For accessing the other nodes, the logical composition engine has to browse the narrative structure. The logical composition has also to associate properties to hyperlinks - Xlinks - for managing annotation, hiding, sorting and direct guidance. All interactions between a user and the web page are also represented in this template in order to respond to users' requests. The database will provide several templates which will be indexed with user's tasks, type of fragments, user's category, user's level of expertise, etc. Then, several templates can be available for a given type of content. By means of these templates, adaptation may take place at this stage.

Physical Composition: finally, the physical composition has to map some presentation rules on the web page. The final process of this architecture is concerned by the design of the web pages of a special report. The final layout of each page may be tailored to the user's preferences: print size, color, and so on and/or use standardized styles from corporate, SMEs or institution style sheets. The physical composition has also to manage the adaptive navigation. From author specification or user stereotypes or user preferences, he has to hide, to annotate, etc; the different types of hyperlinks in a web page. There is a style sheet for each template. It is one way for mapping a presentation on a web page. Indeed, a java process can be applied to an XML structure to provide a web page.

The above description has presented the semantic composition engine architecture and the process for delivering a special report to a user. Now, we present the management of revisiting and versioning in a virtual special report.

4   Revisiting and Versioning

Computing a document on the fly is very interesting because it is cheaper to produce a single virtual document which can be the source of numerous real documents according to a user's requests than to prepare all these documents in advance. Nevertheless, a real document is ephemeral, that is to say, no real documents are stored, each one is computed at run-time. Readers have an expectation that documents found once will be available on a subsequent search. In fact, they expect to retrieve the same document in the same state. So the system needs enough information to recreate the document as it was. It is called revisiting purposes which may lead to bookmark an I-Component. In fact, there is no URL to store because of the dynamic generation of the document, so we need to recreate the document and to display the same I-Component.

Thanks to the enrichment capabilities of virtual special reports, it is necessary to manage versioning [15]. Version control is a central issue for special report management, readers need to retrieve a former version of the document, may be because they have already read it or because they want to be aware of the life cycle of this report. They also need to go forward and backward in time through changes in order to develop their own analysis of the situation.

Revisiting and Versioning are very closed together but these are two different issues. Even if we often intertwine them. The main difference between them concerns the domain, providing revisiting features requires the storage in a user model of all the data enabling the semantic composition engine to compute the same real special report again. On the other hand, the versioning process is related to the metadata schema and the special report ontology, that is to say it works directly on documents, structures and so on. According to versioning purposes, revisiting requires to have in the user model the version number of the last visited special report.

4.1   Version Management

Versioning management is related to enrichment features and to the metadata schema. The author will be able to add or remove all the elements of the special report model - I-SubReport, I-Structure, I-Component - and also the relationship between I-Components. We provide, by default, the latest version of the element except if the user asks for a particular version.

The metadata schema (Table 1) provides metadata information about fragments. The semantic composition engine uses the schema for information retrieval. It matches content specification against metadata. The current version of the metadata schema consists of six parts:

Now, according to the special report model and the metadata schema, we manage versioning features as follows:

– The I-PublishedReport does not have versioning purposes, because if the author changes the main I-SubReport, we create a new I-PublishedReport.
– An I-Component: This exists only inside an I-Structure and it works as a small information retrieval service. We do not have versioning for this kind of element, because the internal information retrieval features are not updated. If needed, a new I-Component is created. But relationships between I-Components can change, so we add a validity period (cf. fig. 3, R4 (m-n)) to relations. This property corresponds to the list of the I-Structure's version in which this relation is valid.

Table 1. The Metadata Schema

MD.1	General	General information about the resource	Unique Instance
MD.1.1	Identifier	Unique Identifier	Single Value
MD.1.2	Title	Title given by the author	Single Value
MD.1.3	Authors	One or more authors for the resource	Unsorted List
MD.1.4	Description	Short description of the resource	Single Value
MD.1.5	Language	Language of the resource	Single Value
MD.2	Life cycle	Entries for versioning purposes	Unique Instance
MD.2.1	Version	Version number of the resource	Single Value
MD.2.2	Status	Status of the resource (draft, final ...)	Single Value
MD.2.3	Authors	Authors of the version	Unsorted List
MD.2.4	Date	Date of the version	Single Value
MD.3	Meta Metadata	Information about metadata	Unique Instance
MD.3.1	Creator	Author of metadata	Single Value
MD.3.2	Validator	Reviewer of metadata	Single Value
MD.3.3	Language	Language of metadata	Single Value
MD.3.4	Date	Date of metadata	Single Value
MD.4	Technical	Technical information about the resource	Unique Instance
MD.4.1	Location	Where the resource can be found?	Single Value
MD.4.2	Format	Format of the resource	Single Instance
MD.4.2.1	Type	Type of the resource (ppt, doc, html, ...)	Single Value
MD.4.2.2	Size	Size of the resource in Kbytes	Single Value
MD.4.3	Requirements	What is required to read the resource?	Single Instance
MD.4.3.1	Software	Software names and version	Unsorted List
MD.4.3.2	Hardware	Hardware description	Unsorted List
MD.5	Classification	Data about the content and reporting features	Unique Instance
MD.5.1	Domain	Description related to the domain	Unsorted List
MD.5.1.1	Concept	Concept name	Single Value
MD.5.1.2	Level	Level of knowledge required	Single Value
MD.5.2	Reporting	Reporting classification	Single Instance
MD.5.2.1	Resource Type	Type of resource (Interview, report ...)	Single Value
MD.5.2.2	Edition	Edition concerned	Single Value
MD.5.2.3	City	City concerned	Single Value
MD.6	Rights	Use conditions of the resource	Unique Instance
MD.6.1	Copyrights	Copyrights or licenses	Single Value
MD.6.2	Access	Access restrictions	Single Value
MD.6.3	Cost	Cost needed	Single Value
MD.6.4	Publisher	Publisher identity	Single Value
MD.6.5	Remarks	Usage remarks	Single Value

- The I-Structure is composed of a set of I-Components and a link to the first I-Component which is the root of the I-Structure. Two changes can be applied to an I-Structure. First, the root can be replaced, and next the set of I-Components can be updated. An I-Component can only be added. Indeed, an I-Component may be not relevant on a new version, but has to be present for a previous one. For each new version we have to increase the set of I-Components and to give the validity period of the root (cf. fig. 3 (k-n)).
- The I-SubReport is composed of a set of I-Structures and a data collection (in our case, this is a list of articles selected by the author). Between two versions of I-SubReport, these two sets can be updated (inserts). For each new version we store the new sets.

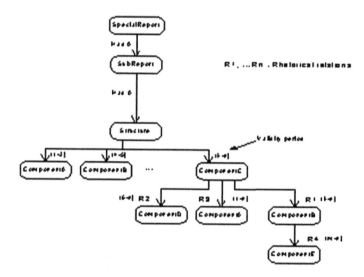

Fig. 3. Versioning Application on an Instance of the Special Report Model

For each new version, we instantiate a new element of the special report model. We associate the metadata information related to the "Lifecycle part". This will enable us to use information retrieval methods to find the relevant version. Instead of managing versions via numbers like many versioning systems, we manage version via the date. In Press Institutions, especially daily local newspapers, several editions are printed every day according to different geographical areas. It is therefore more relevant for a reader to ask for the special report of a particular date, than the third version of the special report. According to this versioning management, retrieving the correct version is in fact a filtering process.

4.2   History and Revisiting

As well as the metadata schema useful for versioning features, the user model is necessary for history and revisiting issues. The current version of the user model (Table 2) is an individual model because it deals with individual features, unlike stereotype models which are about user class features. The user model consists of five parts: personal, preferences, knowledge, history and session.

   Comments: Personal: The geographical area is relevant for a local daily newspaper, and the professional activity (economist, fisherman, student, etc.) will be used to provide some stereotypes of needs in the future; Knowledge: The estimated level of knowledge about some domain concepts. At present, it is given by the reader;

   History: It stores all features required to retrieve the last special report(s). Then, the semantic composition engine will be able to deal with revisiting and versioning. We plan to add two new entries about readers' Behavior and Background.

   We have to store all data needed to recreate a web page. According to our special report model, these data are: the I-PublishedReport ID, the I-Structure ID, the I-Component ID and the date for retrieving the relevant version. The I-SubReport ID is not necessary because we can obtain it via the date and the I-PublishedReport ID. Concerning the versioning issue, the I-PublishedReport ID and the date chosen by the user are sufficient to recreate the same special report. Then we will store the user's bookmark in the appropriate section of his individual model. Concerning history purposes, these are necessary for two reasons. First, the system has to propose navigational guides to the reader. In this case, it has to show the path covered by the reader. Next, it is interesting to be able to show, on another visit, the element already visited or elements newly added since the last version. In the first case, we have to store the path exactly, that is to say, an ordered list of elements where something can be found more than one time. In the second case, we just need a list of elements without duplicates, but with the date of the last visit. This date is very useful in order to re-open a document in the same configuration the user left it. We will use in the user model, the history section, and the current session.

5   Adaptation

Our semantic composition architecture is composed of three engines. Each one is able to offer different types of adaptation to readers.

1. **Semantic Composition:** at this level, the engine adapts the special report structure and the content to the user. By means of the authoring tool, the author is able to select the I-Component content. The authoring tool chooses some metadata entries for specifying this content, at least the classification section (5.1.1 concept name, 5.2.1 resource type) implicitly. Moreover, it has to ensure the consistency of the special report. In other words, an article may be referred in several I-Components according to the author, but not elsewhere. An I-Component may have several contents which are variants

Table 2. The User Model

UM.1	Personal data	Personal data concerning the user	Unique Instance
UM.1.1	Identity	His identity	Single Instance
UM.1.1.1	Last name	His last name	Single Value
UM.1.1.2	First name	His first name	Single Value
UM.1.1.3	Age	His age	Single Value
UM.1.2	Login	Unique identifying data	Single Instance
UM.1.2.1	Login name	The login name	Single Value
UM.1.2.2	Password	The corresponding password	Single Value
UM.1.3	Classification	Classification data	Single Instance
UM.1.3.1	Location	Where does he live?	Single Value
UM.1.3.2	Professional Activity	What kind of job? (economist, fisherman, student, etc.)	Single Value
UM.1.3.3	Role	The role in the application (author, reader ...)	Single Value
UM.2	Preferences data	Data about the preference of the user	Unique Instance
UM.2.1	Interest	Topics of interests	Single Instance
UM.2.1.2	Topic	A list of topics	Unsorted List
UM.2.2	Adaptation	Adaptation preferences	Unsorted List
UM.2.2.1	Element	An adaptable element (link ...)	Single Value
UM.2.2.2	Rule	A method of adaptation (annotation ...)	Single Value
UM.3	Knowledge	Data about the knowledge of the user	Unique Instance
UM.3.1	Domain	Knowledge about the domain	Unsorted List
UM.3.1.1	Element	A domain concept	Single Value
UM.3.1.2	Level	A level of knowledge	Single Value
UM.4	History data	Data about access to special reports	Unique Instance
UM.4.1	Access	Access log	Unsorted List
UM.4.1.1	Report ID	Which special report has been accessed	Single Value
UM.4.1.2	Structure ID	Structures used	Single Value
UM.4.1.3	Component ID	Component read	Single Value
UM.4.1.4	Date	Date of access	Single Value
UM.4.2	Bookmark	Bookmark data	Unsorted List
UM.4.2.1	Report ID	Identifier of the special report	Single Value
UM.4.2.2	Structure ID	ID of the structure in the special report	Single Value
UM.4.2.3	Component ID	ID of the comp. in the structure	Single Value
UM.4.2.4	Date	Date of the storage, for retrieving the relevant version	Single Value
UM.5	Session data	Data concerning the current session	Unique Instance
UM.5.1	Choice	Stores the first choices of the user	Single Instance
UM.5.1.1	Special Report ID	The Special Report chosen	Single Value
UM.5.1.2	Structure ID	The structure chosen	Single Value
UM.5.2	Current	Stores curr. data about reading path	Single Instance
UM.5.2.1	Special Report ID	The current Special Report	Single Value
UM.5.2.2	Structure ID	The current structure	Single Value
UM.5.2.3	Fragment ID	The current fragment	Single Value
UM.5.3	Device	Description of the current device	Single Instance
UM.5.3.1	Software	Software names and version	Unsorted List
UM.5.3.2	Hardware	Hardware description	Unsorted List

due to knowledge level, technical requirements or versioning. As soon as a new article is included in a special report, the authoring tool has to check if another specification matches this article. In this case, more metadata entries has to be added in the specification. We shall have to learn what are the relevant implicit metadata entries in order to help the authors. The composition engine can match the following user model entries: topics of interests and knowledge against the classification entries in metadata. If there are not compatible with, the I-Component is deleted from the I-Structure. The resulting structure with the corresponding content becomes the user adapted special report.

2. **Logical Composition:** the logical engine may select the relevant template according to the resource type, the user task — for instance reading —, the device, etc. for computing the next XML web page. The templates will have metadata entries which will be used to select the most relevant one. They will be indexed with user's tasks, type of fragments, user's category, user's level of expertise, etc.The composition engine determines the XML page content and the corresponding navigation tools. Hyperlink annotation will be defined at this level by means of properties associated to hyperlinks - Xlink.

3. **Physical Composition:** the layout engine selects a style sheet, at least, according to the template. This style sheet has to manage adaptive navigation according to user's preferences (annotation, hiding, direct guidance).

6   Perspectives

In this paper, we have presented our framework which consists in delivering adaptive special report according to an author oriented viewpoint. Authors have know-how which enables them to choose document contents and to organize them in one or more consistent ways by means of narrative structures. Authors can share and reuse these narrative structures. A particular knowledge elicitation method is used to formalize this knowledge because they are unable to explicit this knowledge. This method relies on theories and methods stemming from cognitive psychology and psycholinguistics. The reusability of this knowledge leads to Knowledge management. It aims to exploit an organization's intellectual assets for greater productivity, new value, and increased competitiveness[2].

We have proposed a semantic composition engine which delivers a user adapted special report by means of a user model and metadata. This composition engine is also studied for another European project called CANDLE which concerns with distance learning. In this paper, we have considered the management of revisiting and versioning because of the non persistent state of virtual documents. Our system has to ensure that a dynamic document can be recreated every times in the same state for a particular reader.

We plan to offer a kind of free browsing mode which will use a narrative structure as a guide. In other words, the intelligent search engine will not be limited to

---

[2] http://www.aifb.uni-karlsruhe.de/WBS/ontoknowledge/

the information space dedicated to the special report. Indeed, the content specification of each I-Component will be applied to the entire database. A reader will be able to access all articles fitting the different content specifications and then to get articles closely related the current I-Component.

In the future, readers' strategies will be managed by adding enough metadata to compute their structures on the fly according to user's goals. For instance, a clustering process can be applied to geographical (or temporal) criteria present in the metadata and according to a domain ontology. For a local newspaper, which has several issues organized by editions (geographical areas), readers use this criteria for information retrieval from its website.

References

1. Brusilovsky, P., Methods and techniques of adaptive hypermedia. User Modeling and User-Adapted Interaction, 1996. 6(2-3): p. 87-129.
2. Watters, C. and M. Shepherd. Research issues for virtual documents. in Workshop on Virtual Document, Hypertext Functionality and the Web. 1999. Toronto.
3. Berners-lee, T., Weaving the Web. 1999, San Francisco: Harper.
4. Decker, S., et al., Knowledge Representation on the Web. 2000, On to Knowledge Project: http://www.ontoknowledge.org/oil/papers.shtml.
5. Decker, S., et al. Ontobroker: Ontology Based Access to Distributed and Semi-Structured Information. in Conference on Database Semantics. 1999. Rotorua, New Zealand: Kluwer Academic Publishers.
6. Ardissono, L., L. Console, and I. Torre. Exploiting user models for personalizing news presentations. in 2nd Workshop on Adaptive Systems and User Modeling on the WWW, AH'99 and UM'99. 1999: Einhdoven University of Technology, Computer Science Reports.
7. Domingue, J. and E. Motta. A Knowledge-Based News Server Supporting Ontology-Driven Story Enrichment and Knowledge Retrieval. in 11th European Workshop on Knowledge Acquistion, Modelling, and Management (EKAW '99). 1999.
8. Mann, W.C. and S.A. Thompson, Rhetorical Structure Theory: Toward a functional theory of text organization. Text, 1988. 8(3): p. 243-281.
9. Christophides, V., Electronic Document Management Systems. 1998, UCH/FORTH: http://www.ics.forth.gr/~christop/.
10. Decker, S., et al., The Semantic Web - on the respective Roles of XML and RDF. 1999. http://www.ontoknowledge.org/oil.
11. Bray, T., et al., Extensible Markup language (XML) 1.0, (Second Edition). 1998, W3C: http://www.w3.org/TR/2000/REC-xml-20001006.
12. Adler, S., et al., Extensible Stylesheet Language (XSL) Version 1.0. 2000, W3C: http://www.w3.org/TR/xsl/.
13. Fensel, D., et al. On2broker in a Nutshell. in the 8th World Wide Web Conference. 1999. Toronto.
14. Fensel, D., et al. On2broker: Semantic-Based Access to Information Sources at the WWW. in World Conference on the WWW and Internet, WebNet 99. 1999. Honolulu, Hawai, USA.
15. Vitali, F. Versioning hypermedia. in ACM Computing Surveys. 1999.

Tailoring the Recommendation of Tourist Information to Heterogeneous User Groups

L. Ardissono, A. Goy, G. Petrone, M. Segnan, and P. Torasso

Dip. Informatica, Università di Torino
Corso Svizzera 185
I-10149 Torino, Italy
{liliana,goy,giovanna,marino,torasso}@di.unito.it
http://www.di.unito.it/~seta

Abstract. This paper describes the recommendation techniques exploited in INTRIGUE (INteractive TouRist Information GUidE), an adaptive recommender system that supports the organization of guided tours. This system recommends the places to visit by taking into account the characteristics of the group of participants and addressing the possibly conflicting preferences within the group. A group model is exploited to separately manage the preferences of heterogeneous subgroups of people and combine them, in order to identify solutions satisfactory for the group as a whole.

1 Introduction

Web-based information systems have become very popular tools to retrieve specialized information. In particular, the provision of tourist information is extremely appealing, as it supports the search for up-to-date information about services and attractions, without relying on books or travel agencies. The development of Web-based tourist guides is however challenged by the variety of user needs to be satisfied during the presentation of the information. Users are typically interested in different types of attractions (pieces of art, scientific attractions, natural parks, etc.). Moreover, most people do not travel alone, so that possibly conflicting requirements have to be taken into account when recommending the places to visit. Therefore, the presentation of tourist information requires personalized travel guides, satisfying individual information needs; e.g., see [17,25,26,21,24].

In this paper, we present INTRIGUE (INteractive TouRist Information GUidE), a Web-based adaptive system that provides information about tourist attractions and services, such as accommodation and food. In the following presentation, we focus on the techniques for the generation of the personalized recommendations tailored to the preferences of the group of participants.

INTRIGUE supports the user in a combined search for tourist attractions, based on orthogonal criteria, i.e., category-based and geographical search. Moreover, the system dynamically generates multilingual presentations, by exploiting efficient template-based NL generation techniques. Our current prototype

S. Reich, M.M. Tzagarakis, P.M.E. De Bra (Eds.): OHS/SC/AH 2001, LNCS 2266, pp. 280–295, 2002.

presents information about the city of Torino and the surrounding Piedmont area, in Italian and in English. The system assists the user in the organization of a tour by providing personalized recommendations about attractions and services. Moreover, it offers an interactive agenda that supports the scheduling of the tour, by considering both the user's needs and the constraints concerning the opening hours, the average visit time for the selected places, and so forth.

As far as the recommendation functionality is concerned, INTRIGUE deals with a structured model of the group of people traveling together, to manage the possibly conflicting preferences of the subgroups. This approach supports alternative recommendation criteria, which the user can select to receive suggestions customized according to specific viewpoints. For instance, the system supports the suggestion of a solution that satisfies all the participants in a more or less a uniform way. However, also the search for solutions focused on the preferences of specific subgroups is available (in our prototype, we consider children and disabled people). In this way, the user can ask for suggestions focused on particular perspectives. As noticed in [7], an essential feature for an intelligent system is the explanation of the reasons for its own suggestions. This aspect becomes even more crucial for group recommendations, where there is no immediate correspondence between the user's preferences and the system's decisions. For this reason, we have developed an explanation technique supporting a clarification of the evaluation strategies adopted by the system in the recommendation. This technique enables the system to specify which properties are most suitable for the characteristics of the various subgroups, therefore helping the user to select the items to include into the agenda in a very informed way.

The paper is organized as follows: Section 2 describes the structure and the management of the group model; section 3 describes the recommendation criteria used in the system to provide users with personalized suggestions tailored to a possibly heterogeneous tourist group. Section 4 describes some related work and section 5 closes the paper, outlining some future work.

2 Management of Group Models in INTRIGUE

2.1 User Groups

The management of heterogeneous groups having different and potentially conflicting preferences is essential to enhance the recommendation task in several application domains, other than the tourism one. For instance, consider the management of personalized television services and the suggestion of items to purchase in a group environment.

In some cases, group preferences have been managed by exploiting stereotypical models that describe the preferences of the group as a whole. For instance, in the TV domain, family models have been used to customize Electronic Program Guides to the standard preferences of groups formed by adults and children. Although this approach suits the applications having a small number of typical user groups to be considered, it is not flexible enough to manage the cases where the

groups can be highly heterogeneous and there are many possible combinations
of user classes. Tourist services represent an interesting example of this case,
because people having very different preferences and requirements may join the
same tour, which should be organized by taking into account the interests of all
the participants. To this extent, a different group model is needed, in order to
avoid a combinatorial explosion in the number of models to be described. In particular, the management of the user group should be considered as orthogonal
with respect to the management of different user classes.

Ideally, a group model could be managed as the integration of one individual
user model for each member of the group. However, this approach would not
scale up when large groups are considered. Moreover, to address individual preferences, the system would need individual descriptions of the group members,
therefore imposing strong overhead on the user interacting with the system.

We adopt a different approach to overcome the drawbacks of the previous
ones: we consider a group as a set of people that can be partitioned into a
limited number of subgroups.[1] Each subgroup is modeled as a class of users
having similar preferences and the preferences of the whole group can be inferred
by combining the preferences of its subgroups. Moreover, the influence of each
subgroup on the system's recommendation is evaluated. A subgroup could be
particularly influent either because it represents a very significative portion of
the tourist group, or because its members belong to a class having special needs;
e.g., children and disabled people.

The types of (sub)group to be considered and their relevance are domain dependent and have to be defined on the basis of the personalization requirements
to be addressed. For instance, in a tourism domain, groups with special needs,
such as children and disabled, could be given maximum relevance to take their
needs in particular account. However, other groups could be considered; for example, animals could be "members" of the group, with specific preferences, e.g.,
the one for places where they are accepted. In the next sections, we describe the
management of group models adopted in our system.

2.2   Structure of the Group Model

INTRIGUE exploits a structured group model, where uniform subgroups are
represented as distinct entities. A subgroup model is associated to each *homogeneous subgroup* of people planning the tour together. Each subgroup model is
structured in three portions:

- The "Characteristics" section provides information about the characteristics
  of the participants, acquired by the system by questioning the user via a
  registration form. For instance, Figure 1 represents a subgroup of people
  aged between 46 and 55, with a human science background, full mobility
  capabilities, partial vision capabilities and interested in arts and history.

---

[1] In the simplest case, the group is formed by homogeneous people and consists of a
single subgroup.

Characteristics:
    Age: 46-55;
    Background: human_science;
    Mobility: full;
    Vision: partial;
    Interest_for_arts: yes;
    Interest_for_history: yes;
    Interest_for_science: no;
Preferences:
    Special_transportation_systems:
        Importance: 0; *Values*: missing: 0.3; some: 0.4; present: 0.3;
    Special_facilities_for_vision:
        Importance: 0.8; *Values*: missing: 0.1; some: 0.4; present: 0.5;
    Historical_value:
        Importance: 1; *Values*: low: 0.05; medium: 0.1; high: 0.85;
    Artistical_value:
        Importance: 1; *Values*: low: 0.05; medium: 0.35; high: 0.6;
    Scientific_value:
        Importance: 0.5;
Group Information:
    Cardinality: 5;
    Relevance: 0.4

Fig. 1. An example subgroup model for the tourism domain.

– The "Preferences" portion specifies the system's predictions for the subgroup preferences. Each preference is represented as a slot and includes:

  • An "Importance" facet specifying the importance of the preference to the subgroup. For instance, the travelers represented by the model shown in Figure 1 have no interest in special transportation systems (the importance is 0). In contrast, their interest in the historical value of tourist attractions is extremely strong (importance = 1).

  • A probability distribution over the values of the preference. For instance, the described tourists very likely prefer attractions having high historical value ("high" is dominant in the distribution), while the probability that they prefer attractions with low historical value is almost null.

– The "Group Information" section stores general information about the subgroup. Each subgroup has a *cardinality*, specifying the number of people in it, and a *relevance*, representing an estimate of the weight that the preferences of a prototypical member of the subgroup should have on the selection of tourist attractions to be recommended. The relevance ranges from 0 (null relevance), to 1 (maximum one). In our example, there are five people in the subgroup and it has a medium relevance (0.4).

2.3   Knowledge about User Classes

We manage the presence of users having different preferences and requirements by exploiting stereotypical information that describes the characteristics of the various user classes. The tourist population can be segmented according to different perspectives; for instance, we can consider their interests in different aspects of tourist attractions, (e.g., historical value), their knowledge about arts or science, or their mobility and vision capabilities. These perspectives influence different sets of preferences, which the system can exploit to evaluate a tourist attraction. For our prototype, we have specified the following perspectives, each one corresponding to a cluster, that includes a set of stereotypes representing the tourist classes described from that viewpoint:

- "Age_range" perspective: the traveler population is segmented by ranges of age. The main goal is to distinguish children from adults and to model interests for special activities (such as playing) accordingly. The only relevant user's characteristic is "age", but the stereotypes predict specific interests for activities, types of documentation about tourist places, length of the visit, and so on.
- "Interests" perspective: in this cluster of stereotypes, the tourists' interests are modeled. People are segmented into groups characterized by different educational backgrounds (e.g., historical, technical, etc.), also depending on the explicit interests stated by the user in the registration form. This cluster makes predictions on the preferences for different types of tourist attractions: e.g., some places may have a noticeable value from the historical viewpoint, others may excel in scientific or technological aspects.
- "Mobility_capabilities" perspective: the population is segmented to characterize different mobility capabilities. The preferences concern the reachability of places and the availability of special transportation systems.
- "Vision_capabilities" perspective: this segmentation concerns the travelers' sight and makes it possible to describe the preferences of people having full, partial, or null vision capabilities.

2.4   Representation of User Classes

The stereotypical information is stored in a knowledge base, where it is organized as a set of clusters, each one associated to a different perspective: e.g., age, mobility and vision capabilities. A cluster contains a set of stereotypes, representing the classes of tourists forming the partition: e.g., the "vision_capabilities" cluster includes three stereotypes, representing the people having complete, partial and null vision capabilities. Similar to the representation defined for the SeTA system [3], a stereotype contains a set of classification data, describing the characteristics of travelers belonging to the represented class, and a set of preferences, describing the typical requirements of such people for properties of the tourist attractions. For instance, the stereotype describing people with null vision capabilities has only one significant classification data, i.e., the "vision",

PRIMARY-SCHOOL
Classification data:
    Age: up_to_5: 0.0; 6-11: 1.0; 12-14: 0.0; ...; 46-60: 0.0; more_than_60: 0.0;
Preferences:
    Play_activities:
        Importance: 1; *Values*: null: 0.0; low: 0.05; medium: 0.45; high: 0.5;
    Reading_material:
        Importance: 0.8; *Values*: null: 0.05; introductory: 0.2; specialized: 0.05;
                                scholastical: 0.7;
    Length_of_visit:
        Importance: 1; *Values*: short: 0.6; medium: 0.35; long: 0.05;
    Background_knowledge:
        Importance: 1; *Values*: low: 0.9; medium: 0.1; high: 0.0;
    ...
Relevance: 1;

Fig. 2. Stereotype describing primary-school children.

which is a trigger for the stereotype. Moreover, the main predicted preference concerns the availability of vocal presentation devices.

As clusters represent different viewpoints for describing people, the stereotypes belonging to different clusters may be based on different classification data, although some data may be exploited by more than one cluster. Moreover, they make predictions on distinct sets of preferences (those significant from the described viewpoint). For instance, the stereotype described in Figure 2 belongs to the Age_range cluster and describes primary school children, aged from 6 to 11.

The stereotypes also specify the relevance of the represented group ("Relevance" slot). The relevance predicted by a stereotype S represents the weight that the preferences of a prototypical tourist belonging to S should have on the selection of tourist attractions. This parameter ranges in $[0..1]$, where 0 denotes null relevance and 1 represents the maximum relevance. In order to take into account the fact that some subgroups, such as children, have strong requirements on the organization of a tour, the related stereotypes predict a relevance equal to 1 (e.g., see the "PRIMARY-SCHOOL" stereotype in Figure 2). Instead, most of the other stereotypes have medium or low relevance.

2.5   Management of Subgroups within a Tourist Group

At the beginning of the interaction, the user visiting the Web site is asked how many people are going to travel together. Then, the system asks her to distribute such people into relevant subgroups, on the basis of a set of pre-defined features. Currently, the main user features we have considered concern the range of age (to deal with children and elderly) and the mobility and vision capabilities; however, the system can be configured to take into account other features, such as social and cultural aspects. For each subgroup, a registration form is displayed, in order to provide the system with information about the interests of the related travelers, the cardinality of the subgroup, and other similar information. The fields of the forms are not mandatory, but the system's suggestions can be more focused, if information about each subgroup is provided. Each subgroup model is initialized with the preferences of a generic traveler, corresponding to an adult without special requirements. This initialization enables the system to have a basic description, in case the direct user does not fill in the forms.

The system initializes each subgroup model by exploiting stereotypical information about tourists, according to the techniques developed for the SeTA system. The subgroup characteristics are matched against the stereotypical information; the stereotypes best matching the characteristics of the subgroup are then used to predict the subgroup preferences and its importance. Details about these techniques can be found in [3].

3   Generation of Recommendations for a Tourist Group

3.1   Evaluation of Tourist Attractions

The evaluation of items to be recommended to a heterogeneous tourist group is achieved in two steps. First, items are separately evaluated and ranked with respect to each subgroup. Then, the subgroup-related rankings are combined to obtain the overall ranking, from the viewpoint of the whole group. In the following, we will focus on the subgroup-related evaluation of items. Then, in section 3.2, we will discuss the combination of the separate rankings to generate the system's recommendations.

Given the preferences of a homogeneous subgroup, items are ranked by exploiting the same techniques used in the SeTA system for the recommendation of products. As such techniques are extensively described in [3], we only sketch them in the following.

Tourist attractions are represented as entities described by features providing different types of information: e.g., geographical information, category, logistic information, and so forth. In the evaluation of a tourist attraction, the system exploits the *properties* of the item. Properties are features that provide a qualitative evaluation of the attraction. For instance, we take into account the historical or artistic value of an attraction, how much background knowledge is required to appreciate it, or whether the place offers play areas for children ("play_activities" in Figure 2).

The degree of matching (henceforth, *satisfaction score*) between an item and a subgroup model is evaluated by analyzing the preferences of the subgroup towards the properties of the item, stored in the subgroup model. Each property is matched against the related preference to establish an individual score.[2]

---

[2] This score is a decimal value in [0..1], where 1 represents perfect compatibility with the preference, while 0 represents total incompatibility. In this evaluation, the importance of the preference in the subgroup model is used to tune the influence of less relevant properties, when they are not compatible with the subgroup preferences.

The overall satisfaction score of the item results from the merge of the individual scores of its properties. Two individual scores, X and Y, are combined by exploiting the following formula:

$$SATISFACTION\_SCORE(score_X, score_Y) =$$
$$score_X * score_Y / (score_X + score_Y - score_X * score_Y)$$

This formula, described in [2], takes values in the $[0..1]$ range. It is additive and therefore supports and incremental evaluation of the overall satisfaction score of an item. Moreover, it is particularly selective: being based on the product operator, it returns a 0 satisfaction score for any item having at least one null individual score. This selective power is essential in the tourism domain, as it enables the system to dramatically downgrade the evaluation of items incompatible with basic requirements of the traveler subgroups. For instance, a tourist place without a transportation system suitable for disabled people cannot be recommended as a good solution to a group of tourists with mobility problems.

3.2   Recommendation Criteria

INTRIGUE provides the user with alternative recommendation criteria to support her in the selection of the attractions for the tour. The reason for providing different recommendation criteria is that no specific recommendation method can satisfy all the possible requirements. For instance, the user may want to see separate recommendations for each subgroup and compare the lists by themselves. Alternatively, she may prefer to be provided with a single recommendation list, representing a synthesis of the suggestions, in order to avoid the analysis of multiple and possibly long recommendation lists. However, even in this case, different criteria could be applied to generate the list. For instance, items unsuited for at least one subgroup might need to be ignored, although they are interesting options for other groups. Moreover, the recommendations could be fair, trying to satisfy all the subgroups in a uniform way, or they could be biased towards the preferences of the most influent subgroups.

In our system, we have included three recommendation modalities, which the user can choose from by clicking on buttons available in the user interface. See the buttons at the top of Figure 3: "Separate listing by groups", "Unique listing (method 1)", "Unique listing (method 2)". We describe these recommendation criteria referring to a scenario where a user similar to the one described in Figure 1 inspects the civil buildings in Torino. The user is organizing a tour with some children and impaired people. In this case, the system generates three subgroup models: one for the subgroup including the direct user, the others for the two homogeneous subgroups traveling with her.

Separate Listing by Group. In this modality, the system shows separate lists, one for each subgroup, with items sorted on the basis of the rankings previously evaluated for each subgroup. The best ranked elements for each subgroup are at the top of the lists, while the worst ones are at the bottom.

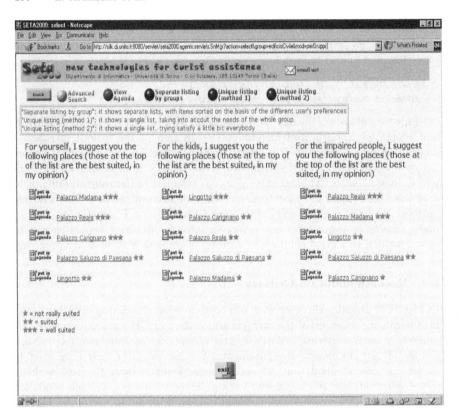

Fig. 3. Separate listing of tourist attractions

Figure 3 shows the system's recommendations, reporting the suggestions for the subgroup including the direct user in the first column, for the children in the second one and for the impaired people in the third one. Notice that each item is associated with an icon (stars), which represents the satisfaction score obtained by the item and supports an easy identification of the best items for each group.

This type of recommendation enables the direct user to select the interesting attractions in an informed way, taking into account the ranking of each item in each subgroup-related list. However, it may be confusing if there are too many subgroups to be considered, because the user should compare several permutations of the items, which may result in a certain overhead.

Preferential Satisfaction Listing (Method 1). In this modality, the system displays a single, sorted list of items representing the suggestion for the whole group. The overall ranking of items is obtained by merging all the subgroup-related rankings in a weighted way, depending on the cardinality and the rele-

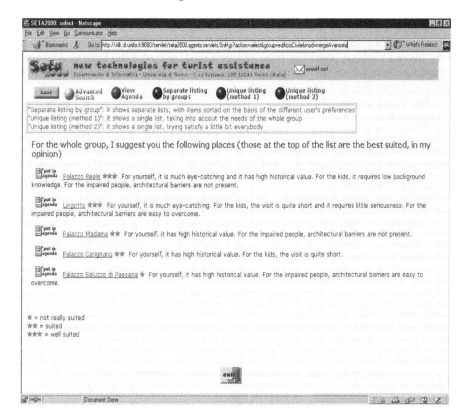

Fig. 4. Unique listing of tourist attractions

vance of the various subgroups. Thus, the system's suggestions take into account the presence of large homogeneous subgroups, and that of subgroups with special needs. The overall score S of an item is evaluated by combining the satisfaction scores S_{UM} associated to the item for each subgroup. In our example:

$$S = inf_{direct\_user} * S_{direct\_user} + inf_{children} * S_{children} + inf_{impaired} * S_{impaired}$$

For each subgroup, the associated weight (inf_{UM}) represents the influence of the subgroup's preferences within the whole group and is evaluated according to the following formula:

$$inf_{UM} = relevance_{UM} * cardinality_{UM} \,/\, total\_cardinality$$

where $relevance_{UM}$ is the relevance of the subgroup, $cardinality_{UM}$ is the number of its members[3] and $total\_cardinality$ is the total number of tourists forming the overall group. In this way, special subgroups can be privileged in a flexible way, depending on the portion of the overall group they represent.

---

[3] Relevance and cardinality are retrieved from the subgroup model.

Figure 4 shows the preferential listing recommendation for the same group of tourists considered in Figure 3. The tourist attractions are sorted according to the overall ranking, resulting from the weighted merge of the individual group rankings. In this case, the stars next to the items represent their overall ranking, related to the whole group of tourists.

This type of recommendation is useful to provide the user with suggestions supporting her in the selection of the items to add to the agenda. In fact, the first items in the list are the best ones for the group considered as a whole, possibly with special attention to the preferences of the most influent subgroups. However, other strategies could be exploited to weight the influence of the subgroups; for example, the group relevance alone could be used, without considering the cardinality, in order to maximize the influence of special subgroups (or, in alternative, the cardinality alone could be used). We are investigating the possibility of providing the direct user with methods to select the parameters to be considered for the evaluation, therefore supporting further personalization forms in the recommendations.

Uniform Satisfaction Listing (Method 2). As an alternative to the preferential satisfaction listing, which sorts tourist attractions in a biased way, the user may be interested in receiving a fair recommendation, where the suggestions uniformly satisfy all the subgroups. To this extent, we have introduced a third modality, where the system shows a single recommendation list whose items are sorted to achieve uniform satisfaction for each subgroup. In this case, the satisfaction score obtained by an item with respect to each subgroup is explicitly used as a *degree of satisfaction* for the subgroup itself: an item with a satisfaction score equal to 1 increases the satisfaction of a subgroup in a maximal way, while an item with a 0 satisfaction score does not modify it. The recommendation list is generated in order to achieve uniform satisfaction for all the subgroups. We do not describe this method in detail, but the idea is the following: to build the recommendation list, at each step, the system selects, out of the set of items to be sorted, the one maximally increasing the satisfaction degree of the subgroup with the lowest satisfaction degree. The aim is to raise the group satisfaction degree as much as possible.

3.3   Explanation of the System's Suggestions

Although the explanation capability is an essential feature, few recommender systems offer this functionality and most of them specify rather naive reasons for the system's suggestions. For instance, NetPerceptions [23] bases the explanation mechanism on collaborative filtering information and motivates its own positive and negative suggestions by relating them to the selections (or rejections) performed by people with selection histories similar to those of the current user. As another example, NLSA [12] motivates its recommendations by highlighting the features of items satisfying the user's explicit requirements, but does not support explanations including more information which can help the user in her selections. More interesting, News Dude [7] explains its own recommendations by analyzing analogies and differences among the items suggested in previous recommendations and already inspected by the user.

INTRIGUE supplements its own recommendations with articulated explanations, which explicitly refer to the preferences of the subgroups of tourist. This feature is particularly important to produce informative and transparent explanations because a recommended item may suite different subgroups due to different properties.

As shown in Figure 4, in the unique listing modalities each item is coupled with a sentence specifying, for each subgroup, the most important properties determining the suggestion of the item.[4] For instance, "Palazzo Reale" (Royal Palace) is a good suggestion for the subgroup including the direct user since it is much eye-catching and has high historical value; moreover it is also good for children because its visit requires low background knowledge. Finally, it suits disabled people because it has no architectural barriers.

Notice that the generated explanations only include a subset of the properties satisfying the preferences in the subgroup model: in fact, they only report the most relevant preferences of the subgroup. For instance, the recommendations for children in Figure 4 are focused on properties such as the background knowledge required to appreciate the attraction and the length of the visit.

The contextually relevant properties for a subgroup are selected by exploiting the stereotypical information: given the set of properties satisfying the preferences of a subgroup model, the properties to be mentioned are selected by taking into account the importance of the related preferences in the stereotype describing the tourist class characterizing the subgroup. For instance, as shown in Figure 2, children's preferences concern properties such as the availability of play areas, length of the visit and required background knowledge.

The linguistic form of the explanations are automatically generated by exploiting template-based Natural Language Generation techniques (see [2]), on the basis of a language independent internal representation of the item properties. In this way multilinguality is supported.

4   Related Work

The typical tourist information Web sites are static hypertexts and provide non-personalized information about attractions and services available in a town, or in a region. These systems suffer from two major drawbacks: first, they cannot provide users with information focused on specific interests (the only way to search for specific information is typically provided as an embedded search engine). Second, they rely on static descriptions, which become obsolete in a short time and have to be manually revised by the site administrators. Another type of site are the e-travel agencies, like, for instance, Expedia [15]; their main goal is

---

[4] The presentation of the most suited properties is not displayed in the separate listing by group due to space constraints on the screen. However, information about items and their properties can be retrieved by asking for their detailed presentation pages.

to offer discount airfare, flight, hotel, cars, vacation packages reservations. However, these sites only help the user to gather information or to make reservations and do not support her in the organization of a trip or a tour of a city.

Some dynamic hypermedia systems have been designed to generate the presentations "on the fly", possibly tailoring contents and styles on the basis of the application of personalization strategies; e.g., see [14,22,9,10] and [19] for an overview. For instance, AVANTI [17] was designed as a kiosk system which generates customized presentations of the services and tourist attractions available in a town. The goal was to support alternative interaction media and personalization strategies were exploited to tailor the presentations to the individual user's interests. More recently, intelligent virtual guides have been designed to personalize the visit of a museum, taking into account several factors such as the user's interests, domain expertise, the fact that the user was visiting the place for the first time, and also the (physical) navigation style within the museum [25, 21]. In particular, there is a strong interest in the development of context-aware applications, supporting a selective presentation of information, based on the physical location of the user [20,13,11,18].

From a related perspective, special attention has been paied to the development of systems supporting the individual user's search for information, by providing her with personalized recommendations. For instance, see [8,7,16]. Finally, some researchers have defined techniques to support the user in the definition of her own search criteria, therefore leading to the configuration of her own information service [6].

5   Discussion

Our work is focused on the provision of multilingual, personalized recommendations for groups of people planning a visit to a given geographical area. Different from on-site kiosks and context-aware applications, the role of our system is in assisting the user to schedule the tour, not in guiding the group during the visit. Therefore, physical context has a marginal role and is exploited only when the schedule of the trip is considered, to estimate, for instance, the appropriate transfer times from one tourist attraction to another.

The main contribution of this paper concerns the management of a *group model*, where the characteristics, interests and preferences of the various components of the group are taken into account to tailor the recommendations in a suitable way. The management of a group model and the group-oriented personalization distinguishes our system from the other recommender systems, which typically tailor the suggestions to the individual user. In the case of a single user, her preferences may be more or less articulated, but are unique. In contrast, a group of people traveling together may have conflicting preferences (and needs) and the generation of a recommendation which addresses the requirements of all the people in the group is much more complex. In order to address this issue, we have considered the group as composed of subgroups, having homogeneous preferences and needs. Moreover, we have designed different recommendation criteria, which the user can select to get different types of suggestion from the system. These criteria include the separate ranking for subgroups, a uniform merge of the preferences of all the subgroups, and a weighted recommendation, where the subgroups have different influence on the system's rankings. Another important aspect is the capability to explain why a recommendation has been made: when the system presents the lists of tourist places to be visited, a sentence specifying the most relevant properties determining the suggestion is generated.

All the Web pages of the INTRIGUE user interface are dynamically generated, according to the following steps: first, the information to be displayed is selected; then, the linguistic descriptions are generated, by exploiting a template-based Natural Language Generator (see [2]) and an XML object, representing the content of the page, is produced (see [5]). Finally, the XML object is transformed into a HTML page to be interpreted by a standard browser, by exploiting XSL transformations. Our goal is to have a representation of the personalized content of each page independent from the actual user interface implemented by the system. For instance, the XML object could be fed to a different module, that generates a user interface for a different medium (e.g. a mobile), or stores the personalized content in a database for further processing.

We have not yet focused on the adaptive presentation of tourist attractions. However, the generation module could be easily extended with the techniques developed for the SeTA system, in order to filter the features of an attraction to be presented, on the basis of the user's interests [2,3]. We are also working on improving the scheduling facility to realize a "virtual travel-agent" able to help the user to organize her day tour, including hotel and meal arrangements.

INTRIGUE is based on the multi-agent architecture of SeTA, instantiated on the tourism domain and updated with the introduction of the agent managing the interactive agenda. Details about this architecture can be found in [1,4].

We have planned to test the recommendation and explanation functionalities of the system with users in the next future. In particular, we would like to evaluate the system on some typical scenarios, such as a family visiting a town, a tour to be organized for the a group of students or the organization of a spare day for some people visiting a town for business reasons. In all these cases, we will evaluate the recommendation capabilities of the system by comparing the tourist attractions actually selected by the user (by adding them to the agenda) with those suggested by the system. Moreover, we will collect, from a selected number of users, individual feedback on the usefulness and effectiveness of the system's alternative recommendation criteria and explanation capabilities.

References

1. Ardissono, L., Barbero, C., Goy, A., Petrone, G.: An agent architecture for personalized Web stores. In: Proc. 3rd Int. Conf. on Autonomous Agents 182–189, Seattle, WA (1999)
2. Ardissono, L., Goy, A.: Dynamic generation of adaptive Web catalogs. In: Adaptive Hypermedia and Adaptive Web-Based Systems. Lecture Notes in Computer Science, Vol. 1892. Springer Verlag, Berlin (2000) 5–16

3. Ardissono, L., Goy, A.: Tailoring the interaction with users in Web stores. User Modeling and User-Adapted Interaction 10(4) (2000) 251–303

4. Ardissono, L., Goy, A., Petrone, G., Segnan, M.: A software architecture for dynamically generated adaptive Web stores. In: Proc. 17th IJCAI 1109–1114, Seattle, WA (2001)

5. Ardissono, L., Goy, A., Petrone, G., Segnan, M., Torasso, P.: Dynamic generation of personalized tourist information on the Web. In: Proc. of 12th ACM Conference on Hypertext and Hypermedia, Aarhus, Denmark (2001)

6. Bauer, M., Dengler, M.: InfoBeans - configuration of personalized information assistants. In: Proc. 1999 Int. Conf. on Intelligent User Interfaces 153–156, Los Angeles, CA (1999)

7. Billsus D., Pazzani, M.: A personal news agent that talks, learns and explains. In: Proc. 3rd Int. Conf. on Autonomous Agents 268–275, Seattle, WA (1999)

8. Burke, R.D., Hammond, K.J., Young, B.C.: The FindMe approach to assisted browsing. IEEE Expert (1997) 32–39

9. De Carolis B., de Rosis, F.: User-adapted image descriptions from annotated knowledge sources. In: Proc. 3rd Workshop on Adaptive Hypertext and Hypermedia 13–23, Sonthofen, Germany, (2001)

10. De Carolis, B., de Rosis, F., Pizzutilo, S.: Adapting information presentation to the 'user in context'. In: Proc. IJCAI Workshop on AI in mobile systems 13–18, Seattle, WA (2001)

11. De Carolis, B., de Rosis, F., Pizzutilo, S.: Context-sensitive information presentation. In: Proc. UM'2001 Workshop on User Modelling in Context-Aware Applications, Sonthofen, Germany (2001)

12. Chai, J., Horvath, V., Nicolov, N., Stys-Budzikowska, M., Kambhatla, N., Zadrozny, W.: Natural Language Sales Assistant - a Web-based dialog system for online sales. In: Proc. 13th Innovative Applications of Artificial Intelligence Conference 19–26, Seattle, WA (2001)

13. Cheverest, K., Davies, N., Mitchell, K., and Smith, P.: Providing tailored (context-aware) information to city visitors. In: Proc. International Conference on Adaptive Hypermedia and Adaptive Web-based Systems 73–85, Trento, Italy (2000)

14. Dale, R., Green, S.J., Milosavljevic, M., Paris, C.: Dynamic document delivery: Generating natural language texts on demand. In: Proc. 9th Int. Conf. and Workshop on Database and Expert Systems Applications, Vienna (1998)

15. Expedia.com. http://www.expedia.com

16. Fink, J., Kobsa, A.: A review and analysis of commercial user modeling servers for personalization on the World Wide Web. User Modeling and User-Adapted Interaction, Special Issue on Deployed User Modeling 10(2-3) (1997) 209–249

17. Fink, J., Kobsa, A., Nill, A.: Adaptable and adaptive information for all users, including disabled and elderly people. New review of Hypermedia and Multimedia 4 (1999) 163–188

18. Fischer, G., Ye, Y.: Exploiting context to make delivered information relevant to tasks and users. In: Proc. UM'2001 Workshop on User Modelling in Context-Aware Applications, Sonthofen, Germany (2001)

19. Kobsa, A., Koenemann, J., Pohl, W.: Personalized hypermedia presentation techniques for improving online customer relationships. The Knowledge Engineering Review 16(2) (2001) 111–155

20. Marti, P., Rizzo, A., Petroni, L., Tozzi, G., Diligenti, M.: Adapting the museum: a non-intrusive user modeling approach. In: Proc. 7th Int. Conf. on User Modeling 311–313, Banff, Canada (1999)

21. Marucci, L., Paternò, F.: Logical dimensions for the information provided by a virtual guide. In: Proc. International Conference on Adaptive Hypermedia and Adaptive Web-based Systems 359–362, Trento, Italy (2000)

22. Milosavljevic, M., Dale, R., Green, S.J., Paris, C., Williams, S.: Virtual museums on the information superhighway: Prospects and potholes. In: Proc. Annual Conference of the International Committee for Documentation of the International Council of Museums, Melbourne (1998)

23. Net perceptions. http://www.netperception.com

24. Paris, C., Wan, S., Wilkinson, R., Wu, M.: Generating personal travel guides - and who wants them? In: Proc. 8th Int. Conf. on User Modeling 251–253, Sonthofen, Germany (2001)

25. Petrelli, D., De Angeli, A., Convertino, G.: A user centered approach to user modelling. In: Proc. 7th Int. Conf. on User Modeling 255–264, Banff, Canada (1999)

26. Wilkinson, R., Lu, S., Paradis, F., Paris, C., Wan, S., Wu, M.: Generating personal travel guides from discourse plans. In: Adaptive Hypermedia and Adaptive Web-Based Systems. Lecture Notes in Computer Science, Vol. 1892. Springer Verlag, Berlin (2000) 392–85

Application of ART2 Networks and Self-Organizing Maps to Collaborative Filtering

Guntram Graef and Christian Schaefer

Telecooperation Office (TecO), University of Karlsruhe, Vincenz-Priessnitz Str. 1,
76131 Karlsruhe, Germany, Tel.: +49 (721) 6902-89, Fax: -16,
{graef}@teco.edu

Abstract. Since the World Wide Web has become widespread, more and more applications exist that are suitable for the application of social information filtering techniques. In collaborative filtering, preferences of a user are estimated through mining data available about the whole user population, implicitly exploiting analogies between users that show similar characteristics. These preferences are then normally used to filter content or functionality of an application. Two important factors for the quality of the filtering process are the number of users and the amount of information (such as observed behaviors) available about each user. Another factor is the number of objects in the pool of the application that can be considered during the filtering process. Today in most cases memory based approaches to collaborative filtering are used. Unfortunately with O(#users * #items) those do not scale well. Therefore we implemented a model based approach using two different types of neural networks and benchmarked them against a widely used memory based approach. Especially with ART2 networks we obtained some encouraging results.

1 Introduction

The World Wide Web has been established as a major platform for information and application delivery. The amount of content and functionality available often exceeds the cognitive capacity of users. This problem has also been characterized as information overload [15].

Various approaches exist that address this issue, such as search engines [7], web catalogs or filtering techniques based on user profiles, such as collaborative filtering [21].

In collaborative filtering, user profiles are generated that describe user preferences in relation to items within a specific domain. Depending on the application, items can e.g. be Web resources, components [14], services [12], or products [1]. Initial knowledge about user preferences can be obtained either explicitly such as from ratings by users [21] or implicitly through behavior analysis [19] [13]. For each user a vector is generated with one entry for each known item. The profile vectors are then used as input for either a memory based or a model based method to compute item recommendations by exploiting information stored in profiles that show similarities to a given profile. An often used memory based method is the *Mean Squared*

S. Reich, M.M. Tzagarakis, P.M.E. De Bra (Eds.): OHS/SC/AH 2001, LNCS 2266, pp. 296-309, 2002.

Differences Algorithm [21]. As illustrated in figure 1, a given profile D is compared to profiles of other users to find the n nearest neighbors i.e. the n most similar profiles that are not equal to D. For this purpose a vector distance metric is employed. In the example, n=2 and thus profile A and C are selected. A target vector is then computed as the average of the neighbor vectors. Depending on the type of the application, the target vector is used to recommend items or to find estimates for blank parts of the original user profile.

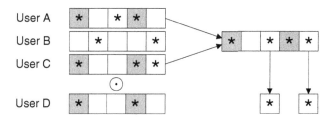

Fig. 1. Memory based collaborative filtering

In model based approaches such as [10] [6], all available profile vectors are first learned by a model. Later single profile vectors can be applied to the model to either obtain a target vector or directly receive recommendations. Figure 2 illustrates this.

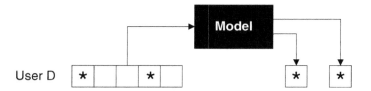

Fig. 2. Model based collaborative filtering

A model usually is smaller in size than the whole set of profile data and no any-to-any matching of profiles is necessary which often leads to performance problems in memory based approaches. On the other hand, an abstraction is performed that usually leads to an information loss and the adaptability of the model to changes to a profile is an issue.

Some applications of collaborative filtering can be found in [21], [17], [22] and [14].
In the first part of this contribution we describe two memory based approaches to collaborative filtering using self-organizing maps (SOMs) [16], and Adaptive Resonance Theory (ART) networks [9]. In the second part of the paper we perform an evaluation with two sets of test data from real world applications and compare the two approaches with a widely used memory based approach.

2   Using Neural Networks for Collaborative Filtering

A large variety of neural networks have been described [20]. Neurons are modeled after nerve-cells in animals. Quite popular is the McCulloch-Pitts Neuron [8] shown in figure 3 (left). The activation of a neuron j is computed by comparing a threshold value θ_j to the weighed input $w_{ij}s_i$. In effect, the neuron performs pattern recognition with the angle between input and weight vector being a measure of conformity. To obtain an adaptive filter this angle is also used during learning, instead of the output value that is used in supervised learning. The weight vector of the neuron is then adjusted towards the input vector as shown in figure 3 (right). This is called unsupervised learning. An important parameter is the learning rate δ that determines how quickly the weight vector is adjusted. Usually a high learning rate is used at the beginning which is then decreased when more input vectors are learned.

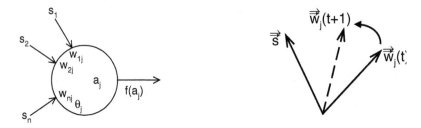

Fig. 3. McCulloch-Pitts Neuron (left), Adjustment of a weight vector to an input pattern (right)

Neurons are connected to form networks where the output signal of one neuron is used as input signal for other neurons. Competitive learning can be realized by organizing McCulloch-Pitts Neurons in a layer and presenting an input pattern to each neuron and then only allowing the neuron with the highest activation to produce an output signal. Thus the neuron layer responds to each input pattern with a specific neuron. It independently classifies all patterns into clusters.

Two types of competitive learning are described with the Adaptive-Resonance-Theory [9] and Self-Organizing Maps [16].

2.1 Self-Organizing Maps

In Self-Organizing Maps (SOMs) [16] not only weights are important but also the location of neurons within the layer. Similar neurons that classify similar patterns are closely located. During the learning process a spacial distribution is created so that neighbor neurons are activated by similar signals. Following the biological example, neurons are arranged in spaces of low dimensionality. This is why the term "map" is used. A topology preserving mapping is attained that maps highly dimensional input patterns to few spacial dimensions. Thus, a strong compression of dimensionality is performed.

Usually, two dimensional maps are used for classification tasks since they allow for greater flexibility in neighborhood relations than one dimensional maps while allowing for easier computations than maps with more than two dimensions. As shown in figure 4 (left) for an example of three neurons, each neuron of the map is fully connected to the input layer. The weight vectors are thus of the same dimensionality as the input vectors. The neurons at the border of the map have less neighbors than those in the center. This leads to an undesired preferential treatment of some neurons. To avoid this, the map is projected to the surface of a sphere [3]. In figure 4 (left) the neighborhood of a neuron is shown in the case of a spherical mapping.

During the learning phase competitive learning is used to determine a winner neuron for each pattern in the training set. But now not merely the winner neuron is adjusted according to the training pattern but also all neighbor neurons. The learning process of a neuron is not independent from other neurons which is why a global learning method must be used [5].

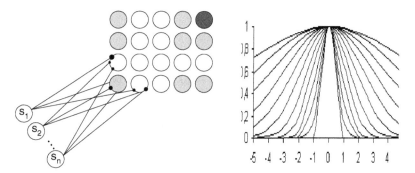

Fig. 4. 2-dimensional SOM with input signal ($s\{n\}$), weighted connections showing neighborhood relations (gray) of a neuron (black)

In each learning step the neuron with the strongest activation by the external signal is determined. If for the McCulloch-Pitts neurons the additional conditions are met that the sum of all weights is constant and the input signal are normed, then the winner neuron k can be determined by applying the euklidian norm.

The weight adjustments of the winner neuron are performed according to the formula that describes the learning rule for competitive learning: $w_j(t+1) = w_j(t) + \delta(t)*(s-w_j(t))$. The adjustment of the neighboring neurons j depends on their distance d_{jk} from the winner neuron k. The strength of the adjustment is described as a function of the distance. With this function $h_{jk}(t)$ and learning rate $\delta(t)$ the following learning rule is true: $w_{ij}(t+1) = w_{ij}(t) + \delta(t) * h_{jk}(t) * (s_i - w_{ij}(t))$.

In [16] and in [5] the calculation of the adaptation strength is performed with the Gauss bell: $h_{jk}(t) = -d_{jk} / e^{2\alpha(t)* 2\alpha(t)}$. At the beginning of the learning phase the general structure of the map must develop. After some time smaller details should manifest themselves on the map. Therefore at the beginning even neurons that are relatively distant are adjusted, while later only local adjustments are performed. Figure 4 (right) shows how through the dependence of the Gauss function on the learning duration the neighborhood is affected less and less by the learning process.

Stability and Plasticity

The application of a SOM to a classification problem is only interesting if there are more patterns than neurons. A neuron must be able to represent more than one pattern of a cluster. If the patterns greatly differ, after each learning step the weight vector is adjusted towards the applied pattern but away from previously learned ones. Thus the neuron "jumps" within the cluster. To avoid this problem and to obtain a stable net, the learning rate is reduced in order that later changes only slightly modify the weight vector. This way a convergence is forced.

To create a clustering for a set, representative samples must be presented to the map several times during the learning phase. If the net shall be able to learn new patterns even after the learning phase, the learning rate can't be reduced too much and the influence on the neighborhood during the learning process must stay rather strong. Thus, the ability of the net to be shaped after the learning phase can only be maintained if stable weights are abandoned. A stable net can't be adjusted. This problem is called stability-plasticity problem and has been addressed in [9] with the Adaptive-Resonance-Theory.

2.2 Adaptive Resonance Theory

On the SOM the number of neurons is fixed and can't be changed. If during the learning phase a pattern is applied to which no neuron strongly responds, a neuron is selected pretty much by random and adjusted to that pattern. In the worst cases that neuron had already been adjusted optimally to a class of patterns from the training set. By adjusting the weights to the new pattern the weight vector representing that class is changed which results in the classification being unlearned. In that case weights won't stabilize.

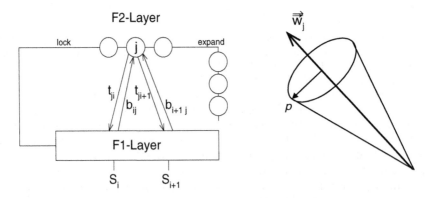

Fig. 5. Set-up of an ART network (left) and attentiveness cone of a weight vector (right)

The Adaptive-Resonance-Theory solves this problem by making the neuron layer adaptive. This means new neurons can be added step by step if a pattern does not match any existing neuron closely enough. Furthermore, a winner neuron can reject the pattern if the similarity is too low. The winner neuron therefore sends its weight vector back to the input layer and only learns the new pattern if it lies within a cone around the weight vector [20]. The size of the cone is determined by the vigilance parameter ρ. Figure 5 (right) shows the attentiveness cone.

The net contains two layers F1 and F2. F2 is the competitive layer and consists of a set of ordered neurons that do not constitute any neighborhood relations. For each input pattern a winner neuron is determined in that layer. The F1 layer controls the classification. If a pattern is not within the attentiveness cone the F1 layer blocks the winner neuron for that pattern. Between the layers weighted connections exist in both directions. Figure 5 (left) shows the set-up.

During the learning process a pattern is applied to the F1 layer. Through the weights that are directed upwards the neuron with the strongest activation is determined by computing the scalar. By applying the weight vector that is directed downwards, the F1 layer checks if the pattern lies within the attentiveness cone. If that is the case, both weight vectors are adjusted to the pattern. Otherwise the F1 layer blocks the winner neuron during the further processing of the pattern and tries to locate another winner neuron. If none of the existing neurons fits, then a new neuron that matches the pattern is added. A detailed description of the F1 layer and the learning process can be found in [11].

The described approach makes sure that the net always converges to a stable state and still maintains plasticity. A potential disadvantage is that under certain circumstances the optimal number of classes can be greatly surpassed [5]. Thus the extension of the competitive layer F2 is limited to a maximum number of neurons. After the limit has been reached, no new neurons will be added and rejected patterns must be discarded.

The Adaptive Resonance Theory exists in two versions. One version is restricted to binary input patterns while the ART2 networks that we selected for our research have been designed to process analog input patterns.

3 Applied Model

In the previous sections two neural networks have been introduced that are able to cluster a training set without supervision and to classify patterns applied after a learning phase. The nets can therefore be used to assign a profile to a class of similar profiles. Information is stored in the weight vectors of the neurons. Besides classification this allows for another application of the nets, as described in the following section.

The weight vectors of the neurons in the competitive layer are also called reference vectors. During each step of the learning phase, the weight vectors are adjusted towards an applied pattern. In the case of competitive learning a weight adjustment is only performed if a similar enough pattern is used. Then the weight vector converges towards the average of all learned patterns. It more or less describes each learned pattern. The weight vector is thus a "codebook" for the represented class.

In an ART2 network, the weight vectors that are directed downwards are the reference vectors. For the learning process in an ART2 net two different learning methods can be applied. But only the slower one of the two methods produces a reference vector. In contrast to a SOM the weight vectors are not normed. Still, they converge i.e. the vector norm converges towards a constant value $1/(1-d)$ whereas d is the constant output of a winner neuron. To reach that limit a large number of learning steps is required which is why usually convergence is forgone.

In the SOM the normed weight vector also describes the "learning history" of a neuron. However, in that case during the learning phase the reference vector is also influenced via neighborhood relations. But since the neighborhood contains similar neurons this does not necessarily have a negative effect. It is rather assumed that this modification of the reference vector is desirable since it prevents neurons to specialize too strongly on a small number of similar patterns.

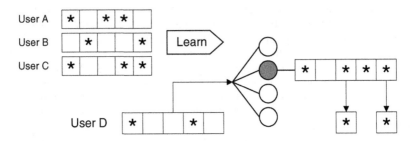

Fig. 6. A neural network as a model for generating predictions. Asterixes mark user interest.

The ability to classify and the formation of reference vectors form the basis for using neural networks as a model in collaborative filtering. Figure 6 shows the set-up.

The first step is to determine the network parameters. The learning rate and the number of learning steps are empirical values and can be chosen similar for every application. In contrast the network size must be estimated individually for different data sets. If the network is too large, neurons specialize too much on a few patterns. Is the network too small the neurons generalize too much and the reference vector becomes useless. As an indicator for estimating the network sizes the number of profiles is used. It is assumed that with a large number of profiles more different behavioral patterns i.e. more independent profiles exist than with a smaller number.

In an ART2 net the similarity parameter must be specified. It can be set automatically during the learning process. A maximum value is used for initialization. If during the learning process a pattern of no neuron can be accepted the parameter is decreased until the pattern can be assigned to a neuron.

After the determination of the profile and the initialization of the weights, the network learns the existing profiles. After the learning process has been completed the network is able to classify profiles and to assign them to a reference vector that can be used as a basis for compiling recommendations.

Learning

From the database a number of representative and expressive profiles are compiled to a training set that is then learned by a neural network. Less expressive profiles are those that are only sparsely populated.

The higher the dimensionality of the input vectors the more difficult it becomes for a neural network to a achieve a useful clustering because the number of independent patterns that do not show similarities increases. For each of those patterns an individual neuron must be learned.

If in addition to this, the training set contains sparsely populated profile vectors, the network must use a large part of its resources or neurons for the classification of vectors with low expressive value. The result is a network that does badly represents the training set. Thus only profiles that contain a minimum number of entries should be selected for training.

Both SOMs and ART networks possess the ability to learn after completion of the initial learning phase. If the profile of a user changes it can be learned again. However, this leads to an advantage for profiles that change frequently over profiles that seldom change because it is learned more often. In the worst case, other profiles might be unlearned as the weight vector shifts towards the re-learned profile.

The re-learning of changed profiles can be handled best by the SOM because in that case the global structure of the map needn't be modified. A changed profile usually is still similar enough to the original profile to be represented by the same neuron or at least one of its neighbors. Thus it is unlikely that existing patterns are unlearned. Changes can be performed localy. On the other hand the ART2 network has problems if the changed profile lays no longer within the similarity cone of the neuron that it had been assigned to before. In that case the profile will be assigned to a new neuron and over time the optimal clustering of the training set will be destroyed.

If a new profile is added that has no similarities to existing profiles, it can easily be added to the ART2 network while the SOM would have to adjust its global structure, which would have to be done by re-learning the whole training set. Thus a SOM tends to forget patterns when new patterns are learned.

It is also possible to add new items after a network has been trained. For this purpose the number of input neurons must be increased because a new dimension is added to the profile vectors. In both cases the extension is easily performed by adding a new initial weight to each neuron. To avoid violating the requirement of equal weight sums it only needs to be ensured that the initial weight values stay within a small interval.

Requests

After the training phase the network is ready to classify profiles. To generate recommendations for a user his or her user profile is applied to the network. Each neuron of the competitive layer computes its activation and a winner neuron is determined. This neuron represents the class of the profile. Instead of generating a target profile from all profiles of this class, the reference vector of the neuron is used i.e. the target profile has already been generated when computing the reference vector during the learning phase. As in the case of the *Mean Squared Differences Algorithm*, the target vector is compared to the applied profile and recommendations are made for items that appear to have been underused by the user.

When determining the winner neurons, a scalar product must be computed for each neuron of the competitive layer. The complexity of a request for recommendations thus depends on the number of items and the number of neurons: $O(\#neurons * \#items)$. The number of neurons in the network does not depend on the number of users but on the number of relevant user clusters. This factor tends to be smaller by orders of magnitude and can be treated as a quality of service parameter.

Limitations

A winner neuron is determined by choosing the neuron with the highest activation. This means, only the similarity between input vector and weight vector is recognized. But if two vectors are opposite to each other this can also carry potentially useful information.

4 Evaluation

Three requirements for neural networks can be identified: Requests for recommendations must be processed quickly, the recommendations should be of high quality and the network should be able to adapt to changes to profile data during run-time. The first experiments presented here have been performed to test if those requirements were met when using two test data sets. The performance of the neural networks has been compared to memory-based Collaborative Filtering based on the *Mean Squared Differences Algorithm*. After presenting our first experiments, the learning duration, selection of parameters and the dependence of the quality of recommendations on the training set will be discussed. Based on those criteria SOMs and ART2 networks will be compared.

4.1 Test Data

We used two test data sets. Most results presented here have been obtained by using the publicly available EachMovie data set [18]. It contains 2.811.983 ratings on a scale from 1 to 5 for 1628 movies by 72.916 users. As in [4] we randomly selected a subset of 2000 users that had a minimum of 80 entries in their profiles. In each profile 30 entries are then randomly selected as control set while the others are used as input for the filtering algorithms. To test the performance of the different methods with sparse profile data from a different domain, we used data that we obtained in a large intranet E-Commerce application, Eurovictor II [14]. The data describes the intensity with which employees have accessed different services of the application.

4.2 Response Time and Quality of Predictions

For our experiments we used a 10x10 SOM and an ART2 network for a maximum of 50 neurons. We also used *Mean Squared Differences Algorithm* with a neighborhood size of 20. We used the EachMovie data set. To simulate a growing database, we did three experiments using 20%, 60% and 100% of available profile entries, with 30 control set entries in each case that we used to evaluate the computed recommendations.

The three different subsets have been used as training sets for the neural networks and as input for the memory based method. Afterwards one, three, five and 30 recommendations have been computed and compared to the control set of 30 hidden profile entries. The results of those experiments can be found in figure 7 (left). As can be seen, the ART2 network performed significantly better than the memory based method while the SOM produced results of the lowest quality.

Each time recommendations were computed the response time has been measured. As expected and shown in figure 7 (right), the performance of the neural network based methods mostly scales with the number of items, while the number of users has a much less significant influence. The three test sets contain profile entries for 400, 1200 and 2000 of users. While the memory based approach has to calculate scalars for all users, the neural networks only need to compute 50 and 100 scalars respectively

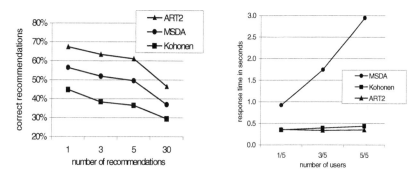

Fig. 7. Quality of results (left) and response time with growing number of users (right)

4.3 Adaptivity

A third important requirement besides quality of recommendations and performance is the ability of the neural networks to adapt during run-time. The networks can't relearn all profiles whenever a single profile changes since the complete learning process takes a considerable amount of time, in the case of our test sets several minutes. Therefore new or changed profiles must be (re-)learned by the network without repeating the initial learning phase.

We performed an experiment to test the ability of our networks to adapt to changes or additions of profiles. The same test data as in the previous experiments was used. This time we started with 400 profiles that we randomly selected from the complete set of 2000 user profiles and used them as training data on the networks. Then we randomly selected 800 profiles that were learned by the networks, then 1200, 1600 and finally all 2000. Please note that those data sets were not disjunct and some profiles were learned more often than others. Then, recommendations were generated and compared to the control set of 30 profile entries that were not used for training.

Figure 8 (left) shows the results of the experiment using a SOM. To unlearn as few patterns as possible when updating the network, the map's learning rate is reduced from 0.8 to 0.5. There is only a slight difference in the quality of the obtained results. The SOM shows a high degree of adaptivity.

Figure 8 (right) shows the corresponding results for an ART2 network. To preserve the knowledge of previously learned patterns the number of learning steps has been reduced from 10 to 5. The quality of predictions decreased in our experiments and after (re-)learning all profiles from the 5 training subsets the quality of the recommendations fell to the level of what we obtained using our *Mean Squared Differences Algorithm* implementation. The neurons have not been adapted to profile changes in a step by step manner. Modified profiles have been rejected as dissimilar to existing neurons and have been assigned to new neurons. This prevented an optimal clustering of the input data.

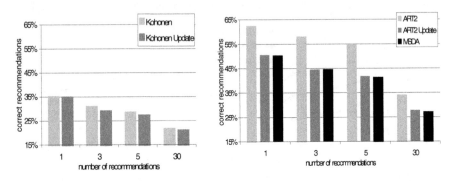

Fig. 8. Quality of results when gradually updating the network compared to relearning all data

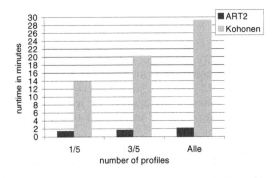

Fig. 9. Learning duration for 400, 1200 and 2000 profiles

4.4 Learning Speed

The decrease of prediction quality that occur after updates of an ART2 network can be countered by occasionally relearning the whole data set. Figure 9 shows that compared to a SOM an ART2 network can be trained fairly quickly. The same test data and networks as in the previous experiments were used. The comparatively slow learning speed of the SOM results from the complex computation of neighborhood relations using the Gauss bell. The learning speed can be increased by using a slightly less exact linear function. The duration for (re-)learning a single profile from our training set was on average 0.06 seconds with an ART2 network and between 0.5 and 1 second for a SOM.

4.5 Choice of Parameters

For most parameters of the neural networks standard values can be used. Two important parameters that have to be set are the number of learning steps (*epoch*) and the size of the network In the case of our ART2 networks ten learning steps have been enough, often the network stabilized even faster.

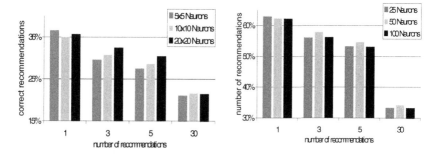

Fig. 10. Quality of results in relation to network size

For the SOM we also used ten learning steps. The map needs a global learning process and can then make more and more fine grained local weight adjustments while decreasing the learning rate. This fine grained learning phase needs much longer and can't be completed after ten learning steps. We performed experiments with up to 100 steps without being able to observe any measurable improvements. The most important parameter is the network size which means the number of neurons in the competitive layer. In order to decrease run-time during profile evaluation the network size should be constant and as small as possible. But the quality of recommendations also depends on the number of neurons. Thus, depending on the number of relevant clusters in the profile set more or less neurons are necessary.

When using SOMs, too few neurons lead to an instability while too many neurons prevent a useful classification. The ART2 network only uses new neurons when a pattern does not lie within a cone of attentiveness. Thus the number of neurons in an ART2 network can never be too high. The number of neurons in an ART2 network is only limited for performance reasons. If the set maximum number of neurons has been reached and a new pattern does not lie within the attentiveness cone of a neuron then the cone radius is increased automatically until the pattern can be assigned to a neuron. Figure 10 (left) shows that in the case of a SOM in the range of 25 to 400 neurons only small differences in quality can be observed with our test data. Figure 10 (right) shows that there is also no significant difference when increasing the number of neurons in an ART2 network from 25 to 100.

4.6 Influence of Training Set

To test the influence of the population of the training set on the quality of results obtained with the three collaborative filtering methods, we performed two more experiments using the Eurovictor II data set. Since that data set is smaller and very sparsely populated we chose 16 neurons as the network size for both the ART2 network and the SOM and only computed 5 recommendations per profile. The Eurovictor II data set contains 770 profiles, only 91 with 5 or more entries.

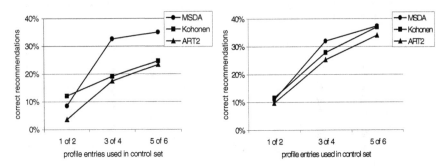

Fig. 11. Results with E-Victor data set: all profiles (left), only profiles with 5+ entries (right)

Figure 11 (left) shows results using all profiles as training set and figure 11 (right) visualizes the results that were obtained only using profiles with 5 or more entries. In both cases three different query sets have been created: These are sets that contain profiles with two or more, four or more and six or more entries respectively and use one, three or five of those entries for the control set. The result shows that the neural networks' performance is affected negatively by the sparsity of the training data. With very sparse data our memory based implementation produced better quality results.

5   Conclusion

We have described two model based approaches to collaborative filtering based on Self-Adaptive Maps and ART2 networks. When evaluating them with test data from two real life applications we found out that ART2 networks produce even better results than a widely used memory based approach if the profile vectors in the training data are not sparsely populated. The model based algorithms needed by several orders of magnitude less memory and less computations to produce recommendations. The ART2 network proofed to be adaptive but the quality of predictions still degraded slowly after more and more changed profile vectors were (re-)learned suggesting that it is necessary to relearn the complete data set once in a while. In the near future we want to include other memory based algorithms into our comparison, such as suggested in [10] or [6]. We also plan to explore whether it is possible to improve results further by combining several methods, including the neural network models explored in this contribution.

References

[1]   AMAZON.COM, Amazon Homepage: http://www.amazon.com (accessed: May 2000)
[2]   R. ARMSTRONG, D. FREITAG, T. JOACHIMS, T. MITCHELL, WebWatcher: a learning apprentice for the World Wide Web, in: AAAI Spring Symposium, Stanford, U.S., pp. 6-12.
[3]   W. BENN, O. GOERLITZ, Semantic Navigation Maps for Information Agents, in: Proceedings of the 2nd Intl. Workshop on Cooperative Agents, Lecture Notes in Artificial Intelligence 1435, Springer-Verlag, Heidelberg, 1998,
[4]   D. BILLSUS, M. J. PAZZANI, Learning Collaborative Information Filters, in: Proceedings of the 15th Intl. Conference on Machine Learning, Morgan Kaufmann Publishers, 1998
[5]   H.BRAUN, J.FEULNER, R.MALAKA, Praktikum Neuronale Netze, Springer Verlag, 1996
[6]   J. S. BREESE, D. HECKERMAN, C. KADIE, Empirical Analysis of Predictive Algorithms for Collaborative Filtering, in: Proceedings of the 14th Annual Conference on Uncertainty in Artificial Intelligence, pp. 43-52, 1998
[7]   S. BRIN, L. PAGE, The Anatomy of a Large-Scale Hypertextual Web Search Engine, in: Proceedings of the 7th World Wide Web Conference, 1998
[8]   G. A. CARPENTER, Neural Network Models for Pattern Recognition and Associative Memory, 1989, in: G. A. Carpenter and S. Grossberg, Pattern Recognition by Self-Organizing Neural Networks, MIT Press, 1991
[9]   G. A. CARPENTER, S. GROSSBERG, ART2: Self-Organization of Stable Category Recognition Codes for Analog Input Patterns, 1987, in: G. A. Carpenter and S. Grossberg, Pattern Recognition by Self-Organizing Neural Networks, MIT Press, 1991
[10] M. K. CONDLIFF ET AL., Bayesian Mixed-Effects Models for Recommender Systems, in: Proceedings of the ACM SIGIR Workshop on Recommender Systems: Algorithms and Evaluation, 22nd Intl. Conf. on Research and Development in Information Retrieval, 1999
[11] L. FAUSETT, Fundamentals of Neural Networks, Prentice Hall International Inc., 1994
[12] M. GAEDKE, C. SEGOR, H.-W. GELLERSEN, WCML: Paving the Way for Reuse in Object-Oriented Web Engineering, ACM Symposium on Applied Computing, Italy, 2000
[13] G. GRAEF, Adaptation of Web-Applications Based on Automated User Behaviour Analysis, 2nd Annual Conference on World Wide Web Applications, Johannesburg, 2000
[14] G. GRAEF, M. GAEDKE, Construction of Adaptive Web-Applications from Reusable Components, in: Lecture Notes on Computer Science, 1st Conference on Electronic Commerce and Web Technology, Springer-Verlag Heidelberg, 2000
[15] D. K. HAWES, Information literacy in the business schools, in: Sep/Oct Journal of Education in Business, 70, pp 54-62, 1994
[16] T. KOHONEN, Self-Organizing Maps, Springer-Verlag, Heidelberg, 1997
[17] J. A. KONSTAN ET AL., Applying Collaborative Filtering to Usenet News, in: Communications of the ACM, Vol. 40, No. 3, pp. 77-87, 1997
[18] P. MCJONES, EachMovie collaborative filtering data set, DEC Systems Research Center, http://www.research.compaq.com/SRC/eachmovie/.
[19] D. M. NICHOLS, Implicit Rating and Filtering, in: Proceedings of the Fifth DELOS Workshop on Filtering and Collaborative Filtering, Budapest, 1997
[20] R. ROJAS, Theorie der Neuronalen Netze, Springer Verlag, Heidelberg, 1993
[21] U. SHARDANAND, P. MAES, Social information filtering: algorithms for automating "word of mouth", in: Human factors in computing systems (CHI'95), Denver, USA, 210-217
[22] A. M. A. WASFI, Collecting User Access Patterns for Building User Profiles and Collaborative Filtering,in: Proceedings of the International Conference on Intelligent User Interfaces, pp. 57-64, 1999.

METIOREW: An Objective Oriented Content Based and Collaborative Recommending System

David Bueno[1], Ricardo Conejo[1], and Amos A. David[2]

[1] Department of Languages and Computer Science, University of Málaga,
29071, Málaga, Spain.
{bueno, conejo}@lcc.uma.es
[2] LORIA, BP 239, 54506 Vandoeuvre, FRANCE.
adavid@loria.fr

Abstract. The size of Internet has been growing very fast and many documents appear every day in the Net. Users find many problems in obtaining the information that they really need. In order to help users in this task of finding relevant information, recommending systems were proposed. They give advice using two methods: the content-based method that extracts information from the already evaluated documents by the user in order to obtain new related documents; the collaborative method that recommends documents to the user based on the evaluation by users with similar information needs. In this paper we analyze some existing Web recommending systems and identify some problems which we try to solve in our system METIOREW.

1 Introduction

The size of Internet has been growing very fast and many documents appear every day on the Net. Users find many problems in obtaining the information that they really need. In order to help users in this task of finding relevant information on the Web *recommending systems* are proposed.

In order to recommend a document to a user some systems use solely the content of the documents. To do so, documents are represented with a set of features eg. title, author, keyword, etc. The user model/profile is constructed from the user evaluations using just the features of the documents. That's why they are called *content-based recommending systems.*

A pure *collaborative recommending system* offers documents to the user because other users with similar interest have already evaluated it. The problem with this kind of system is related to the new documents. Until somebody evaluates them the system has no information regarding their relevance. Another important problem lies in the number of users of these systems. The lower the number of users the lower the probability of evaluating the documents with the same interest.

The content-based method has been used in the Information Retrieval area with interesting results. But the idea of completing the recommended documents with other documents that have been retrieved by other users with similar characteristics looks like very promising. This *hybrid solution* is more efficient than both applied separately.

S. Reich, M.M. Tzagarakis, P.M.E. De Bra (Eds.): OHS/SC/AH 2001, LNCS 2266, pp. 310-314, 2002.

In section 2 we will see the work that has been done in this area focusing on the advantages and disadvantages of each. In section 3 we will describe our Web Recommending system METIOREW that tries to solve most of the identified problems in the systems of section 2. Section 4 describes the state of development of this system and the lines that we are following.

2   Related Work

In this section we will analyze the characteristics of the most representative recommending systems that apply some of the methods explained above. In the group of content based system we have WebWatcher. [1] ,Letizia [10], Syskill & Webert [13] and PTV [7], and TechFinder. Systems that implement an hybrid model are FAB [2] MOVIELENS [8], Casper/Jobfinder [14], GASs [3], and WebCobra [16]. We will summarize here some limitations of these systems and present how we have tried to solve the problems in our system METIOREW.

The first problem is in the creation of a model of a user on which the system has little or no information. This is a typical problem in User Modeling. One of the solutions to this problem is through the use of stereotypes [15] . Letizia, Syskill, Webert and Casper have difficulties at the beginning to give advice to the user because the model is empty. In MOVIELENS and FAB, a little training is needed by the system that offers a list of films or documents respectively that the user evaluates. This evaluation is used to create the initial model. WebWatcher and WebCobra begin to create the model using some initial keywords that nearly fix the model to them.

Another important problem that we have found in these systems is the global vision of the people's interests. It seems that people will always want to find the same information in the web. Letizia, FAB, PTV, MOVIELENS or WebCobra don't define the concept of goal or objective. But even the systems that define it are very restrictive or let the user have only one goal. For example WebWatcher allows one goal restricted to technical reports, Syskill & Webert allows the selection of a limited number of topics for which some index has been manually constructed, GASs supposes that many people have the same single goal.

The last important concept is related to the manipulation of the history. Everybody has bookmarks in his Web browser with the most relevant URLs. From the systems analyzed only[1] MOVIELENS allows the review of evaluated documents.

3   METIOREW Description

METIOREW is a collaborative and content-based Web recommending system. It recommends documents to the user by trying to solve the problems presented in section 2. The first aspect of METIOREW is that it is objectives oriented where an objective expresses an information need. We can relate users and objectives in the following manners in an Information Retrieval System a) a user's information needs can evolve, b) the user can have the same information need at different times and c)

---

[1] The information we have from these systems is based on the content of their publications

different information needs can be related. The same methodology is used in METIORE [6].

METIOREW allows the user to review the documents already evaluated through the user's history. The user also has the possibility to modify the evaluations attached to the documents. This can be interpreted as an "intelligent bookmark" organized by objectives and evaluated documents sorted in order of their relevance to the objectives.

The problem of how to make recommendations to users at the beginning has also been carefully studied in METIOREW. The user inserts an objective (In natural language, but it's used just as a label) and a list of keywords that helps to create the initial model for this objective. As this model is not strong enough, the system looks for another user with a similar objective (initially using this list of keywords). Then for the new user two models are managed simultaneously to give him recommendations: his own model and the most similar model found in the system. The second model is used until the new user's model is significant.

3.1 Architecture

The final goal of METIOREW is to find the most relevant Web pages for the current user's objective. The pages will come from Web robot search, supervised navigation and collaborative retrieval. The architecture of the system is agent [12] oriented.

We have a *Personal Agent* who controls the users' identification, management of objectives, supervised navigation, history of activities, generation of recommendations and the reception of user feedback. There is a *Search Agent* for each user objective that will look for information in a web index like Altavista or Google. It constructs the queries using the most representative keywords of the user model for this objective. The *keyword agent* analyzes the documents' content and obtain its parameters. The *Collaborative Agent* offers relevant information to the user taking as reference documents that have already been evaluated by other users with similar objectives to the current user's objective. Finally the *mail agent* is activated with a timer defined by the user (for example once day or once week). Its mission is to examine the list of recommendations generated by the collaborative and search agent and send the N best links for each objective to the user by mail.

3.2 User Model

The user model keeps all the information needed to personalize the interactions with the user. In METIOREW we keep diverse information such as documents evaluated, synthesis of keywords, related objectives or interesting documents to recommend. The model is objective oriented. This means that for each user we can have several models depending on the different information needs. With this representation the same user will be able to work in different sessions with different objectives, but with the possibility of review past sessions through the information acquired by the system. The user's relevance feedback is fundamental to make the personalized recommendations.

3.3 Calculation of the Degree of Relevance

In this section we describe briefly the methods used to calculate the degree of similarity a) between a document and the user model (keyword synthesis), b) between two objectives and c) how we extract the relevant keywords from the documents and the model.

Obtaining relevant keywords. The keyword agent will obtain the features to describe the web page. Using the Term Frequency TFIDF with a list of stop words for English and Spanish and with the Porter's algorithm. It is expected that this will provide the best m words that describe the document.

Classifying new pages in the user model. After each evaluation by the user, the synthesis of the keywords in user model is updated. This is done by increasing by one the frequency of the evaluation for each keyword that represents the document evaluated. When a new page arrives the system must predict how the user will evaluate it. To do that we compare the vector of features of this document with the user model for the current objective using an adaptation of the Naive Bayes [9] that has been proved to be a good classifier in [9] [11] [17].

Objectives similarity. To find similar models it is necessary to compare different objectives. For this we use the Pearson Correlation [4]

Obtaining representative features for searching. To create a vector that represents the model of the current objective we calculate the probability of correctly evaluation for each feature. Sorting this we obtain the n best keywords to be used by the *search agent*.

4 Future Work

The system presented here is in the phase of development and we are planning its trial in a real situation. This trial will be composed firstly by the analysis of information collected by the system, basically efficiency in recommendations and percentage of correct prediction of feedback. Besides that, we elaborate a questionnaire to be filled in by the users in order to make a correlation between the system's proposal and the user's opinion. We are also working on the improvement of the *personal agent* as a 3D agent in the style of Pazzani [5] which gives the user a more human interaction with the computer.

References

1   Armstrong, R., Freitag, D., Joachims, T., & Mitchell, T. (1995). "Webwatcher: A learning apprentice for the world wide web". AAAI Spring Symposium on Information Gathering from Heterogeneous Distributed Environments

2.   Balabanovic, M., & Shoham, Y. (1997). "Combining Content-Based and Collaborative Recommendation". Communications of the ACM, 40(3)

3.   Barra, M. (2000). "Distributed Systems for Group Adaptivity on the Web". Adaptive Hypermedia and Adaptive Web-Based Systems Springer-Verlag

4.   Billsus, D., & Pazzani, M. (1998). "Learning Collaborative Information Filters". Proceedings of the International Conference on Machine Learning Madison, Wisc.Morgan Kaufmann Publishers
5.   Billsus, D., & Pazzani, M. (1999). "A Hybrid User Model for News Story Classification". Proceedings of the Seventh International Conference on User Modeling (UM '99) Banff, Canada
6.   Bueno, D., & David, A. A. " METIORE: A Personalized Information Retrieval System". 8 International Conference on User Modeling.UM'2001
7.   Cotter, P., & Smyth, B. (2000). "WAPing the Web: Content Personalisation for WAP-Enabled Devices". Adaptive Hypermedia and Adaptive Web-Based Systems Springer-Verlag
8.   Good, N., Schafer J. , Konstan, J., Borchers, A., Sarwar, B., Herlocker, J., & Riedl, J. (1999). "Combining collaborative filtering with personal agents for better recommendations". In Proceedings of the Sixteenth National Conferenceon Artificial Intelligence
9.   Kononenko, I. (1990). "Comparison of Inductive and Naive Bayesian Learning Approaches to Automatic Knowledge Acquisition". Current Trends in Knowledge Adquisition, 190-197
10. Lieberman, H. (1995). " Letizia: An Agent That Assists Web Browsing". International Joint Conference on Artificial Intelligence Montreal, CA.
11. Mitchell, T. M. (1997). "Machine Learning". The McGraw-Hill Companies, Inc.
12. Nwana, H. (1996). "Software Agents: An Overview". Knowledge Engineering Review
13. Pazzani, M., Muramatsu, J., & Billsus, D. (1996). "Syskill & Webert: Identifying interesting web sites". AAI Spring Symposium on Machine Learning in Information Access . URL= http://www.parc.xerox.com/istl/porjects/mlia/papers/pazzani.ps.
14. Rafter, R., Bradley, K., & Smyth, B. (2000). "Automated Collaborative Filtering Applications for Online Recruitment Services". Adaptive Hypermedia and Adaptive Web-Based Systems ItalySpringer-Verlag
15. Rich E. (1979). "User Modeling via Stereotypes". International Journal of Cognitive Science, 3, 329-354
16. Vel, O., & Nesbitt, S. (1997). "A Collaborative Filtering Agent System for Dynamic Virtual Communities on the Web". URL= http://citeseer.nj.nec.com/de-collaborative.html.
17. Versteegen, L. (2000). "The Simple Bayesian Classifier as a Classification Algorithm". URL= http://www.cs.kun.nl/nsccs/artikelen/leonv.ps.Z.

Integrating User Data and Collaborative Filtering in a Web Recommendation System

Paolo Buono, Maria Francesca Costabile, Stefano Guida, and Antonio Piccinno

Dipartimento di Informatica, Università di Bari, via Orabona 4, 70125 Bari, Italy
{buono, costabile}@di.uniba.it

Abstract. Web-based applications with a large variety of users suffer from the inability to satisfy heterogeneous needs. Systems should be capable of adapting their behavior to the user's characteristics, such as goals, tasks, interests, which are stored in user profiles. Filtering techniques are used to analyse profile data and provide recommendation to the users to help them navigating in the site and retrieving information of interest. We describe here the approach we have adopted in FAIRWIS (Trade FAIR Web-based Information Services), a system that offers on-line innovative services to support the management of real trade fairs as well as Web-based virtual fairs. The approach is based on the integration of data the system collects about users, both explicitly and implicitly, and a classical collaborative filtering technique in order to provide appropriate recommendations to the user in any circumstances during the visit of the on-line fair catalogue.

1   Introduction

Web-based applications with a large variety of users suffer from the inability to satisfy heterogeneous needs. For example, a Web bookstore offers the same selection of best sellers to customers with different reading preferences. A Web museum offers the same "guided tour" and the same narration to visitors with very different goals and interests.

Personalisation is a process of gathering and storing information about visitors of a Web site, analysing the stored information, and, based on this analysis, delivering the right information to each visitor at the right time. A personalisation component should be capable to recommend documents and/or other Web sites, promote products, make appropriate advice, target e-mail, etc. Personalisation is increasingly used as a mean to expedite the delivery of information to a visitor, making the site useful and attractive so that the visitor is stimulated to return to it. For this, personalisation is becoming an expected feature of e-business Web sites.

Big companies use different methods to personalize their Web sites. Many successful sites, such as Amazon.com, Yahoo.com, and CNN.com, use rich profile information as the basis for providing valuable services; they are considered models for those who want to personalise their site, but we have to consider the huge computing power they require. This is also a reason why most Web sites do not provide yet any personalisation feature.

S. Reich, M.M. Tzagarakis, P.M.E. De Bra (Eds.): OHS/SC/AH 2001, LNCS 2266, pp. 315-321, 2002.

The work presented here is related to the EU founded project called FAIRWIS (Trade FAIR Web-based Information Services). This project aims at offering on-line innovative services to support the management of real trade fairs as well as Web-based virtual fairs. In recent years, some Web-based information sites have been made available, providing information both on trade fair events and on companies participating in these fairs. However, these data are not organised in an integrated, homogeneous and comprehensive way, since are usually presented in a rigid pre-designed company oriented style. Moreover, currently available Web sites exploit static data that it is difficult to update and to put on-line in an appropriate format. FAIRWIS has a real time connection with an underlying database to guarantee coherence of data and up-to-date status. Another unique feature of FAIRWIS is provided by the User Profile Engine (UPE) that is the personalisation module. In the analysis, we have performed of fair Web sites worldwide, none was found to show any personalisation feature. Therefore, UPE provides a significant added value towards a system that can fit the users needs as better as possible.

The approach we have implemented in UPE to build the user profiles and provide recommendations is based on the integration of data the system collects about users both explicitly and implicitly and a classical collaborative filtering technique in order to provide appropriate recommendations to the user during the visit of the on-line fair catalogue. Our main objectives in designing UPE were to create a personalization component that should have limited cost and scale well to small computers. We were also sensitive to the so-called *cold-start problem*, that is the lack of information about users at the beginning of their interaction with the system. For this reason, UPE exploits all possible information that can be collected about the users.

The paper is organized as follows. In Section 2, we describe general approaches for collecting and exploiting user information. Section 3 discusses the rates provided by the FAIRWIS users about the Web pages they visit. Section 4 presents UPE in more details, and Section 5 concludes the paper.

2   Collecting and Exploiting User Information

The objective of collecting user information is to create a profile that describes user characteristics. The more common techniques are explicit profiling, implicit profiling, and use of legacy data:

- *Explicit profiling*: each user is asked to fill in a form when visiting the Web site; this method has the advantage of letting users specify directly their interests.
- *Implicit profiling*: the user's behaviour is tracked automatically by the system. This method is generally transparent to the user. Often, user registration is saved in what is called a cookie that is kept at the browser and updated at each visit. Behaviour information is generally stored in a log file.
- *Legacy data*: they provide a rich source of profile information for known users.

The above methods can be combined to produce comprehensive profiles. This is what we have done in FAIRWIS. The generated user profiles are analysed in order to present or recommend documents, items, or actions to the user. Making recommendations is a very challenging step. Rule-based and filtering techniques are the best known for analysing profile data and making appropriate recommendations.

Rule-based techniques exploit a set of rules specified in the system in order to drive personalisation. Cross-selling is an e-business example of the rule-based technique: a rule could be specified to offer product X to a customer who has just bought product Y; for example, a customer of a book might be interested in current or previous books by the same author or in books on the same subject.

Filtering techniques employ algorithms to analyse profile data and drive presentations and recommendations. The most common filtering techniques are: simple filtering, content-based filtering, and collaborative filtering [5]. *Simple filtering* relies on predefined classes of users to determine what content should be displayed or what service should be provided. For example, employees of the Research department may access some functionality not available for employees of other departments. Therefore, specific pages will be presented to the Research department employees.

Content-based filtering works by analysing the content of the objects to generate a representation of the user's interests. The analysis needs to identify a set of key attributes for each object and then fill in the attribute values. For example, in e-commerce users are often asked to provide rates for each attribute of a product. In this way, content-based filtering analyses the rates provided by the users to determine, for any product, which other product of the same category has the closest rates and could then be recommended to a user who got interest in the first product. This technique is most suitable when the objects are easily analysed by the computer and the user's decision about object suitability is not very much subjective. However, recommendations are limited to objects related to those the visitor has considered during his or her navigation, and there is no provision for user qualification.

Collaborative filtering collects visitor opinions on a set of objects, using rates provided explicitly by the users or implicitly computed, to form peer groups and then learns from the peer groups to predict a particular user's interest in a item. Instead of finding objects similar to those a user liked, as in content-based filtering, collaborative filtering develops recommendations by finding visitors with similar tastes. Recommendations produced by collaborative filtering are qualified based on the peer group's response and are not restricted to a simple profile matching. However, this method requires a large user base in order to find a peer group for each visitor. This might imply a long learning curve, because at the beginning, when the number of participating visitors is small, the quality of recommendations will be low. The results improve gradually as the number of participating users increases. The more objects two users have rated similarly, the closer the two users are.

For examples of systems incorporating a personalisation components based on content-based and/or collaborative filtering see [2, 6].

3 User Rates for Providing Recommendations

UPE (User Profile Engine) is a personalisation module. In the current implementation in FAIRWIS, UPE works as a recommender system that provides personalized suggestions about pages users might find interesting in the on-line fair catalogue available in the system. The recommendations are generated on the basis of different types of rates that the system gets from the user interaction or computes trough an algorithm of collaborative filtering.

The rates collected by the system during the user interaction may be both implicit and explicit. They are explicit if users tell the system what they think about an item. For example, the user may give a rate of 5 to an element of the fair catalogue he or she has found very interesting by filling an appropriate form shown on the screen. Even if explicit rating is fairly precise, it has disadvantages, such as: 1) stopping to enter explicit ratings can alter normal patterns of browsing and reading; 2) unless users perceive that there is a benefit providing the rates, they may stop providing them.

Implicit rating is much more difficult to determine. Oard and Kim divide implicit rating into three categories [7]: rating based on examination, when a user examines an item; rating based on retention, when a user saves an item; rating based on reference, when a user links all or part of an item into an other item. Some criteria to determine user preferences from implicit rating were established in [3]. In FAIRWIS, by taking into account the structure of the system currently developed by the other partners of the project, we may only consider the following events, and each one has been associated with a weight that highlights the importance of that event for collecting information about the user interests: a) access to a Web page (we gave different weights to the home page and the other pages); b) print and/or save action (the user that does this is highly interested on that page or item); c) download of specific files included in download areas; d) image zoom.

Even if implicit rates are difficult to determine, they have the following advantages: 1) every interaction with the system (and every absence of interaction) can contribute to implicit rating; 2) can be gathered for free; 3) can be combined with several types of implicit rates for a more accurate rating; 4) can be combined with explicit rates for an enhanced rating.

Indeed, the method that is quite effective is the mixed technique implicit/explicit rating and we implemented it in FAIRWIS, as it will be described in the next section. However, especially in the case of sites with many pages, we can be in a situation that some pages have not been evaluated by the current user (neither explicit nor implicit rates are available). To overcome this situation, we used an algorithm of collaborative filtering. It predicts user interests on a not yet evaluated item by taking into account a database of existing rates provided by other users. Such a database is a set of rates $u_{i,j}$ corresponding to the evaluation of user i on the item j. If I_i is the set of items on which user i has expressed a rate, it is possible to define the average rate for user i as:

$$\bar{u}_i = \frac{1}{|I_i|} \sum_{j \in I_i} u_{i,j} \tag{1}$$

It is also possible to compute the evaluation of the current user (indicated with a subscript a) based on information on the current user and on a set of weights calculated from the user database. We can assume that the predicted rate of current user expected for item j, i.e. $p_{a,j}$, is a weighted sum of rates of other users:

$$p_{a,j} = \overline{u}_a + k \sum_{i=1}^{n} w(a,i)(u_{i,j} - \overline{u}_a) \qquad (2)$$

where n is the number of user in the database with non zero weight, and k is a normalisation factor such that the absolute values of the weights sum to unit. Weights $w(a,i)$ reflect distance, correlation, or similarity between each user i and the current user. They are computed by using Pearson's correlation [4]. The expression that identifies the weight $w(a,i)$ which relates the current user a with user i is:

$$w(a,i) = \frac{\sum_{j}(u_{a,j} - \overline{u}_a)(u_{i,j} - \overline{u}_i)}{\sqrt{\sum_{j}(u_{a,j} - \overline{u}_a)^2 \sum_{j}(u_{i,j} - \overline{u}_i)^2}} \qquad (3)$$

where summations over j are computed on all items which have been evaluated by the users a and i.

4   The User Profile Engine in FAIRWIS

We describe in this section the current use of UPE in FAIRWIS. The main types of users addressed by FAIRWIS are: i) fair organisers; ii) exhibitors, namely responsibles of companies that exhibit their products or activities in the fair; iii) professional visitors, who visit the fair for business reasons rather than fun.

The user profiles managed by UPE have a static component and a dynamic one. The static component consists of a set of information that identifies each user and doesn't change, e.g., name, nationality, type of users. This information comes from the registration forms that exhibitors and professional visitors are required to fill.

The dynamic component of user profile includes user preferences. UPE obtains this information by different type of rates: explicit rates, for instance interest rates for catalogue pages; implicit rates, obtained by tracking user navigation; computed rates, obtained by collaborative filtering techniques to supply the preferences not expressed by users, either implicitly or explicitly.

The reasons for collecting these different types of data is to be able to provide recommendations in any situation. UPE is composed of several modules, each one computing recommendations based on some types of rates. Since we are interested in suggesting catalogue pages that the user did not visit yet, UPE first considers the recommendations derived by the rates computed by the collaborative filtering algorithm. If they are not enough, the UPE module that identifies the recommendations based on explicit, implicit, and computed rates is considered.

UPE stores individual user profiles, but also assigns the users to a kind of stereotype [8], each stereotype characterised by specific values of the attributes considered in the user profile; these stereotypes are called *segments*. Segments are used to provide recommendations even to a user who just registered, because in the registration form the user provided enough data to be assigned to a segment, and thus UPE gives as recommendations those relative to the segment the user belongs to. They are computed using all rates available for every user belonging to that segment.

It may also happen that the segment doesn't contain enough information for recommendations, or the user is not a registered one but he or she is just surfing the Web catalogue. In this case, UPE provides recommendations based only on the current page the user is visiting, computing them by considering the rates of the other users that have already visited that page. In other words, the system will suggest the pages indicated as interesting by most users who were also interested in the page the user is currently looking at.

Referring to the collaborative filtering algorithms, it is well known that these algorithms are very useful but they do not scale well because of their computational complexity. We are reducing the algorithm complexity by using some heuristics. For example, UPE doesn't re-compute all the weights in formula (3), but it does it only for those pairs of correlated users, in which at least one of the two users has interacted with the Web site and has modified a number of rates higher than a certain threshold.

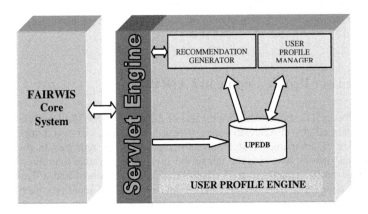

Fig. 1. UPE architecture and the communication with FAIRWIS Core system.

Figure 1 shows the main modules of UPE. The User Profile Manager implements the collaborative filtering algorithm and stores the computed rates into the database (UPEDB). It also computes the implicit rates on the basis of events monitored by the system, and stores them into UPEDB. The Recommendation Generator computes the recommendations. To show them on the Web page, UPE needs to communicate with the FAIRWIS Core system that manages the Web interface. The communication between UPE and the Web application is based on Java Servlet technology. The servlets (Servlet Engine) insert into UPEDB static user information coming from the registration form filled by the user in the FAIRWIS Web site, update UPEDB with the dynamic information coming from the user interaction, calls the appropriate methods that give recommendations, and communicate them to the Web application. UPE has been developed using Windows NT, Java and SQL-Server 7.0. The shown architecture using the Servlet Engine permits the use of UPE as an independent component that can be portable to other systems.

5   Conclusions

In this paper, we have described the FAIRWIS personalization component that currently works as a recommendation system. The approach is based on the integration of data collected both explicitly and implicitly from the user interaction and a collaborative filtering technique.

It is worth nothing that UPE has been designed to be an independent module that can be integrated in any system, with which the communication is done through Java Servlet technology. Moreover, UPE manages a complex user profile that can be better exploited   to provide different types of personalisation. The current behaviour as a recommender system is due to constraints imposed by the actual structure of the FAIRWIS Core system.

Acknowledgement. The support of European Commission through grant FAIRWIS IST-1999-12641 is acknowledged.

References

1. Brusilovsky, P., Stock, O., Strapparava, C. (eds.): AH2000 Proceedings of the International Conference on Adaptive Hypermedia and Adaptive Web-Based Systems. Trento, Italy, August 28-30, 2000.
2. Bueno, D., Conejo, R., David, A.A.: METIOREW: An Objective Oriented Content Based and Collaborative Recommending System. In this volume.
3. Claypool, M., Le, P., Waseda, M., Brown, D.: Implicit Interest Indicator. Computer Science Technical Report Series, WPI Computer Science Department, Worcester, Massachussets, http://citeseer.nj.nec.com/claypool00implicit.html (2000).
4. Hogg, R.V. & Tanis, E.A.: Probability & Statistical Inference. Collier Macmillan International Editions (1977).
5. IBM High-Volume Web site team: Web Site Personalisation. January 2000, http://www7b.boulder.ibm.com/wsdd/library/techarticles/hvws/personalize.html.
6. Kobsa, A., Koenemann, J., Pohl, W.: Personalized Hypermedia Presentation Techniques for Improving Online Customer Relationships. To appear in *The Knowledge Engineering Review* (2001).
7. Oard, D., Kim, J. Implicit Feedback for Recommender Systems. In Proceedings of AAAI Workshops on Recommender Systems (1998).
8. Rich, E.: Stereotypes and User Modeling. In Kobsa, A., Wahlster, W. (eds.): User Models in Dialogue Systems. Springer-Verlag (1989), pp. 35-51.

Adaptive Hypermedia System for Supporting Information Providers in Directing Users through Hyperspace

Yoshinori Hijikata, Tetsuya Yoshida, and Shogo Nishida

Graduate School of Engineering Science
Osaka University
1-3 Machikaneyama, Toyonaka
Osaka 560-8531, Japan
{hijikata,yoshida,nishida}@nishilab.sys.es.osaka-u.ac.jp

Abstract. This paper introduces a rule-based adaptive hypermedia system that allows the information providers to easily direct users to their own personalized navigation paths. In order to reduce the information providers' efforts in creating navigation rules, we simplified the format of these rules and offer an authoring tool that verifies the navigation rules. This tool also guarantees the adequacy of the navigation path.

1 Introduction

The applications of the WWW are diversifying into such areas as electronic commerce, marketing and education [5]. In these kinds of application, the information providers or the Web masters often want to direct their users through hyperspace as desired according to each user's preferences and status [3]. Some researchers have been studying these kinds of user navigation aids in the research field of adaptive hypermedia [2]. Many adaptive hypermedia systems implement user-navigation guidance created by the information providers, using methods that allow the information providers to describe the navigation rules defined in advance[1]. However this method leads to the following problems:

1. Information providers have great difficulty describing the navigation rules as they move towards fine-grained navigation control.
2. It becomes difficult to predict the resulting states for various kinds of users, because the navigation dynamically varies according to each user.

This research aims to construct an adaptive hypermedia system that reduces the burden on information providers and prevents errors in the navigation rules. We propose a system solving the above problems by the following mechanisms:

1. A simplified format for navigation rules.
2. An authoring tool that examines the navigation rules.

S. Reich, M.M. Tzagarakis, P.M.E. De Bra (Eds.): OHS/SC/AH 2001, LNCS 2266, pp. 322–326, 2002.
© Springer-Verlag Berlin Heidelberg 2002

Existing rule-based adaptive hypermedia systems [1] do not focus on providing mechanisms and functions that can reduce the burden on information providers for creating and verifying navigation rules. In the proposed system, (1) destination options are determined by hiding links so that information providers can direct users accurately, (2) long-term and short-term user information can be used in the navigation rule, because it is generally important to consider users from both perspectives [4], and (3) the format of user information is also simple, because the format of navigation rule is simple.

2   Navigation Method

2.1   Class and Hypermedia Model

In the hypermedia model of our system, every node has a "class". The reason why we introduced the notion of class is to allow information providers to describe the navigation rules by generalizing and specializing the characteristics and meanings of the navigation rules. The identity of the node is represented by a number and node classes are represented by alphabetic characters. Some of the nodes have navigation rules (explained later) as created by the information provider.

2.2   User Model

Since our system simplifies the format of navigation rule, we also make our user model simple. We use pairs consisting of a property and a value (we call "user parameter") for modeling the user's long-term information. We also use a browsing history (we call "path history") for modeling the user's short-term information. The user parameter is represented as a value from some range. The information provider assigns a meaning to the user parameter according to his/her navigation control. The user, the information provider, or some other person sets the value of a parameter. The path history is represented concisely as the sequence of classes of the nodes the user has visited, and indicates the order of information the user has browsed. If the user browsed nodes in an order such that their classes were $C \to A \to B \to B \to A$, the path history is represented as $CABBA$.

2.3   Navigation Rule

This system decides which links to hide based on a navigation rule that may be associated with the current node. In the source part of the rule, the information provider should describe the path history that the user will follow or the range of user parameter. In the target part of the rule, the information provider should describe the links that should be displayed by the node ID or by the class of the node that is the target of the link. The system hides all links that are not referenced in a navigation rule as links to be displayed.

3   Authoring Tool

3.1   Objective

Generally an authoring tool is important for an adaptive hypermedia system. Therefore our system provides an authoring tool that helps the information provider in describing the navigation rules. This tool examines the execution results of the navigation rule before they are incorporated into nodes. This aims for correct navigation with fewer errors and for simplification of the information provider's efforts to describe the navigation rules. We focused on detecting the following two kinds of problems because they can happen in any kind of content and are very likely to be related to navigation errors:

1. Dead end: There is a possibility that all links are hidden and the user cannot go anywhere after reaching a node with a navigation rule. This dead end problem could be caused by a bad navigation rule. Were a dead end to appear, it would force the user to stop searching in hyperspace.
2. Loop: As seen in the WWW, we can use a loop effectively, for example as a link for returning to a top page. However our concerns are that there may be unintended loops or the user may not be able to follow a loop that the information provider intended the users to follow. This is because the system hides links dynamically, which could cause problems for user navigation.

4   Evaluation

4.1   Objective and Method

We implemented the system using the C++ language We quantitatively evaluated whether the authoring tool reduced the time that the information provider required for describing the navigation rules (description time) and reduced the number of errors in the navigation rules. We created 6 tasks for the experiment.

Ten information providers participated in the experiment as subjects. These subjects were divided into two groups. The subjects of one group (Group A) described navigation rules without the authoring tool. The subjects of the other group (Group B) described navigation rules with the authoring tool.

4.2   Results

Table 1 shows whether or not the subject described the navigation rules without an error, and the error ratio. In Table 1, Subjects a-e were in Group A and Subjects f-j were in Group B. A circle shows that there is no error and an X shows that there are errors. We can see a significant difference between the two groups. Figure 1 is a graph of the relationship between the description time and the error ratio. Although we cannot guarantee high and negative correlation, we see an apparent relationship that as the description time becomes longer the error ratio gets smaller.

The overall results, showing significant differences in the error ratio, indicate that the authoring tool reduced the numbers of navigation errors. We can

Table 1. Error in the navigation rule.

Sub-ject	Task 1 2 3 4 5 6						Error ratio(%)	Sub-ject	Task 1 2 3 4 5 6						Error ratio(%)
a	O	O	O	O	X	O	17	f	O	O	O	O	O	O	0
b	O	O	O	O	X	X	33	g	O	O	O	O	O	O	0
c	O	X	O	O	X	O	33	h	O	O	O	O	X	O	17
d	O	X	O	O	X	O	33	i	O	X	O	O	O	O	17
e	O	O	O	O	X	O	17	j	O	O	O	O	O	O	0

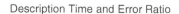

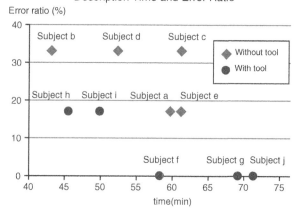

Fig. 1. Time for describing and error ratio

recognize the effectiveness of the authoring tool also on the description time, because of the fact that the description time tends to get longer as the error ratio becomes smaller and the error ratio becomes smaller when the subjects use the authoring tool. This again shows that the authoring tool reduced the information providers' efforts in describing the navigation rules.

5 Conclusions

The authoring tool that checks the execution of the navigation rules enables information providers to direct users more reliably and reduces the information providers' efforts to describe the rule.

References

1. Adaptive hypertext and hypermedia, http://wwwis.win.tue.nl/ah/
2. Brusilovsky, P. L.: Methods and techniques of adaptive hypermedia, User Modeling and User-Adapted Interaction, Vol.6, No.2-3, (1996), 87–129

3. Miller, M. and Wantz, L. J.: Computed web links: The cool link model, Proc. of 2nd Workshop on Adaptive Hypertext and Hypermedia (1998)
4. Rich, E.: Users are individuals: Individualizing user models, international journal of man-machine studies, Vol.18 (1983) 199–214.
5. Yanagisawa, A. and Matsumoto, H.: Internet value chain marketing, SCC (1998)

A Complementary Approach for Adaptive and Adaptable Hypermedia: Intensional Hypertext

William W. Wadge[1] and Monica M.C. Schraefel[2]

[1] Department of Computer Science
University of Victoria
Victoria, B.C., Canada
wwadge@csr.uvic.ca
[2] Department of Computer Science, University of Toronto
Toronto, ON, Canada M5S 3G4
mc@dgp.toronto.edu

Abstract. We describe a methodology and an authoring/publishing tool for adaptable and/or adaptive Web documents. Our approach is based on intensional logic, the logic of assertions and expressions, which vary over a collection of contexts or possible worlds. In our approach the contexts are sets of values for parameters which specify the current user profile as supplied by the current Web page URL, and the latest user input. The author produces generic (multi-version) source in the form of HTML with extra markup delimiting parts that are sensitive (in various ways) to the parameters. This source (in what we call Intensional Markup Language) is translated into program in a Perl-like language called ISE (Intensional Sequential Evaluator). To generate the appropriately adapted individual pages, the server runs the ISE program in the appropriate context. The program produces HTML that, when displayed in the user's browser, is rendered into the desired adaptation of the requested page. Although this intensional approach was originally designed to work without any explicit user model, we can extend it (and make the documents adaptive as well as adaptable) simply by incorporating a user model that monitors the user and computes some of the profile parameters.

1 General Adaptive/Adaptable Architecture and the Role of Parameters

The goal of adaptive and adaptable hypertext[1] is in many respects to accessing the right information easier for users, but at the same time the mechanisms to

---

[1] By adaptive hypermedia, we refer to hypermedia systems which primarily rely on a user model to support the delivery of user-specific content (see, for instance, [1]-[5]). By adaptable, we mean that users select from a variety of parameters to adapt the hypertext to their needs. A stateless version of adaptable hypertext can be created in client-side JavaScript, for instance, in which users can change the color of the background of a page dynamically. The server side approach described here can maintain the state of such a change across any other page selections made on that site.

S. Reich, M.M. Tzagarakis, P.M.E. De Bra (Eds.): OHS/SC/AH 2001, LNCS 2266, pp. 327–333, 2002.
© Springer-Verlag Berlin Heidelberg 2002

support this goal can greatly complicate the task for the content creators and publishers. In general there are many different possible states (configurations) of a user model - many different possible user profiles. In adaptable hypermedia, there are likewise multiple possible instances (or versions) of a domain object, such as the large color view of an image with English captions or the small, black and white one with French captions. The publishing system is therefore responsible in each case for delivering a whole family of variants of a document (one for each possible profile or domain instance), rather than one single mono- lithic document. It becomes necessary to develop a system that can render these families in an efficient way, which will avoid overloading either the system, or the content creators.

In the following sections of this paper, we describe a methodology and an authoring/publishing tool which can be understood as the result of using inten- sional logic to formalize these general observations about adaptive/adaptable architecture. We hope by this to provide a general front-end or author-based tool, which will facilitate the authoring of versionable, web-based hypermedia which can then be supported by either adaptive, adaptable or both kinds of inputs.

2   The Intensional Approach

Our approach is based on intensional logic [10], a natural choice for versioning, since it is the logic of assertions and expressions which vary over a collection of contexts or possible worlds. In our approach the contexts are sets of values for parameters which specify the user profile (if one exists), current page, and user input.

The intensional (possible-worlds) approach to versioning was originally de- veloped by Plaice and Wadge [6] for use in configuring families of programs from families of components. Most software configuration tools work bottom-up, and allow the user to create a variant of the program by selecting different variants of the components. In intensional versioning, by contrast, each variant is de- scribed/determined by a "version expression" assigning values to parameters. For example, the expression

```
processor:ppc+OS:8+language:french
```

might indicate the French language version for a PPC Macintosh running OS 8.

A particular version of a program is configured, as usual, by assembling particular versions of components. In intensional versioning, however, the com- ponent choices are not arbitrary; instead, they are determined by the expression for the version requested. For this to work it is necessary that each variant of each component be labeled with a version expression. In the simplest case, when configuring version V of a program, we use version V of each component. How- ever in general we do not require that each component have a version whose label is exactly V. If there is no such component, we are allowed to choose a component whose label is strictly more generic than V, in that it omits some of the parameter values prescribed by V.

For example, suppose that we wanted the French PPC OS 8 version described above. It may be that there is no version of the (say) windowing component which has exactly that label, but that there is one with the label processor:ppc+OS:8. We can use this component, the justification being that the windowing component is language independent.

In general, although we do not require that there be a component labeled V, we insist that among the more generic alternatives there is one which is best in that it is the most specific. If there is a most specific alternative component, that one must be taken. If there is no such best alternative, the configuration attempt is abandoned.

The net effect of the best-generic-alternative or best-fit rule is that a relatively small number of component variants can form the basis for a much larger family of program variants. The leverage comes from the fact that different versions of the program can share the same versions of particular components (for example, as the French and English programs PPC OS 8 share the PPC OS 8 windowing component). The more generic relationship between versions is thus an inheritance relationship, so that more specific versions inherit (that is, use by default) more generic versions of components.

3   IHTML, ISE, and IML

The system presented here is the latest stage in an effort, as described in [7], begun in 1996, to produce an authoring/publishing system based on an intensional versioning scheme analogous to the one just described for programs.

In these systems authors define Web sites as linked collections of pages, each of which can exist in many different versions. A request issued by a browser consists of a conventional URL together with a version expression. The server software generates the requested version of the requested page by combining the particular version expression with the (usually generic) source.

The first such system was Intensional HTML [12], a minimal extension of ordinary HTML. Initially, the most important feature of IHTML was that it allowed multiple source files for the same page, each labeled (as above) with a version expression. When a request arrives for a particular version of a particular page, the IHTML server (an Apache server plug-in) uses the best-alternative rule described above to select the appropriate source file.

In generating the actual HTML all the copy and most of the mark up is duplicated verbatim. Links, however are specialized, so that they connect analogous versions of pages. For example, the IHTML source for page A might contain an ordinary-looking link to page B. When a request arrives for the HTML source of (say) version language:french+level:expert of page A, the link is changed to lead to the language:french+level:expert version of page B.

IHTML also allowed what we call transversion links: these are links which connect one version of a source page with a different version of the target page.

With transversion links the author can allow the user to change parameter values (and therefore adapt the target page) simply by following a link.

IHTML worked well enough for small sites but as a markup-only system proved to impractical for larger projects. In 1998 Paul Swoboda, then an MSc student, decided to abandon markup as the basis for intensional Web versioning. He designed and implemented ISE (pronounced "iz-ee"), which is to Perl as IHTML is to HTML [8]. As a full featured algorithmic language, there is no a priori limitation on the kinds of features it can support. Also, since it has functions and procedures, sophisticated versioned Web sites do not necessarily translate into extremely large ISE programs.

4   Intentional Markup Language

As a programming language, ISE is inherently more complex than a markup system. We therefore developed the Intensional Markup Language, IML, as a front end to retrieve the obvious advantages of markup authoring.

IML is, like IHTML, a markup language which extends HTML. However, since IML is implemented on top of a full programming language, there is also no a priori limit on the power of intensional markup. The decisive improvement of IML over its precursor IHTML is that IML is readily extensible. IML is implemented by macro processing - each intensional tag in a Web page is defined by a macro. When the Web page is processed by the server, the macro is translated into ISE code. When all these tags are replaced by their ISE definitions, the result is an ISE program. The pieces of the non-ISE Web page, including the HTML markup, are enclosed in quotes and appear as the arguments of print statements. The intensional tags expand to form complex control structures governing the execution of these print statements.

Adding new constructs or control structures involves adding definitions for new macros to a file. These definitions can be intricate, but only have to be written once, and then can be used by authors who have no knowledge of ISE or (for that matter) of any other programming language. Moreover authors can use the macro facility to define new tags in terms of existing ones; these macros replace tags not with ISE but with text marked up with simpler tags. This allows large numbers of non-programming authors to use, directly or indirectly, the expertise of (a few) coders familiar with Perl-made-ISE.

We note that the current version of IML's markup [11] is, effectively, the Groff macro format whose line-oriented syntax is far less flexible than HTML/XML conventions. We are currently developing an XML-styled macro system to better blend IML into Web page authoring practices.

5   Publishing Modes

One advantage of the approach described here is that it is possible to produce useful, version-based or "adaptable" sites with only a simple or implicit UM. The documents produced earlier using IHTML fall into this last category. This

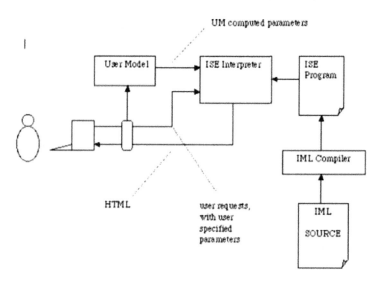

Fig. 1. Model-neutral IML architecture for versioning in which UM parameters can be processed through the ISE architecture to render a blended adaptable and adaptive page.

kind of site is referred to as "adaptable" rather than "adaptive" because the variations are the result of the user making explicit choices (mainly by choosing links) rather than the system determining that selection. Even a very simple UM can greatly improve the effectiveness of a site. For example, the UM could reason at the reader's language preference by examining the IP address associated with the user's request. Or it could supply the parameter values which specify the date and time (definitely something the reader should not have to provide).

As has been previously published [7] there are a number of advantages in using of an intensional/adaptable system as a precursor to a user model based system, such as making it cheap to add adaptive effects like stretch text, or assessing where a site might benefit from more adaptivity based on frequency of use of adaptable shifts made by users in any part of the site. Most user model-based adaptive systems, as per [2] and [3] can be well integrated with the ISE, adaptable framework. Our approach to publishing (Fig.1) puts only one constraint on the nature of the model: that it be able to pass on the relevant parts of its current state as a set of values for parameters.

6   Conclusions and Research Directions

In this paper we have presented a mechanism for letting authors author versionable hypertext without being primarily constrained by how those versions will be delivered, whether by user-determined link choices or UM parameter determination in which the author specifies general defaults first, then overrides where appropriate. We suggest that this intensional approach to handling versionable content, as embodied in the IML methodology, can act as general front-end tool for preparing versionable content to be delivered to a user, whether the versioning is managed by an adaptive or adaptable approach. We are currently engaged in a large-scale, intensional hypertext project with Biomedical Communications at the University of Toronto. The intensional architecture will be used to support two, multi-user sites: one on breast cancer for care givers and those interested in the subject, and one for medical students and surgeons on the sentinel node biopsy procedure. These sites will also be the test bed for evaluating the intensional approach for user-determined content adaptation. We look forward to reporting on these results.

Acknowledgements. We thank Michael Milton and Adele Newton of the Bell University Labs Research Program at the University of Toronto for their continued support of this research. Thanks also to Paul Swoboda and Neil Graham for their development efforts and insights throughout the lifecycle of IML.

References

1. Brusilovsky, Peter: Methods and techniques of Adaptive Hypermedia. Adaptive Hypertext and Hypermedia. Kluwer Academic Publishers, Amsterdam (1998) 1–43.
2. De Bra, Paul, Calvi, Licia: Towards a Generic Adaptive Hypermedia System. Proceedings of the 2nd Workshop on Adaptive Hypertext and Hypermedia HYPERTEXT'98, Pittsburgh, USA, June 20-24, (1998) 5–12.
3. DeBra, Paul: Design Issues in Adaptive Hypermedia Application Development. 2nd Workshop on Adaptive Systems and User Modeling on the WWW. Toronto (1999) 29–39.
4. Kushmerick, Nicholas McKee, James and Toolan, Fergus: Towards Zero-Input Personalization: Referrer-Based Page Prediction. In: Brusilovsky, P., Stock, O., Strapparava, C. (eds.): Adaptive Hypermedia and Adaptive Web-Based Systems International Conference, AH 2000, Trento, Italy, August (2000). Proceedings. Springer-Verlag, Lecture Notes in Computer Science, Vol. 1892, 133–143.
5. Petrelli, Daniela, Baggio, Daniele and Pezzulo Giovanni: Adaptive Hypertext Design Environments: Putting Principles into Practice. In: Brusilovsky, P., Stock, O., Strapparava, C. (eds.): Adaptive Hypermedia and Adaptive Web-Based Systems International Conference, AH 2000, Trento, Italy, August (2000). Proceedings. Springer-Verlag, Lecture Notes in Computer Science, Vol. 1892, 202–213.
6. Plaice, J. and Wadge, W. W.: A New Approach to Version Control, IEEE Transactions on Software Engineering, March (1993) 268–276.
7. Schraefel, M.C. "ConTexts: Adaptable Hypermedia."" In: Brusilovsky, P., Stock, O., Strapparava, C. (eds.): Adaptive Hypermedia and Adaptive Web-Based Systems International Conference, AH 2000, Trento, Italy, August (2000) Proceedings. Springer-Verlag, Lecture Notes in Computer Science, Vol. 1892, 369–375.
8. Swoboda, P. Practical Languages for Intensional Programming, MSc Thesis (Computer Science), University of Victoria, Canada (1999)
9. Wadge, W. Intensional Logic in Context. Intensional Programming II, World Scientific Publishing, Singapore (2000) 1–13.

10. Wadge W., Brown, G., Schraefel, M. C., Yildirim T.: Intensional HTML, Proc 4th Int. Workshop PODDP '98, Springer Verlag LNCS 1481 (1998) 128–139.
11. Wadge, W. Intensional Markup Language. Peter Kropf, Gilbert Babin, John Plaice, Herwig Unger (eds.): Distributed Communities on the Web, Third International Workshop, DCW 2000, Quebec City, Canada, June 19-21 (2000). Proceedings. Lecture Notes in Computer Science, Vol. 1830, Springer (2000) 82–89.
12. Yildirim, Taner. Intensional HTML Masters Thesis, U of Victoria, Canada. (1997)

Vol. 2234: L. Pacholski, P. Ružička (Eds.), SOFSEM 2001: Theory and Practice of Informatics. Proceedings, 2001. XI, 347 pages. 2001.

Vol. 2235: C.S. Calude, G. Păun, G. Rozenberg, A. Salomaa (Eds.), Multiset Processing. VIII, 359 pages. 2001.

Vol. 2236: K. Drira, A. Martelli, T. Villemur (Eds.), Cooperative Environments for Distributed Systems Engineering. IX, 281 pages. 2001.

Vol. 2237: P. Codognet (Ed.), Logic Programming. Proceedings, 2001. XI, 365 pages. 2001.

Vol. 2239: T. Walsh (Ed.), Principles and Practice of Constraint Programming – CP 2001. Proceedings, 2001. XIV, 788 pages. 2001.

Vol. 2240: G.P. Picco (Ed.), Mobile Agents. Proceedings, 2001. XIII, 277 pages. 2001.

Vol. 2241: M. Jünger, D. Naddef (Eds.), Computational Combinatorial Optimization. IX, 305 pages. 2001.

Vol. 2242: C.A. Lee (Ed.), Grid Computing – GRID 2001. Proceedings, 2001. XII, 185 pages. 2001.

Vol. 2243: G. Bertrand, A. Imiya, R. Klette (Eds.), Digital and Image Geometry. VII, 455 pages. 2001.

Vol. 2244: D. Bjørner, M. Broy, A.V. Zamulin (Eds.), Perspectives of System Informatics. Proceedings, 2001. XIII, 548 pages. 2001.

Vol. 2245: R. Hariharan, M. Mukund, V. Vinay (Eds.), FST TCS 2001: Foundations of Software Technology and Theoretical Computer Science. Proceedings, 2001. XI, 347 pages. 2001.

Vol. 2246: R. Falcone, M. Singh, Y.-H. Tan (Eds.), Trust in Cyber-societies. VIII, 195 pages. 2001. (Subseries LNAI).

Vol. 2247: C. P. Rangan, C. Ding (Eds.), Progress in Cryptology – INDOCRYPT 2001. Proceedings, 2001. XIII, 351 pages. 2001.

Vol. 2248: C. Boyd (Ed.), Advances in Cryptology – ASIACRYPT 2001. Proceedings, 2001. XI, 603 pages. 2001.

Vol. 2249: K. Nagi, Transactional Agents. XVI, 205 pages. 2001.

Vol. 2250: R. Nieuwenhuis, A. Voronkov (Eds.), Logic for Programming, Artificial Intelligence, and Reasoning. Proceedings, 2001. XV, 738 pages. 2001. (Subseries LNAI).

Vol. 2251: Y.Y. Tang, V. Wickerhauser, P.C. Yuen, C.Li (Eds.), Wavelet Analysis and Its Applications. Proceedings, 2001. XIII, 450 pages. 2001.

Vol. 2252: J. Liu, P.C. Yuen, C. Li, J. Ng, T. Ishida (Eds.), Active Media Technology. Proceedings, 2001. XII, 402 pages. 2001.

Vol. 2253: T. Terano, T. Nishida, A. Namatame, S. Tsumoto, Y. Ohsawa, T. Washio (Eds.), New Frontiers in Artificial Intelligence. Proceedings, 2001. XXVII, 553 pages. 2001. (Subseries LNAI).

Vol. 2254: M.R. Little, L. Nigay (Eds.), Engineering for Human-Computer Interaction. Proceedings, 2001. XI, 359 pages. 2001.

Vol. 2255: J. Dean, A. Gravel (Eds.), COTS-Based Software Systems. Proceedings, 2002. XIV, 257 pages. 2002.

Vol. 2256: M. Stumptner, D. Corbett, M. Brooks (Eds.), AI 2001: Advances in Artificial Intelligence. Proceedings, 2001. XII, 666 pages. 2001. (Subseries LNAI).

Vol. 2257: S. Krishnamurthi, C.R. Ramakrishnan (Eds.), Practical Aspects of Declarative Languages. Proceedings, 2002. VIII, 351 pages. 2002.

Vol. 2258: P. Brazdil, A. Jorge (Eds.), Progress in Artificial Intelligence. Proceedings, 2001. XII, 418 pages. 2001. (Subseries LNAI).

Vol. 2259: S. Vaudenay, A.M. Youssef (Eds.), Selected Areas in Cryptography. Proceedings, 2001. XI, 359 pages. 2001.

Vol. 2260: B. Honary (Ed.), Cryptography and Coding. Proceedings, 2001. IX, 416 pages. 2001.

Vol. 2262: P. Müller, Modular Specification and Verification of Object-Oriented Programs. XIV, 292 pages. 2002.

Vol. 2263: T. Clark, J. Warmer (Eds.), Object Modeling with the OCL. VIII, 281 pages. 2002.

Vol. 2264: K. Steinhöfel (Ed.), Stochastic Algorithms: Foundations and Applications. Proceedings, 2001. VIII, 203 pages. 2001.

Vol. 2266: S. Reich, M.M. Tzagarakis, P.M.E. De Bra (Eds.), Hypermedia: Openness, Structural Awareness, and Adaptivity. Proceedings, 2001. X, 335 pages. 2002.

Vol. 2267: M. Cerioli, G. Reggio (Eds.), Recent Trends in Algebraic Development Techniques. Proceedings, 2001. X, 345 pages. 2001.

Vol. 2271: B. Preneel (Ed.), Topics in Cryptology – CT-RSA 2002. Proceedings, 2002. X, 311 pages. 2002.

Vol. 2272: D. Bert, J.P. Bowen, M.C. Henson, K. Robinson (Eds.), ZB 2002: Formal Specification and Development in Z and B. Proceedings, 2002. XII, 535 pages. 2002.

Vol. 2273: A.R. Coden, E.W. Brown, S. Srinivasan (Eds.), Information Retrieval Techniques for Speech Applications. XI, 109 pages. 2002.

Vol. 2274: D. Naccache, P. Paillier (Eds.), Public Key Cryptography. Proceedings, 2002. XI, 385 pages. 2002.

Vol. 2275: N.R. Pal, M. Sugeno (Eds.), Advances in Soft Computing – AFSS 2002. Proceedings, 2002. XVI, 536 pages. 2002. (Subseries LNAI).

Vol. 2276: A. Gelbukh (Ed.), Computational Linguistics and Intelligent Text Processing. Proceedings, 2002. XIII, 444 pages. 2002.

Vol. 2277: P. Callaghan, Z. Luo, J. McKinna, R. Pollack (Eds.), Types for Proofs and Programs. Proceedings, 2000. VIII, 243 pages. 2002.

Vol. 2284: T. Eiter, K.-D. Schewe (Eds.), Foundations of Information and Knowledge Systems. Proceedings, 2002. X, 289 pages. 2002.

Vol. 2285: H. Alt, A. Ferreira (Eds.), STACS 2002. Proceedings, 2002. XIV, 660 pages. 2002.

Vol. 2300: W. Brauer, H. Ehrig, J. Karhumäki, A. Salomaa (Eds.), Formal and Natural Computing. XXXVI, 431 pages. 2002.

Lecture Notes in Computer Science

For information about Vols. 1–2194
please contact your bookseller or Springer-Verlag

Author Index